A LITERARY HISTORY OF ENGLAND

LONGMANS, GREEN AND CO. LTD.

39 PATERNOSTER ROW, LONDON, E.C.4
6 OLD COURT HOUSE STREET, CALCUTTA
53 NICOL ROAD, BOMBAY
167 MOUNT ROAD, MADRAS

LONGMANS, GREEN AND CO.

55 FIFTH AVENUE, NEW YORK
221 EAST 20TH STREET, CHICAGO
TREMONT TEMPLE, BOSTON
128–132 UNIVERSITY AVENUE, TORONTO

A LITERARY HISTORY OF ENGLAND

BY

BERNARD GROOM, M.A.

SENIOR ENGLISH MASTER AT CLIFTON COLLEGE

LONGMANS, GREEN AND CO.
LONDON ◆ NEW YORK ◆ TORONTO
1929

PREFACE

THE nature of this book may be described in a few words. It is an attempt to give a short critical account of the greater English writers, with the background—intellectual, political, or social—which best helps to explain their work. As there is a clear literary tradition from the age of Chaucer to the beginning of the present century, such a book becomes a brief Literary History of England. The first and last chapters are in the nature of Introduction and Epilogue.

The book is recommended to the attention of those who are concerned with English Literature as a means of higher education, and as a key to the thought and culture of the English people. In Schools, it is intended particularly for those who are studying English Literature as a special subject in the Higher School Certificate, and similar examinations. It is also designed for students in other subjects, especially the historian and the classical scholar, who wish to supplement their knowledge by a general acquaintance with English Literature. To the University student it is offered as a new introductory treatment of the subject.

I cherish the extravagant hope that this book may exercise some slight influence on the future course of advanced studies in English. In my own time, the demands of Anglo-Saxon literature and philology on the energies of the University student were certainly exorbitant, and in spite of changes, here and there, in a more liberal direction, the situation does not seem to have greatly improved. For an adequate appreciation of the English writers from Chaucer onwards, some acquaintance with classical literature, or with English history, is at least as necessary as a detailed knowledge of Anglo-Saxon grammar; and even the study of *Beowulf* is not more essential, it seems to me, than that of the *Iliad*, or the *Æneid*, or the Reformation in England, or the Revolution of 1688. To admit the claims of these and other subjects to a place in the scheme of English studies would, I know, involve many difficulties of re-organization; yet the attempt must surely be made, sooner or later, if the Honours " School " of English is to flourish as it deserves. Signs of a movement in the direction I have indicated are already visible in certain places, and with that movement it is my hope that this book may in some small measure co-operate.

My thanks are due to the Delegates of the Clarendon Press for their kind permission to print certain extracts from the Oxford " Chaucer," and to my former pupil, Mr. O. E. Holloway, of Balliol College, for much useful help in the correction of proofs.

CLIFTON COLLEGE,
June 1929.

CONTENTS

CHAPTER I

OUR DEBT TO THE ANGLO-SAXONS

CHAPTER II

CHAUCER AND HIS AGE

CHAPTER III

THE RENAISSANCE AND THE REFORMATION

CHAPTER IV

SPENSER

CHAPTER IX

THE RESTORATION

CHAPTER X

THE AUGUSTAN AGE

CHAPTER XI

THE EIGHTEENTH CENTURY : POETS AND NOVELISTS

CHAPTER XII

THE EIGHTEENTH CENTURY : DR. JOHNSON AND HIS CIRCLE

CHAPTER XIII

THE EIGHTEENTH CENTURY : LATER POETS

CHAPTER XIX

THE VICTORIAN AGE: THE NOVEL

CHAPTER XX

SOME FEATURES OF CONTEMPORARY LITERATURE

LITERARY HISTORY OF ENGLAND

CHAPTER I

OUR DEBT TO THE ANGLO-SAXONS

IT is natural to feel some curiosity about the earliest monuments of our literature. A few questions must occur at once. Of what nature is the language used by our most ancient writers? What ideas of life does their literature express? What manners does it reflect? What are its literary merits? These questions, at least, are likely to enter the minds of many persons; and, on being answered, they will probably lead to one more : What are the qualities which raise old writings above the level of antiquities and historical documents, and give them a living interest for the present generation? In other words, when does English Literature, properly so called, begin?

I

The foundations of our language were laid by the Teutonic tribes which migrated from the Continent to Great Britain in the early centuries of the Christian era. Jutes, Saxons and Angles all spoke dialects of that great family of tongues of which German, Danish, Dutch, Norwegian and Swedish are members. By the end of the seventh century, dialects of Teutonic origin were being spoken over the larger part of our island—everywhere except in the extreme North and the extreme West. An Englishman of to-day, suddenly transported to those times, would soon recognise many of his commonest words under a thin disguise. For instance, "bring" would be represented by "bringan"; "book" by "bōc"; "wood" by "wudu"; "life" by "līf"; "man" by "mann"; "one" by "ān"; "white" by "hwīt." Some words, like "word" itself, have undergone no change in spelling, though the letters represent different sounds. It is easy to frame sentences every word of which has its equivalent in the vocabulary of our Anglo-Saxon ancestors. "Goodbye; I am sorry that you must go so soon"; "How many loaves shall I buy to-day?"; "The evil that men do lives after them"[1]—these sentences are composed wholly of words derived from Anglo-Saxon, though in some instances their functions have changed. A printed line of modern English, even if the subject is highly technical, generally contains many more words of Anglo-Saxon than of foreign origin; and in colloquial English the proportion of native words is much higher.

Is Anglo-Saxon, then, the earliest form of the English language? The question is one to which a categorical answer, whether negative or affirmative, is impossible. But when one has considered all the features which distinguish the language of our own time from the dialects of King Alfred's, there seem to be as many differences of degree as make up, in the aggregate, a difference of kind. In the first place, it was not until some centuries after the Norman Conquest that the unity of the English tongue began to emerge from chaos. In the Anglo-Saxon era there were at least four main dialects : the Northumbrian, the Mercian, the West-Saxon and the Kentish. At one time, Northumbria was the chief centre of political power and literary culture : later, the supremacy passed to Wessex; but at no time before the Conquest could any man say : "The language that I speak is standard English; other forms are mere provincial dialects." The influx of new words into certain parts of the country during the Norse and Norman invasions made matters worse. Local peculiarities were exaggerated. It was not until the fourteenth

---

[1] The form of "them" has been affected by Norse influence.

century that one dialect, the East Midland, began to rise above its rivals into the position of Standard English.

Moreover, the grammar of Anglo-Saxon was in many respects widely different from the grammar of modern English. The Anglo-Saxon dialects belong to the class of languages known as " synthetic," while modern English, by contradistinction, is called " analytic." In other words, Anglo-Saxon grammar depends largely on the use of inflexions, English grammar very much less. Many of the grammatical relations which we can express by the use of prepositions, pronouns, and auxiliary verbs were expressed in Anglo-Saxon by changes within the body of nouns and verbs, or by terminations. The Anglo-Saxon noun had four cases : nominative, accusative, genitive and dative, and it had different forms for the singular and plural. Our possessive *'s* and plural *-s* (from *-es* and *-as*, terminations of a masculine declension) are almost the only remains of the old inflexions. The functions performed in Anglo-Saxon by the other case-endings of nouns are fulfilled in our language by the position of words in a sentence, and the use of various prepositions, such as *by, with, to, from, at*, etc. In modern English, for example, the speaker of the sentence, " I saw the king," indicates that the last two words are in the objective case by placing them after the verb. In the same sentence put into Anglo-Saxon, " Ic seah thonë cyning," it is the accusative form of the word " thonë " (of which the nominative is " se ") that shows the relation of the last two words to the verb. Similarly, " Thaēm cyningë " (which is the dative of " se cyning ") corresponds, approximately, to the phrase " to the king." Anglo-Saxon has less elaborate inflexions than Greek or Latin ; but its system of verbs and pronouns, as well as of nouns, is extremely complex when compared with that of modern English. Since a date even before the Norman Conquest, our language has been moving towards the goal of an " analytic " ideal. The Conquest, with its introduction of Norman French as a co-habitant with English, accelerated the process ; and by Chaucer's time, three centuries later, a great many old terminations had been lost or simplified. But even Chaucer's English, with its frequent case-endings, especially the final -*e*, shows the change as far from complete. Nor have we even to-day got rid of every grammatical superfluity. For instance, we no longer differentiate between the singular and plural of the definite article : the addition of -*s* to the noun with which it is coupled is enough to mark the plural. Yet we still use the plural forms " these " and " those " ; though there is no more ambiguity in the strange phrase " *this* men " than in the familiar " *the* men." Still, such anomalies are rare ; and the practical spirit of our race is well expressed in our love of energetic mono-syllables, and the general adaptation of the means to the end. Certainly, Anglo-Saxon but faintly expresses the English spirit as we now understand it to be ; while modern English, in its essentials unchanged since Tudor times, is a significant product of the national genius.

In vocabulary, also, the changes have been great. Some words have dropped out, but many more have been added. The Anglo-Saxon vocabulary was in some respects superfluously rich. It was particularly rich in synonyms. For instance, *wer*, *guma*, and *mann* all mean " man," and there is little difference between them in use. In poetry, especially, this wealth of words is noticeable. For " boat," there is the common *bāt*, and also the more poetic *flota*. The sea was known not only by its plain name (*sǣ*), but also by descriptive synonyms such as " swan's road " and " gannet's bath." These imaginative words are among the most attractive features of Anglo-Saxon literature ; but it was natural that they should die with the old forms of poetry to which they belong. On the other hand, our vocabulary has been immensely enriched both from foreign sources and the cultivation of our native possessions. Hence has arisen the composite character of our language. This quality, under the same general conditions, will be found in nearly every department of thought and activity. First, there will be a small substratum of native words ; next, a layer of ancient borrowings, some perhaps dating from before the Norman Conquest ; lastly, a great collection of new words, some formed from Anglo-Saxon roots but with different meanings ; more, derived from the chief contributory tongues, such as Scandinavian, French, Latin and Greek. Imagine a walk in the country, preferably in a hilly region when the landscape will be varied. If you look round and name the features and objects you see, many of the commonest will certainly take their names from Anglo-Saxon words. *Earth, sun, wood, tree, hill, grass, stream ; road, house, bridge, lane, path ; man, child, horse, bird ; oak, ash, birch* are all of native origin. *Street* and *wall* are also Anglo-Saxon, but not strictly Teutonic, for they are derived from two Latin words (*Strata via* and *vallum*) which our ancestors learned from Roman civilisation. *Sky* is not of Anglo-Saxon but of Scandinavian origin—one of the many common words (e.g. *cast, take, same, law*) which we owe to the Norse invasions. *Cloud* is native, but has changed its meaning ; for it originally meant a " lump of earth," and was later applied to a lumpish " cumulus " cloud. *Wheat, oat, barley, wine, bread* and *beer* are of Anglo-Saxon origin ; but *beef, mutton, pear* and *cherry* have come to us from French. Of the now living Continental languages, French has nearly always been our chief source of enrichment ; and we still borrow from it, though less freely than before. The influx of words derived from Latin, already considerable in the fourteenth century, steadily grew until the seventeenth ; it then slackened, but has not ceased yet. At the Renaissance, Greek began to make its great contribution, and in recent years has added many words to our scientific terminology. And since English has become the language of a World Empire, we have been enriching our vocabulary from almost every region under heaven.

The destinies of Anglo-Saxon, then, were great ; for it was to become the parent tongue of one of the most important of languages. Anglo-Saxon survives, as an ancestor survives in his descendant. It did not die with the Norman Conquest, though its character, even then, was rapidly changing. Another hundred years, and the old name for the language is no longer adequate. About the middle of the twelfth century the last addition was made, at Peterborough, to the Anglo-Saxon Chronicle ; and that date may be chosen to mark approximately the beginning of " Middle English."

II

It is a pity that the Anglo-Saxons did not describe the details of their daily lives. Novels, memoirs and familiar letters were the inventions of a later age. Literature was in the hands of " clerks," whose main objects were edification and instruction. The times were unfavourable to the free and full development of literary genius. Even Cædmon and Cynewulf, the chief among Anglo-Saxon poets, are shadowy and half-mythical figures. The story of how Cædmon's tongue was miraculously unloosed, and how he was bidden to sing the story of the Creation is typical of the literary history of those times. Most Anglo-Saxon poetry, both in style and matter, takes the reader into a region more remote from our minds than the Old Testament or the *Iliad*. *Beowulf*, the roots of which are in the Pagan past, has few of the splendid qualities which give the epics of Homer an undying freshness. Its style is somewhat monotonous, its human interest is faint, and it is full of puerilities. Many of the other long poems in Anglo-Saxon elaborate stories from the Bible and record the lives of saints. In a few of these, such as *The Dream of the Rood*,[1] there are gleams of poetry, but in general their value is slight. It is to the prose works of Alfred and his successors and to certain shorter poems that we must go to find any clear reflection of Anglo-Saxon life.

The most vivid picture which is given in classical literature of our Teutonic ancestors is found in the *Germania* of Tacitus. The Roman historian describes the Germans as free from all the vices of civilisation. They have, it is true, the rude elements of a State in their institution of the " comitatus," and they preserve a superstitious respect for the primitive virtues of loyalty and courage. Eating and drinking are their chief delights ; and they love prolonged

[1] An Introduction, by Cynewulf, to his poem *Elene*.

sleep after their excesses. They despise labour, thinking it a disgrace to win by toil the food that can be obtained in a single day's hunting. Of the value of gold they have little conception; but, like the savages, they have a passion for worthless finery. They sacrifice to gods of their own, and practise divination. Such is the picture painted by Tacitus. But the conversion of the Anglo-Saxons to Christianity and their contact with the remains of Roman and Celtic civilisation wrought wonders. The West Saxons of Alfred's time were, in comparison with their ancestors before the migration, a highly civilized and industrious people. Christianity had elevated their moral character and had brought them into touch with a culture which, though but the shadow of what it had been, was still the greatest in the world. The Anglo-Saxons produced their own martyrs to the faith, and more than one ecclesiastic of European fame, most notably the Venerable Bede. When the first Norse invasions threatened this civilisation, its latent strength was shown under its great champion, King Alfred (848–901). As soon as he had stemmed the torrent, he set to work to repair the damage. Learning and literature revived under his inspiration. No Anglo-Saxon document is more interesting than the king's lament for the scarcity of books and the ignorance of the clergy. Formerly, he tells us, books had been plentiful and the clergy well instructed; but now it was a rare thing for a man to be able to read even his mother-tongue. Alfred was anxious that the study of Latin should recover its lost ground; but he was not less zealous for native literature. He translated four works, each considered in those days as particularly important in its own province. These were the *Consolation of Philosophy* by Boethius, the *Universal History* of Orosius, the *Ecclesiastical History* of Bede, and the *Pastoral Care* of St. Gregory, the last being a work on the duties of the clergy. To Alfred we owe the *Voyages of Ohthere and Wulfstan*, the former of whom had rounded the North Cape. To Alfred also, or to Alfred's impulse, we owe the initiation of the Anglo-Saxon Chronicle, which, written at various monastic centres, such as Winchester,

Abingdon, and Peterborough, recorded the most noteworthy events, year by year, through evil days and through good, right up to the reign of King Stephen.

The art of prose continued to flourish after Alfred's death. Large parts of the Bible were translated into Anglo-Saxon. Perhaps the best prose of all is that of Ælfric, whose *Lives of the Saints* (early eleventh century) contains passages of eloquence and concise expression which are rarely matched before the revival of prose under the Tudors. A renewed series of Norse raids damaged and almost destroyed the tradition of West Saxon culture. One of the last pieces of Anglo-Saxon prose, before the language began to show signs of hopeless decay, is a tragic and despairing sermon by Archbishop Wulfstan, delivered when the violence of the raiders was at its height, and prophesying the imminent end of the world.

Amid the general atmosphere of strife and failure, the modern reader welcomes any records of peaceful and settled life. He is glad to come across the little " charms," verses recited to ward off evil from men, beasts and crops. The " Riddles " describe common things with pleasing touches of observation. But it is in such poems as *The Wanderer* and *The Seafarer* that we come into closest contact with the Anglo-Saxon spirit. It is a spirit of stubborn endurance, scarcely illumined by hope, yet surveying its destiny with a mixture of fatalism and clear-sighted courage. The first lines of *The Seafarer* give little foretaste of the spirit of Drake and Nelson, but they lack neither nobility nor imagination. Here is a literal translation of them :

I will utter about myself a true lay and relate my adventures ; how in days of toil, I often endured a time of hardship ; have undergone bitter cares of heart, known on the ship many times of suffering, the dire rolling of waves. There at the prow the rigorous night-watch oft occupied me, when, tormented by cold (the prow) dashed against the cliffs. My feet were numbed with frost, with cold fetters ; cares sighed passionately about my heart ; hunger tore within the heart of a sea-wearied one. The man whose lot is happily cast on earth knows not how I haunted the icy sea during the winter with the steps of an exile,

8

deprived of my companions, hung about with icicles : the hail
fell in showers. There I heard nothing but the sea resounding,
the ice-cold way ; sometimes the song of the swan. I found
my pleasure in the gannet's laughter and the sound of the
sea-bird instead of the laughter of men, the singing sea-gull
instead of mead-drinking. The storms beat against the sea-cliff
where the icy-feathered tern makes answer ; full oft the dewy-
feathered eagle screamed around . . .

The imagination of the Anglo-Saxon often found its
natural abode in the gloomier regions of thought.

III

The quality of poetry depends largely upon its form.
Some literatures possess a vocabulary and a metre which by
themselves lead the poet a long distance towards perfect
expression. Others suffer from disadvantages which the
greatest genius cannot wholly overcome. The character
of Anglo-Saxon poetry is closely connected with its metrical
laws.

The metre of Anglo-Saxon poetry is based on the
principle of alliteration. Every line is divided into halves,
each of which contains two strongly accented syllables : of
these, three—two in the first half and one in the second—
must begin with the same letter. A line from one of the
last alliterative poems, *The Vision of Piers Plowman*, will
illustrate the system :

So on a May morning   on Malvern Hills.

Here are four accented syllables : May, morn-, Mal- and
hills ; three of them alliterate. In the best days of Anglo-
Saxon poetry there were rules determining the relation of
unaccented to accented syllables, but, even so, the metre
presented little difficulty to the poet beyond the task of
finding three words having the same initial letter. The
disadvantages of this metre are evident. It is arbitrary
without being strict. It imposes vexatious limitations, yet
it has small musical charm. Further, it invites the writer
to attempt expression in one line ; and if he fails, or suc-

ceeds imperfectly, to try again in the next. With this last tendency, the Anglo-Saxon vocabulary co-operated. Its abundant synonyms gave rise to a practice which is familiar to us from Old Testament poetry, namely, parallelism. A sentence is uttered and then repeated, with little or no change of meaning, but in different words. " Until I had brought him into my mother's house, and into the chamber of her that conceived me," as the poet says in the Song of Solomon ; and the lines already quoted from *The Seafarer* also illustrate the principle.

Such are the main features of Anglo-Saxon verse. Both style and metre are highly dangerous to any writer who is inclined to be prolix. The author of *Beowulf* yields to his temptations, and tells his story with an excessive number of repetitions. His very theme repeats itself. We are told how the beer-hall of the Danish King Hrothgar suffers from constant depredations by a monster, half man, half beast, whose name is Grendel. The thanes who, after feasting, sleep in the hall, can never be certain that one of them will not be missing when the next day dawns. Beowulf, as a famous hero, is besought to deliver the Danes of their enemy. He consents, and Grendel, on his next visit to the beer-hall, receives a surprise. There is a terrific combat, in which the monster's arm is wrenched off and he escapes only to die. Soon, however, Grendel's mother attacks the hall to avenge her son ; and Beowulf is summoned to deal with this new peril. He is victorious after a fierce struggle in her lair, and is overwhelmed with thanks by the grateful king. But Beowulf's tasks are not yet over. Years after, his own people are afflicted by the devastations of a " fire dragon." The champion, though stricken in years, delivers the land, but he perishes in the conflict.

The story is worth repeating, for *Beowulf* is a great "antiquity," if not a great poem. Certain resemblances to the language of Homer suggest that there was, in the remote past, an epic tradition common to the Aryan peoples. The courtesy shown by Hrothgar to Beowulf, and the relations between the king and his " comitatus " of nobles are matters of high historical interest. But as a work of literature, *Beowulf* has very great faults. Its three main actions resemble each other too closely to sustain the reader's interest, nor is the poem redeemed by its style, in spite of passages, here and there, of grim power.

It is not to *Beowulf*, but to the shorter poems in the epic manner that we must look for the finest achievements of Anglo-Saxon poetry—to the old fragment, called *The Fight of Finnsburh*, or to the late poem of triumph on Athelstan's victory over the Danes in 937, *The Battle of Brunanburh*. But none of these contains anything so noble as the concluding lines on the last desperate stand of the defending army against the invaders of Essex in 993. *The Battle of Maldon* records a defeat, but a defeat in which the vanquished rose to supreme heroism. These lines of Anglo-Saxon at least deserve to be known to every English reader:

Byrhtwold maþelode,　　bord hafenode,
sē wæs eald genēat,　　æsc ācwęhte,
hē ful baldlīce　　beornas lǣrde :
" Hige sceal þe heardra,　　heorte þe cēnre,
mōd sceal þe māre,　　þe ūre mægen lȳtlað.
Hēr līþ ūre ealdor　　eall forhēawen,
gōd on grēote ;　　ā mæg gnornian
sē ðe nū fram ðīs wīgplegan　　węndan þęnceð.
Ic eom frōd fēores ;　　fram ic ne wille,
ac ic mē be healfe　　mīnum hlāforde,
be swā lēofan męnn　　licgan þęnce."

Byrhtwold spoke,　　he grasped his shield,
He was an aged companion,　　he brandished his spear,
Full boldly he　　spake to his men,
" The spirit must be the sterner,　　the heart the braver,
The mind the greater,　　as our might grows less.
Here lies our chief　　hewn to pieces,
The good man in the dust.　　Ever may he mourn
Who now from this war-play　　thinks to withdraw.
Aged am I ;　　I will not yield,
But by his side,　　close to my lord,
To a man so dear,　　mean I to lie."

IV

The foregoing description may give the reader some help in deciding how far Anglo-Saxon literature is a part of English literature. Here and there, it is true, may be recognised glimpses of the English spirit : but for the most part one moves in a world which is strangely unfamiliar. Of humour, which is so strong a feature of our later literature, there is scarcely a trace. Nature is a mysterious power, to be dreaded rather than loved. Life is regarded, not so much as a great adventure, as a gloomy ordeal. It is true that a more hopeful spirit is felt in the prose of Alfred and others; but Anglo-Saxon prose is the vehicle of instruction rather than imagination, and it is to the poets that one must go for the deeper interpretation of life.

Nor have our best writers at any time drawn much inspiration from the Anglo-Saxons. There are, indeed, a few exceptions. Milton, for example, may have known *The Fall of the Angels ;* Tennyson modernised *The Battle of Brunanburh.* With such rare signs of indebtedness, one may well compare the universal chorus of praise in honour of Chaucer. Strangely enough, alliterative verse, which seems at first so antiquated, has never wholly died, but survives in an altered form. As an ornament of style, though not as a principle of metre, alliteration has its uses. This most of our great poets have known ; and in such a line as Milton's

> Than *f*ables yet have *f*eigned or *f*ear conceived,

the emphasis falls naturally and effectively on three words beginning with the same letter, just as it does in *Beowulf.* Far more important is our debt to the Anglo-Saxon language. But these things we have absorbed into our national life unconsciously : and there is but little for which we should return to Anglo-Saxon literature in the spirit in which the hero of the *Æneid* was bidden to seek out the ancient home of his race : " Antiquam exquirite matrem."

CHAPTER II

CHAUCER AND HIS AGE

CHAUCER is a poet whom men have united to honour. Of his admirers, Spenser and Dryden have perhaps uttered the most memorable praise. Spenser invented the happy title, " Well of English undefiled " ; and Dryden expressed the joy which every reader takes in the abounding life of the *Canterbury Tales*. Actually, it is the humanity of Chaucer that keeps his work alive ; but to discerning readers his style is scarcely less delightful. Chaucer owes his success as a writer partly to his natural gifts and partly to his good fortune. He would have won distinction in any circumstances ; but his century, his social position, even his native dialect, were all in his favour. Ever since the Norman Conquest the conditions which made his work possible had been slowly maturing. His way was prepared by generations of artificers in language and metre, some of whom have left work which has not been wholly eclipsed by that of their great successor.

I

When Chaucer began to write in the fourteenth century, the composite character of the English language had already been fixed. The tongue of the conquered people had first sunk to the level of a despised dialect, spoken still, but not by men of the highest authority and best culture. Norman-French was, for many years, the language of the great. But very soon the defeated Anglo-Saxon tongue began to absorb portions of the Norman vocabulary, and to frame its sentences somewhat in the Norman manner.

13

It is easy to see the advantages of this speech to the two races, which, however hostile, were bound to communicate. By the end of the twelfth century this new language was already being used in both prose and verse, especially in works of instruction and improvement, like the much-read *Moral Ode*. Many Norman-French words have survived in modern English. Some are revealed by their form, e.g. *castle, beast, feast,* which preserve an " s " which has disappeared from the corresponding words in Parisian French. Many words from France indicate a dominant people, e.g. *baron, court, mansion, justice.* The process of borrowing, thus begun, was soon extended. The frequent intercourse between England and France during the thirteenth and fourteenth centuries led to an immense influx of new words, some of which seem to have been first used by Chaucer himself.

French influence soon affected the technique of verse. Metre in those days was important, even if there were no good poets ; for the common people much preferred to receive their instruction, sacred or profane, in a form which was easy to remember. Words arranged metrically make a far deeper impression than prose on simple minds. There were many who preferred the alliterative manner, but the system of scansion by feet, as used by the French, soon became its rival. To show that English adapts itself well to this foreign fashion was an important work ; and we owe a debt, even to the tedious Orm, for his effort to " reform our numbers." Orm was a monk who flourished in the early thirteenth century, and wrote a work, expository and homiletic, extending to thousands of lines. His title to fame is the inflexible regularity with which he hammers out his verses, never deviating from the rhythm of the opening two :

> Þiss bóc iss némmnedd Órrmulúm,
> Forrþí þatt Órrm itt wróhhtë.

This is a well-known metre. It resembles the familiar 8 : 6 of hymns, though, as was natural in the days of sounded final *-e's*, Orm uses the feminine ending and makes it 8 : 7.

If Orm's two lines are repeated, we get the "ballad-stanza," one of the most common of English measures (8 : 6, 8 : 6). The first of his two lines is octosyllabic (four iambic feet) : and it was soon found that a succession of these suits many kinds of poetry, whether lyrical or narrative. Thus, as early as the thirteenth century, English verse was beginning to assume the shape we know ; and there were better writers contemporary with Orm, such as the author of the *Moral Ode*, who did not despise the saving grace of variety.

There was good verse of many kinds in Middle English before Chaucer's time. One of the best of the longer poems is *The Owl and the Nightingale*, in which the contrasted character of the two birds is brought out with telling satire and shrewd observation. Some of the lyrics made a special appeal to modern readers. The *Love-Rune* of Thomas de Hales, which was written in the thirteenth century, is both beautiful and accomplished. Here is a charming stanza on a favourite mediæval theme, " Where are the snows of yester-year ? "

> Hwer is Paris and Heleyne
>   þat weren so bryht and feyre on bleo,[1]
> Amadas, Tristram, and Dideyne,
>   Yseudë and allë þeo [2] ;
> Ector wiþ his scharpe meyne,[3]
>   And Cesar riche of worldës feo ? [4]
> Heo beoþ iglyden ut of þe reyne,
>   So þe schef is of þe cleo.[5]

In some of the popular songs, too, there is a freshness which gives a foretaste of the Elizabethan spirit. This is especially true of the delightful part-song, " Sumer is i-cumen in."

II

The fourteenth century was a great epoch in English Literature. Chaucer's pre-eminence long cast his con-

---

[1] Hue.   [2] Those.   [3] Power.   [4] Wealth.
[5] They have departed from the kingdom (of earth) as the corn has from the hillside.

temporaries into the shade : and even to-day less is commonly known about them than they deserve. It is true that prose, as represented, for example, by *The Travels of Sir John Mandeville*, makes a poor display by the side of *The Canterbury Tales ;* but the poets are on a different plane. Of Chaucer's two great contemporaries one was named William Langland (or Langley) : the name of the other has perished ; but he is known, from the dialect in which he wrote, as the West Midland Poet. Both were deeply imbued with the spirit of the times, yet there was a wide difference between them. The West Midland Poet was above all an artist—a lover of romance and of natural beauty. Langland had an intense moral zeal, his whole view of life was coloured by his enthusiastic dreams of reform. Another poet whose name must at least be mentioned is John Gower, whose *Confessio Amantis* is, like Chaucer's great work, a collection of tales in verse.

By the fourteenth century, the Catholic Church, after performing incalculable services to mankind, was beginning to show signs of inward corruption. Thinking men, for the most part, still upheld her institutions, while they condemned the worldliness of her prelates. Dante (1265–1321), the greatest of mediæval poets, held that the Catholic Church and the Mediæval Empire were both divinely appointed, but that each had trespassed on the province of the other. He denounced with fiery vehemence the unworthy successors of St. Peter, and their neglect of the simple but uncompromising commands of their Master. In England, the worldliness of the Church was exposed in different ways by three of the greatest men of the age, by Wycliffe, by Chaucer, and by Langland.

The last-named of the three was born in Shropshire about 1330. Little is known about the course of his life, and even the correct form of his name is uncertain. Apparently he was in minor orders, and lived much in London. A few further details, such as the severity of his manner and the names of his wife and daughter, can be gathered from his poem, *The Vision of William concerning Piers the*

Plowman, which was, in a real sense, his lifework, for it occupied him at intervals from before 1362 till 1398. It appeared in three versions; and we are thus able to follow the growth of his ideas from his early manhood till the end of his life.

The Vision of Piers the Plowman, like many poems of the time, is in the form of a dream. Its style is old-fashioned, and the author uses the alliterative metre. The opening lines bring the subject swiftly before the reader :

> In a somer seson   whan soft was the sonne,
> I shope me in shroudes [1]   as I a shepe [2] were,
> In habite as an heremite   unholy of workes,
> Went wyde in this world   wondres to here.
> Ac on a May mornynge   on Maluerne hulles
> Me byfel a ferly   of fairy me thou3te. [3]

He sees a " Field full of folk," men of every class and occupation. Holy Church appears to the dreamer, and informs him that it is man's duty to seek for Truth, that " works " by themselves are vain, and that love alone leads to salvation. These words are heard by the multitude, and much bewilderment is caused by the mention of Truth. Can this be some new saint ? Even a palmer who has visited many shrines can give no information. At this moment, Piers the Plowman comes forward. He has laboured for fifty years, doing his duty to God and man, and his honest character and straightforward life make him a fit leader. An allegorical pilgrimage is now described, and the poet is free to depict the innumerable snares that lead men out of the way of truth. All things spiritual and temporal are passed in review, the government of England and the state of the Church. Episodes abound, and, in the later versions, the personality of Piers himself changes bewilderingly. At first, he is the type of righteous man who seeks salvation by doing his duty in charity ; but towards the end of the poem, he is merged into the figure of Christ. Langland thought little about the clearness of his plan,

---

[1] Garments.   [2] Shepherd.
[3] There befel to me a wonder of enchantment, it seemed to me.

and the task of discovering remedies for the abuses of his age was beyond his powers. Yet the main lines of his thought are clear. He sees how justice is sold and the poor are plundered, while the rich give way to avarice and ostentation. The Church, though making the highest professions, is unfaithful to her task. None of her servants are more unworthy than the Friars, who have utterly forsaken the ideals of poverty and service as instituted by their founder. The hope of the world, in the poet's view, is a return to the morals and religion of primitive Christianity. Langland thus belongs to a well-known type of Englishman. He anticipates both Bunyan and Wesley : he is a reformer, though not an iconoclast. His greatest power is shown in his satirical pictures, such as the description of the Seven Deadly Sins, and in his visionary and prophetic passages, especially in the great lines on the Passion and the Resurrection. His impatience of systematic thought, his certainty that right and wrong are eternally distinct, his keenness to discern the knave from the true man, are all qualities of mind and character which his countrymen, after the lapse of more than six centuries, still recognise in their midst.

That four of the finest poems in Middle English, *Sir Gawain and the Green Knight*, *Patience*, *Cleanness* (or *Purity*), and *The Pearl*, were all the work of the same anonymous writer is probable, but not certain. There are, however, good grounds for the conjecture. All four are written in the West Midland dialect, and belong to the second half of the fourteenth century. Only the first- and last-named shall be considered here. *Sir Gawain and the Green Knight* belongs to a very important body of literature, the mediæval romances, and it is the finest specimen of that class in English. Romance was the most popular form of literature in Western Europe during the Middle Ages. In England, in France, in Italy and in Spain, men loved to hear recited in verse the adventures of the world's great champions. Romance has countless ramifications, but, as an old French poet tells us, there are only three " matters " (or cycles) of which any man need take note : the cycles of France, of

Britain and of Rome. The French cycle dealt with the exploits of Charlemagne and his twelve peers. The cycle of Rome included the various legends connected with the fall of Troy, and the settlement of the Trojans in Italy. The heroes of the British cycle were King Arthur and the Knights of the Round Table.

Sir Gawain and the Green Knight is raised above most of the romances by its energetic style, its powerful descriptions of nature and its strong human interest. An account of the plot—which is full of miraculous adventure—will give some idea of romance in general, as well as of this romance in particular. The Knights of the Round Table are seated in their hall one Christmas Day, when they are surprised by the sudden entrance of an immense knight clad in green, and mounted on a green horse. Riding up through the throng, he offers to receive a blow from any one present, provided that his assailant shall, within a year, accept a blow from himself. The challenge is taken up by Sir Gawain. He raises his sword and severs the stranger's head from his shoulders. But, to the general amazement, the Green Knight picks up his head and rides out of the hall, charging Sir Gawain, as he goes, to remember his promise. In the following winter, Sir Gawain sets out to find the stranger's castle. His way lies through a wild, mountainous country, which is very powerfully described. Arriving at the castle, he is courteously entertained by an old man and his beautiful wife. After the separation of the party, the lady pays a visit in private to her guest, and offers him her love ; but Gawain, who is the soul of honour, stedfastly resists the temptation. At length, he is prevailed upon to accept a green silk girdle, which, he is told, will preserve him from death when the time for his ordeal arrives. Thus protected, he receives the appointed blow, which causes merely a slight wound. The trial being over, the identity of Sir Gawain's hosts is revealed. The old man is the Green Knight, and the Lady is Morgan le Fay, whose great desire is to humiliate the knights of the Round Table. Such were the stories which pleased our mediæval ancestors ; but the real merit of the poem lies in the handling, and in the power of certain scenes, such as that of Gawain's temptation.

The Pearl reflects another side of the mediæval character. It is an elegy in allegorical form, and is written with great skill in a metre of almost insuperable difficulty. The poem consists of stanzas which are grouped in sections of five. The concluding line throughout the section is the same (or nearly so), and it is repeated at the beginning of the section that follows, so that all the stanzas are linked together. The whole has much the effect of a sonnet-sequence. The "Pearl," which gives the poem its title, represents the author's little daughter, whom he has lost by death. One day in August, he falls asleep in a green arbour, and dreams that he is standing by the side of a beautiful river, which flows over gems instead of stones. On the farther bank appears a maiden of exquisite beauty, wearing a large pearl in the midst of her bosom. She greets the dreamer as her father; but her words astonish him, for when she died she was a child, and now is a queen. But she explains that all the blessed are kings or queens, and tells him the parable of the Labourers in the Vineyard to prove that in the Kingdom of Heaven all are equal and receive the same reward: those who toiled for but one hour, and those who bore the burden and heat of the day. She also obtains for her father a glimpse of the New Jerusalem; but when he sees how narrow is the stream which separates him from bliss, he attempts to cross, and in the attempt is awakened from his dream.

The Pearl is perhaps the most beautiful poem in Middle English. Its charming descriptions of nature and the pathos of the situation harmonise perfectly with the intricate music of the verse. The stanza that follows is the last one in the section on the Labourers in the Vineyard:

> At þe date of day of evensonge,
> On oure byfore þe sonne go doun,
> He seȝ þer ydel men ful stronge,
> And sayde to hem wyth sobre soun:
> "Wy stonde ȝe ydel þise dayeȝ longe?"
> Þay sayden her hyre watȝ nawhere boun.

" Gotȝ to my vyne, ȝemen ȝonge,
And wyrkeȝ and dotȝ þat at ȝe moun."
Sone þe worlde bycom wel broun ;
  þe sunne watȝ doun, & hit wex late ;
To take her hyre he mad sumoun ;
  þe day watȝ al apassed date.

" At the time of day of evensong, one hour before the sun does down, he saw there some idle men of great strength, and said to them in earnest tone : ' Why stand ye idle through the length of this day ? ' They said their wages were nowhere ready for them. ' Go into my vineyard, young yeomen, and work and do what ye may.' Soon the world became very dark ; the sun was down and it grew late ; he had them summoned to take their wages. The day had quite passed its limit."

III

Our knowledge of the life of Geoffrey Chaucer is somewhat meagre. He was born about 1340, in the middle class of society. He was appointed one of the " valets " of the king's household ; and it is thus natural that his earliest writings should reflect the manners of the Court. One of his first poems was *The Book of the Duchesse*, written in memory of the wife of John of Gaunt, Chaucer's patron. In 1372 he was sent to Italy on a diplomatic mission, and in 1374 he was appointed to the important office of Comptroller of the Wool Customs. Four years later, he visited Italy for a second time, and in 1382 received the Comptrollership of Petty Customs. Chaucer had thus become a high official in the Civil Service ; and before long he was allowed to appoint deputies to perform his duties. It is possible that during this season of comparative leisure (about 1385) he occupied himself with the *Canterbury Tales*. In 1386, however, his good fortune deserted him. John of Gaunt went to Spain, and the chief power in the State was seized by his brother, the Duke of Gloucester, who had friends of his own to promote. Chaucer was deprived of both his offices, and, for a time, was in difficulties. He continued his great work, however, and on the return of John of Gaunt received a new appointment. But his prosperity does not seem to have been renewed, for in 1399 he bewailed his poverty in the half-humorous

Compleint to his Empty Purse. The new king, Henry IV, granted the poet a pension, which he did not enjoy for long, as he died in the following year.

Chaucer's genius was refined by travel and experience. The great event in his life was his first visit to Italy. Until that time he had lived in an atmosphere of Anglo-French culture, and his early writings, which are in the courtly manner, are accomplished rather than original. Italy, in the fourteenth century, was the intellectual centre of Europe, and no greater fortune could befall a man of letters than a sojourn in the cities of Lombardy. The first half of the fourteenth century was a brilliant prelude to the Renaissance. Dante, the author of the *Divina Commedia*, was born in Florence in 1265. He was followed by Petrarch, the poet and scholar (1304–1374), and by Boccaccio (1313–1375), author of the *Decamerone*, a famous collection of stories in prose. Giotto (1267–1337) had begun the great age of painting by his frescoes at Padua and Florence ; and somewhat earlier St. Thomas Aquinas (*d.* 1274) had produced the crowning work of mediæval philosophy. Chaucer soon became acquainted with the best Italian poetry of the time.

On his return to England, he began to produce a series of works which, though less famous than the *Canterbury Tales*, are scarcely inferior. The best of the " Italian group " is *Troilus and Criseyde*, which was founded on *Il Filostrato*, a poem by Boccaccio. *The Knight's Tale*, which was afterwards fitted into the Canterbury scheme, tells of the rivalry of two lovers, Palamon and Arcite : it also has an Italian source, Boccaccio's *La Teseide*. *The Legende of Good Women* is an unfinished collection of stories and was put forward as a " palinode " or recantation, written to atone for Chaucer's alleged injustice to women in his portrait of Cressida. From Dante he borrowed some hints for his curiously unequal poem, *The Hous of Fame*, and also the terrible story of Ugolino of Pisa, which is included among the tragedies of *The Monk's Tale*. Petrarch furnished the tale of Patient Griselda, which is told by the Clerk of Oxford on the way to Canterbury. But it was not only for narrative material that Chaucer was indebted to the Italians. He owes them the inspiration derived from their great art, and confesses as much in his allusion to Petrarch and the "heigh style he endyteth." Nearly all that is best in Chaucer is contained in the work of this Italian period and in the delineations of English life which occupied the years that followed.

IV

Chaucer is second to no English poet in the art of narrative. Other writers have greater moments, but none such even excellence. The *Canterbury Tales* were originally designed to beguile the time; and their power to do so is unimpaired to this day.

The invention of a story in a sense belongs to the man who tells it best. No one, for instance, could deny that *The Pardoner's Tale* is really Chaucer's, though it is of Eastern origin and has been told many times. It illustrates splendidly its author's skill in pure narrative. The story begins by telling how three rioters one morning, drinking in a tavern, hear the clink of the bell which is rung when bodies are carried to the grave. They ask who has died, and are informed that it is one of their old companions:

> And sodeynly he was y-slayn to-night,
> For-dronke,[1] as he sat on his bench upright;
> Ther cam a privee theef, men clepeth Deeth[2];
> That in this contree all the peple sleeth,
> And with his spere he smoot his herte a-two,
> And wente his wey with-outen wordes mo.

The three revellers burst into imprecations on hearing this news. Who is this false traitor, Death, who slays all their comrades? Let him be slain himself! And so they swear that Death shall die as soon as they can lay hands on him. Meantime, they leave the tavern, and are just about to cross a stile, when they see an old man who gives them a timid greeting. The proudest of the three answers by brutally asking why he lives so long, to which the old man replies that he must abide the will of God:

[1] Excessively drunk.   [2] Whom men call Death.

> Ne deeth, allas ! ne wol nat han my lyf ;
> Thus walke I, lyk a restelees caityf,
> And on the ground, which is my modres gate,
> I knokke with my staf, bothe erly and late ;
> And seye, " leve moder, leet me in ! "

On hearing these words about Death, the revellers swear that they will learn where he dwells, from the old man. He answers meekly that if they will have it so, he can direct them :

> " Turne up this crooked way,
> For in that grove I lafte [1] him, by my fey,
> Under a tree, and ther he wol abyde."

The sinners rush towards the spot and find—not the grisly form they expect—but a hoard of treasure ; " wel ny an eighte busshels " of gold. All thoughts of Death vanish from their minds. They are now only concerned with the means of conveying the treasure away without arousing suspicion. It is resolved that one of them shall go and buy provisions while the others remain and keep watch over the hoard ; then, at the fall of night they can separate, each taking his share. So lots are cast ; and the youngest, on whom it falls, is sent to the town. But as soon as his back is turned, one of the remaining two hints that he has a device whereby they may add their companion's share to their own portions.

> " Thou woost [2] wel we be tweye,
> And two of us shul strenger be than oon,
> Look whan that he is set, and right anoon
> Arys, as though thou woldest with him pleye ;
> And I shal ryve him thurgh the sydes tweye [3]
> Whyl that thou strogelest with him as in game,
> And with thy dagger look thou do the same ;
> And than shal al this gold departed be,
> My dere freend, betwixen me and thee ;
> Than may we bothe our lustes [4] al fulfille,
> And pleye at dees right at our owene wille."

But the youngest of the revellers, as he walks towards the town, also revolves a plan of treachery. He cannot forget the beauty of the florins :

[1] Left.   [2] Knowest.   [3] Two.   [4] Desires.

"O lord!" quod he, "if so were that I mighte
Have al this tresor to my-self allone,
Ther is no man that liveth under the trone
Of god, that sholde live so mery as I."

Covetousness prepares a way for the fiend to enter his heart. As soon as he reaches the town, he calls upon an apothecary and demands some poison:

that he might his rattes quelle [1];
And eek ther was a polcat in his hawe,[2]
That, as he seyde, his capouns hadde y-slawe.[3]

The poison is given him, and the "ryotour" hastily mingles it with the wine, keeping a bottle pure for his own use. Then straightway he returns to his companions.

What nedeth it to sermone of it more?

as the Pardoner asks. The youngest of the three is killed, and the others then drink the poisoned wine. The story ends with a grim suggestion of the two sinners' last sufferings.

But Chaucer can do more than give new life to an old story. He has the novelist's gift of revealing the human heart and unravelling the complexities of sentiment. His deepest study of human nature is *Troilus and Criseyde*, which in one sense is an offshoot of mediæval romance, and in another, a great novel in verse. The story is almost entirely a mediæval creation, though it was generally accepted as part of the great Trojan cycle. We hear something in the poem of Hector and Achilles; the pagan deities are frequently mentioned, and there are touches of local colour in the geography; for example, "Simoys" flows through Troy. But in all essentials, in manners, in ideas, in sentiments, the poem is mediæval. This is one of its greatest charms. *Troilus and Criseyde* is as much a study of contemporary life as *Vanity Fair*. All our interest is concentrated on the three main characters: on Troilus, the passionate and faithful lover; on Criseyde, whose inconstancy is made so human; and on the busybody, Pandarus, who, as the friend of Troilus and uncle of Criseyde, is deeply

[1] Kill.   [2] Hedge.   [3] Slain.

involved in the whole love affair. The ceremonial visit of
farewell paid by the Trojan ladies to Criseyde on the eve
of her departure to the Greek camp, is wonderful in its
observation of social feelings. In such scenes as this,
Chaucer seems wholly modern. Cressida, who goes for a
while to her father, Calchas, has faithfully promised to
return to Troy by an appointed day. But the difficulties
of her situation—she is a Greek woman in love with a
Trojan warrior—and the importunities of Diomede, another
lover, break down her constancy, and she never returns.
Troilus's feelings as he waits for her with Pandarus, on the
city walls, are described in a passage which well illustrates
Chaucer's power in the higher kind of narrative :

> Til it was noon, they stoden for to see
> Who that ther come ; and every maner wight,[1]
> That cam fro fer, they seyden it was she,
> Til that they coude knowen him a-right,
> Now was his herte dul, now was it light ;
> And thus by-japed [2] stonden for to stare
> Aboute nought, this Troilus and Pandare.
>
> To Pandarus this Troilus tho [3] seyde,
> " For ought I wot, bi-for noon, sikerly,[4]
> In-to this toun ne comth nought here Criseyde.
> She hath y-now to done, hardily,
> To winnen from hir fader, so trowe I ;
> Hir olde fader wol yet make hir dyne
> Er that she go ; god yeve [5] his herte pyne ! " [6]
>
> Pandare answerde, " It may wel be, certeyn ;
> And for-thy lat us dyne, I thee biseche ;
> And after noon than mayst thou come ayeyn."
> And hoom they go, with-oute more speche ;
> And comen ayein, but longe may they seche
> Er that they finde that they after cape ; [7]
> Fortune hem bothe thenketh for to jape.[8]
>
> Quod Troilus, " I see wel now, that she
> Is taried with hir olde fader so,
> That er she come, it wol neigh even be.
> Com forth, I wol un-to the yate [9] go.
> Thise portours been unkonninge [10] ever-mo ;

---

[1] Every kind of person.   [2] Fooled.
[3] Then.   [4] Certainly.   [5] Give.   [6] Pain.
[7] Gape, seek.   [8] Mock.   [9] Gate.   [10] Unskilful.

And I wol doon hem holden up the yate
As nought re were,[1] al-though she come late."

The day goth faste, and after that comth eve,
And stil come nought to Troilus Criseyde.
He loketh forth by hegge, by tree, by greve,[2]
And fer his heed over the wal he leyde.
And at the laste he torned him, and seyde :
" By god, I woot hir mening now, Pandare !
Al-most, y-wis, al newe was my care.

Now douteles, this lady can hir good ;[3]
I woot,[4] she meneth ryden prively.
I comende hir wysdom, by myn hood !
She wol not maken peple nycely [5]
Gaure [6] on hir, whan she comth ; but softely
By nighte in-to the toun she thinketh ryde,
And, dere brother, thenk not longe t'abyde.

We han nought elles for to doon, y-wis.
And Pandarus, now woltow trowen me ?
Have here my trouthe, I see hir ! yond she is.
Heve up thyn eyen, man ! maystow not see ? "
Pandare answerde, " Nay, so mote I thee ! [7]
Al wrong, by god ; what seystow,[8] man, wher art ?
That I see yond nis but a fare-cart.[9] . . . ."

The wardein of the yates gan to calle
The folk which that with-oute the yates were,
And bad hem dryven in hir bestes alle,
Or al the night they moste bleven there.
And fer with-in the night, with many a tere,
This Troilus gan hoomward for to ryde ;
For wel he seeth it helpeth nought t'abyde.

V

With this skill in narrative is mingled a gift of many-sided humour. Half the Canterbury pilgrims, as they file before the reader of *The Prologue*, raise a smile. Pandarus is perhaps the greatest comic figure in our literature before Falstaff. Chaucer's humour is a part of his rich humanity,

---

[1] As though nothing were the matter.   [2] Grove.
[3] Knows what is good for her.   [4] Know.   [5] Curiously.   [6] Stare.
[7] So may I thrive.   [8] Seest thou.   [9] Travelling-cart.

and it sometimes almost startles us with its realism. The Pardoner, for instance, as he harangues the Pilgrims on the deadly sins, forgets that he is addressing a cavalcade and drops into his pulpit manner :

> " If any wight be in this chirche now . . ."

Equally unexpected and equally Chaucerian is Chanticleer the cock's translation of a Latin phrase for the benefit of his wife, Dame Pertelote, in *The Nonne Preestes Tale* :

> For also siker as [1] *In principio,*
> *Mulier est hominis confusio—*
> Madame, the sentence [2] of this Latin is,
> " Womman is mannes joye and al his blis."

The whole of that tale, in which the Cock and the Hen argue learnedly on the cause of dreams, supporting their rival theories by an array of authorities, after the manner of mediæval disputations, is a masterpiece.

Chaucer loves fun at his own expense. In *The Hous of Fame* he dreams that he is carried up to heaven by an eagle. In mid-air he speculates on the reason for this sudden seizure, and, for a moment, imagines that Jove perhaps intends to " stellify " him. The flattering thought is soon dispelled by the eagle :

> For Joves is not ther-aboute—
> I dar wel putte thee out of doute—
> To make of thee as yet a sterre.

The poet is also humiliated on the road to Canterbury. The tale which he puts into his own mouth is a ridiculous romance called *The Tale of Sir Thopas.* The host endures this ditty until the beginning of the second " fit," but then can contain himself no longer :

> " No more of this, for goddes dignitee,"
> Quod oure hoste, " for thou makest me
> So wery of thy verray lewednesse [3]
> That, also wisly god my soule blesse,
> Myn eres aken [4] of thy drasty [5] speche ;
> Now swiche a rym the devel I biteche ! [6]
> This may wel be rym dogerel," quod he.

---

[1] Just as surely as.   [2] Meaning.   [3] Flat ignorance.
[4] Ache.   [5] Worthless.   [6] I consign to the devil.

28

A mild protest is uttered by the discomfited poet, but he consents to make another attempt, and begins "a litel thing in prose." But the humour of Chaucer is feebly illustrated by specimens, for it springs up from the depths of his nature and pervades his whole work.

VI

While his contemporaries were dreaming dreams and weaving allegories, or entangling themselves in the web of mediæval philosophy, Chaucer found a means of speaking direct to the hearts of future generations. He painted life as he saw it ; and he saw it with so observant an eye that his epoch has become one of the vivid epochs of history, comparable even to the age of Cicero and the age of Shakespeare.

The English people have, perhaps, beyond all others, shown a passion for individual liberty. In political life they have offered a steady resistance to despotic rule ; in private life they have generally shown strong independence of character. English fiction abounds in pictures of highly original men and women ; the dramas of Shakespeare surpass all others in richness and variety of characterisation. Chaucer is the first of a long line of English authors who have found in their countrymen inexhaustible opportunities for observation. Our literature has been largely moulded by our people ; and a short road to success, in fiction and drama, has been the power to " create " character. There are few things more alive than Chaucer's work at its best. No poet has ever set before his readers a livelier array of figures than the Canterbury pilgrims. All are discriminated by the happiest touches. " Even the ribaldry of the low characters is different: the Reeve, the Miller, the Cook are several men, and distinguished from each other as much as the mincing Lady-Prioress and the broad-speaking gap-toothed Wife of Bath." Yet, with all his zest for low life, as Dryden describes it, Chaucer is able to paint noble portraits ; that of the Knight, for example, and that of the Poor Parson. It was a picturesque age ; and the outward appearance often revealed a man's character as well as his rank and calling. Thus, the Knight's " bismotered habergeoun " is an indication of his activity ; the Prioress's motto " Amor vincit omnia " of her sentimentality ; the Scholar's thread-bare " courtepy " of his unworldliness ; and the Shipman's sunburnt skin of his seafaring life. Delight in the motley spectacle was Chaucer's inspiration. To have preserved the everyday poetry of his age is one of Chaucer's greatest achievements.

Chaucer also belongs to the line of English poets who have delighted in the countryside. His descriptions are short, but they are extremely fresh and vivid. The Prologue to *The Legende of Good Women* is memorable for its charming tribute to the poet's favourite flower. With the advent of every May, he throws aside his books and goes forth " to ben at the resureccioun " of the daisy :

> And doun on knees anon-right I me sette,
> And, as I coude, this fresshe flour I grette ;
> Kneling alwey, til hit unclosed was,
> Upon the smale, softe, swote [1] gras,
> That was with floures swote embrouded [2] al . . .

His description of the Reeve's dwelling is a charming picture in two lines :

> His woning [3] was ful fair upon an heeth,
> With grene treës shadwed was his place.

Like Virgil and Dante, he loves the simile drawn from nature :

> And as in winter leves been biraft, [4]
> Eche after other, til the tree be bare,
> So that ther nis but bark and braunche y-laft, [5]
> Lyth [6] Troilus, biraft of ech wel-fare . . .

And he is not afraid to bring into his verse the homely names of the wayside English hamlets :

> Wite [7] ye nat wher ther stant [8] a litel toun
> Which that y-cleped [9] is Bob-up-and-doun,
> Under the Blee, in Caunterbury weye ?

---

[1] Sweet.   [2] Embroidered.   [3] Dwelling.   [4] Torn off.   [5] Left.
[6] Lies.   [7] Know.   [8] Stands.   [9] Called.

VII

A mixture of genius and luck put Chaucer, in nearly all issues, on the winning side. He was not always consistent ; but his better self knew that neither long-winded allegory, nor marvellous adventures, nor astrology, nor metaphysics, nor any of the delights of the Middle Ages, was true matter for poetry. Nor was he ever enticed by the revival of alliteration. He would probably have been content to dismiss the whole subject in the words of his own Parson :

> I can nat geste—*rum, ram, ruf*—by lettre.

In metrical skill, Chaucer stands high among our greatest writers. He introduced the heroic couplet into English verse, and he handled the decasyllabic line with a mastery which was the envy and despair of the following century. The loss of the final sounded -*e* from the language misled English readers for three hundred years into supposing that Chaucer was a rude metrist. But the discovery that final syllables are sounded according to strict rules of grammar and scansion revealed him as one of the masters of English verse.

It was fortunate alike for Chaucer and for his country that he should have been born in London and bred to the Court, for it was thus natural that he should use the East Midland dialect, which was spoken at both universities, and at Court and in the capital. The balance was already weighted heavily in favour of East Midland, and when the immense prestige of Chaucer was cast into the scale in the fifteenth century, the East Midland dialect was clearly destined to become the standard language of England. Thus, while the language used by many another writer of the century was fated to dwindle into an obscure rustic dialect, Chaucer's was to spread to the farthest ends of the earth.

CHAPTER III

THE RENAISSANCE AND THE REFORMATION

BETWEEN Chaucer's death in 1400 and the advent of a
" new poet " announced by the appearance of Spenser's
Shepherd's Calendar, in 1579, there were no English writers
of the first order. This fact is more intelligible than such
facts often are : for even if a man of great genius had been
born in the fifteenth or early sixteenth century, he would
have found the conditions hostile to literature. He would
have been like one who strives to build on shifting sand.
The fifteenth century was an age of dissolution. The
great institutions of the Middle Ages were being threatened
all over Western Europe. In Europe, the Catholic Church
was rapidly approaching the most serious dispute it had
ever known—a dispute destined to rend asunder the whole
of Christendom. In England, feudal society was breaking
up, and in the course of the century was to destroy itself
in the suicidal Wars of the Roses. Even the English
language seemed to be in decay. Its changes rendered the
works of the past useless as models in poetry, and writers
could find no sure standards to govern their practice. But
beneath the surface new forces were beginning to stir.
The Revival of Learning was to provide a new culture
common to the whole of western Europe. Out of the
religious conflict was to emerge a new Church, while the
ancient one was to reveal its latent vitality. In England,
the strong government of the Tudors rose out of the ruins
of feudalism, and ended the years of anarchy. Poetry itself
began to show signs of life as soon as the features of the
new language began to take shape. At the same time, the

invention of printing by movable types opened out prospects for literature such as had never been dreamed of. If the fifteenth century in England was in appearance a period of decay, the sixteenth was one of preparation. The signal for a great outburst of intellectual activity long held in restraint was the defeat of the Armada in 1588.

I

The Renaissance is the name given to a series of changes which transformed the intellectual life of Europe. The "other-worldliness" of the mediæval saints, the view that this present life is of small account save as a prelude to eternity, was exchanged for a passionate desire to reach the summit of wisdom within man's allotted days. The authority of the Church in all matters of the mind was challenged by the great advances in secular learning. New knowledge of the physical universe was won by astronomers and explorers. The place of a Europe united under one Catholic system was taken by a collection of independent states, France, Spain, Holland and England, each possessing a strong national spirit. The writers of Greece, known hitherto only in translation, were studied in the original tongue; and at the same time the sense of nationality created a desire among men to adorn the literature of their own lands. In countries where the Reformation prevailed, a great change took place in the religious life of the people, and the problems of theology came more and more to occupy men of serious temper in every walk of life.

II

The birthplace of the Renaissance was Italy. Even before the introduction of Greek, that country was a great home of learning. The spirit of Petrarch revived in Pope Nicholas V, who reigned from 1447 to 1455, and collected the manuscripts which formed the nucleus of the Vatican Library. In 1453 occurred an event which had vast consequences. The Eastern Empire, which stretched back to the days of Constantine the Great, and had preserved the continuity of the ancient world, had long been exposed to attacks of the Turks. At last, Constantinople fell, and numerous Greek scholars fled westwards, taking their manuscripts with them. In Italy, where they were welcomed with great enthusiasm, Greek literature soon became an object of passionate curiosity and daily conversation. Scholarship under the patronage of such men as Lorenzo dei Medici flourished as never before ; and great works, like Poliziano's translation of Homer into Latin, were begun and completed with buoyant eagerness. The enthusiasm soon spread north of the Alps. Erasmus (1466–1536), a native of Rotterdam, became one of the most influential of all Renaissance scholars. He had studied in Italy, and later taught at both Oxford and Cambridge. Among his friends was Sir Thomas More, the great English humanist. Erasmus combined the enlightenment which is the best result of learning with an accurate sense of style seldom known during the Middle Ages. In his *Praise of Folly* (1508) he makes game of superstition and priestly impostures ; while his *Colloquies* and *Letters* show a mastery of classical Latin unsurpassed since the days of the Roman Empire. Greek soon found a place in the curriculum of our schools and colleges. In England, as in Italy, many great men desired nothing more than to be associated with some eminent service to learning. Cardinal Wolsey, for instance, founded Christ Church, and Dean Colet St. Paul's School, where in the next century Milton, the greatest of our Renaissance poets, was educated. The proudest in the land coveted the reputation for scholarship ; and Queen Elizabeth, in the midst of her business and pleasure, continued to cultivate her Latin and her Greek to the end of her life.

English literature contains some excellent descriptions of the Renaissance spirit. No writer has depicted it better than Browning, whose poem *The Bishop orders his Tomb at St. Praxed's Church* is entirely true to the character of that age. The dying prelate, with his children clustered round him, exults in the bad Latin of his rival's epitaph :

> Aha, ELUCESCEBAT quoth our friend ?
> No Tully, said I, Ulpian at the best !

Nor is there any exaggeration in the picture which Browning gives in *A Grammarian's Funeral*. There were men in Holland and elsewhere as intent as the Grammarian on the foundations of scholarship, and equally willing to make their lives a martyrdom if only they might " settle *Hoti's* business." But while some men faithfully performed the " spade-work " of scholarship, others aimed at encyclopædic learning. An instance of this type was the Florentine, Pico della Mirandola, who, though he died young, left a deep impression on the minds of the learned all over Europe; " the miracle and phœnix of the world " he is called by the Elizabethan poet Daniel. Pico's life was written by Sir Thomas More, in a short work which sets forth those qualities of mind which the most eminent men of the Renaissance most admired :

He was not of the condition of some folk (writes More), which to be excellent in one thing, set all other aside ; but he in all sciences profited so excellently that, which of them soever ye had considered in him, ye would have thought that he had taken that one for his only study. . . .

To the bringing forth of so wonderful effects in so small time, I consider five causes to have come together. First an incredible wit ; secondly a marvellous fast memory ; thirdly, great substance (by which to the buying of his books, as well Latin as Greek and other tongues, he was especially holpen : seven thousand ducats he had laid out in the gathering together of volumes of all manner of literature) ; the fourth cause was his busy and infatigable study ; the fifth was the contempt or despising of all earthly things.

III

The New Learning operated variously on various minds. It made some men wise and others pedantic. Admiration for the classics deprived certain scholars of their good sense, but fortunately the Renaissance in England was immediately followed by the Elizabethan Age, when the nation was high in spirit and particularly self-confident. Hence, while some men wanted to re-model all things after the Greek and Roman fashion, others vindicated the right of Englishmen to follow their own ways.

The minute attention to style, the critical discussion of every word in Latin and Greek, naturally affected men's use of their own language. Shakespeare's Holofernes is no doubt studied from life, and Ben Jonson has drawn a character who jots down in a note-book every new word that takes his fancy. One clergyman of the sixteenth century devised an extraordinary jargon of Anglo-Latin, a sufficient specimen of which is the date of a certain letter, " the penult of the month sextile." But though the Renaissance produced much folly of this kind, it enriched our language with hundreds of valuable words. Many were introduced obscurely, but some can be assigned to their originators. There were, in the sixteenth and seventeenth centuries, plenty of writers who, besides being great scholars, had the finest feeling for the spirit of their own tongue. Hooker, Bacon, Milton and Browne were men of this kind. If they coined a new word, it was to express a new idea, and they generally avoided barbarous formations. The *Pseudodoxia Epidemica* of Sir Thomas Browne, according to Mr. Pearsall Smith, contains new formations " by the hundred, and has probably given currency to more words in the English language than any one book since the time of Chaucer." As instances, he names *hallucination*, *insecurity*, *retrogression*, *precarious*, *incontrovertible*, *antediluvian*. Words of this kind poured into English during the Renaissance. Those derived from Latin were by far the more numerous, though Greek also made a large contribution. The period of enrichment extended to about the middle of the seventeenth century.

The art of poetry naturally attracted the attention of scholars both wise and foolish. Towards the end of the sixteenth century an attempt was made to write English verse according to the classical system. Sir Philip Sidney gave some countenance to these " barbarous experiments," and one writer, after much labour, struck out the following hexameter :

Tityrus, happily thou liest tumbling under a beech-tree.

Success in this direction being but slight, an attack was made upon the use of rhyme. Strangely enough, the movement was supported by two men, one of whom had considerable, the other supreme, skill in rhyming verse— Campion and Milton. In the Preface to *Paradise Lost* Milton slips for a moment into a churlish tone, and calls rhyme "the invention of a barbarous age, to set off wretched matter." But Daniel, in his *Defence of Rhyme*, rose above such prejudices, and expressed the nobler spirit of the Renaissance in words which silence the pedant once and for all :

Methinks we should not so soon yield our consents captive to the authority of antiquity, unless we saw more reason ; all our understandings are not to be built by the square of Greece and Italy. We are the children of nature as well as they ; we are not so placed out of the way of judgment, but that the same sun of discretion shineth upon us ; we have our portion of the same virtues as well as of the same vices. . . . It is not books, but only that great book of the world and the all-overspreading grace of heaven that makes men truly judicial.

In the sphere of imagination, the influence of the classical literature was great, especially through its mythology. A number of legends had been known to the Middle Ages, through Ovid and other Latin poets ; but the effect of these stories in the far grander form they wear in Homer and the Greek dramatists was intoxicating. The poets seized on the ancient myths with all the eagerness of children. To us, frequent allusions to fiery Phœbus and watery Neptune are tiresome, and it is difficult to capture the spirit of the age when such allusions were still fresh. Perhaps the entrancing effect of mythology is best seen in the works of the painters. To an art occupied solely with religious subjects—austere Madonnas and ascetic saints— the ancient deities brought the breath of a brighter and fresher world. The sacred legends and moral allegories, which had been enough for Giotto and Fra Angelico, did not satisfy the men of the sixteenth century such as Leonardo, Correggio and Titian. The Venetians especially gloried in the pagan gods and goddesses, and loved to depict the sleeping Venus and the triumphing Bacchus. Something of this spirit is felt in the *Epithalamion* of Spenser, and both *The Faerie Queene* and *Paradise Lost*, as well as a hundred inferior works, owe part of their glory to the spell wrought by the legends of Greece and Rome.

It was natural that the poets of the Renaissance should be stirred to emulation by the great works of antiquity. In what, they asked, had the classical writers most excelled? Few scholars of the sixteenth century would have questioned that in describing the wrath of Achilles and the wanderings of Odysseus, the human imagination had made its supreme effort. " A heroic poem, truly such, is undoubtedly the greatest work the soul of man is capable to perform." Such was the Renaissance view, expressed in the words of Dryden. The sixteenth century was rich in poems which, by their length and variety of incident, though not always in their structure and style, are true descendants of the *Iliad* and the *Æneid*. Some of these works are as near to mediæval romance as to classical epic. The *Orlando Furioso* of Ariosto (1516) and the *Gerusalemme Liberata* of Tasso (1576) are, perhaps, best described as " romantic epics," and to the same class belongs *The Faerie Queene* (1590–1596). Spenser, in particular, allowed himself almost infinite licence of digression. But *Paradise Lost* (1667) is far more nearly an epic. It is a poem severely wrought, showing that passion for perfect form and perfect style which, to the more scholarly men of the Renaissance, was almost a religion.

IV

The Revival of Learning was only one phase of the Renaissance. Other activities, besides the enthusiasm for the classics, acted on literature almost as potently, though less directly. Between the middle of the fifteenth and the end of the seventeenth century, men's ideas of the Heavens and the Earth underwent a complete change. During the Middle Ages the physical sciences had been, not dead indeed, but dormant. At the Renaissance, they entered upon that progressive movement which is now generally supposed to have no limit. The effect of the new science was at once exhilarating and disturbing. Mediæval thinkers had believed in a small symmetrical universe which the imagination could conceive with ease. They had supposed human affairs to be the centre of the whole terrestrial and celestial system. The earth, according to them, was in the middle of the universe, and Jerusalem in the middle of the earth. To inquire deeply into the secrets of nature was an occupation not worthy of an immortal being. The highest subjects for contemplation were the truths of religion, and for the humbler purpose of education the Seven Liberal Sciences (Grammar, Logic and Rhetoric; Arithmetic, Geometry, Music and Astronomy) were deemed sufficient. All knowledge of animate and inanimate Nature that men could need, might, it was supposed, be found in, or deduced from, the Bible and the works of Aristotle. By the shock of discovery the old simple notions of the earth and the heavens were rendered untenable. The voyages of Vasco da Gama, Magellan, Cabot and Columbus revolutionised men's ideas of the globe. The investigations of Copernicus, Galileo and Newton acquainted men with the motions of the earth and planets and with the immensity of the universe. The mediæval dream of the world as " a limited space, bounded by actual crystal walls and a material firmament " was shattered ; and in its stead came " our own conception of nature, with its unlimited space, its innumerable suns, and the earth but a mote in the beam."

Many great men of the Renaissance lived to witness only the beginning of this movement. But the new facts were, in themselves, less significant than the general atmosphere of discovery and expansion. To the men of action, especially the Elizabethan seamen, the knowledge of new lands came as a challenge which it would be base to ignore :

> You brave heroic minds,
>   Worthy your country's name,
>   That honour still pursue ;
>   Go, and subdue !
> Whilst loitering hinds
>   Lurk here at home with shame.

So wrote Michael Drayton in his poem *To the Virginian Voyage*. To poets, the revelation of the new world without was a stimulus to explore the world within. The greatest character of the Elizabethan stage was moved to wonder when he compared the mortal part of our nature, " this quintessence of dust," with the immensity of the human mind. " What a piece of work is a man! How noble in reason! . . . In apprehension, how like a god!" Marlowe, a contemporary of Shakespeare, was fascinated by the thought of men like Faust, who

> Still climbing after knowledge infinite,

would endure no obstacle to their ambition ; and Chapman, another Elizabethan dramatist, expressed through one of his characters man's claims to unlimited freedom :

> There is no danger to a man, that knows
> What life and death is : there's not any law
> Exceeds his knowledge ; neither is it lawful
> That he should stoop to any other law.

In a spirit as bold, Bacon plans his great revolution of the sciences. " Wonder," he says, in the calmer language of philosophy, " is the seed of knowledge." And looking forward into the future, he declares " these times are the ancient times, when the world is ancient," and again : " I cannot but be raised to this persuasion, that this third period of time will far surpass that of the Grecian and Roman learning."

The great outburst of confidence which is so evident in the last decade of the sixteenth century was, in part, the result of England's victory over the Armada. The event produced a great sense of security ; it was also a signal triumph for the Reformation. The exploits of our sailors continued to assert their equality with the Spaniards and to inflame the pride of the nation. Patriotism is one of the chief notes of Elizabethan literature. Sometimes it is mingled with fulsome compliments to the reigning sovereign. Sometimes it shines out undimmed by all base exultation. Nowhere is a nobler patriotism expressed than in certain speeches of Shakespeare, above all in John of Gaunt's praise of England in *Richard II*.

V

The Reformation, though to some extent a political movement, was also the cause and effect of profound religious and moral changes. It was, in one sense, an off-shoot of the Renaissance ; for one of the first concerns of scholars was to make the whole Bible, or at least the New Testament, accessible to the laity. The mediæval Church-men had given many writings (the Lives and Miracles of Saints, for example) an importance equal to that which they ascribed to the canonical books. They had never encouraged the reading of the Bible as a whole. But as soon as scholars began to study the New Testament in the original tongue, without comment or curtailment, many began to wish that this book, the very fountain-head of Christian doctrine, might be opened to all men. Erasmus, who remained a Catholic to the end of his life, worked hard to achieve this object. " I wish," he said, " that even the weakest woman might read the Gospels and Epistles of St. Paul. I wish that they were translated into all languages, so as to be read and understood not only by Scots and Irishmen, but even by Saracens and Turks. But the first step to their being read is to make them intelligible to the reader. I long for the day when the husbandman shall sing portions of them to himself as he follows the plough, when the weaver shall hum them to the tune of his shuttle, when the traveller shall while away with their stories the weariness of his journey." Erasmus himself translated the New Testament into Latin ; other men translated the Bible, or portions of it, into the vernacular. Before long, the Psalms and the Gospels became as familiar to thousands of men and women in the Protestant countries as Erasmus had dreamed. In England, the various efforts which were made during the sixteenth century to produce a satisfactory translation of the Bible culminated in the marvellous success of the Authorised Version, published in 1611. This fact is by far the most important event in the history of our literature which is directly traceable to the Reformation. "The Bible," it was said, "is the religion of Protestants."

VI

The indirect influence of the Reformation on our literature has also been great, for it has left an enduring mark on the minds of the people and on the framework of society. In the whole history of Christianity, no change so profound has ever taken place. Of course, many Englishmen were quite incapable of appreciating the real nature of the Reformation. Many, also, were indifferent ; only the minority, who troubled themselves deeply with religious matters, felt the full severity of the conflict. The nation as a whole was willing to give up belief in Transubstantiation, and to become Protestant. But the matter did not end there. No one could altogether escape the sense of change wrought in the whole aspect of life by Henry VIII's severance with Rome. The Pilgrimage of Grace shows how quickly popular sentiment was affected. The mediæval Church was no doubt deeply rooted in the hearts of many people. In the north and west, especially, the old loyalties were strong. Love of the Church was intertwined with the whole of life. For centuries the course of the year had been marked by festivals and holy days. Here a well, there an ancient shrine, recalled miracles of help and healing. The walls of the churches were gay with paintings, and from their niches looked down the rudely carved features of saint and apostle. The monasteries, in spite of all their faults, had performed great services to education, and many continued their work up to the time of their dissolution. Was all this to be changed ? Was a complete breach to be made with the past—with the Old England which had been Christian for a thousand years, and had given birth to saints so famous as Edward the Confessor and Thomas of Canterbury ? All to whom ancient ties were dear felt some pang, as one by one the signs of the old religion began to disappear.

The Reformation called upon men to examine a thousand practices which, however beautiful, rested on mere tradition, not on the Word of God. Thus a conflict was begun which split the nation asunder, and divided the minds of many men against themselves. The battle did not end with the Act of Supremacy, or even with the Church Settlement of Elizabeth. Under a new form, the old strife continued. Respect for the past, loyalty to tradition, the desire to worship God in the " beauty of holiness "—all these, it was felt, would be endangered by a triumphant Puritanism. Many joined the Cavalier party in defence of these things ; something of the old loyalty and reverence may be heard in the best of the Cavalier lyrics. The same spirit awoke to life in the later speeches of Burke, when he lamented the decay of chivalry. It survived in the Toryism of Scott. It largely inspired the Oxford movement. In various forms, religious, imaginative and sentimental, it lives to this day.

The desire to purify religion, and to reform the Church according to its original pattern, stirred feelings no less deep. After the reigns of Henry VIII and Mary, the zeal of each side was embittered by the memory of persecution. But even before the days of Smithfield, there had been a stern " enthusiasm " among the Reformers which admitted of no compromise. Protestantism threw a new and terrible burden on the conscience. The belief that a man will be judged by his actions is, of course, inherent in all forms of Christianity. But during the Middle Ages, this truth had been half forgotten. Intellectual assent to dogmas was held to cover a multitude of sins. Even the phrase " good works " was often interpreted to mean such acts as penances and pilgrimages. But the Protestant Reformers restored the term to its true meaning. To them " good works " were those acts by which a man seeks to perform the bidding of Christ. At a Diet which met at Augsburg in 1530 to draw up the Protestant Confession of Faith, the way to salvation was clearly defined. " Christian perfection," it was said, " is this : to fear God sincerely, to trust assuredly that we have, for Christ's sake, a gracious and merciful God ; to ask and look with confidence for help from Him in all our affairs, according to our calling, and outwardly to do good works diligently and to attend to our vocation. (True perfection) doth not consist in going about begging, or in wearing a black or a grey cowl." Thus a man's acts and beliefs received a new and tremendous significance. The priest could do little ; the whole burden was thrown on the individual. No wonder that some of the greatest men of the seventeenth century were, like Cromwell, afflicted with a " religious melancholy." No wonder that, like Bunyan, they read the one true Book with a passionate desire for guidance through the " wilderness of this world." Something of the old Puritan fervour was lost in time, but much remained. It revived in the zeal of Wesley and the deep religiousness of Cowper. It has left a permanent mark on our life and literature, and it has helped to form the conscience of the nation.

CHAPTER IV

SPENSER

A DISTINCTION is sometimes drawn between the poetry of interpretation and the poetry of escape. There are those who wish a poem to " say something." They are not satisfied unless they can carry away with them a definite sense of its meaning. Life, they say, is a serious affair and poets are nothing if not men of vision ; they should therefore illuminate life. If they describe a mountain or a sunset, they should make the reader learn to look at these things with more discerning eyes. If they write a tragedy, they should leave the spectator more at peace or more at war with the world ; at any rate, not unchanged in his attitude. Readers who demand this interpretation of life from poetry are likely to feel some impatience with Spenser, who certainly helps one to escape from the world rather than to understand it. But is there not much merit in a poem which fills the ear with music, and delights the imagination with a succession of pictures ? Abraham Cowley certainly knew in what spirit Spenser must be read : " I was infinitely delighted," he says, " with the stories of the knights and giants and monsters and brave houses, which I found everywhere there ; and by degrees with the tinkling of the rhyme and dance of the numbers, so that I think I had read him all over before I was twelve years old, and was thus made a poet." Even those who have lost their taste for marvellous adventure may still enter the enchanted world of *The Faerie Queene*, if they have kept their love of beautiful language.

I

Versification in England, after the death of Chaucer, became almost a lost art. Of his followers, only those in Scotland showed any of their master's skill. The English "Chaucerians," Lydgate, Occleve, and the rest, were amazingly incompetent, and it was not till the sixteenth century that better days arrived. The language was getting past the stage of transition, and the time had come to remaster the art of verse. Sir Thomas Wyat (1503–1542) and the Earl of Surrey (1516–1547) were pioneers in the work; yet even Surrey, the more polished writer of the two, lacks the confidence of real mastery. Still they formed a new school of poetry. Both wrote sonnets of a kind, those of Surrey being tolerably correct, and he attempted blank verse. The mid-century produced some poets who had got beyond the alphabet of versification, and were beginning to learn the secrets of expressive rhythm. Such were Thomas Sackville, Earl of Dorset (1536–1608), George Gascoigne (1525–1577), and that paragon of his age, poet, scholar, soldier and courtier, Sir Philip Sidney (1554–1586). In 1579, when Spenser published his first work, *The Shepherd's Calendar*, the tide of poetry was rising fast. No one since Chaucer had ever handled verse with such skill as Spenser showed in the various and elaborate metres of his poem, and Chaucer was far behind the new poet in lyrical power. It was not, however, as a lyrical poet that Spenser was to produce his most famous work, though he rose to great heights in the *Epithalamion* and *Prothalamion*. He belongs, above all things, to the order of Ariosto and Tasso, the masters of the Romance of Chivalry.

II

Edmund Spenser was born in London in 1552. After his education at the Merchant Taylors' School and at Pembroke College, Cambridge, he entered the household of the Earl of Leicester, and, in 1580, became secretary to

Lord Grey de Wilton, Governor of Ireland. In these earlier years, Spenser had had plenty of opportunity for discussing questions of literature with his friend Gabriel Harvey, a Cambridge scholar somewhat older than himself. He had also lived at Court, had learnt the art of flattering the Queen, had been in love, and had adopted the views of a moderate Puritan. Such matters as these were in his mind when he wrote *The Shepherd's Calendar*, a poem of twelve ecologues. Under the pastoral form of this work, one can trace the dim outline of Spenser's own thoughts and experience. But his skill in graceful embroidery is what strikes the reader most. Already Spenser is a master of rhythm and of poetic language. His duties in Ireland left him time to meditate his great poem, the first three books of which were published in 1590. Three more were completed, and the whole six appeared in 1596. Spenser also wrote a number of shorter poems which were published under the title of *Complaints*, in 1591 ; some sonnets called *Amoretti*, and *Epithalamion*, in 1595 ; and *Four Hymns*, inspired by Plato's philosophy, to *Beauty*, to *Love*, to *Heavenly Beauty* and to *Heavenly Love*, in 1596. These shorter poems give much more direct expression to Spenser's thoughts than *The Faerie Queene*, though even in them his mind is seen as through a glass, darkly. Sometimes, however, one meets passages of almost startling directness. There are some lines in *Mother Hubbard's Tale* in which Spenser utters his disgust at the disappointments endured by a courtier with all the idiomatic force of true satire :

> Full little knowest thou, that hast not tride,
> What hell it is in suing long to bide :
> To loose good dayes that might be better spent ;
> To wast long nights in pensive discontent ;
> To speed to-day, to be put back to-morrow ;
> To feed on hope, to pine with feare and sorrow ;
> To have thy Princes grace, yet want her Peeres ;
> To have thy asking, yet waite manie yeeres ;
> To fret thy soule with crosses and with cares ;
> To eat thy heart through comfortlesse dispaires ;
> To fawne, to crowche, to waite, to ride, to ronne,
> To spend, to give, to want, to be undonne.

Pope himself could hardly have written with more vigour and terseness.

The last part of Spenser's life was a tragedy. In 1598 a great rebellion in Ireland burst out, and many of the Protestant settlers were driven from their estates. Spenser was one of those who suffered. Kilcolman Castle, his home, was burnt down, and one of his children perished in the fire. He returned to London and died soon after, in 1599—according to Ben Jonson, " for lack of bread."

III

That Spenser was a contemporary of Shakespeare and of Bacon is one of the anomalies of the Elizabethan Age. In many ways the author of *The Faerie Queene* seems to be two centuries behind his time. Had a poet of Chaucer's age chosen King Arthur and Fairyland for his subject, and made the whole work an allegory of the virtues and vices, there would have been nothing to cause surprise. But, in the meanwhile, the modern world had been born. In Spenser's time, many men still loved romantic legends, but they knew that these belonged to an ancient world of chivalry, and that they reflected manners and ideas which had departed for ever. Spenser was not wholly unlike Don Quixote, who had read so many romances that at last he saddled his horse and rode forth as a knight-errant ; for *The Faerie Queene* brings King Arthur and the knights of the Round Table into the company of Queen Elizabeth and Philip of Spain, and mingles the world of fairies and satyrs with the world of Protestants and Catholics. The Renaissance taught Spenser to read Greek, and it deepened his love of poetry, but it did not make him a man of his age.

The Faerie Queene is both a romance and an allegory. " I labour to pourtray in Arthur," says Spenser, " the image of a brave knight, perfected in the twelve private moral virtues, as Aristotle hath devised, the which is the purpose of these first twelve books." Though Arthur represents the all-embracing virtue of magnanimity, and though he intervenes

48

in moments of crisis, he is but a shadowy figure in the half-finished poem. The heroes and heroines of the separate books are much more real to the imagination. Each book is devoted to a particular virtue, and the incidents represent the struggle of that virtue with its foes. In the First Book the hero is the Red Cross Knight, typifying Holiness. In the second it is Sir Guyon, the Knight of Temperance. Britomart, a female warrior, is the champion of Chastity in the Third Book. Cambel and Triamond, who represent Friendship, are the central figures of the Fourth. Sir Artegall and Sir Calidore, the Knights of Justice and Courtesy, are the champions of the Fifth and Sixth. The connecting link between the various books was to have been supplied by the Twelfth, " where," as Spenser says, in a letter to Sir Walter Raleigh, "I devise that the Faery Queene kept her annual feast twelve days, upon which twelve several days, the occasions of the twelve several adventures happened, which being undertaken by twelve several knights, are in these twelve books severally handled and discoursed." Thus, the origin of the exploits of which we read is never completely revealed, as Spenser plunges *in medias res*, and had reserved the chronological beginning for the last book of the poem.

The allegorical purpose is also explained in the author's own words. "The general end of all the book," says Spenser, "is to fashion a gentleman or noble person in virtuous and gentle discipline." He names several other poets who, as he supposes, wrote with a similar object: Tasso, Ariosto, Virgil, and even Homer, "who in the persons of Agamemnon and Ulysses hath ensampled a good governor and a virtuous man, the one in his *Ilias*, the other in his *Odysseis*." So we are back again in the Middle Ages, when a story was never a mere story, but also a guide to right action and to orthodox belief. Spenser was not the poet to throw light on the problems of his own day. In fact, he disliked his age and longed to escape. By the antique language of his poem, by his chivalric conceptions, by his miraculous stories of errant knights, distressed ladies, enchanters, satyrs and saracens, he shows his preference for the past over the present. It is not that he is blind to contemporary events. On the contrary, his impressionable nature is affected by them as by everything else. A historical allegory is interwoven into the fabric of his poem. Philip of Spain, Mary of Scotland, Lord Grey de Wilton, the troubles in Ireland, the Mar-Prelate controversy, are all introduced under a disguise. But these matters discerning readers may, if they like, discreetly ignore. If, as Hazlitt said, they do not meddle with the allegory, the allegory will not meddle with them. Spenser is serious enough, no doubt, in his morality and religion, and in his admiration for the chivalrous past. But in these things he differed little from many other men. It is his sense of beauty that makes him a poet.

IV

The Faerie Queene, to borrow the title of an Elizabethan anthology, is a " gorgeous gallery of gallant inventions." Nowhere is poetic fancy more fertile. History and legend are ransacked for their spoils, and elements of the most diverse origin—classical, Christian, mediæval and modern— are fused together with a boldness unsurpassed even in that age of anachronisms. To realise the richness of Spenser's mind, one should pass in review the scenes of a single book. The adventures of the Red Cross Knight alone are a long romance. One picture succeeds another : Una and her lion, the plots of Archimago ; the House of Pride ; the wiles of Duessa ; the fate of Fradubio, turned into a tree ; the errors of the Red Cross Knight ; the craft of Orgoglio ; Despair and his victims ; the penance of the hero and his final victory over the dragon. The poet's fancy continues its flight with unflagging wing through all the six books. Sir Guyon in the Cave of Mammon, Malbecco escaping from his burning house and sleeping among satyrs, Brito-mart's passage through the flames into the house of Busirane, the exploits of Talus, the iron-man—these, and a score of other incidents show the poet's inexhaustible power of fantastic invention. Spenser's skill in narrative is of a

peculiar kind. He does not impress the reader with the
reality of what he describes, but charms him into a dreamlike acceptance of impossible visions. The nature of his
art is well illustrated by the story of the Red Cross Knight
and the Dragon. This fight is the culminating event of
the First Book. The Red Cross Knight had set out on his
quest accompanied by Una, or Truth. His strength sufficed
him to overcome the monster Error, but he fell a victim
to Archimago, and forsook Una in favour of Duessa, who
impersonates False Religion. He passes through many
troubles, and is nearly overcome by Despair, but at length
gains strength necessary for his great ordeal. The Dragon
approaches him, " Halfe flying, and halfe footing in his
hast " :

> His flaggy wings when forth he did display,
>   Were like two sayles, in which the hollow wynd
> Is gathered full, and worketh speedy way :
>   And eke the pennes, that did his pineons bynd,
>   Were like mayne-yards, with flying canvas lynd,
> With which whenas him list the ayre to beat,
>   And there by force unwonted passage find,
> The cloudes before him fled for terrour great,
> And all the heavens stood still amazed with his threat.

> His huge long tayle wound up in hundred foldes,
>   Does overspred his long bras-scaly backe,
> Whose wreathed boughts when ever he unfoldes,
>   And thicke entangled knots adown does slacke,
>   Bespotted as with shields of red and blacke,
> It sweepeth all the land behind him farre,
>   And of three furlongs does but little lacke ;
> And at the point two stings in-fixed arre,
> Both deadly sharpe, that sharpest steele exceeden farre.

> But stings and sharpest steele did far exceed
>   The sharpnesse of his cruell rending clawes ;
> Dead was it sure, as sure as death indeed,
>   Whatever thing does touch his ravenous pawes,
>   Or what within his reach he ever drawes.
> But his most hideous head my toung to tell
>   Does tremble : for his deepe devouring jawes
> Wide gaped, like the griesly mouth of hell,
> Through which into his darke abisse all ravin fell.

> And that more wondrous was, in either jaw
> Three ranckes of yron teeth enraunged were
> In which yet trickling bloud and gobbets raw
> Of late devoured bodies did appeare,
> That sight thereof bred cold congealed feare :
> Which to increase, and all at once to kill ;
> A cloud of smoothering smoke and sulphur seare
> Out of his stinking gorge forth steemed still,
> That all the ayre about with smoke and stench did fill.
>
> His blazing eyes, like two bright shining shields,
> Did burne with wrath, and sparkled living fyre ;
> As two broad Beacons, set in open fields,
> Send forth their flames farre off to every shyre,
> And warning give, that enemies conspyre,
> With fire and sword the region to invade ;
> So flam'd his eyne with rage and rancorous yre :
> But farre within, as in a hollow glade,
> Those glaring lamps were set, that made a dreadfull shade.

Formidable as the monster is, he is not victorious. He seems unaware of his own advantages, and the dreadful tail which, one would think, might have dashed man and horse to the ground, remains useless. Indeed, the knight is by far the more active combatant : but there is a limit to his powers of endurance :

> Faint, wearie, sore, emboyled, grieved, brent
> With heat, toyle, wounds, armes, smart, and inward fire
> That never man such mischiefes did torment ;
> Death better were, death did he oft desire.

The fight is not fought on equal terms, for the Red Cross Knight receives supernatural aid. Succoured by the Tree of Life, he gains power to deal the final blow. Thus, the allegory is deepened, but the conflict, as a trial of strength, loses interest. One remembers the Dragon more vividly than the fight ; and as to the issue, there is not a moment's serious anxiety.

V

But *The Faerie Queene* contains things better than brilliant unrealities. Spenser did not stand in much awe of his own Dragon ; but there were many things in which he believed sincerely, and when he writes of these, his poetry both interests and moves the reader. Like a true Elizabethan and Platonist, he thought deeply on Love and Friendship ; his treatment of these matters in Books III and IV of *The Faerie Queene* is full of subtlety. Further, his life amid the anarchy of Ireland compelled him to ponder on the foundations of Government and the nature of Justice. The picture in Book V of the Giant who wished to test everything in his balances, and then reconstruct the world after more rational principles, has an interest for all times. The speaker is a " leveller," who conceals his subversive designs under specious promises :

> Therefore I will throw down these mountaines hie,
>   And make them levell with the lowly plaine :
> These towring rocks, which reach unto the skie,
>   I will thrust downe into the deepest maine,
>   And as they were, them equalize againe.
> Tyrants that make men subject to their law,
>   I will suppresse, that they no more may raine,
> And Lordings curbe, that commons over-aw ;
> And all the wealth of rich men to the poore will draw.

Spenser is nowhere more excellent than in his allegorical pageants. There are two of special magnificence, the Masque of Cupid in Book III and the Procession of the Vices in Book I. In depicting Queen Lucifera and her evil Counsellors, Spenser had just the opportunity he needed. He had the sanction of the past—both painters and poets in the Middle Ages had loved to represent the Deadly Sins. He had his feelings as a Puritan to give reality to the picture, for, after all, Spenser was not wholly miscalled by Milton our " sage and serious " poet. Further, he had the artist's desire to outdo all predecessors in wealth of imagery and richness of language. The Vices ride in procession, each being mounted according to his character. The First in the troop

> Was sluggish Idlenesse the nourse of sin ;
>   Upon a slouthfull asse he chose to ryde,
> Arayd in habit blacke, and amis thin,
> Like to an holy Monck, the service to begin.

He is followed by Gluttony, "Deformed creature, on a filthie swyne":

> In greene vyne leaves he was right fitly clad,
>> For other clothes he could not weare for heat,
> And on his head an yuie girland had,
>> From under which fast trickled downe the sweat:
>> Still as he rode, he somewhat still did eat,
> And in his hand did beare a bouzing-can,
>> Of which he supt so oft, that on his seat
> His dronken corse he scarse upholden can,
> In shape and life more like a monster, than a man.

Avarice is mounted on a "Camell loaden all with gold."

> Two iron coffers hong on either side,
>> With precious metall full, as they might hold;
>> And in his lap an heape of coine he told;
> For of his wicked pelfe his God he made,
>> And unto hell him selfe for money sold;
> Accursed usurie was all his trade,
> And right and wrong ylike in equall ballaunce waide.

Envy follows on a "ravenous wolfe."

> And next to him malicious Envie rode,
>> Upon a ravenous wolfe, and still did chaw
> Betweene his cankred teeth a venemous tode,
>> That all the poison ran about his chaw;
>> But inwardly he chawed his owne maw
> At neighbours wealth, that made him euer sad;
>> For death it was, when any good he saw,
> And wept, that cause of weeping none he had,
> But when he heard of harme, he wexed wondrous glad . . .

> And him beside rides fierce revenging Wrath,
>> Upon a Lion, loth for to be led;
> And in his hand a burning brond he hath,
>> The which he brandisheth about his hed;
>> His eyes did hurle forth sparkles fiery red,
> And stared sterne on all, that him beheld,
>> As ashes pale of hew and seeming ded;
> And on his dagger still his hand he held,
> Trembling through hasty rage, when choler in him sweld.

Spenser's elevation of mind is shown, above all, in his representation of moral crises. The Red Cross Knight, having forsaken Una, is almost ruined by the wickedness of his enemies. In his dejection he encounters Despair, who offers him a dagger ; and the motives to self-destruction are urged with all the seductive power of Spenser's languorous verse :

> Who travels by the wearie wandring way,
>   To come unto his wished home in haste,
> And meets a flood, that doth his passage stay,
>   Is not great grace to helpe him over past,
>   Or free his feet, that in the myre sticke fast ?
> Most envious man, that grieves at neighbours good,
>   And fond, that joyest in the woe thou hast,
> Why wilt not let him passe, that long hath stood
> Upon the banke, yet wilt thy selfe not passe the flood ?

> He there does now enioy eternall rest
>   And happie ease, which thou doest want and crave,
> And further from it daily wanderest :
>   What if some litle paine the passage have,
>   That makes fraile flesh to feare the bitter wave ?
> Is not short paine well borne, that brings long ease,
>   And layes the soule to sleepe in quiet grave ?
> Sleepe after toyle, port after stormie seas,
> Ease after warre, death after life does greatly please.

VI

Spenser's influence on English poetry has been immense. He has been justly called " the poet's poet." Men of the most diverse gifts have admired and imitated him. He is the inventor of one of the most individual and romantic styles in literature, the chief marks of which are the metre and the vocabulary. The " Spenserian stanza " of nine lines, intricately rhymed and ending with an Alexandrine, was revived by Thomson and others in the eighteenth century, and has since been imitated by many great poets. Byron and Shelley both used it, each subduing its character to his own genius. But the spirit of the stanza has been more finely recaptured by two poets who were more akin in temperament to its inventor—by Keats in *The Eve of St. Agnes*, and by Tennyson at the beginning of *The Lotus-Eaters*.

Spenser, more than any other writer, is the founder of

our " poetic diction." The type of mind which seeks its home in the ideal, or in the romantic past, is known in many ages. Spenser's imagination was of this order, and his genius created a style to suit it. " He writ no language," said Ben Jonson, contemptuously ; but the very remoteness of his style is its commendation. " He cherished words," says one of his best critics, " which though still in use were rapidly passing out of fashion, and the sustained colouring and atmosphere of his style is thus given by a constant use of words which are found in Marlowe, Shakespeare or Sidney, perhaps once or twice. *Eftsoons, ne, als, whilom, uncouth, wight, eke, sithens, ywis*—it is words like these continually woven into the texture of his diction which . . . give it the Spenserian colour." The practice of preserving old words has been of great service to our poets, and Spenser is the chief founder of this art. He also enjoys the rare distinction of having added words of his own coining to our language. Three examples are : *blatant, elfin* and *braggadocio*. The fact, perhaps, seems small, yet it indicates that *The Faerie Queene* has won a place not only in the admiration of poets but in the memory of the English people.

CHAPTER V

SHAKESPEARE: HIS STAGE AND HIS WORKS

SHAKESPEARE's position as the first of English writers cannot be challenged. The phrase of Matthew Arnold, "Others abide our question, thou art free," still expresses an almost universal feeling, if we regard the supreme merits of Shakespeare's plays. But our greatest writer is not well served by mere adulation. He was a man, writing for men, an author with a living to make. He belonged to an age which, though great in action and imagination, was in some respects half barbarous. He was himself careless over trifles, and often deficient in taste. He wrote for an audience of which a noisy brawling multitude formed a considerable part. The stage on which his plays were performed was designed in a way of its own, and in all its mechanical contrivances would seem very clumsy to modern notions. No intelligent and candid reader of Shakespeare's plays can help feeling puzzled by some things in them, and repelled by others. To do him justice, we must make some effort to understand the conditions under which he wrote. Fortunately, the history of the Elizabethan theatre is itself full of romantic interest. The study of it would repay the time spent, even if its final reward were not the illumination of our greatest poet.

The Stage

I

For a glimpse of our theatre in its earliest form, we must look back into the tenth century. In those days, the Church was the one institution which fostered the finer feelings of men. It accepted the task of satisfying all desires : hence the great festivals of the year were landmarks in the intellectual, as well as the religious lives of the people. Christmas and Easter were seasons on which all the resources of imagination were lavished. The deepest emotions were aroused by the services, so that a mere touch of art was enough to render them highly dramatic. The priests rose to the occasion, and by a few deft additions to the accepted ritual made the great story of the Resurrection the first drama to be played in Christian England. No better description can be given of what took place than the directions for the ceremony as performed in Winchester Cathedral :

While the third lesson is being chanted, let four brethren vest themselves. Let one of these, vested in an alb, enter as though to take part in the service, and let him approach the sepulchre without attracting attention, and sit there quietly with a palm in his hand. While the third respond is being chanted, let the remaining three follow, and let them all, vested in copes, bearing in their hands thuribles with incense and stepping delicately as those who seek something, approach the sepulchre. These things are done in imitation of the angel sitting in the monument and the women with spices coming to anoint the body of Jesus. When therefore he who sits there beholds the three approach him like folk lost and seeking something, let him begin in a dulcet voice of medium pitch to sing *Quem quæritis*. And when he has sung it to the end, let the three reply in unison, *Jhesum Nazarenum*. So he, *Non est hic : surrexit sicut prædixerat. Ite, nuntiate quia surrexit a mortuis*. At the words of this bidding, let those three turn to the choir and say, *Alleluia ! resurrexit Dominus !* This said, let the one, still sitting there and as if recalling them, say the anthem, *Venite et videte locum*. And, saying this, let him rise and lift the veil and show them the place bare of the cross, but only the cloths laid there in which the cross was wrapped. And when they have seen this, let them set down the thuribles which they bare in that same sepulchre, and take the cloth and hold it up in the face of the clergy, and as if to demonstrate that the Lord has risen and is no longer wrapped therein, let them sing the anthem *Surrexit Dominus de Sepulchro*, and lay the cloth upon the altar. When the anthem is done, let the priest, sharing in their gladness at the triumph of the King, in that, having vanquished death, He rose again, begin the hymn *Te Deum laudamus*. And this begun, all the bells chime out together.[1]

The dramatised services were, as may be imagined, immensely popular. The Church had set on foot a movement, the issue of which no one could foresee. By degrees, the people took these ceremonies into their own hands. They themselves became actors in the sacred drama, and they increased its scope more and more until it embraced a large part of Biblical history. The end of it was that a set of plays came into being which represented the entire scheme of man's destiny as set forth by the Church. The first story to be enacted was the Creation. This was followed by scenes from Old Testament History, such as Abraham's sacrifice, the building of the Ark, and Jonah's journey to Nineveh. The culminating play represented the Passion, and the series was concluded by the Last Judgment. The control of these performances was in the hands of the Trade Guilds, who divided the various parts among themselves. These sacred dramas are known as Mystery or Miracle Plays. Four cycles have survived: the York, the Towneley, the Chester and the Coventry Plays.

II

By the fifteenth century, Miracle Plays were already losing their hold, and their place was being taken by a new form of drama, founded not on the Bible but on the religious conception of the struggle between Good and Evil in the life of man. These new dramas are known as Morality Plays and are in the form of allegories. Instead of patriarchs and prophets, the characters are now such beings as " Bonus Angelus," " Malus Angelus," " Mundus," " Belial," " Caro," " Repentance," and " Riches." It may be thought from this description that the Church had recovered its hold on the drama. This is partly true—at

[1] *Trans.*, E. K. Chambers.

least, several Morality Plays reflect the religious contro-
versies of the time. Some, such as *Lusty Juventus*, which
belongs to the middle of the sixteenth century, are written
from the Protestant side and ridicule Popish superstitions.
A few of the Morality Plays reveal considerable dramatic
skill and have justified the attempt to revive them in
recent years. One, in particular, is really impressive when
well played. This is *Everyman*, which is almost a minor
classic in our literature, and shall therefore be shortly
described in illustration of the type to which it belongs.

The character who gives his name to the play is a
flourishing citizen. He is in the full enjoyment of this
world's good things, when a Messenger suddenly arrives
with the news that he is imperatively called upon to take
a long journey. Everyman anxiously calls his friends about
him, hoping to find one who will bear him company.
Friendship, Kindred and Goods appear in succession.
All greet their friend cheerfully, but on hearing the nature
of his request shrink back with various excuses. Everyman
becomes more and more troubled, for the hour of his
departure is drawing near and the Messenger becomes
increasingly urgent. At last, a better counsellor, Good
Deeds, makes his appearance. He gives the dying man
sobering but wholesome advice, commanding him to seek,
not the worldly help of his boon companions, but the aid
of Repentance and the good offices of the Church. The
minutes are now running out. Five wits, Kindred, Beauty,
Strength and Discretion, forsake Everyman in turn. Only
Good Deeds remains with him till the end. As the play
closes, Everyman sets forth on his long journey.

Morality Plays survived well into the sixteenth century.
But by that time the Elizabethan theatre was beginning
its great career, and even such excellent works as *The
Three Ladies of London* (1584), one of the last Moralities,
could not keep alive a dying tradition. But the Morality
Plays were long remembered, and something of their spirit
survived. Allusions to the " Vice " are common enough
in Shakespeare, and the popular figure of the Clown is
probably a relic of the Devil who was often placed in

ludicrous and humiliating situations. In the works of Ben Jonson, especially, the spirit of the Morality Play lived on. He loved to draw characters dominated by some particular quality or "humour." In such creations as Morose and Sir Politic Would-be, one may recognise descendants of the abstract figures who typified the Virtues and Vices in the old plays.

III

Love of dramatic entertainments possessed a strong hold on the generations just before Shakespeare. For courtly and ceremonial occasions, for Christmas revels and marriages at great houses, the refined but somewhat stiff performances known as Masques were in request. These plays were best performed either in a stately hall, or the grounds of a large house. The costumes were splendid ; and the dialogue was varied by music and pageantry. In *The Tempest*, Prospero contrives a Masque in honour of Miranda's betrothal to Ferdinand, and Juno and Ceres address each other in formal speeches full of classical allusions. For learned audiences, a play modelled on the manner of Seneca called *Gorboduc*, or *Ferrex and Porrex*, had been written by Sackville and Norton in 1562. In the early 'eighties John Lyly began producing a series of comedies (*Campaspe*, *Endymion*, *The Woman in the Moon*, and others), which combine some effective situations with a display of not very profound learning and a great deal of "euphuistic" language. Contemporary with Lyly, or a little later, were the "University Wits," who sometimes took their subjects from classical sources, but generally made them fit for average men and women. Chief among these writers were Peele, Greene, and above all, Marlowe, the author of *Doctor Faustus* and *Edward II*.

More homely audiences were entertained by plays of a ruder kind called Interludes. This name, it will be remembered, is given by Bottom to the tragedy of *Pyramus and Thisbe*, which the hard-handed mechanics played before Theseus and his court. Most interludes are amusing in a somewhat popular way. *The Four P's*, *Ralph Roister Doister* (*cir.* 1553) and *Gammer Gurton's Needle* (printed 1575) are perhaps the best known. All are farcical, and it will be sufficient to give a very short account of one of them. Gammer—that is, Grandmother—Gurton has lost her needle, and a search of the whole house is made in vain. At length the party become weary and give up their efforts in exhaustion. The husband, Gaffer, sits down with the rest, whereupon the needle is immediately discovered, for his wife, who had been mending his breeches, had left it sticking in the cloth. The story indicates the taste of a popular Tudor audience. The generation for which Shakespeare wrote had, no doubt, been trained to appreciate higher things, but the love of horseplay dies hard, and the " groundlings " of The Globe were perhaps as boisterous a crew as ever clapped and hissed before a stage. Not that they were incapable of higher feelings. Their patriotism, for instance, was always ready to catch fire, and they followed intently the history of their own country. As early as 1560, a chronicle play, called *King Johan*, the work of one Bale, had appeared. It is a rude piece, without construction, but it deserves to be remembered as the forerunner of Shakespeare's Histories.

IV

Elizabethan plays were designed for the Elizabethan theatre, and we must not be surprised if they do not wholly suit the conventions of our own stage. It was not until the latter part of the sixteenth century that theatres were first built in England. Before that time plays had commonly been acted at inns, built round a courtyard. A scaffolding raised in the centre, or at one end, provided a rude stage in view of spectators sitting in the galleries or standing on the ground. Many persons, no doubt, were awkwardly placed ; but it mattered little, for the audience of those days went to hear a play rather than to see it. Stage scenery was of the simplest kind. Notices rapidly brought in and removed indicated the various scenes, such as " A wood," " Rome, the Forum." These arrangements would seem crude to an audience accustomed to regard the drama as a spectacle, yet they suited Shakespeare and his contemporaries, and enabled them to bring on scene after scene in quick succession.

Inns, such as the Red Lion, the Bull, the Bel Savage, and the Cross Keys, served Londoners for a time as theatres, but later, buildings were erected for the purpose, the earliest being the Theatre and the Curtain, both of them at Shoreditch. Soon the theatre quarter was shifted to the Bankside, and there, between London Bridge and Blackfriars, were built the Globe, the Swan and several others. To some extent the plan of an inn was reproduced. The theatres were round or polygonal. About half-way into the middle projected a raised platform, visible on all sides to the audience, who were seated tier above tier or crowded together on the floor of the house. On this stage or platform, naked to the gaze, without screen or curtain, most of the action took place. Some distance back from the front of the stage was a curtain hung before a door and forming a recess—a useful receptacle for unnecessary properties, and for characters killed in the frays so dear to an Elizabethan audience. But the recess had a still greater value. All but the entrance was hidden from view : it therefore served as a cavern, or an antechamber, or any other place suitable to a stratagem or deed of darkness. Many well-known incidents in Shakespeare were acted upon this hidden stage. Polonius concealed by the arras, Caliban in his den, crying, " There's wood enough within," Desdemona lying smothered on her bed, were all behind the dividing curtain. In modern theatres the curtained portion has become the main stage ; and it would seem odd to us to listen to a dialogue spoken almost in the middle of the theatre. Yet such, in Shakespeare's time, was the custom. To deliver an important speech an actor would come to the very front of the open stage and utter the words with all the power of his voice.

Above the curtained recess was a space used sometimes as a musicians' gallery ; sometimes, on rare occasions, as a third stage. The direction " enter above " means that the actor was to make his appearance in this part of the theatre. In *Richard II* the upper stage represents the battlements of the castle from which the king harangues his captors. In *Antony and Cleopatra* it serves as the tower into which the dying Antony is drawn, and instances may easily be recalled in which it represents a balcony or upper storey. All these contrivances were both simple and effective. By their means, plays of many scenes could be acted with a speed which in our theatre would be impracticable. *Hamlet*, uncurtailed, is a prodigiously long work for a modern stage, but in an Elizabethan theatre its length would be scarcely noticed.

The actors of Shakespeare's time were all males. Women's parts were taken by boys or by young men with voices more or less suitable. Actresses did not make their appearance until the Restoration. The exclusion of women from the stage is another surprise to those who consider that a play should produce the illusion of reality. But literal truth was as little desired by the Elizabethan dramatist as historical accuracy was sought by Renaissance painters. Just as Paul Veronese depicts Alexander the Great as a contemporary Venetian, so Cæsar and Coriolanus would appear on the boards of the Globe in the dress and beards of the time. It was to the imagination rather than the senses that an appeal was made ; and the imagination was to be stimulated, but not surfeited. " Oh, pardon," says the chorus in *Henry V*, apologising for the narrow limits of the theatre,

> Since a crooked figure may
> Attest in little place a million ;
> And let us, ciphers to this great accompt,
> On your imaginary forces work . . .
> For 'tis your thoughts that now must deck our kings.

The realities of life, however, were not without their influence on the conventions of the stage ; and the fact that the persons dressed as women were really males, smoothed the way for the disguises which are so common in Shakespeare's plots. It was natural enough to make

Viola dress as a page when the actor playing the part was, as all knew, a boy or young man himself.

The presence of the groundlings—talking, eating, and interrupting—must have been a sore annoyance to dramatists who aspired to write good as well as popular plays. Ben Jonson blames the poets who brought on monsters and " machines " for the delight of the uncritical, and Shakespeare himself, as we may learn from *Hamlet*, had his own difficulties with the groundlings. Actors, it seems, would sometimes spoil a good speech by adding something of their own to amuse the " barren " spectators. In the eyes of many, the theatres were no doubt intended for much the same purpose as the Bear Garden which stood not far away on the Bankside. A play without physical violence and sensational episodes would be " caviare to the general." It needed supreme skill to adapt the demands of the groundlings to the purposes of art ; and nothing in Shakespeare deserves higher praise than the skill with which he performed this most difficult task. Even in his greatest tragedies, he admits scenes of violence and fighting, and he does not dare to exclude the popular Clown and Fool. The miracle is that the clowns in *Hamlet* and the fool in *King Lear* are brought so triumphantly into the poet's scheme, that instead of spoiling the tragedy, they render it more tragic still.

The Works of Shakespeare

I

Shakespeare's dramatic career extended from about 1590 to 1613.[1] In the space of those twenty-three years he passed through every phase of artistic development. He began as an immature young man, with some knowledge of the theatre, but little power to interpret life, and scarcely any literary style. Within four years he was producing masterpieces, still " early works," but full of poetry and passion. Two years more and he had reached maturity.

[1] The dates assigned to Shakespeare's plays in the following pages are only approximate and conjectural.

Henceforth his work, though changing year by year, shows that close grasp of life which belongs to a man at the height of his powers. We may name the years 1596 to 1600, Shakespeare's early middle period. It was then that he produced many of his best Comedies and Histories. Between 1601 and 1609 all the great tragedies from *Julius Cæsar* to *Coriolanus* were written : in this later middle period his genius reached its culmination. The plays composed between 1610 and 1613 are definitely " late." There is no sign of decay—the poet has passed into a new phase of his art. But he has come into smoother waters after a night of turmoil.

The few facts known about Shakespeare's life throw scarcely any light on his works. He was born at Stratford-on-Avon in 1564, and died there, as a man of property with a coat of arms, in 1616. That he was one who read life with his own eyes and regarded books as at best only a commentary is evident in every page of his works. Coming up to London as a young man with a wife to support, his chief object was naturally to earn a living. He evidently found employment in the theatre quarter ; it is said, by looking after the horses of playgoers. The tradition that he was of a " sweet " and affable nature is well established, and his friendliness was no doubt of great value to him at this period. At any rate, his rise in the early twenties was rapid : by the time he was twenty-six he had already produced his first comedy, *Love's Labour's Lost*. It is a clever work, without the humanity of style that keeps old books sweet. Shakespeare hits off some absurd characters he had noticed—a pedantic schoolmaster, and an affected phrase-maker. He experiments in various metres and he displays facility in rhyming. But these things do not make an old play live, nor is there much genius in the poet's treatment of the central theme. A young man, Biron, and his companions sequester themselves for the purpose of study and meditation, and vow to abjure all feminine society. But the retreat is visited by the Princess of France with some other ladies, and the scheme of the hermitage falls to the ground. Biron and his friends conceal their backslidings from each other as long as possible, but each is detected at last, and the play ends with the triumph of Hymen. There is some skill in the working out of the plot, but even the most living of the characters, Biron, is little more than a shadow.

During the two years that followed this early attempt, Shakespeare produced two other comedies, *The Comedy of Errors* and *The Two Gentlemen of Verona*. The first is a farce of mistaken identities with little human interest; the second is a more mature work, and one of the characters, Speed, may rank among Shakespeare's minor comic creations. At the same time he was at work on the three parts of *Henry VI*, but here he was the collaborator of other men, and his contributions cannot be discriminated with certainty. *Richard III*, a melodramatic history with some powerful passages, such as Clarence's dream, is also the work of these years. But two plays of this early period stand out above all the rest: these are *Romeo and Juliet* (1592) and *A Midsummer Night's Dream* (1594).

These plays are the crown of Shakespeare's youth. *Romeo and Juliet* is one of the supreme love poems of the world. It is the story of a great passion and its tragic outcome. Never were the meeting of lovers and their farewell so steeped in poetry as in this story of old Verona. Romeo is a less interesting character than the heroes of the later tragedies; indeed, he is as much a type as an individual. He is in love with love, and his heart is like dry tinder even before he goes to the Capulets' ball. His meeting there with Juliet is conceived not only as a crisis in his life but also as a romantic incident to be described with all the tenderness of lyrical verse:

Romeo : If I profane with my unworthiest hand
      This holy shrine, the gentle fine is this :
  My lips, two blushing pilgrims, ready stand
      To smooth that rough touch with a tender kiss.

Juliet : Good pilgrim, you do wrong your hand too much,
      Which mannerly devotion shows in this ;
  For saints have hands that pilgrims' hands do touch,
      And palm to palm is holy palmers' kiss.

The style is that of an Elizabethan sonnet; and indeed, throughout these early plays, it is often Shakespeare's own voice that we hear. But, in the agony of despair, Romeo bursts into a passionate cry that anticipates the poet's tragic style :

> O here
> Will I set up my everlasting rest,
> And shake the yoke of inauspicious stars
> From this world-wearied flesh.

The incidents and characters which contrast with the two lovers and their fate show how strong was the poet's sense of drama even in this lyrical play. The death of the gay Mercutio, the domestic despotism of the Capulets, and the old nurse's babbling in season and out of season, all belong to a world which revolves on another axis than that of love, yet all are brought into harmony with the central love story.

A Midsummer Night's Dream seems in some ways an earlier work than *Romeo and Juliet*. Shakespeare thought little of life when he wrote this play, but much of poetry. We watch the entanglements of the four lovers with a detachment like that of Puck himself. A passion which is created by the potency of a love-juice strikes no deep chord of sympathy ; but the charm of faery-life, the strange fantasy of Titania's love for the " translated " Bottom, and the exquisite imagery drawn from old rustic England make up as rich a poem as was ever conceived. Shakespeare never gave his imagination so free a rein as in this play ; and it is like him to revel in the contrast between the courtly King of Fairies and the naïve absurdities of the Athenian mechanics. He knew, no doubt, that this was to be his last work of pure fancy, and perhaps the thought was in his mind when he made Theseus say to Hippolyta of "the most lamentable comedy" of *Pyramus and Thisbe* :

Thisbe : The best in this kind are but shadows ; and the worst are no worse if imagination amend them.

The best of Shakespeare's historical dramas, with the exception of *Henry VIII*, one of his latest works, were written between 1593 and 1598. The line which separates these plays from the rest is far from distinct. *Richard II*, for instance, is as much a tragedy of character as *Hamlet*; and in *Henry IV*, Part I, we are engrossed by Falstaff, not by the king who gives the play its title. Shakespeare's Histories, indeed, are greatly unlike the old chronicle plays which preceded them. Peele's *Edward I*, for instance, is rather a pageant than a drama. The scenes follow each other in chronological order, and the work is like a portion of Holinshed or Froissart versified for the stage. Shakespeare was not content with so crude a treatment. He tried to reconcile the facts of history with the form of drama. In *Richard II* and *Henry IV* he came about as near to success as the nature of the problem allowed him. *King John* is not the equal of these, yet in this play too, Shakespeare produced something far beyond a mere chronicle. As a king's tragedy, the work is greatly inferior to *Richard II*. John is a much less interesting figure than Richard. He is a stage villain, and his crimes are not made very credible. But it is in the subordinate scenes and characters that Shakespeare shows his power. The Bastard Faulconbridge is the master spirit of the play, and he dominates every company in which he finds himself. His disrespect for mere rank, his strong unimaginative nature, and his practical sense make him a typical Englishman of a certain kind. The story of Arthur has all the pathos which one would expect from Shakespeare. The young prince's speeches, indeed, do not ring perfectly true—they are spoilt by affectation ; but Constance, Arthur's mother, is a most tragic figure in her maternal grief :

> *Pandulph :* You hold too heinous a respect of grief.
> *Constance :* He talks to me that never had a son.
> *King Philip :* You are as fond of grief as of your child.
> *Constance :* Grief fills the room up of my absent child,
> Lies in his bed, walks up and down with me,

> Puts on his pretty looks, repeats his words,
> Remembers me of all his gracious parts,
> Stuffs out his vacant garments with his form ;
> Then have I reason to be fond of grief.

The four plays which begin with *Richard II*, and end with *Henry V*, form a continuous historical sequence. The first shows the misgovernment and overthrow of one of the feeblest rulers who ever occupied a throne. Although the events are historical, Shakespeare sets the character of Richard in so clear a relation to his fall, that we seem to be watching a story created by pure imagination. At first, we can only feel contempt for the weakly violent, self-pitying and poetising monarch, but as his misfortunes close around him, he begins to move compassion. He has virtues which become a private station, though he utterly wants the strength of a ruler. The style has an elegiac beauty, which does not altogether suit the rugged John of Gaunt or the astute Bolingbroke ; but in the concluding scenes it is admirable. The final mood of the play has more of pathos in it than tragedy, for Richard throughout suffers rather than acts, and he has not the greatness of a tragic hero. It is to the pity of men that the picture of the degraded king appeals :

> No man cried, " God save him " ;
> No joyful tongue gave him his welcome home :
> But dust was thrown upon his sacred head,
> Which with such gentle sorrow he shook off,
> His face still combating with tears and smiles,
> The badges of his grief and patience,
> That had not God, for some strong purpose, steel'd
> The hearts of men, they must perforce have melted,
> And barbarism itself have pitied him.

So the patient, resolute, and diplomatic Bolingbroke becomes king ; but in the opening speeches of *Henry IV* he already shows himself weary of rule. Richard has become a legendary figure, almost a saint, and there are some who speak of his deposition as a crime. Thus the stage is set for new troubles, and we are already attending with interest to the king's political and domestic problems,

when suddenly the whole character of the play is transformed. Falstaff enters, and from that moment until his
rejection at the end of Part II, he is the life of the whole
drama, leaving only a fraction of our thoughts available
for the public weal. The whole play is, indeed, admirable :
the Prince of Wales, Hotspur and Owen Glendower are
all splendidly alive ; but who can compete with Falstaff ?
He is so full of life that every one pales before him, like
candles in the presence of the sun. There is endless mirth
in his audacious lies, his preposterous assumptions and his
reckless gaiety at his own expense. Like Hamlet and
Cleopatra, he is a creation of " infinite variety." But he is
far more than a jester—he is a man whose attitude towards
life implies a profound criticism of the world and its ways.
To win a solid reputation, men must suppress many impulses
and perhaps maim a genial nature. But Falstaff has taken
the measure of life and concluded that the esteem of the
world is not worth its cost. He has thus arrived at an
advanced age, totally unspoiled by life, but without its
visible honours. His companions, it is clear, do not really
despise him ; indeed, he can inspire very wholesome fear.
But how can an elderly toper, who lays himself open without
a qualm to the imputation of lying and gluttony, hope for
outward respect ? He does not hope for it, but dismisses
all thought of honour in one of those wonderful Shakespearian soliloquies which are perfect alike in style and
penetration :

Prince of Wales : Why, thou owest God a death. (*Exit*)
Falstaff : 'Tis not due yet ; I would be loath to pay Him before His
day. What need I be so forward with Him that calls not on me ? Well,
'tis no matter ; honour pricks me on. Yea, but how if honour prick me
off when I come on ? how then ? Can honour set to a leg ? no : or take
away the grief of a wound ? no. Honour hath no skill in surgery, then ?
no. What is honour ? a word. What is that word, honour ? air. A
trim reckoning ! Who hath it ? he that died o' Wednesday. Doth he feel
it ? no. Doth he hear it ? no. It is insensible, then ? yea, to the dead.
But will it not live with the living ? no. Why ? detraction will not
suffer it : therefore, I'll none of it. Honour is a mere scutcheon : and so
ends my catechism.

But though Falstaff is proof against the allurements of

honour, he has his weak spot. He has a strong affection, almost a passion, for the Prince. In the second part of *Henry IV*, Shakespeare emphasises the grosser side of Falstaff's character, and as the old king fails in health it becomes clear that the Eastcheap revels cannot last into the new reign. None the less, when Falstaff hears that Henry IV is dead and hurries up from Justice Shallow's in order to be at the new king's coronation, we catch some of the old man's buoyant confidence. But no: Henry V is one

> Who, moving others, are themselves as stone,
> Unmoving, cold, and to temptation slow.

He casts off Falstaff at once and for ever, and his old friend's heart is broken. The master of men straightway begins his brilliant reign. The trumpets sound, the fleet gathers at Southampton, and the reader is swept away on that glorious tide of conquest which ends in the triumph at Agincourt. *Henry V* contains some noble passages, and patriotism never inspired a more stirring eloquence than that of the king's address to his troops on St. Crispin's day. Yet if one part of this play stands out above the rest, it is the Hostess's description of Falstaff's death. Nothing that Shakespeare had yet written has such moving power.

Thus, the whole series of four plays is a human drama. The events of history are scarcely more than a background. What absorbs our attention is the conflict of character. Richard, who is better as a man than as a king, stands in strong contrast to Henry V, who is better as a king than as a man. Throwing a glorious light over the two middle plays is the genial figure of Falstaff, who has almost succeeded in turning history itself into comedy, when, by a sudden turn of fortune, he is crushed by the fatal necessities of state.

III

Shakespeare's period of great comedies opens with *The Merchant of Venice*, written about 1597. He had already produced *All's Well that Ends Well* and *The Taming of the Shrew*, and he had degraded Falstaff from a great comic figure into a buffoon in *The Merry Wives of Windsor*, written, it is said, at the request of Queen Elizabeth, who desired to see " the fat knight in love." None of these three plays deserves to rank with *The Merchant of Venice*, or with the works which immediately followed it : *Much Ado about Nothing*, *As You Like It*, and *Twelfth Night*. These plays have certain features in common, and it seems natural to group them together as " romantic comedies."

A light atmosphere of unreality hovers over these four plays. The poet makes us laugh and sigh over the follies and mischances of men, but it is not his design that we should be deeply stirred. We are never quite in the real world, though we are never far away from it. The plot is often ludicrously improbable. A wooer wins a bride by choosing from a number of caskets marked with different inscriptions ; a merchant borrows a sum of money on the security of a pound of his own flesh ; a lady is driven from home by her uncle, and wanders off into a forest, accompanied by her cousin, in disguise. By a series of almost imperceptible touches, the poet dispels much of our disbelief, and as the web of circumstance becomes more and more entangled, an old legend or a romantic intrigue affects us with half the seriousness of real life. The fanciful events take place in scenes as fanciful. One play takes us to the Forest of Arden, where an exiled Duke lives an idyllic life with his faithful followers. In another, the scene is Illyria, the ground of which seems to infect every one who sets foot on it with the disease of love.

Nothing could be more inappropriate than to judge these plays by their plots. It is not the story that one enjoys, but the art of Shakespeare. Each play is a web of many colours. It is the unexpected that happens. Rosalind, who has seemed half a boy, falls in love and becomes wholly a woman. Beatrice, who has set no bounds to her wit, is touched to the quick by Hero's suffering, and forgets everything but her affection. Sunlight and shadow pass over the stage in turn, and the most diverse characters are

73

brought into contact with each other. The melancholy Jacques crosses the path of Touchstone, the fool. The drunken knights, Sir Andrew and Sir Toby, take part in the gulling of Malvolio, Puritanical and " sick of self-love." Every play is a complex pattern of contrasts. The poet's task is to keep us from attending too much to the darker elements. If there is a villain in the piece, our thoughts are not allowed to dwell on his villainy. In *Much Ado About Nothing*, the crime of Don John and Borachio even contributes to the general harmony, for it is the means of bringing the love between Beatrice and Benedick to a head. Tragedy is often in the air, but it is held in suspense by the equilibrium of forces.

As You Like It is probably the most perfect of all these comedies. It is free from discordant elements ; and its poetry, its woodland atmosphere and its songs are full of charm. It has, too, its graver side in the pathetic fidelity of old Adam and the subtle relation of Jacques to the other characters. *Much Ado About Nothing* is the weakest of the four, but it is redeemed by the rich comedy of Dogberry and the sparkling contests between Beatrice and Benedick. In *Twelfth Night*, perhaps, the poetry is most exquisite. There is much jesting and make-believe in this Christmas play, but sometimes the poet passes into the region of real feeling. It is then that his comedies become most delicately beautiful. The sentimental Duke Orsino, who feeds on an imaginary passion for Olivia, has awakened a real passion in the heart of Viola. She is disguised as a boy and is employed as Orsino's messenger. " Make no compare," says the Duke :

> Between that love a woman can bear me,
> And that I owe Olivia.

Viola :   Ay, but I know . . .

Duke :   What dost thou know ?

Viola :   Too well what love women to men may owe ;
> In faith, they are as true of heart as we.
> My father had a daughter loved a man,
> As it might be, perhaps, were I a woman,
> I should your lordship.

Duke :   And what's her history ?

Viola :   A blank, my lord.   She never told her love,
But let concealment, like a worm i' the bud,
Feed on her damask cheek.

The words are as near to tears as words can be, yet the Duke notices nothing.   Nor does he regard the yet clearer hint in Viola's next declaration :

Duke :   But died thy sister of her love, my boy ?
Viola :   I am all the daughters of my father's house,
And all the brothers too : and yet I know not . . .

Harmony, which is the perfection of a Shakespearian comedy, is not disturbed by these finer emotions.   But the gulling of Malvolio leaves behind an unpleasant feeling, and one is moved to sympathy rather than laughter by his last defiant words :

I'll be revenged on the whole pack of you.

Close to the theatres on the Bankside stood a Bear-garden, where animals were baited by dogs.   It seems as if an Elizabethan audience found a certain pleasure in the baiting of a man.   The treatment of Shylock probably gratified the groundlings who, no doubt, felt that the villain had got his due.   But it is clear enough to a later age that Shakespeare has dealt with the lonely Jew in a spirit of noble humanity.   The only question which the critic can ask is whether he has not overstrained his scheme in thus introducing a tragic figure into the gay world of Venetian pleasure-seekers.   *The Merchant of Venice* contains elements which cannot be brought into perfect harmony. At the one extreme are the young, the fortunate and the beautiful, uttering their thoughts in half lyrical verse.   At the other extreme is the persecuted Jew, to whom life is an affair of bitter earnest, and whose natural mode of expression is an intense and naked prose :

Hath not a Jew eyes ? hath not a Jew hands, organs, dimensions, senses, affections, passions ? fed with the same food, hurt with the same weapons, subject to the same diseases, healed by the same means, warmed and cooled by the same winter and summer as a Christian is ? if you prick us, do we not bleed ?

75

if you tickle us, do we not laugh ? if you poison us, do we not die ? and if you wrong us, shall we not revenge ?

Perhaps the most serious emotion in *The Merchant of Venice*, after the mingled wrath, vindictiveness, avarice and patriotism of Shylock, is the friendship between Antonio and Bassanio. The Elizabethans wrote beautifully about friendship. Its strength and its trials are a constant theme in Shakespeare's comedies. The lines which describe Antonio's affection for his friend strike a deeper note than many of the love speeches exchanged by the various couples :

> *Salarino :* And even then, his eye being big with tears,
> Turning his face, he put his hand behind him,
> And with affection wondrous sensible,
> He wrung Bassanio's hand, and so they parted.
> *Salanio :* I think he only loves the world for him.

IV

Shakespeare's greatest tragedies were written between 1601 and 1609. The first of the series is *Julius Cæsar*, the last, *Coriolanus*. One play, called a comedy, belongs to this period, the sombre and powerful, but somewhat unequal *Measure for Measure*.

The tragedies differ from the plays which precede them in giving the poet freer scope. In writing the histories, Shakespeare had taken as his groundwork the events of a reign. In writing the comedies he had dramatised a story. As we have seen, he contrives to escape from many of the limitations imposed by his plan. Neither the history nor the story is the most important thing. But in writing the tragedies, Shakespeare chose a plot which he could treat with entire seriousness. The atmosphere of make-believe which hangs over the comedies is dispelled, and we look down upon the real world of men. In each tragedy, the action revolves round matters of deep and lasting importance, and the central figure in each is a man of outstanding character.

The hero of *Julius Cæsar* is undoubtedly Brutus. It

is true that, in a sense, Cæsar dominates the action, but it is as a power half supernatural rather than as a living man. In the region where skill and calculation still count, Brutus is the figure who draws most attention. His character and his mistakes determine the fate of the other conspirators. He is not born for action. He cannot judge men, for he lives in a world of principles and ideals. Something in his nature gives him an ascendancy over his associates, and they yield to him even when they know they are right. By a series of misjudgments, of which the most fatal was the permission granted to Antony to address the mob after Cæsar's death, Brutus ruins the conspirators' cause. He loses everything the world can give or take away, but he keeps his idealism. Almost his last words are :

> In all the world
> I found no man but he was true to me.

His character has far less passion and far less subtlety than Hamlet's, but it has a grave and beautiful charm. The other conspirators, especially Cassius and Casca, are excellently drawn. Antony is a masterpiece. The play is full of beautiful episodes, especially the scenes of Portia's fears before the murder, and of Brutus's quarrel with Cassius. *Julius Cæsar* is the first of Shakespeare's plays after *Richard II* which can be called a " tragedy of character," but it far surpasses that early work in the success with which it represents a whole world of men, actuated by varying motives, yet drawn irresistibly into the same sphere of action.

It is easy to see why *Hamlet* should be the most widely read, the most discussed and probably the most beloved of all Shakespeare's plays. The hero is, perhaps, the most wonderfully conceived character in all literature. As long as men are superior to their environment, as long as they fail in action because they are great in imagination, as long as happiness is out of the reach of those who need it most, and the good things of the world turn sour to the taste because of one defect which cannot be done away—so long will readers find in the poetry of *Hamlet* some consolation for the harshness of life. Those who are too young or too fortunate to read books in this spirit, will still delight in the incomparable romance of this play. Hardly any drama creates a more breathless suspense than the opening sentences exchanged in the bitter cold on the ramparts at Elsinore. From the first scene to the last, our attention is on the strain ; and even after the climax of excitement has been reached in Claudius's guilty cry, " Give o'er the play," the poet still draws on our emotions in the poignant interview between Hamlet and his mother, the pathos of Ophelia's madness, and the penetrating realism of the graveyard scene. The conclusion of the play is, perhaps, better read than acted, for no visible conflict on the stage has any power to move the spectator after all the drain on his imaginative sympathies.

It has been well said of *Othello* that it is Shakespeare's best stage play. The plot has an extraordinary directness and concentration. The relations of Othello with Desdemona and Iago provide less food for philosophy than the workings of Hamlet's mind, but they form a superb drama. Fate has brought Othello into contact with the one man who can compass his ruin. Of Iago's motives, little is said, but his methods are those of an artist. Chance may seem to aid his designs ; but he had skill to make use of any chance, and a hundred accidents would have served his turn as well as Desdemona's loss of her handkerchief. There is hardly anything so pathetic in Shakespeare as the misunderstanding between Othello and Desdemona. The demand on our feelings is almost intolerable :

The pity of it, Iago ! O Iago, the pity of it, Iago !

But it is not the object of tragedy to carry painfulness to unendurable limits. Shakespeare transforms pity into admiration, and Desdemona's falsehood, by which she lays the guilt of her death on herself, at once consummates and relieves the tragedy. Few instances of Shakespeare's genius are more striking than his power to sustain the drama from this point onwards. Other dramatists might have written the scene of Othello's disillusionment, but

78

no one else in the world could have composed the matchless poetry of his last speech.

Hitherto, Shakespeare's heroes had been men whose fine qualities are marred by a fatal defect. Even Othello is, on the whole, a noble character. But in his next tragedy, *Macbeth*, the "hero" is a man of guilt—a man of rich endowments, but none the less a criminal who stops at nothing to gain his ends. The great moral issues at stake are not revealed at first. The whole action is raised to a supernatural plane by the appearance of the witches, and the first impression which Macbeth makes is that of a great and heroic commander. Even when his purposes begin to take shape, his imaginative terrors hold our condemnation in check and every other feeling is lost in sympathetic emotion. No sooner has Macbeth won the crown than he begins to pay his debt to heaven. Yet our sympathy is not wholly destroyed by all the sins which he heaps upon his head. One murder involves another ; but crimes have now become punishments. The further Macbeth advances in the path of evil, the more terrible becomes his isolation. It is a wonderful testimony to the sympathy he evokes, that even after he has dyed the land with blood, he still awakens pity when he bewails his lot :

> And that which should accompany old age,
> As honour, love, obedience, troops of friends,
> I may not look to have.

The spiritual desolation of this man who has given away his "eternal jewel" is complete. Life has utterly lost its meaning :

> It is a tale
> Told by an idiot, full of sound and fury,
> Signifying nothing.

In no drama is the moral order of the universe brought home with such power to the imagination. The lot of Lady Macbeth is as frightful as her husband's. At first, her nerves had been the stronger and her will the firmer, but her collapse is also swifter and more complete. Pity, which she does not awaken till near the end of the play, is paid in full measure in the tremendous scene of her sleep-walking.

King Lear, the last of Shakespeare's four chief tragedies, is the least suited to the stage. The elements themselves take part in this primæval drama : thunder and lightning seem to Lear the allies of his tiger-hearted daughters. By the imagination alone can the great warfare between good and evil be fitly realised. There is hardly anything to make the tragedy a popular work. The language by turns seems to freeze and to burn, but it does not charm. The devotion of Cordelia is too near to martyrdom to place her among Shakespeare's other heroines ; and the jests of the half-witted Fool are too bitter to provoke a smile. One can well understand how a young man like Keats had to brace himself for the ordeal of reading this tragedy. In the characters of Goneril and Regan evil seems incarnate. The thought of their ingratitude drives Lear to the brink of madness, and his realisation of their true nature brings down upon them some of the most terrible curses ever uttered. Furious passion and diabolical cruelty form the dark background of this play, and against these forces loyalty and love seem to avail nothing. One cannot wonder at Albany's words as he looks into the depths of human depravity :

> It will come,
> Humanity must perforce prey on itself,
> Like monsters of the deep.

But the darkness of this dark play is not unrelieved. Little consolation can be drawn from the undoing of Goneril, of Regan, and of Edmund ; and the death of Cordelia seems to mock all our hopes of justice. Indeed, the view of many critics that the tragedy should not end with so unspeakable a calamity cannot be wholly ignored. Yet the truth is not so black as the darkest forebodings of the play suggest. In spite of Cordelia's fate, we feel that in the general course of things, love will outlast hatred and ingratitude. Goodness shines the brighter after its passage through the furnace, and it is significant that the last lines of the play leave the future in the hands of the few faithful characters who survive the catastrophe.

V

The plays which Shakespeare wrote after *King Lear* are among his very finest works, but his art was obviously passing into a new phase, one that is best described as "lateness." He begins to take the liberties of a man who has conquered every difficulty of his art. In *Antony and Cleopatra*, the scene is shifted from place to place with a rapidity which even to the imagination is startling, and on the stage is almost preposterous. In *The Winter's Tale*, he leaps over a whole generation, and persons who are children in one act are grown men and women in another. The liberties he takes with language and metre are justified by their felicity, but they often defy all custom and rule.

King Lear was followed by *Timon of Athens* in 1607; and the next two years produced *Antony and Cleopatra* and *Coriolanus*. Then came the late comedies, *Cymbeline*, *The Winter's Tale*, and *The Tempest*. In 1613, appeared *Henry VIII*, a play not wholly by Shakespeare.

Timon of Athens is altogether inferior to the tragedies which it immediately followed, and the greatness in certain speeches of *Troilus and Cressida* is not sustained through the whole of that disillusioned play. But in *Antony and Cleopatra* Shakespeare's powers are again at their height. The play is less of a tragedy than *Hamlet* or *Othello*, for it contains less conflict. Antony is suffering from the "dotage" of love when the play opens, and though he succeeds in breaking away from the "grave charm" which is ruining his career, he makes little resistance when Cleopatra "nods" him back to Egypt. He has made his choice—"all for love, and the world well lost." But though the play is less mighty as a whole than some of the earlier tragedies, nothing of Shakespeare, as Coleridge says, gives a stronger impression of "angelic power." As often happens, the style reflects the nature of the work, and the style of *Antony and Cleopatra* shows, perhaps, as consummate a mastery over language as any man ever possessed. Nothing in Shakespeare is more magical than the cry of Cleopatra to her handmaid when the asp is at her bosom :

> Peace, peace ! dost thou not see my baby at my breast,
> That sucks the nurse asleep ?

An examination of the vocabulary of this play brings one as near to the secret of Shakespeare's style as it is possible to get. Take a single instance, his use of the word " gild." In the sonnets, a simple and obvious metaphor is drawn from the word :

> Full many a glorious morning have I seen,
> Flatter the mountain-tops with sovereign eye
> Kissing with golden face the meadows green,
> *Gilding* pale streams with heavenly alchemy.

In *Hamlet*, the word is used to imply corruption by bribery :

> Offence's *gilded* hand will shove by justice.

In *Antony and Cleopatra* the word is used with still greater expressiveness. The primary meaning of colour is retained, but it is combined with the secondary meaning of corruption. In a single epithet Shakespeare suggests the horrors of a military march in winter. " Thou didst drink," says Cæsar to Antony,

> The *gilded* puddle,
> Which beasts would cough at.

The boldest metaphors form the very stuff of the style. Indeed, there seems no limit to Shakespeare's power of finding new uses for familiar words. In three lines, there are as many metaphors :

> All come to this ? the hearts
> That *spaniel'd* me at heels, to whom I gave
> Their wishes, do *discandy*, melt their sweets
> On *blossoming* Cæsar.

The last of the tragedies, *Coriolanus*, is a work of great intellectual power, imbued with the austere political and military spirit of early Rome. Its tone is often grandly heroic, and often harsh, and sometimes one feels that there is little to choose between the inhuman patrician and the hateful demagogues who fill the five acts with their bitter strife. But the three latest comedies are among the most attractive of all Shakespeare's plays. Undoubtedly, *The Tempest* is the most beautiful, though *The Winter's Tale* contains one of the loveliest poetic scenes ever written by man. In *The Tempest*, Shakespeare returns to his old practice of uniting the most diverse beings in the same plot. Not even Titania and Bottom are so incongruous as the persons who meet on the enchanted island—Ariel, the " tricksy spirit," and the half-beast Caliban ; the drunken. mariners and the shipwrecked courtiers from Naples But the plot is far simpler than that of any early play. It is a plain story of an ancient wrong righted. Chance brings the usurper face to face with the lawful Duke of Milan, whose exile thus comes to a happy conclusion ; while the marriage of Ferdinand and Miranda blots out the enmity of the older generation. Moreover, the whole action takes place in a few hours and within the limits of Prospero's island, so that the latest comedy has a simplicity all its own. It is not wonderful that many readers—Shelley, for instance —should have loved *The Tempest* above all the poet's other plays, for it unites nearly all Shakespeare's more winning qualities—exquisite feeling with wild fantasy, unrestrained merriment with perfect expression. Through the whole play, the surf is heard breaking on the reefs of the island, and the atmosphere is salt with the sea air. The very metaphors of Miranda are drawn from the waves :

> And now I pray you, sir,
> For still 'tis *beating* in my mind, your reason
> For raising this sea-storm ?

and the language of the sea lends beauty even to the despair of Alonso :

> Therefore my son i' the ooze is bedded, and
> I'll seek him deeper than e'er plummet sounded,
> And with him there lie mudded.

VI

The superiority of Shakespeare to contemporary dramatists was not so evident in his own century as it is in ours. Ben Jonson, indeed, admitted that Shakespeare was without a rival ; but some preferred Jonson himself ; others upheld the claims of Fletcher to be at least the equal of both. Time has so altered these views that many readers would now refuse even the second place to Jonson and Fletcher, and would award it to Shakespeare's co-eval, Christopher Marlowe (1564–1593).

In Marlowe's short career as a dramatist, he produced four plays, *Tamberlaine*,[1] *The Tragical History of Dr. Faustus*, *The Jew of Malta*, and *Edward II*. They are the works of an extraordinary mind, a man of dæmonic energy, filled to the brim with the dauntless intellectual daring of his age. As a poet, he must always be remembered as the first man who revealed the power of English blank verse. Others, like Peele, had written sweet and limpid lines, but Marlowe's verse sounded with thunderous energy. The splendour of *Tamberlaine* arises chiefly from the superb vaunts of its hero, the Scythian tyrant. Often monotonous, and sometimes absurd, these speeches are redeemed by the constant recurrence of vigorous lines, like the promise

> To ride in triumph through Persepolis !

In *Dr. Faustus*, Marlowe rises to heights worthy of his romantic theme. The story of the scholar who aspired to infinite knowledge bears some analogy to that of the shepherd-king's struggle for boundless power, but there can be no comparison between the two works, judged as plays. *Tamberlaine* has some fine qualities as a poem, but *Dr. Faustus* contains one of the supreme passages in our dramatic literature. The verse catches again and again the note of great poetry, as in the speech when Faustus calls up a spirit from the dead :

> Was this the face that launched a thousand ships
> And burnt the topless towers of Ilium ?
> Sweet Helen, make me immortal with a kiss !

---

[1] *Tamberlaine* appeared in two parts.

But the climax of the poem is the great despairing speech of Faustus, in his last hour of grace. The excellence of the work lies wholly in its serious parts, the " comic relief " being of very inferior quality. Of Marlowe's other two plays, *Edward II* is by far the better. The earlier parts do not rise much above the level of the ordinary chronicle play, but as the action proceeds, the interest grows, and the scene of Edward's murder mingles horror with pity in a manner fully comparable to the close of *Richard II*. No one can do justice to Marlowe who does not also read his narrative poem, *Hero and Leander*.

The strength of Ben Jonson (1573 ?–1637) lay principally in comedy. He studied the manners of his time with the keen eye of the social satirist. His favourite characters are men dominated by " humours," a word to be used, he tells us, when " one peculiar quality "

> Doth so possess a man, that it doth draw
> All his affects, his spirits, and his powers,
> In their confluctions, all to run one way,—
> This may be truly said to be a humour.

Jonson's first characteristic play, *Every Man in His Humour* (1598), gives a foretaste of better things to come. For instance, Captain Bobadil, the boastful soldier, already shows his creator's store of comic observation. *Every Man out of His Humour*, and *The Poetaster*—the latter an amusing attack on its author's literary foes, Marston and Dekker— both show some advance in power, and then in 1605 came the first of Jonson's four great comedies, *Volpone*. The sub-title of this play is *The Fox*, the name being given to a crafty jester who pretends to be dying that he may extract gifts from the swarm of legacy-hunters who cluster round his bed. The stratagems by which Volpone and his " parasite " Mosca delude their victims are developed with uproarious humour ; yet through all the overflowing mirth, the author keeps a tight hold on the action, and brings it to an end at exactly the right moment. The fun of Jonson's next play, *Epicoene, or the Silent Woman* (1609), has a little faded ; parts of it drag heavily, yet it is brightened by moments of truly Rabelaisian jesting. The *dénouement* is brought about by the revelation of a secret kept alike from the victim on the stage and the spectators in the theatre—a new thing, apparently, in English drama. The plot of *The Alchemist* (1610) turns upon a gigantic imposture. The fraud is perpetrated by a rascally servant who is in temporary possession of his master's house, and uses it as an alchemist's laboratory for finding the philosopher's stone. Victims great and small are drawn by the scheme, the chief among them being one Sir Epicure Mammon, whose dreams of limitless wealth show Jonson's power as a poet. *Bartholomew Fair* (1614) is rich in scenes of bustle and vivacity, but it has not the close construction of the earlier comedies. Of Jonson's other plays, the most notable are the Roman tragedies, *Sejanus* (1603), and *Catiline* (1611).

The truth of Jonson's saying about Shakespeare, " He was not of an age, but for all time," is only brought home to us when we examine the work of other dramatists. Shakespeare's men and women are so " universal " that they tell us comparatively little about the ways of Elizabethan England ; but the work of his contemporaries is an inexhaustible mine for the social historian. This is a part of their real value. It is true that Jonson's men and women are mostly " types," and that they fail to awaken the deepest human interest. Yet they are studied with marvellous observation from manners which once flourished with a vigorous life, and it must be an exacting reader who finds nothing to amuse him in the fantastic " humours " of Tribulation Wholesome and Zeal-in-the-Land Busy. Some of the other dramatists belong to a definite sphere of social life, and owe part of their interest to the fidelity with which they paint its manners. Thomas Dekker, for instance, was a true citizen of London, a lover of its tradesmen and 'prentices, familiar, too, with its darker life. His *Shoemaker's Holiday* (1599), with its central figure, Simon Eyre, the lovable and absurd Lord Mayor of London, still breathes the charm of honest labour and innocent follies. John Fletcher, on the other hand, and his collaborator, Francis Beaumont, wrote for Court circles. They loved to magnify the greatness of kings, and thereby flatter the monarchical pride of James I. Their best work—*Philaster* (? 1610), *The Maid's Tragedy*, *A King and No King* (1611)—has a certain gloss of refinement. Its authors were clearly men of the world as well as poets. They gave great attention to their plots, which are artfully constructed, and full of sudden surprises. Love is their favourite theme, and they delight also to deal with strained and painful emotions. The most famous feature of Fletcher's verse is his use of an extra final syllable, which gives his lines a plaintive lingering note. Beaumont and Fletcher were highly contemptuous of the bourgeois taste in drama ; and in their excellent comedy, *The Knight of the Burning Pestle*, they make great sport of the city's insatiable appetite for the romantic exploits of apprentices.

Of the remaining later Elizabethan dramatists, Chapman, the translator of Homer, and Middleton, author of some famous plays, such as *The Changeling*, and *A Game of Chess*, must at least be mentioned. John Webster was one of the most remarkable of all the great group. He was a writer of extraordinary but unequal power, whose fame rests principally on two plays, *The White Devil*, or *Vittoria Corombona* (about 1608), and *The Duchess of Malfi* (about 1614). Webster was a tragic poet with an amazing insight into the nature of mental suffering and depravity. His men and women are mostly un-moral Italians of the Renaissance, whose lives are dominated by passion and controlled by cunning. In a strange world of cruelty and guile, one figure stands supreme, that of Vittoria Corombona, a character depicted with an intensity which is one of the wonders of our stage. Webster had great gifts as a poet, and a command of language at once simple and vivid. Lines such as these are not, perhaps, in Shakespeare's manner, but they are not unworthy of Shakespeare :

> O thou soft natural Death, that art joint-twin
> To sweetest slumber ; no rough-bearded comet
> Stares on thy mild departure ; the dull owl
> Beats not against thy casement ; the hoarse wolf
> Scents not thy carrion ; Pity winds thy corse,
> Whilst Horror waits on princes.

The traditions of the theatre were ably maintained in the reign of Charles I by Philip Massinger, who wrote both tragedy and comedy with the competence of a well-educated poet. His best-remembered piece, *A New Way to Pay Old Debts* (? 1625), is a comedy, the central figure of which, Sir Giles Overreach, is a vigorously-drawn " type " worthy of Jonson. Signs of loss in poetic power were, however, beginning to appear, though the old spirit of imagination still broke out at moments—in Ford's play, *The Broken Heart*, for instance. But the decline in verse-technique was a sure sign of decadence : some lines in the later plays dissolve into prose through sheer metrical weakness. The actual end, however, came from without, for the theatres were closed by Act of Parliament in 1642.

CHAPTER VI

THE ELEMENTS OF PROSODY

In every good poem there is something old and something new. The beauty of the language is never wholly the work of the author ; part of it was in the words before, part has been added by his skilful handling. The structure of the verse, too, owes something to the poet, but it also owes something to his predecessors. Every great poet is an heir who improves his inheritance. Hence, for an accurate love of verse, one should have some notion of a writer's debt to the past. Much may be learnt by tracing a great poet's gradual self-deliverance from the forms which he has inherited from others, and his progress towards the freedom of perfect self-expression. Such reading demands some acquired knowledge as well as natural taste. Of the knowledge, no part is more necessary than some acquaintance with the history of metres.

I

The metres used in English poetry are very numerous and very complex. A reader of modern verse may well be bewildered by the variety of forms which are at the command of the poet. His best plan will be to examine our metres at some period of our literature when they were in a simpler form. The foundations of our verse were laid in the Middle Ages. But, as we have seen, there was an almost complete break between the age of Chaucer and the age of Spenser ; practice acquired in the fourteenth century was of no use to the men of the sixteenth, who spoke a language so changed as to be almost new. The art of versification was re-learnt by Wyat, by Surrey, and by the other predecessors of Spenser. But these men were, in general, students rather than masters. The mere forms of verse may be studied in their work, but the variety which gives life is absent. It is to the Elizabethans themselves and to their immediate successors that we must look for the true foundations. These men, with all their love of freedom, did not forget that the essence of metre is a certain regularity. They were always experimenting and were restless in their search after new effects ; yet on the whole they avoided extravagance. The laws of English verse and the principles of liberty may both be studied in the age of Shakespeare and Milton.

II

Iambic verse was preferred by the Elizabethans to all other forms. They used it not only for drama but for most of their lyrics. Trochaic verse came next in favour, but at a long interval. For dactylic and anapæstic measures they had little liking ; these, indeed, were of small importance in English poetry before the early eighteenth century. On a broad survey of our literature, the Elizabethans seem somewhat prejudiced in their neglect of triple measures ; but in their general preference for iambic metres over all others, they were undoubtedly in the right.

Iambic Metres.—(*a*) Of the shorter iambic measures little need here be said. Lines of one or two feet hardly maintain an independent existence. Even those of three feet are less often used by themselves than in combination with longer lines. But the line of *four* feet, commonly called octo-syllabic, is one of the most important measures in English poetry. It is older than Chaucer and was still fresh in the days of Rupert Brooke. It has often been used consecutively in poems running into hundreds of lines. Its province is somewhat limited. As the metre of a long poem, it is less weighty than decasyllabic verse, and lends itself to speed rather than force. Butler, for instance, appropriately uses it in his burlesque satire, *Hudibras*, but it would not suit the more formal and calculated manner of Pope. Octosyllabic lines, too, make an excellent metre for the martial romances of Scott, but they would be intolerable in a true epic or a drama. As the basis of a lyrical stanza, however, the line has no such limitations. In short passages, it is perfectly adapted to express weighty feelings, as in Matthew Arnold's lines :

> We cannot kindle when we will
> The fire that in the heart resides,
> The spirit breatheth and is still,
> In mystery our life abides :
> But tasks in hours of insight willed,
> May be in hours of gloom fulfilled.

(*b*) The decasyllabic line (*five* iambic feet) is in English poetry what the hexameter is in Greek and Latin, and the Alexandrine in French. For epic, for drama, for narrative, and for satire it has no rival, and it almost rivals the octosyllabic line as a lyrical measure. It was the principal line of Chaucer, of Spenser, of Shakespeare, of Milton, of Dryden, of Pope—there is no end to the list. To-day, it is as full of vitality as ever. It can be used with rhyme and without, in couplets and in stanzas. Moreover, it is quickly responsive to the mood of the writer. There is not one great poet who has not given it the impress of his own character. Its great feature is its naturalness. It is the metre into which English speech most readily shapes itself, and, indeed, prose-writers sometimes slip into decasyllabics without any intention. The octosyllabic and the decasyllabic lines are those which permit the greatest variety in the handling ; and to this quality is due their position at the head of English measures.

(*c*) Lines of *six* iambic feet are called *Alexandrines*. They are not uncommon in Elizabethan poetry, but have since become rare, except in certain stanzas. Drayton wrote a long poem *Polyolbion* (1613–1622) in Alexandrines ; but the lines have an irrepressible tendency to fall into two halves : they have neither the continuity nor the flexibility of decasyllabics. But though the line does not lend itself to consecutive verse, it produces an admirable effect in combination with others. The Spenserian stanza owes much of its music to its concluding Alexandrine; and writers of Pindaric or irregular verse are often indebted to the extra foot of this line for an impressive "rounding-off." There is a fine instance in the conclusion of Milton's *Blest Pair of Sirens*:

> O may we soon again renew that song
> And live with Him in heaven, till He ere long
> To His celestial consort us unite,
> To live with Him and sing in endless morn of light.

(*d*) The line of *seven* feet is the longest of the iambic order which has an established place in English verse. It was a great favourite in early Elizabethan poetry and is often called the "fourteener" or "septenarius." It was used, as we have seen, by certain early Middle English writers, and it was equally popular with the men who were restoring our versification in the sixteenth century. It has a pronounced rhythm which appeals to inexperienced ears, but seems a little elementary to those who are acquainted with the subtler harmonies of other metres. The Tudor and Elizabethan poets were particularly fond of what they called "Poulter's measure," that is, an Alexandrine followed by a "fourteener":

> Shall I thus ever long, and be no whit the neare?
> And shall I still complain to thee, the which me will not hear?
> Alas! say nay! say nay! and be no more so dumb,
> But open thou thy manly mouth and say that thou wilt come.

These lines, from a poem which appeared in 1552, would obviously appeal to an age which was just beginning to be educated in rhythmic feeling; but the metres used by Spenser, Marlowe and Shakespeare soon made the "fourteener" seem old-fashioned. It does not, indeed, lend itself to elevation or varied expression. But when this same line is split into two unequal halves, it often becomes a fine lyrical tune:

> Drink to me only with thine eyes,
> And I will pledge with mine.

This is the 8 : 6 combination so familiar in lyrical verse.

The octosyllabic line, disengaged from the shorter half, has a flexibility of which the unwieldy seven feet are incapable. A number of measures are based on the division of the "fourteener." A certain little stanza of Herrick's, for instance :

> What needs complaints,
> When she a place
> Has with the race
> Of saints ?

is nothing but this line cut into four pieces and "tagged" with rhyme :

What needs / complaints / when she / a place / has with / the race / of saints / ?

Trochaic Metres.—A peculiarity of trochaic metres in English is that the last foot of a line is generally curtailed of its second syllable so that the verse ends with a strong accent. A foot which is shortened in this way is said to be "catalectic." Longfellow's *Hiawatha* is written in lines of four complete trochaic feet, but the plan would have caused great difficulty if rhyme had been used. Ben Jonson's *Hymn to Diana* illustrates the commoner and more convenient method :

> Queen and huntress, chaste and fair,
> Now the sun is laid to sleep,
> Seated in thy silver chair,
> State in wonted manner keep :
> Hesperus entreats thy light,
> Goddess excellently bright.

Next to the line of four feet, that of eight is probably the most fit for English verse. It is employed with great musical beauty in a short poem by Tennyson :

> Row us up from Desenzano, to your Sirmione row !
> So they rowed, and there we landed, " O venusta Sirmio ! "
> There to me thro' all the groves of olive in the summer glow
> There beneath the Roman ruin where the purple flowers grow,
> Came that " Ave atque Vale " of the Poet's hopeless woe,
> Tenderest of Roman poets nineteen hundred years ago,
> " Frater, Ave atque Vale "—as we wander'd to and fro
> Gazing at the Lydian laughter of the Garda Lake below
> Sweet Catullus's all-but island, olive-silvery Sirmio !

Anapæstic and Dactylic Metres.—The Elizabethans seldom wrote lines in triple feet. Ben Jonson, indeed, uses anapæsts—a little awkwardly—in his poem beginning :

See the Char / iot at hand / here of Love / ;

and Shakespeare gives a dactylic ending to Ariel's song :

Merrily, / merrily, / shall I live / now,
Under the / blossom that / hangs on the / bough.

But it was not until the eighteenth century, with its taste for *vers de société*, that the real uses of triple feet were discovered. For a long time, anapæsts and dactyls seemed a little frivolous. Barham used them freely in *The Ingoldsby Legends*, the mood of which they exactly suit. Wordsworth and Coleridge, Byron and Shelley attempted, not always with success, to give triple feet a more honourable position among English metres ; and the task was victoriously accomplished by the skill of Tennyson, Browning, and Swinburne. A remarkable instance of the way in which even short dactylic lines may be subdued to a tragic mood is in Hood's *Bridge of Sighs*. Anapæsts are finely used by Browning in *Saul* and elsewhere, but with the aid of numerous " substitutions "—a principle explained in the next paragraph.

III

The great feature of English verse is its freedom. We may count the syllables, name the feet and classify the metres of our poets, and yet leave the secret of their verbal music as inexplicable as ever. The magic of verse does not submit to explanation. Every poem, nay, every line that has any life, has a character of its own ; and how can we define the laws of freedom, or circumscribe a variety which is infinite ? The fact remains, however, that at this late day in the history of our poetry, certain means of attaining freedom have themselves become conventions. These we may describe, and therefore, if we write verse, may imitate. To every original poet, however, the eternal

problem will still present itself; and it is a problem which
he must solve in his own way if he is to solve it at all.
Some of the commonest means of attaining variety in
English verse are well illustrated in two of Milton's early
poems, *L'Allegro* and *Il Penseroso*. No one can read these
works without feeling that the spirit of life within them is
renewed at every line. To say exactly how this is done is
impossible; yet we may note a few of the metrical devices
which contribute to the general effect. *L'Allegro*, after
the invocation, leads off with an octosyllabic couplet:

> But come, thou Goddess, fair and free,
> In Heav'n yclept Euphrosyne;

but the next line has only seven syllables, the weak accent
of the first foot being omitted:

> And by men, heart-easing Mirth.

Throughout the poem these two types of line are mingled,
so that the cadence is sometimes iambic, sometimes trochaic.
But this is not all. Milton often substitutes a complete
trochee for the opening iamb, so that the metrical scheme
is as follows:

$$/ \ast \quad \ast / \quad \ast / \quad \ast /^1$$

In the four following lines each of the three types is
illustrated:

> (a) Oft on a plat of rising ground,
> (b) I hear the far-off curfew sound,
> (c) Over some wide-water'd shore,
> (d) Swinging slow with sullen roar.

In line (a), a trochee is substituted for the opening iamb.
Line (b) is a normal octosyllabic (four iambic feet). Lines
(c) and (d) have each only seven syllables, the omission of
the first producing a trochaic effect which well suits the
sense. The occasional use of double or *feminine* rhyme,
as in the couplet:

> And join with thee calm Peace and Quiet
> Spare Fast, that oft with gods doth diet,

---

[1] The line indicates a strong, and the asterisk a weak, syllable.

provides Milton with yet a fourth type of line. Thus the metrical scheme is itself full of variety, apart from the many devices, too subtle for definition, by which the poet gives his verse its changing music.

The principle of substituting some " equivalent " foot for the ordinary iambic is of still greater importance in the decasyllabic line. This verse is one of the easiest to write, and therefore, unless varied, one of the most monotonous. Open the works of any early Elizabethan dramatist and you will find this kind of writing :

(a) The warlike soldiers ‖ and the gentlemen,
(b) That heretofore ‖ have filled Persepolis
(c) With Afric captains ‖ taken in the field,
(d) Whose ransom made them march in coats of gold,
(e) With costly jewels ‖ hanging at their ears,
(f) And shining stones ‖ upon their lofty crests,
(g) Now living idle ‖ in the walled towns,
(h) Wanting both pay ‖ and martial discipline,
(i) Begin in troops ‖ to threaten civil war,
(j) And openly exclaim ‖ against their king.

By the time he has read ten lines of such writing, the reader is already weary of its monotony. Eight of the lines are self-contained, as the final comma shows, and in rhythm are very nearly identical. Line b, it is true, begins with a trochee, but that is the sole exception in a passage of fifty feet. Further, in all those lines where there is any marked pause, or cæsura, it falls very near to the middle. In line a, for instance, the pause is after the fifth syllable :

The warlike soldiers ‖ and the gentlemen.

In line b, it is after the fourth :

That heretofore ‖ have filled Persepolis.

All the other lines in which there is any clear pause follow one or other of these two types, except the last line of the piece, where the cæsura follows the sixth syllable. Had blank verse been able to do no better than this, it would have had a poor career. Fortunately, the poetic resource and venturesome spirit of the Elizabethans were equal to the task of creating variety. No one met the difficulties with half the skill of Shakespeare. Step by step, he moved farther away from the monotonous technique of his masters. At the climax of his powers, his versification has a variety as wonderful as that of his imagination itself.

The latest of Shakespeare's plays show the freedom of his technique at its height. But in those of the middle period, he is already master of a versification far more varied than any one could have dreamed of ten years before. Compare the following passage from *Julius Cæsar* with the lines last quoted :

> *Brutus :* This is a sleepy tune.   O murderous slumber,
> Lay'st thou thy leaden mace upon my boy,
> That plays thee music?   Gentle knave, good-night ;
> I will not do thee so much wrong to wake thee :
> If thou dost nod, thou break'st thy instrument ;
> I'll take it from thee ;   and, good boy, good-night.
> Let me see, let me see ;   is not the leaf turn'd down
> Where I left reading?   Here it is, I think——

Here, as in the earlier piece, most of the lines are still end-stopped, yet how livingly they express the meditative mood of the speaker ! The verse lingers as the thoughts of the weary soldier linger :

> I will not do thee so much wrong to wake thee **. . .**

Note the effect of the extra final syllable in retarding the line. Note, also, how fittingly the normal iambic foot gives way to the spondee in

> I'll take / it from / thee ; and / góod bóy / góod-níght/

How natural, too, is the substitution of two anapæstic feet at the beginning of the line which follows :

> Let me see, / let me see ; / is not / the leaf / turn'd down /

When blank verse could be written in this way, it had already become one of the finest instruments for dramatic expression ever invented.

In his later plays, Shakespeare went further, and seemed to delight in breaking every rule of his earlier verse.

Yet, when his most daring speeches are examined, one sees that there is a purpose in every liberty, and one marvels at the genius which could so unerringly create its own law. The verse of *King Lear* or *The Tempest* when compared with that of *A Midsummer Night's Dream* shows a complete revolution in technique. The change was natural and inevitable. To represent the full force of passion in art, a man must submit to no guide but his own inspiration. Here is the versification of a master, who, having learnt all that rules could teach him, knew that their best use is to be broken :

> *Lear :*   Blow, winds, and crack your cheeks ! rage ! blow !
> You cataracts and hurricanoes, spout
> Till you have drenched our steeples, drowned the cocks.
> You sulphurous and thought-executing fires,
> Vaunt-couriers to oak-cleaving thunderbolts,
> Singe my white head ! And thou, all-shaking thunder,
> Strike flat the thick rotundity o' the world !

The verse of this speech and of the lines that follow has the speed of the wind and the tumult of a tempest. Once more, art baffles analysis, yet here and there we can mark the means which have produced the effect. In the first line, Shakespeare twice substitutes a single syllable for a whole iambic foot. The licence is bold in the extreme, yet no other device could so effectively have represented the passion of the old king :

> Blow, winds, / and crack / your cheeks ! / ráge ! / blów ! /

The late position of the cæsura gives the second and third lines the speed of lightning :

> You cataracts and hurricanoes, || spout
> Till you have drenched our steeples, || drowned the cocks !

The tumultuous effect of triple feet in place of iambics is felt in both the fourth and fifth lines, but especially in the last where it is made more acute by the dentals :

> Strike flat / the thick / rotund / ity o' / the world ! /

Milton, alone among the great poets of the seventeenth century, is Shakespeare's equal in the art of versification.

Broadly speaking, he adopts the same means to obtain the freedom he requires. He varies the position of the cæsura with equal boldness and more deliberately. Observe, for example, how effectively it is placed after the second syllable in the solemn warning of the archangel to Adam:

> Firm they might have stood,
> Yet fell; ‖ remember, | and fear to transgress.

He uses triple feet much more sparingly than Shakespeare, feeling, no doubt, that they are a menace to the elevation of epic verse; but no poet employs the art of substitution more freely or with greater skill. "True musical delight," to quote Milton himself on this subject, "consists only in apt numbers, fit quantity of syllables, and the sense variously drawn out from one verse into another." To this last device—"enjambement," as it is commonly called—Milton's poetry owes much of its infinite variety; but on what principle the sense is variously drawn out is a secret known only to the poet himself. Another device, much employed by Milton, was the use of alliteration, not as a mere ornament, but as an emphasis on the important words and a clue to the intricate music of the verse-paragraph. Milton's art is displayed in every page of his poem, and within the compass of a few lines there is more skill than the critic can describe:

> Thus roving on
> In confus'd march forlorn, ‖ the adventurous bands
> With shudd'ring horror pale, ‖ and eyes aghast
> View'd first their lamentable lot, ‖ and found
> No rest: ‖ through many a dark and dreary vale
> They pass'd, ‖ and many a region dolorous,
> O'er many a frozen, ‖ many a fiery Alp,
> Rocks, caves, lakes, fens, bogs, dens and shades of death,
> A Universe of death, ‖ which God by curse
> Created evil, ‖ for evil only good,
> Where all life dies, ‖ death lives, ‖ and nature breeds,
> Perverse, ‖ all monstrous, ‖ all prodigious things,
> Abominable, ‖ inutterable, ‖ and worse
> Than fables yet have feign'd, ‖ or fear conceiv'd
> Gorgons ‖ and Hydras, ‖ and Chimeras dire.

The position of the cæsura alone indicates the variety of Milton's verse. But that is only one element of his technique. He relies also on "enjambement," though he is careful not to overdo this, and therefore uses a fair proportion of end-stopped lines. No bolder or more effective instance of substitution can be found anywhere than the line :

Rócks, cáves, / lákes, féns, / bógs, déns / and shádes / of déath

where eight of the ten syllables are accented. The triple feet in the line

Abóm / inable, / inútt / erable, / and wórse /

are both natural and expressive, and alliteration is finely used in the last line but one to bind the sense together. The more closely one studies the verse of Milton, the more one is amazed at his combination of the boldest originality with faultless skill.

IV

A great many stanzas are used in our poetry, and every poet is free to create new ones. Our task must be limited to naming and describing some of the most important.

(a) Rhyming couplets, though not classed as stanzas, have been in use since early mediæval times, and they are not likely ever to grow obsolete. The couplet with the most interesting history is the " heroic " couplet, so called because the line of five iambic feet was considered the best metre for " heroic," or epic verse. Chaucer was the first poet to write heroic couplets in English, and since his time the measure has nearly always been held in honour. Thanks to the prestige of Dryden and Pope, it was raised above all other forms of verse in the eighteenth century, and was cultivated in an artificial and epigrammatic form. Cowper pointed out the dangers to poetry of Pope's example, but was content to write in couplets not unlike those of the master he was attacking :

> But he, his musical finesse was such,
> So nice his ear, so delicate his touch,
> Made poetry a mere mechanic art
> And every warbler had his tune by heart.

(*b*) No stanza of three lines has become " classical " in English poetry, though several well-known poems are written in three-lined stanzas ; for example, Crashaw's poem *To his Supposed Mistress* :

> Whoe'er she be
> That not impossible She,
> That may command my heart and me.

(*c*) Four-lined stanzas, when rhymed *abab*, are known as *quatrains*. The most familiar of them in English is the *ballad-stanza* (86 : 86). It was extremely common in our old popular poetry, but its simplicity limits its scope. For the " minstrelsy of the Border," it was excellent, but it is difficult to handle artistically. The greater Elizabethan poets generally preferred more elaborate measures. The ballad-stanza was revived in *Lyrical Ballads* (1798), where it is used in Coleridge's *Ancient Mariner* :

> He went like one that hath been stunned,
>> And is of sense forlorn,
> A sadder and a wiser man,
>> He rose the morrow morn.

Coleridge, however, found that this form of verse can only be redeemed from monotony by frequent variations. He, therefore, seldom writes a stanza which does not, in some way, depart from the normal form. Sometimes he increases the number of lines, and he often uses middle-rhyme. Other varieties of the ballad-stanza are extremely common. The forms 8.6.8.6.8.6. and 8.8.6.8.8.6, are among the more familiar adaptations.

The *heroic quatrain* (rhyming *abab*) is the metre of Gray's *Elegy*. Partly by association, partly by its natural qualities, it is almost an elegaic metre. Wordsworth, for instance, uses it in his *Elegiac Stanzas*, and it is the metre of Sir William Watson's poem, *Wordsworth's Grave*. Its slow movement makes it suitable for serious and meditative verse.

(*d*) Five-lined stanzas occupy a minor place among our verse-measures. The three forms which most commonly occur, rhyming : *ababb*, *abaab*, and *ababa*, are all extensions of the quatrain. Some poets have used the five-lined stanza with very charming effect, Sir Henry Wotton, for instance, a poet of the seventeenth century :

> You meaner Beauties of the Night
>   That poorly satisfy our eyes
> More by your number than your light,
>   You Common-people of the Skies ;
>   What are you when the Moon shall rise ?

(*e*) A quatrain followed by a couplet produces a stanza which, though useful, has no great structural beauty. One associates it with a piece like Cowper's *Castaway*, which was written to relieve a profoundly tragic mood, and without thought of formal charm. Shakespeare's *Venus and Adonis* and Wordsworth's *Laodamia* are among the finest poems written in the six-lined stanza.

(*f*) The most beautiful stanzas have some kind of organic structure, and are not merely a collection of lines. The stanza called " rhyme royal " (so named because King James I of Scotland employed it) has the rhyme-scheme *ababbcc*. This arrangement has a great superiority over the quatrain-and-couplet stanza, as the fifth line links the two parts together. For some centuries after Tudor times, the rhyme-royal was almost wholly neglected, but it was revived by several poets of the nineteenth century.

(*g*) Many eight-lined stanzas are elaborations of simpler forms : the *ottava rima* is of a different order. This stanza was of Italian origin, and it was used by the Elizabethan translator of Ariosto's *Orlando Furioso*. But its great vogue came in the early nineteenth century—in the " mock heroic " writings of Byron, and in certain poems of Keats and Shelley. The *ottava rima* is in decasyllabic verse and has the rhyme-scheme : *abababcc*. The stanza is excellently adapted to the serio-comic style of *Don Juan* :

There's only one slight difference between
Me and my epic brethren gone before,
And here the advantage is my own, I ween
(Not that I have not several merits more,
But this will more peculiarly be seen) ;
They so embellish that 'tis quite a bore
Their labyrinth of fables to read through,
Whereas this story's actually true.

(*h*) The Spenserian stanza of nine lines has a beautiful structure, and is elaborately rhymed : *ababbcbcc*. A form of such difficulty would seem to tax a poet's powers to the utmost, yet the melody of the form is so alluring that many of our poets—Byron, Shelley, Keats, Tennyson, to name a few—studied to master its difficulties, and overcame them so far as to manipulate the stanza with ease.

(*i*) The longest fixed form of verse which demands notice is the sonnet. The " Petrarchan " sonnet, which is a stanza of fourteen lines, consists of two unequal parts : the *octave* (eight lines) and the *sestet* (six lines). The rhyme-scheme of the octave, in its strict form, is : *abbaabba*. The rhyme-scheme of the sestet is not so rigidly fixed. Some writers use the scheme *cdcdcd* ; but there is nothing against the introduction of an extra rhyme, and some such arrangement as *cdecde*, or *cdeced*. It seems best that the sestet should not end with a couplet, but should close in a more sonorous and less epigrammatic manner.

There is another fourteen-lined stanza called, by courtesy, a sonnet, though it differs widely from the true Italian form. This is the " Shakespearian " sonnet, a stanza consisting of three quatrains and a final couplet : *abab, cdcd, efef, gg*. The form has no great beauty in itself, but it has won a place in the hearts of most lovers of poetry by association with the sonnets of Shakespeare.

(*j*) Most of the longest stanzas in our poetry are found in Odes, or in other poems of a high lyrical strain. Some of Keats's odes, for instance, are written in a beautiful stanza of ten lines, devised by the poet himself. Other odes, such as Dryden's *Alexander's Feast*, follow no rule, but are obedient only to the poet's own impulse. Such odes are called in English " Pindaric," perhaps from

recollection of a line of Horace who says that Pindar wrote
" numeris lege solutis." Pindaric free verse offers the
poet great opportunities but no guidance. Hence few,
if any, " Pindaric " odes are perfect, though the best
contain magnificent passages. Perhaps *Alexander's Feast*
comes as near being faultless as any of the kind. Wordsworth's *Ode on the Intimations of Immortality* is a greater
poem, but the rhythm, in certain parts, fails to satisfy the
ear. Tennyson's *Ode on the Death of the Duke of Wellington*
is a fine instance of sustained " Pindaric " verse.

We have only touched the fringe of our subject, and
every reader of poetry, especially modern poetry, will
remember many experiments in verse beside which the older
forms seem modest and simple. In the latter half of the
nineteenth century, a movement towards freedom and
novelty began, and that movement still continues. In
our own time we have seen experiments in " vers libre,"
which seem due partly to a desire for greater freedom than
ever, and partly to a desire to substitute the pattern on the
printed page for the appeal to the ear. To discuss the
newest movements would take us far from our present
purpose. But the example of our older poets is not quite
irrelevant to the matter. Our greatest writers certainly
did not make either novelty or freedom their primary aim.
They studied the laws of verse before they attempted its
liberties. Complete mastery of technique gave them confidence and skill to reach out towards new and wider
regions. " Free " verse is certainly the consummation of
metrical expression ; but its surest masters are our greatest
poets, and its triumphs can be seen nowhere so well as
in the last poem of Milton, *Samson Agonistes*.

CHAPTER VII

PROSE FROM LYLY TO CLARENDON

THE poets of the sixteenth century who prepared the way for the Elizabethans had a clearer, if not an easier, task to perform than the writers of prose. The primary rules of verse are so strict that those who do not keep them are at once detected ; but the rules of good prose are more impalpable. When the Tudor writers had a good model to follow or a plain task to perform, they did excellently. Cranmer, for instance, who wrote many of the prayers in the English Liturgy, reproduced the spirit, the rhythm and the sense of the Latin originals with fine literary feeling. The translators of the Bible who wished to do their duty faithfully, and whose reverence for every word of Scripture well fitted them for their task, met with equal success. Translation, indeed, was one of the chief employments of the age. The translation of Plutarch's *Lives* by Sir Thomas North, of More's *Utopia* by Ralph Robinson, and of Montaigne's *Essays* by John Florio, are all done in a worthy and dignified manner. The Tudor works on education have the same solid merits. *The Book called the Governor*, by Sir Thomas Elyot, and *The Schoolmaster*, by Roger Ascham, are both fit monuments of an age which did so much for schools and colleges. But books which serve very well for educational purposes are often wanting in the higher qualities of literature. The age of Elizabeth seems to have despised the pedestrian merits of the earlier prose. Something more brilliant was wanted. It was not enough to supply one's readers with information, they must be astonished by wit. For some time, prose-writers had been trying to make their style more sparkling, when in 1579 a book appeared which seemed to do this with splendid success, a book which for many years was a model to scores of writers, but has now become one of the bywords of criticism.

I

This was the *Euphues* of John Lyly. With the matter of this book we need not much concern ourselves. It is a work of fiction, but scarcely a novel. The story is of no great interest and the dialogue is as far removed from real life as dialogue can be. It was not Lyly's object to represent conversation as it is, but as it ought to be. Nor did he seek to draw men as they are, so much as to "fashion a gentleman or noble person" in delicate and refined sentiment. His characters are perpetually making long speeches—which no one is rude enough to interrupt—in a style which was supposed to be the perfection of eloquence. The features of this style are very clearly marked, so that a clever man could pick it up as easily as he could pick up versification. Alliteration and antithesis are its chief ornaments, and many phrases are both alliterative and antithetical. "Not only with our lips, but in our lives," is a Euphuistic phrase from the Prayer Book, for Lyly did not invent the style. Another feature is a display of obscure learning and a great parade of authorities. Nothing pleased Lyly better than to illustrate his ideas by the laws of natural history, as in the following characteristic speech :

But can Euphues convince me of flattery, seeing for his sake I break my fidelity ? Can he condemn me of disloyalty when he is the only cause of my disliking ? May he justly condemn me of treachery who hath this testimony as trial of my good will ? Doth he not remember that the broken bone once set together is stronger than ever it was ? That the greatest blot is taken off with the pumice ? That though the spider poison the fly, she cannot infect the bee ? That though I have been light to Philautus, I may be lovely to Euphues ?

Before long, Lyly's book came to be regarded as a type
of all that is unnatural in literary style ; and " Euphuistic "
is now a name generally applied to writers of the time who
thought more of eloquence than of simplicity.   Most of
the earlier Elizabethans affect some sort of verbal dexterity,
some ingenious playing with words, which recalls, more
or less, the features of Lyly's style.   Sir Philip Sidney,
in his pastoral romance, *Arcadia*, is a flagrant offender,
and even so grave a writer as Hooker is not free from the
prevailing fashion.   The best parody of Euphuism ever
written was written by Shakespeare.   It is Falstaff who
speaks it, in the riotous scene at Eastcheap, in which he
impersonates the grieved King of England, confronted by
his scapegrace of a son :

Harry, I do not only marvel where thou spendest thy time,
but also how thou art accompanied ; for though the camomile,
the more it is trodden on, the faster it grows, yet youth, the more
it is wasted, the sooner it wears.   That thou art my son, I have
partly thy mother's word, partly my own opinion ; but chiefly,
a villainous trick of thine eye, and a foolish hanging of thy nether
lip that doth warrant me.   If, then, thou be son to me, here lies
the point : why, being son to me, art thou so pointed at ?
Shall the blessed son of heaven prove a micher and eat black-
berries ? a question not to be asked.   Shall the son of England
prove a thief and take purses ? a question to be asked.   There
is a thing, Harry, which thou hast often heard of, and it is known
to many in our land by the name of pitch : this pitch, as ancient
writers do report, doth defile ; so doth the company thou
keepest : for, Harry, now I do not speak to thee in drink but
in tears ; not in pleasure but in passion ; not in words only
but in woes also . . .

and at this point the " King " diverges into a eulogy of a
" virtuous man," who is, of course, Falstaff himself.

II

Education, as we have noticed, occupied the thoughts
of many Tudor writers ; but even education was subordinate, in the minds of most men, to religion.   In the

sixteenth century, the English people dared to break free from Rome and to form a national Church of their own. After many fluctuations, sometimes backwards in the direction of Catholicism, sometimes forwards in the direction of extreme Protestantism, the Anglican religion reached a state of comparative finality. An Act of Uniformity was passed in 1559, and henceforth it was clear that England had chosen a " middle way." The breach with Rome was definite, but the national Church was to have its fixed beliefs and worship, and it was not to be perpetually rent by new schisms.

An apologist, therefore, was needed to expound and defend the Anglican position, so that Englishmen might understand the theological and historical foundations of their own Church. For this task, evidently, a combination of great powers was needed. The apologist must be learned and devout ; he must also be skilled in controversy and a master of prose. The time created the man, and in 1594, Richard Hooker, who had been deputy Professor of Hebrew at Oxford, and Master of the Temple, published the first four books of *The Laws of Ecclesiastical Polity*, the fifth and last book appearing three years later. The work is a classic both of English prose and of English theology : it states once and for all the grounds for the middle position of the Anglican Church.

Hooker takes a survey of the Articles of Religion, the ritual and the government of the Church of England. He shows that a reformation had been necessary to bring the Church back to a closer conformity with its original pattern. He also shows, with a great display of quotation and argument, that the wishes of the extreme Puritans are in conflict with many of the most ancient practices of Christianity. The idea of a purified Church which has all the augustness but none of the corruptions of antiquity kindles Hooker to a sustained and majestic eloquence. He wishes that God should be worshipped, not with the superstitions of Rome, nor in the plainness of a conventicle, but in the " beauty of holiness." His own nature exemplifies almost all that is best in Anglicanism—its love of " true religion and sound learning," of solemn worship and of charitable action. His style, though touched with a little harmless affectation, is mostly pure, grave and eloquent, and is worthy of his great theme. In the following paragraph he enumerates some of the " helps to Public Prayer " which are derived from a consecrated building :

And concerning the place of assembly, although it serve for other uses as well as this, yet seeing that our Lord Himself hath to this as to the chiefest of all other plainly sanctified His own temple, by entitling it " the House of Prayer," what pre-eminence of dignity soever hath been either by the ordinance or through the special favour and providence of God annexed unto His Sanctuary, the principal cause thereof must needs be in regard of Common Prayer. For the honour and furtherance whereof, if it be as the gravest of the ancient Fathers seriously were persuaded, and do oftentimes plainly teach, affirming that the house of prayer is a Court beautified with the presence of celestial powers ; that there we stand, we pray, we sound forth hymns unto God, having his Angels intermingled as our associates, and that with reference hereunto the Apostle doth require so great care to be had of decency for the Angels' sake ; how can we come to the house of prayer, and not be moved with the very glory of the place itself, so to frame our affections, praying as doth best beseem them, whose suit the Almighty doth there sit to hear, and his Angels attend to further ? When this was ingrafted in the minds of men, there needed no penal statutes to draw them unto public prayer. The warning sound was no sooner heard, but the churches were presently filled, the pavements covered with bodies prostrate, and washed with their tears of devout joy.

III

At a time when many of the gravest minds were occupied with religious controversy and the problems of Church government, one man, equal in intellectual power to all but the greatest of philosophers, was asking how far the thoughts of a layman were usefully employed on ques-tions of theology. He would like more light on " the true limits and use of reason in spiritual things," and holds that "this point well laboured would . . . be an opiate to stay and bridle . . . the vanity of curious speculations, wherewith the schools labour." Francis Bacon, the author of these words, has never perhaps received full justice from his countrymen. It is difficult to pardon a Lord Chancellor who was charged before the House of Lords with bribery, and was on his own confession guilty of " corruption and neglect." Moreover, Bacon's philosophy is often blamed as " materialistic," and his wisdom is felt to be at best a " worldly wisdom." Yet his admirers have put no bounds to their eulogies. Shelley, for instance, speaks of his " superhuman wisdom," and D'Alembert, projector of the French Encyclopædia, calls him " the greatest, the most universal, the most eloquent of philosophers."

It is by his *Essays* that Bacon is best known to the reader of to-day. These little compositions, often no more than a page in length, started the English essay on its long career. Of all essayists, Bacon is the most compact and the most allusive. One is constantly reminded of Ben Jonson's remark on Bacon's eloquence : " his hearers could not cough, or look aside from him, without loss." At first sight, many of the essays seem little more than a mosaic of maxims and quotations ; but by degrees one comes to see how intensely expressive they are of their author's personality. The knotty sentences, the countless allusions, and the abrupt transitions from thought to thought are, in their totality, the mirror of a wonderful mind. They transmit the essence of their writer's nature ; and are, indeed, something like prose sonnets—the private record in the most finished form of their author's experience.

Bacon is perhaps the first writer of English prose whose work reaches a uniformly high standard in both matter and manner. It is amazing how little time has antiquated his essays. At a distance of more than three centuries, they are still a storehouse of wisdom, as fresh and convincing as on the day when they were written. Much that is really quaint and mediæval enters into the work of men like Hooker, and Sir Thomas Browne. But the reader who finds Bacon's *Essays* quaint sees only the surface of them. Time has given a pleasant old-world flavour to these sentences from the essay *Of Studies*, but what is really remarkable is the amount of perennial wisdom which has been compressed into a few words :

Read not to contradict and confute, nor to believe and take for granted, nor to find talk and discourse, but to weigh and consider. Some books are to be tasted, others to be swallowed, some few to be chewed and digested. . . .

Reading maketh a full man ; conference a ready man ; and writing an exact man : and therefore, if a man write little, he had need have a great memory ; if he confer little, he had need have a present wit ; and if he read little, he had need have much cunning, to seem to know that he doth not. Histories make men wise ; poets, witty ; the mathematics, subtile ; natural philosophy, deep ; moral, grave ; logic and rhetoric, able to contend.

In Bacon, the intellect was paramount, and it is therefore in matters of general speculation that his wisdom shines brightest. On topics of ordinary life, he often naïvely reveals his nature, as when in his essay *Of Marriage*, he remarks : " He that hath wife and children hath given hostages to Fortune." Bacon's passion for self-advancement made him master of a worldly-wisdom as complete, perhaps, as any man ever possessed. It is wonderful to read in his essay, *Of Great Place*, of the slippery footholds round about human eminence, and in his essay *Of Ceremonies and Respects*, of the manner in which the great should comport themselves before the eyes of the world :

Amongst a man's peers, a man shall be sure of familiarity ; and therefore it is good a little to keep state ; amongst a man's inferiors, one shall be sure of reverence ; and therefore it is good a little to be familiar. He that is too much in anything, so that he giveth another occasion of satiety, maketh himself cheap. To apply one's self to others, is good ; so it be with demonstration, that a man doth it upon regard, and not upon facility. It is a good precept, generally in seconding another, yet to add somewhat of one's own ; as if you will grant his opinion, let it be with some distinction ; and if you will follow his motion . . . let it be with alleging further reason.

In precepts like these, Bacon seems a kind of Polonius,

before "dotage had encroached upon wisdom." The Renaissance, indeed, had made men far more subtle. Taught by Machiavelli, princes were becoming versed in all the arts of politic deception. The casuistry of the Jesuits was admired and emulated even in Protestant countries, and by none more successfully than by Elizabeth herself. In his cold analysis of the art of governing, no less than in his acute discussion of Simulation and Dissimulation, Bacon shows himself a true child of his time.

It is, however, his passion for knowledge that makes Bacon so magnificent a figure. His dreams of advancing the sciences are most fully developed in his great Latin work, the *Instauratio Magna* (1620–3). Fortunately, however, his views are partially set forth in an English book, *The Advancement of Learning*, which is at once a masterpiece of prose and one of the finest records of intellectual aspiration in existence. The concise style of the *Essays* here gives place to a simpler and freer manner. Bacon does not, like Browne, love grandeur of language for its own sake, but he often rises to a sober magnificence, as in the following passage in which he states the purpose of all intellectual inquiry, namely, the benefit of the human race :

But the greatest error of all the rest is the mistaking or misplacing of the last or farthest end of knowledge. For men have entered into a desire of learning and knowledge, sometimes upon a natural curiosity and inquisitive appetite ; sometimes to entertain their minds with variety and delight ; sometimes for ornament and reputation ; and sometimes to enable them to victory of wit and contradiction ; and most times for lucre and profession ; and seldom sincerely to give a true account of their gift of reason to the benefit and use of men : as if there were sought in knowledge a couch whereupon to rest a searching and restless spirit ; or a terrace for a wandering and variable mind to walk up and down with a fair prospect ; or a tower of state for a proud mind to raise itself upon ; or a fort or commanding ground for strife and contention ; or a shop for profit or sale ; and not a rich storehouse for the glory of the Creator and the relief of man's estate.

In turning away from " the vanity of curious speculations, wherewith the schools labour," and setting his face towards scientific improvements, Bacon marks the emergence of the modern world from the Middle Ages. In an unfinished work, called *The New Atlantis* (published 1627), he speculated on some of the future fruits of knowledge. He imagined an institution called " Salomon's House," a place dedicated to scientific experiment. " The end of our foundation," says one of its " fathers," " is the knowledge of causes, and secret motions of things ; and the enlarging of the bounds of human empire, to the effecting of all things possible." He describes the numerous experiments and wonders of the House : " caves . . . for all coagulations, indurations, refrigerations and conservations of bodies," means " to convey sounds in trunks and pipes in strange lines and distances," and many other marvellous things. This is curious and interesting reading : its historical importance is manifest. Yet there is in Bacon's work something greater than historical importance. There is the living fire of a manly and generous wisdom, of a glowing faith in man's destiny and of an insatiable desire for knowledge. In his grander passages, he lifts us out of small personal interests and narrow pursuits to a serene height from which we can survey the whole field of human activity, and see the beneficent results which would flow from the wise co-operation of man with man.

IV

The stately manner of writing, which in Bacon's work is controlled by its author's severely experimental mind, was also cultivated by certain men of Charles I's reign and the Commonwealth. By them a form of prose was produced, highly complex in its structure and almost poetic in its richness of language. The chief masters of this rhetorical prose are Sir Thomas Browne, Milton, and Jeremy Taylor. Clarendon, whose sentences are often as elaborate as theirs, is simpler in his vocabulary.

Sir Thomas Browne, who was born in London in 1605,

was educated at Winchester and Pembroke College, Oxford, and then settled in Norwich, where he practised as a physician. He continued to live in that city from 1636 till his death in 1682. His most famous book, *Religio Medici*, was published in 1642. It soon became known in the principal Protestant countries and was translated into Latin, Dutch, French and German. None of Browne's later writings attained so wide a vogue, though lovers of the magnificent in prose will find passages at least as impressive in his *Pseudodoxia Epidemica* and *Hydriotaphia*. The occasion of this last work was the discovery of an ancient urn in the neighbourhood of Hornchurch. In his deep and eloquent meditations on time and antiquity, Browne reaches a rhetorical splendour of which only he and a few contemporaries possessed the secret.

The *Religio Medici* could not have been written before the Reformation, nor long after 1660, when the growing recognition of natural laws, with the consequent decline of belief in the miraculous, would have clipped the wings of Browne's speculative fancy. "I have ever believed," he writes, "and do now know, that there are Witches : they that doubt of these do not only deny *them*, but Spirits ; and are obliquely and upon consequence a sort, not of Infidels, but of Atheists." The conflict between his acuteness and his credulity gives Browne's writings a peculiar charm. Whether he writes of the existence of angels, the nature of Heaven and Hell, the seat of the soul, or the resurrection of the dead, there is always something unexpected in what he says and his manner of saying it. Every sentence has the stamp of his individuality. His work is the revelation of a cultured mind at once open to the inquiring spirit of the Renaissance and firmly rooted in the faith of the Reformation. His own position is concisely stated by himself ; "Where the Scripture is silent," he says, "the Church is my Text ; where that speaks, 'tis but my Commentary ; where there is a joint silence of both, I borrow not the rules of my religion from Rome or Geneva, but the dictates of my own reason."

But Browne was greater as an artist than as a thinker.

He has the mind of a contemplative poet, and on such subjects as Time, Death, and Eternity his prose has a resonant magnificence which has never been surpassed. The climax of his meditations in the *Hydriotaphia*, the passage beginning, " Now since these dead bones," is one of the most splendid terminal paragraphs to be found in the whole body of prose literature.

Milton's prose works were written during the interval between the meeting of the Long Parliament and the Restoration of the Stuarts. Most of his writings are concerned with the questions at issue between Parliament and King. At first, he leant towards the Presbyterians ; but in his tract *On the Doctrine and Discipline of Divorce* (1645), he took up an attitude highly offensive to that party. Milton was not only a foe to prelates, but the champion of freedom in every form. His sympathies lay rather with Cromwell and the Independents than with the average members of the Long Parliament. His most famous prose work is the *Areopagitica* (1644), occasioned by a parliamentary order for submitting the press to a censorship. To Milton, man's intellect was a sacred thing ; and the idea of establishing a bureaucratic control over genius stirred his most vehement feelings. It is the proud sense of what man can be by his intellect, his virtue, and his will, that inspires the finest passages of Milton's nobler pamphlets, *Of Reformation in England,* the *Tractate of Education*, and the *Areopagitica*. But a pamphleteer has not only to write rhapsodies. In his more pedestrian passages, Milton betrays some unfitness for his task. He had neither humour nor lightness of touch. He sometimes stooped to virulent abuse. None the less, there was an undoubted sublimity in Milton's career as a publicist. He sacrificed his eyesight to the public cause ; and on the very eve of the Restoration, when Charles's return was certain, he had the courage to write and publish a pamphlet, *The Ready and Easy way to establish a Free Commonwealth.*

Milton's prose has just the qualities one would expect from a knowledge of his nature. Once he touches on a noble thought, his genius lifts him from the ground, its wings bear him aloft and he soars on a majestic flight through the highest heaven of imagination. To know how sublime these passages can be, one must read whole pages together, for it is in the sweep of a sustained effort that the greatness of Milton's powers reveals itself. Yet many of his single sentences, even, have a beauty which bears in miniature the impress of their writer's mind, as this one from *Areopagitica* :

I cannot praise a fugitive and cloister'd virtue, unexercised and unbreathed, that never sallies out and sees her adversary, but slinks out of the race, where that immortal garland is to be run for, not without dust and heat.

Or this :

Many a man lives a burden to the earth ; but a good book is the precious life-blood of a master spirit, embalmed and treasured up on purpose to a life beyond life.

Or this short passage from the same work :

Truth indeed came once into the world with her divine Master, and was a perfect shape most glorious to look on : but when he ascended, and his apostles after him were laid asleep, then straight arose a wicked race of deceivers, who, as that story goes of the Egyptian Typhon with his conspirators, how they dealt with the good Osiris, took the virgin Truth, hewed her lovely form into a thousand pieces, and scattered them to the four winds. From that time ever since, the sad friends of Truth, such as durst appear, imitating the careful search that Isis made for the mangled body of Osiris, went up and down gathering up limb by limb still as they could find them. We have not yet found them all, lords and commons, nor ever shall do, till her Master's second coming ; he shall bring together every joint and member, and shall mould them into an immortal feature of loveliness and perfection.

The greatest writer on the other side in the parliamentary struggle was the Earl of Clarendon (1609–1674). On his banishment in 1667 by the king whom he had done so much to serve, he retired to France where he wrote at leisure one of those enormous histories dear to his century. Clarendon's case had some resemblance to that of Sir

Walter Raleigh, who, when in prison, had solaced himself by writing *The History of the World* (1614). Clarendon was one of the last great masters of the old-world manner. He carries on the tradition of stately prose into an age which had definitely decided for colloquial ease. Less magnificent than Browne, less poetic than Milton, Clarendon is more equable in his prose than either, and his theme has a human interest which is often lacking in their pages. His *History of the Rebellion and Civil Wars in England*, like many other histories, is none the less readable for being written with a very strong bias. The following is Clarendon's character of Cromwell :

Without doubt, no man with more wickedness ever attempted anything, or brought to pass what he desired more wickedly, more in the face and contempt of religion and moral honesty ; yet wickedness as great as his could never have accomplished those trophies without the assistance of a great spirit, an admirable circumspection and sagacity, and a most magnanimous resolution. When he appeared first in the Parliament he seemed to have a person in no degree gracious, no ornament of discourse, none of those talents which use to reconcile the affections of the standers by ; yet as he grew into place and authority, his parts seemed to be raised as if he had concealed faculties till he had occasion to use them ; and when he was to act the part of a great man, he did it without any indecency, notwithstanding the want of custom . . .

He was not a man of blood, and totally declined Machiavel's method, which prescribes upon any alteration of a government, as a thing absolutely necessary, to cut off all the heads of those, and extirpate their families who are friends to the old, and it was confidently reported that in the Council of Officers, it was more than once proposed that there might be a general massacre of all the royal party, as the only expedient to secure the government : but Cromwell would never consent to it ; it may be out of too much contempt of his enemies. In a word, as he had all the wickedness against which damnation is denounced and for which Hell fire is prepared, so he had some virtues, which have caused the memory of some men in all ages to be celebrated ; and he will be looked upon by posterity as a brave, bad man.

The eloquence of seventeenth-century prose is partly the outcome of its deeply religious temper. There were many great preachers in that age, and few have ever depicted man's mortal and immortal lot in words of more searching power than John Donne, Dean of St. Paul's. The stately manner of the pulpit survived the Restoration and was continued by eminent divines such as Barrow and South. In the work of Jeremy Taylor (1613–1667), Bishop of Dromore, pulpit eloquence attained a great height. Through the suavity of his language and the richness of his imagery, as well as by his profoundly human imagination, Taylor is one of the masters of English eloquence. One of his works, *Holy Living and Holy Dying* (1650–1), was for many years a favourite book of devotion among English men and women.

v

The writers of grandiloquent English were men who, for the most part, belonged to an aristocracy of intellect. A simpler kind of prose, often much truer to native idiom, was cultivated by less learned men who had no thought of a European reputation. Some of the best works produced under the Tudors and Stuarts are anonymous. Authorship as a profession hardly existed as yet, and even the testimony of a title-page is often an uncertain guide as to the source of a book's contents.

No anonymous writers in our literature can be compared for importance with the translators of the Authorised Version of the Bible. This work, which appeared in 1611, is the crowning achievement of the Reformation in English Literature. The beauty of the translation is due to the devotion of learned and pious men, to whom the task of rendering the Word of God into the language of the people stirred the deepest religious feelings. The work was carried out by three groups of scholars, sitting at Oxford, at Cambridge, and at Westminster. They had before them the versions of their predecessors of the sixteenth century, and these they accepted as the foundation of their work. A part of the English Bible had been printed in 1525, through the efforts of William Tindale. Coverdale's complete Bible was finished in 1535. These works, as well as the Bible of "Matthew,"[1] the "Great Bible," and the "Bishops' Bible," all had their merits and became dear to their various readers ; but the need for one uniform version was evident. The success of the Authorised Version was complete : it soon supplanted all previous translations, and almost immediately it began its great task of moulding the lives, the thoughts and the speech of millions of English people.

To describe the merits of the English Bible is a difficult task, for not only are they very various, but they are almost inevitably taken for granted. But first, we may notice the unfailing dignity of the language. History, prophecy, myth, poetry, and theology—the Bible contains them all, yet it would be difficult to point to a single sentence unworthy of a sacred volume. Secondly, the style is extremely simple. It is true there are obscure passages due to an imperfect understanding of the original tongues. Yet there are pages innumerable which, in their main drift, the simplest mind can understand ; how else could the Bible have become the Book of the people ? Thirdly, there is hardly one great quality of human expression which is not exemplified with wonderful power. For romantic narrative, it would be hard to surpass the story of Joseph and his Brethren. The Parable of the Prodigal Son is one of the best short stories in the world. The language appropriate to pointed epigram and sententious wisdom is admirably illustrated in the Book of Proverbs. The one satisfactory style of rendering poetry into prose is the style of the Psalms and of Isaiah ; and it would be hard to conceive of verse more poetic than the chapter beginning : " Arise, shine, for thy light is come." What prose is more sublime and simple than that of St. Matthew and St. Luke ? Where is language more moving than in the consolatory chapters of St. John ? No words are more stirring than those of the chapter in the Epistle to the

---

[1] "Matthew" was a pseudonym for John Rogers, whose version of the Bible was founded on Tindale's.

Corinthians beginning : " Though I speak with the tongues of men and of angels." No rhythms are more awe-inspiring than those of the Book of the Revelation.

Of the effect of the Bible on our literature and language, it is also difficult to give any idea. Its influence is by no means limited to the devout. Bunyan, indeed, owes everything to it ; but the debt of Swinburne is also im-measurable. The style of almost all men approaches the Scriptural in moments of emotion. Moreover, the Bible is one of the few works which have contributed an appreci-able number of words to our vocabulary. On this subject one cannot do better than quote the remarks of a great philologist. " To Coverdale," says Henry Bradley, " we owe the beautiful combinations *loving-kindness* and *tender mercy ;* Tindale gave us *long-suffering* and *peacemaker* . . . It will be a surprise to most people to learn that such a familiar and, as we should think, indispensable word as *beautiful* is not known to have been used by any writer before Tindale. . . . The indirect effect of the English Bible on the English vocabulary has been progressive down to recent times. Many words that were already somewhat old-fashioned in 1611 and would in the natural course of things have become obsolete, have been preserved from extinction because of their occurrence in familiar passages of Scripture, though they now belong only to elevated literary diction. Such are *apparel* and *raiment* for ' dress ' or ' clothes ' ; *quick* for ' living ' ; *damsel* for ' young woman ' ; *travail* for ' labour.' The retention of *firmament* (the Vulgate *firmamentum*) in the first chapter of Genesis has given rise to the use of the word as a poetical synonym for ' sky.' " As these examples show, the Bible has not only given us a standard of noble expression, but has also helped to preserve the continuity of the language. No other book could have performed this task so well.

VI

The artless prose of the early seventeenth century has a charm which is lacking in the work of more pretentious men.   The most delightful writer in the simpler manner is Izaak Walton (1593–1683), whose *Compleat Angler* (1653) and *Lives* of John Donne, Sir Henry Wotton, Richard Hooker, George Herbert, and Bishop Sanderson perpetuate a refinement which was natural in his day.   The memoirs of two women, Lucy Hutchinson, and Margaret, Duchess of Newcastle, have something of the same grave charm. How effectively a man could write, who, though the reverse of a professed author, inherited, like the rest of his generation, the tradition of pure English, one may see from certain letters of Oliver Cromwell, as, for instance, that noble message of consolation to his "loving friend, Colonel Valentine Walton," whose son had fallen at the battle of Marston Moor.

CHAPTER VIII

MILTON AND HIS AGE

THE life of John Milton extended from 1608 to 1674. Until the Restoration, he participated in the life of his time, but for his last fourteen years he was a recluse, the relic of an age on which the world looked back with abhorrence. The formative part of a poet's mind is the period of his childhood and youth, and much that is most winning in the poetry of Milton owes a debt to the life of rural England, which was never more humane and gracious than in the years preceding the Great Rebellion.

The reigns of James I and Charles I may be described as the golden age of the English manor-house. The soundest part of the population was to be found in the ranks of the lesser gentry, men who were content with their own pleasant seats and had little desire for the glitter of a corrupt court. These men, who had imbibed something of Renaissance humanism at the Universities, had also a literature in their own tongue, and every Sunday they listened to the harmonious prose of the English Bible and the English liturgy. The practice of vocal and instrumental music was widespread, and the Elizabethan song-books provided an inexhaustible fund of native airs, gay and grave. A good tradition of architecture gave the country-side many dwellings both dignified and homely, for something of the Gothic spirit lingered still, and made a pleasant contrast to the Tudor chimney and gable. The owners of these houses, however, had little mind to sink into a life of mere luxury. They formed the most determined House of Commons which has ever met at Westminster, and though slow to take up arms, they offered from the first a strong, passive resistance to what they considered the encroachments of tyranny. The life of the yeoman and the villager showed something of the same amenities. Country sports and dancing, the bustle of wake and fair, fireside stories of Queen Mab and Robin Goodfellow, gave rustic life a stir and colour to which later years can show no parallel. The lines of Bishop Corbet paint no fancy picture :

> When Tom came home from labour,
>   And Ciss to milking rose,
> Then merrily went your tabor,
>   And nimbly went their toes.

The same cheerful life is mirrored in Milton's *L'Allegro*, and in the poems of Robert Herrick.

I

Love of the country and its life may easily be discerned in the plays of Shakespeare, and in the pastoral poems of Spenser and his contemporaries. But in the seventeenth century one is aware of a new note. The circle of imagination has lessened, but in its place has come the intimate love of home and country. National pride had inspired the Elizabethan poet Drayton to become verse topographer of England, but Herrick is content with a narrower sphere. His chief volume was *Hesperides* (1648), so called from its origin in Devonshire, where its author was Vicar of Dean Prior. The volume is a collection of short pieces, the scope of which is described in the prefatory poem :

> I sing of brooks, of blossoms, birds and bowers,
> Of April, May, of June and July flowers ;
> I sing of May-poles, hock-carts, wassails, wakes,
> Of bridegrooms, brides, and of their bridal cakes ;
> I sing of youth, of love, and have access
> By these to sing of cleanly wantonness ;
> I sing of dews, of rains, and piece by piece
> Of balm, of oil, of spice and ambergris.
> I sing of times trans-shifting, and I write
> How roses first came red and lilies white ;

> I write of groves, of twilights, and I sing
> The Court of Mab, and of the Fairy King ;
> I write of hell ; I sing (and ever shall)
> Of heaven, and hope to have it after all.

Herrick was inspired by two muses, of which the more potent was purely pagan, and his second volume, *Noble Numbers*, shows us far less of the real man. Dean Prior possessed abundant charms for the sensuous nature of an unregenerate priest. May-day ceremonies and fairy mythology inspired him to some delicious and delicate verse. He ranges over the meadows from flower to flower, pausing just long enough to mingle some fragile sentiment with the perfumes and colours which give him so much delight. He begs the daisies not to shut so soon, and in a charming fantasy imagines the other flowers present at the funeral rites of the rose. He has much in common with Horace, an epicurean love of beauty with a half-luxurious regret for its evanescence, two feelings to which he gives graceful expression in his poem *To Daffodils* :

> Fair daffodils, we weep to see
>   You haste away so soon ;
> As yet the early-rising sun
>   Has not attained his noon ;
>   Stay, stay
>   Until the hasting day
>   Has run
>   But to the evensong,
> And having pray'd together, we
>   Will go with you along.
>
> We have short time to stay, as you,
>   We have as short a spring ;
> As quick a growth to meet decay,
>   As you, or anything ;
>   We die
>   As your hours do, and dry
>   Away
>   Like to the summer's rain,
> Or as the pearls of morning's dew,
>   Ne'er to be found again.

Herrick was a Cavalier ; but his love of the country was at least rivalled by two Puritan poets, Milton and

Marvell. There have been closer observers of Nature, but few have equalled Milton in the compressed verbal power of his twin poems, *L'Allegro* and *Il Penseroso*. They were written during their author's early maturity, when he lived a student's life in the village of Horton near Windsor. The descriptions are not localised ; yet it is clear, in spite of the allusion to " mountains " (the word could then be applied to very modest eminences), that they are inspired by the landscape of Southern England. They are more than mere landscape pieces. They are poems of contrasted moods, showing the world as it appears to a cheerful, and to a contemplative mind. None the less, the visible horizon is bounded by the author's native land. It is a sunshiny morning in seventeenth-century England that Milton describes in *L'Allegro* :

> While the plowman near at hand,
> Whistles o'er the furrowed land,
> And the milkmaid singeth blithe,
> And the mower whets his scythe,
> And every shepherd tells his tale,
> Under the hawthorn in the dale.

Equally English is the rainy dawn of *Il Penseroso* :

> Kerchief'd in a comely cloud
> While rocking winds are piping loud,
> Or usher'd with a shower still,
> When the gust hath blown his fill,
> Ending on the rustling leaves,
> With minute drops from off the eaves.

Few poets have received so exquisite a delight from Nature as Milton's friend and fellow-Puritan, Andrew Marvell (1621–1678). His half-dozen best pieces are at once " simple, sensuous, and passionate." Marvell is an imaginative as well as a descriptive writer, and in his poem called *Bermudas*, he pictures the miracles of God in the semi-tropical world which he himself had never seen :

> He hangs in shades the orange bright
> Like golden lamps in a green night.

But he is at his best in that lovely piece, *The Garden*, a

description of the perfect felicity which visits the imaginative man :

> What wondrous life in this I lead !
> Ripe apples drop about my head ;
> The luscious clusters of the vine
> Upon my mouth do crush their wine ;
> The nectarine and curious peach
> Into my hands themselves do reach ;
> Stumbling on melons as I pass,
> Insnared with flowers, I fall on grass.
>
> Meanwhile the mind, from pleasure less,
> Withdraws into its happiness ;
> The mind, that ocean where each kind
> Does straight its own resemblance find ;
> Yet it creates, transcending these,
> Far other worlds, and other seas :
> Annihilating all that's made
> To a green thought in a green shade.

II

The first half of the seventeenth century was certainly one of the most religious periods in our history. Men had not learnt the virtue of toleration—one Edward Wightman was burnt for heresy so late as 1612, and the persecutions of Laud were a sign of the times. But many of the religious virtues, self-sacrifice, devotion, zeal, it possessed in full measure, and the pillory was not more typical of the age than the saintliness of a Herbert, the fervour of a Fox, or the monastic piety of the recluses at Little Gidding. At no time in our history has the union of religion and art been so happily consummated. The best religious poets of that age were not mere versifiers of dogma. They were men whose inward experience found in verse its most natural expression—men such as Donne, Crashaw, Herbert, Vaughan, and Traherne, each of them the master of an original poetic manner.

John Donne (1573–1631) took orders in the Church of England at the age of forty-two. He was a courtier and a scholar, a man of brilliant intelligence and handsome appearance. He had the Elizabethan craving to extract every ounce of pleasure that life could yield, and his poetry shows the versatility of his nature. He wrote satires, love-poems, elegies, sonnets. One great merit is his command of the vividly impressive phrase. Much of his verse is obscure, rough, and technically lax—faults which his temperament encouraged rather than condemned. Flashes of intense expression redeem the oddity of frequent " conceits." In certain of his shorter poems, such as *The Extasie*, and *The Calme*, in some of his sonnets, such as those on Death, and in various lyrical pieces, his power is undeniable. Undoubtedly, he was a great man : there is, in some of his sermons, an almost terrifying eloquence. One of the mightiest of his religious poems is his *Hymn to God the Father*, alike in its solemnity and its originality a true revelation of its author's power :

> Wilt Thou forgive that sin, where I begun,
>   Which was my sin, though it were done before ?
> Wilt Thou forgive that sin through which I run
>   And do run still, though still I do deplore ?
> When Thou hast done, Thou hast not done,
>   For, I have more.
>
> Wilt Thou forgive that sin, which I have won
>   Others to sin, and made my sin their door ?
> Wilt Thou forgive that sin which I did shun
>   A year or two : but wallowed in, a score ?
> When Thou hast done, Thou hast not done,
>   For I have more.
>
> I have a sin of fear, that when I have spun
>   My last thread, I shall perish on the shore ;
> But swear by Thyself that at my death, Thy Son
>   Shall shine as He shines now, and heretofore :
> And, having done that, Thou hast done,
>   I fear no more.

Of the other religious poets, the most considerable figure is perhaps Herbert, though he had neither Crashaw's wealth of sensuous imagery, nor the flashes of imagination which illuminate the mystical verse of Vaughan, as in that wonderful opening :

> I saw Eternity the other night,
> Like a great Ring of pure and endless light,
>   All calm, as it was bright.

Like Donne, George Herbert (1593–1633) had thoughts
of a secular career before he entered the Church.   Finally,
he became Vicar of Bemerton near Salisbury, where he
lived a life of apostolic simplicity.   He was constitutionally
frail, and died of consumption at an early age.   He was
a man of great charity, refinement, and many artistic gifts.
During his short career as a priest, he wrote the lyrics
collected in his volume, *The Temple* (1633).   Most of these
pieces are deeply Anglican in tone : some deal with the
very door, porch, and windows of his church, in a somewhat fantastic manner.   Quaintness and extravagance were
the prevailing faults of the age, and Herbert had his full
share of them.   But in a few pieces his humility and
profound religious temper found faultless expression.
One of these in particular is deservedly well known, for
it is an almost perfect poem, and its touch of quaintness
even adds a charm.   It is characteristically called *The
Pulley* :

> When God at first made man,
> Having a glass of blessings standing by,
> " Let us," said He, " pour on him all we can ;
> Let the world's riches, which dispers'd lie,
>   Contract into a span."
>
> So strength first made a way ;
> Then beauty flowed, then wisdom, honour, pleasure ;
> When almost all was out, God made a stay,
> Perceiving that alone of all His treasure,
>   Rest in the bottom lay.
>
> " For if I should," said He,
> " Bestow this jewel also on My creature,
> He would adore My gifts instead of Me,
> And rest in Nature, not the God of Nature :
>   So both should losers be.
>
> " Yet let him keep the rest,
> But keep them with repining restlessness ;
> Let him be rich and weary, that at least,
> If goodness lead him not, yet weariness
>   May toss him to My breast."

III

During the age of Elizabeth, the principal theme in the great outburst of lyrical poetry had been love. But the subject was handled rather conventionally, and the lover generally approached his mistress in the attitude of a worshipper. High-flown compliments are not incompatible with fine poetry, as may be seen from Ben Jonson's "Drink to me only with thine eyes." But convention is the foe to individuality; and it was chiefly in individuality that the love-lyric gained during the early seventeenth century. Jonson himself had sometimes mingled criticism with compliment:

> Still to be neat, still to be drest
> As you were going to a feast,
> Still to be powdered, still perfumed,
> Lady, it is to be presumed,
> Though Art's hid causes are not found,
> All is not sweet, all is not sound.

The tone was taken up by a group of " Cavalier Poets," of whom Herrick himself was one of the chief. These men flung a careless gaiety, and sometimes a mocking cynicism into their verses. The idealism of Elizabeth's reign was now waning, and a long step had been taken towards the unblushing freedom of Restoration manners. At the Court, complimentary verse was still acceptable, and Carew rose splendidly to the occasion in his lyric beginning:

> Ask me no more where Jove bestows
> When June is past, the fading rose,
> For in your beauty's orient deep
> These flowers, as in their causes, sleep.

But the love-poetry of Herrick is frankly voluptuous, while Sir John Suckling (1609–1642) cheerfully consigns his coy mistress to perdition in the lines: " Why so pale and wan, fond lover?" The outbreak of the Civil War changed the atmosphere, and the clash of arms re-woke the spirit of gallantry. It is heard in the stirring songs of the Marquis of Montrose, but most memorably, perhaps, in the lines of Richard Lovelace (1618–1658) *To Lucasta, Going to the Wars :*

> Tell me not, Sweet, I am unkind,
>   That from the nunnery
> Of thy chaste breast, and quiet mind
>   To war and arms I fly.
>
> True ; a new mistress now I chase,
>   The first foe in the field ;
> And with a stronger faith embrace
>   A sword, a horse, a shield.
>
> Yet this inconstancy is such
>   As you too shall adore ;
> I could not love thee, Dear, so much,
>   Loved I not Honour more.

IV

John Milton walked among the men of seventeenth‧century England and participated in their affairs. But he is too great to be thought of in this narrow historical setting. He was one of the chief figures of the Renaissance, and he belongs to humanity. The main facts of his life have a profound interest, for he is a supreme example of self-dedication to a lofty task.

Milton was born in 1608, at a house in Bread Street, Cheapside, almost under the shadow of St. Paul's and nearer still to the ancient church of St. Mary-le-Bow. The boy was sent first to St. Paul's School, where he became an excellent classical scholar and an adept at versification, and then to Christ's College, Cambridge. He stayed at the University for five years, where he had a distinguished career, in spite of some friction with the authorities. In person, he was somewhat under the middle size, was fair-haired and delicately made, and his general appearance earned him the nickname of " the lady of Christ's." He continued to write Greek, Latin, and English, and in the year 1630 composed his first great poem, the *Ode on the Morning of Christ's Nativity*. The theme of the piece

is the victory of the newly-born Child over the pagan
deities. At the birth of Christ, it is said, the oracles ceased
their utterance, and the story gives Milton an opportunity
of revelling in the music of sonorous names in the manner
so dear to him. But what most delights the reader is
the precision of style and the command over rhythm which
can produce a stanza so simple and yet so beautiful as this :

> See how from far upon the Eastern road
> The Star-led Wizards haste with odours sweet :
> O run, prevent them with thy humble Ode,
> And lay it lowly at His blessed feet ;
> Have thou the honour first, thy Lord to greet,
> And join thy voice unto the Angel Choir,
> From out his Secret Altar touch'd with hallow'd fire.

The next stage of the poet's life was passed at his
father's house at Horton in Buckinghamshire. The elder
Milton, who had retired from his occupation as " scrivener,"
recognised his son's extraordinary powers and allowed him
to lead a life of study and self-culture at home. The idea
of some great poem was taking shape in Milton's mind,
but he was still uncertain as to the subject and the form.
He often turned in thought to the legends of King Arthur,
and made himself well versed in the ancient stories of
Britain. But the scope of his studies was boundless, for
in his determination to choose the highest of themes and
to sing it in a worthy manner, he strove to become familiar
with all that had been best written and best done in the
history of man. He was a complete master of Greek and
Latin literature, and a student of French, Italian and
Spanish. He was also a mathematician and an astronomer,
and was eager to learn the latest theories in those sciences.
Even these years at Horton did not satisfy the student's
ambitions or weary his father's generosity. A journey
had to be taken to Italy, the home of the arts and patron
of students. Milton made a leisurely tour to Florence,
Rome, Naples, and other cities, enjoying everywhere the
conversation of learned men, including Galileo. The
reputation of the young Englishman had gone before him,
and his devotion to learning as well as his skill in languages

made him welcome at the Academies. He was still in Italy when the news reached him of the struggle between Parliament and King. Feeling that this was a matter of concern to every patriotic Englishman, he at once hastened home.

Thus Milton's real ambitions were interrupted at a most critical moment, and the poet felt that he had done little yet to justify his laborious training. Yet there are many readers who take a keener delight in his early poems, *L'Allegro*, *Il Penseroso*, *Comus*, *Lycidas*, and the rest, than in the grander and sterner work of his later maturity. *Comus* certainly expresses much that is most delightful in Milton's genius. It is a Masque, written for a family reunion at Ludlow Castle. Played amid stately surroundings by ladies and gentlemen in the rich costumes of the period, the story of the travelling Lady, separated from her two brothers in a lonely wood, assailed by Comus and his crew of revellers, and finally relieved through the intervention of an Attendant Spirit, must have had a great charm even for those who could not enjoy the finest verse at the first hearing. To those who could, and who also had ears for the music of Milton's friend, Henry Lawes, *Comus* must have given incomparable pleasure. The work is a poem rather than a drama—an exchange of speeches in faultless blank verse, rather than the development of a situation. The speech of the Attendant Spirit at the opening of the poem, and the song " Sabrina fair " would alone prove Milton a great artist.

Lycidas is not so much an elegy on a dead friend as a memorial to great powers denied fulfilment. Its motive is to praise rather than lament. Hence, though Milton mourns over the untimely death of the young Cambridge poet, his tone is distinctly impersonal. It may be that the poem is " artificial." Yet no greater glory could have befallen the name of Edward King than to be linked in perpetuity with *Lycidas*. The poem is one great song of many strains, and the reader's mind is borne through a cycle of varied emotions, from regret to consolation, by the most perfect melody of which language is capable. If there is an apex of the poem, it is that part in which Milton speaks of a matter ever in his thoughts—the aspiration after True Fame.

One complete poem of these early years may be quoted, a simple piece of soaring verse, in which the poet celebrates the union of two great arts :

> Blest pair of Sirens, pledges of Heav'n's joy,
> Sphere-born harmonious Sisters, Voice and Verse,
> Wed your divine sounds, and mixt power employ
> Dead things with inbreath'd sense able to pierce,
> And to our high-rais'd fantasy present,
> That undisturbed Song of pure content,
> Aye sung before the sapphire-colour'd throne
> To Him that sits thereon
> With Saintly shout and solemn Jubilee,
> Where the bright Seraphim in burning row
> Their loud up-lifted Angel trumpets blow,
> And the Cherubic host in thousand choirs
> Touch their immortal Harps of golden wires,
> With those just Spirits that wear victorious Palms,
> Hymns devout and holy Psalms
> Singing everlastingly ;
> That we on Earth with undiscording voice
> May rightly answer that melodious noise ;
> As once we did, till disproportion'd sin
> Jarr'd against nature's chime, and with harsh din
> Broke the fair music that all creatures made
> To their great Lord, whose love their motion sway'd
> In perfect Diapason, whilst they stood
> In first obedience, and their state of good.
> O may we soon again renew that Song,
> And keep in tune with Heav'n, till God ere long
> To His celestial consort us unite,
> To live with Him, and sing in endless morn of light.

V

For the historian and the biographer, the period of Milton's life between his return from Italy and his retirement from public affairs on the fall of the Commonwealth presents great interest. His unfortunate first marriage with Mary Powell, his Latin Secretaryship, his controversy with Charles's defender, Salmasius, are among the best-known things in the biography of great men ; yet they have little bearing on Milton's poetical career. Except a few sonnets—that on the Massacre of the Vaudois, that on his Blindness, and a few others—Milton wrote hardly any verse during these years. Still, it was a matter of immense consequence for him that he came into daily contact with some of the ablest men of action then living, and that he heard debates upon matters of policy affecting the fate of kingdoms. The value of this experience to the future epic poet can be seen in the great debate in Pandemonium, in *Paradise Lost*, Book II.

The Restoration certainly placed Milton's life in some danger, for though he was no " regicide," his published writings and his whole career put his republicanism beyond a doubt. It is possible that he had friends at Court who intervened for him, and no doubt his blindness was a protection. The rest of his life was passed in a kind of honoured obscurity, for though poor and in ill-odour with the Government, he was, we are told, " much visited by the learned." These years were occupied by the composition of three great poems. *Paradise Lost* was first published in 1667 ; *Paradise Regained* and *Samson Agonistes* in 1671, the year of the poet's death being 1674. He was buried in St. Giles's, Cripplegate.

A description of Milton in these later years, by one Jonathan Richardson, is well worth quoting. " I have heard many years since," he says, " that he used to sit in a grey coarse cloth coat at the door of his house, near Bunhill Fields without Moorgate, in warm sunny weather to enjoy the fresh air, and so, as well as in his room, received the visits of people of distinguished parts, as well as quality, and very lately I had the good fortune to have another picture of him from an ancient clergyman in Dorsetshire, Dr. Wright. He found him in a small house, he thinks but one room on a floor ; in that, up one pair of stairs, which was hung with rusty green, he found John Milton sitting in an elbow chair, black clothes, and neat enough, pale but not cadaverous, his hands and fingers gouty, and with chalk stones. Among other discourse, he expressed himself to this purpose : that was he free from the pain this gave him, his blindness would be tolerable."

VI

Paradise Lost is an epic poem in twelve books on the Fall of Man. The authority for the " plot " is the short account in the Book of Genesis of the Temptation and Expulsion of Adam and Eve. For his models, Milton had, in particular, the works of Homer and Virgil, but these, being the stories of human wars and wanderings, could give him little more than the " epic idea." For his conduct of the story, for his conception of the first man and woman, for his idea of the supernatural protagonists, and of the vast arena of their conflict, he had to rely on himself —on the riches of a memory stored up through years of intense study, and on the force of an imagination undaunted by infinity.

The plan of the poem, told briefly, is as follows : The fallen angels are discerned lying in a fiery gulf into which they have been flung after their rebellion against the Almighty. The first to stir out of their trance are Satan and Beelzebub. Summoned by their Leader, the rest arouse themselves and seek footing on firm land. Through the skill of Mulciber, an immense palace is built, in which the rebel angels assemble to hold a debate and council of war. Several plans are proposed, but the advice of Beelzebub, to make war on God's new world inhabited by man, wins universal favour, and it only remains to settle who shall set out in search of the earth. Satan himself undertakes the exploit, and passing to the borders of Hell comes face to face with two terrific beings, Sin and Death. Meantime, the Almighty in Heaven perceives the intention of man's Foe, and though knowing the future, sends down an Angel to protect His creatures. The Garden of Paradise, in the midst of Eden, is now described, and a dialogue takes place between the first parents of men.

In the meanwhile, Satan, having made his way up from Hell, and through the vast intervening mass called Chaos, has discovered the earth and set foot on a mountain in the near neighbourhood of Eden. Overhearing the words that pass between Adam and Eve, he learns that of one tree in the Garden they have been forbidden to eat. A messenger from Heaven now arrives, the Archangel Raphael, whose mission is to instruct Adam on the late Rebellion in Heaven, and the creation of the world; and above all to fortify him in his obedience to the Laws of God. Raphael departs; and Adam, having set forth to the duties of the day—for even Paradise needs its husband-man—Eve is left alone. Now is the Devil's chance. Assuming the fair form of a winged serpent, he summons up all his powers of flattery, awakens Eve's curiosity, and finally prevails upon her to perform the forbidden act. Adam, returning, is startled to find the change in Eve, but he also is induced to eat of the fruit. The consequences of their sin now fall upon them. Angry words arise, and mutual recriminations, and they seek to hide themselves from the face of God. A swift retribution lights on the fallen angels, for, just as Satan arrives in triumph to tell them the happy news, they are all transformed into hissing serpents. The doom of their sin also falls upon Adam and Eve, and the curses of the Fall are pronounced upon them. But their expulsion is delayed a space while another messenger from heaven, this time the stern Archangel Michael, comes to show Adam the future of a world into which, through his act, Sin and Death have entered. When Adam beholds the consequences of his sin prolonged through generations, the plagues, sickness and wars that visit mankind, he is overcome by despair and begs for death; but bidden by the Angel to look further still, he sees the birth of the Son of Man and Redeemer of the World. To Eve, who is asleep, the same consolation is conveyed in a dream. And so the parents of man take leave of their Paradise.

Perhaps no poet ever undertook a task of more appalling difficulty than that of Milton in writing his epic. Even

Dante, the one man who may be compared with him, was
travelling a less unknown path. That Milton was
uniformly successful, no one can assert; yet, even if the
reader turns to a part of the poem which has been most
criticised—that in which God addresses the Hosts of
Heaven, he will hear, in one of those opening lines,

> Thrones, Dominations, Princedoms, Virtues, Powers,

an echo of the whole vast conception. Here, as everywhere, is the hand of the great verbal artist. The theology
which is put into the mouth of the Deity affects various
readers in various ways, though there is hardly one, nowa-
days, who will say a word in defence of it. On strictly
literary grounds, it is more valid to object to the volubility
of the speeches. To have attributed an obscure and
difficult theology to the Almighty, and to have dilated it
into hundreds of lines was certainly a serious error of
taste, especially in one who knew so well the effect of
brevity and of mystery. Nor can anyone pretend that the
poem is equal. The gap which separates Books I and II
from Books VII and VIII is vast indeed. It was so
inevitably, for Raphael's account of the Days of Creation
gave the poet less scope for invention than any other part
of his theme. If *Paradise Lost* is claimed to be great as
a whole, not merely in parts, it is chiefly by reason of the
truth expressed in Coleridge's remark : " John Milton
himself is in every line."

To regard *Paradise Lost* as a mere triumph of style,
however, or to say that it is one of those works which we
may admire but need not read is a most serious mistake.
The vast and vague dimensions of the poet's universe, in
which supernatural beings pass between Heaven and Earth,
between Hell and Chaos, baffle the imagination. But the
figure of Satan, the dominating character in the poem, is
magnificently conceived. Milton wisely avoids direct
description of the Arch-Fiend, and conveys his aspect by
verbal suggestion and imagery. Satan's outward immensity
is indicated by comparisons. By the side of his spear,
for instance :

> The tallest pine
> Hewn on Norwegian hills, to be the mast
> Of some great admiral, were but a wand ;

but it is his courage that is most truly superhuman, the
dauntless tone of his defiance after defeat :

> What though the field be lost ?
> All is not lost ; the unconquerable will,
> And study of revenge, immortal hate,
> And courage never to submit or yield :
> And what is else not to be overcome,
> That Glory never shall his wrath or might
> Extort from me.

The indirect method is also used to convey Satan's
terrific spirit. Wherever he appears, he strikes awe into
the heart of the beholder. There are mighty beings in
Hell, Moloch, the god of war, and Beelzebub, to whom the
fallen angels listen with attention " still as night " :

> Deep on his front engraven
> Deliberation sat, and public care ;
> And princely counsel in his face yet shone
> Majestic, though in ruin : sage he stood
> With Atlantean shoulders fit to bear
> The weight of mightiest monarchies.

Yet even Beelzebub and Moloch share with the other angels
a dread of offending their " great Sultan," their " mighty
Paramount." Even the mysterious " anarch," who rules
over Chaos, grows pale when Satan confronts him in his
realm. Yet Satan is not merely the courageous rebel ; he
is the chief who feels for his followers, and nothing is finer
than the description of the pity which sweeps over him as
he surveys the " fellows of his crime " drawn up for the
first time after their overthrow :

> Thrice he essayed, and thrice in spite of scorn,
> Tears such as angels weep burst forth : at last
> Words interwove with sighs found out their way.

There is much truth in the common remark that Satan is
the real hero of the epic : and there are moments when
he inspires sympathy as well as admiration. His hostility

to the designs of Heaven is sometimes forgotten in the penalties of his fate, as, for instance, when he reviles the bright beams of the sun in the great opening speech of Book IV, exclaiming :

> Me miserable ! which way shall I fly,
> Infinite wrath and infinite despair ?

Equally poignant is the passage where he looks unseen on the felicity of Adam and Eve and contrasts it with his own eternal loneliness. Even in *Paradise Regained*, where he appears shorn of his majesty and corrupted by cunning, he inspires some pity, as in the great outburst that begins :

> 'Tis true, I am that Spirit unfortunate.

Satan is the figure that dominates the reader's thoughts, yet Milton's picture of Adam and Eve is, in spite of some blemishes, fully worthy of his design. As long as the pair are sinless, Milton has to rely much on the verbal splendours of poetry, though, indeed, their innocence is described with a simple directness which could not be bettered :

> So passed they naked on, nor shunned the sight
> Of God or angel, for they thought no ill.

As soon as Eve yields to the tempter, there is a pathos in their situation which Milton describes with more dramatic power than is often admitted. At first, alarm for the mysterious consequences of their sin awakens in them both a petulant irritation. This, as they learn the endless results which are to follow, is succeeded by despair—a despair ennobled in Eve by her love for Adam, and her offer to beg that the punishment may fall on her alone :

> On me, sole cause to thee of all this woe,
> Me, me only, just object of His ire.

In the midst of their overwhelming calamity, they are conscious of some refuge in their mutual love. From this bond arises much of the beauty of the closing scene. Even the pang of expulsion is mitigated by their companionship, and Eve can say to Adam when the moment for leaving Paradise is at hand :

> But now lead on;
> In me is no delay.   With thee to go
> Is to stay here; without thee here to stay
> Is to go hence unwilling.

The same thought softens the actual moment of departure, and adds a note of peace to the sadness of the wonderful conclusion:

> Some natural tears they dropped, but wiped them soon;
> The world was all before them, where to choose
> Their place of rest, and Providence their guide:
> They hand in hand with wandering steps and slow
> Through Eden took their solitary way.

VII

In *Paradise Lost, Paradise Regained,* and *Samson Agonistes,* Milton reached the climax of his powers as an artist in words.   His great merit is an almost unfailing command of what Matthew Arnold calls " the grand style."   He is, it is true, guilty of a few weak lines, but what other great poet, who has written in volume, is not guilty of hundreds?

Milton's skill in evoking the magic of words is certainly unequalled in literature.   It is seen in its simplest form in his numerous lines composed almost entirely of proper names, and his vast knowledge often enables him to choose words more musical and more potently suggestive than those in common use.   He does not say: " In Italian land men called him Vulcan," but with precisely the same meaning, though infinitely finer effect:

> In Ausonian land
> Men called him Mulciber.

He does not say, " Pharaoh and his Egyptian horsemen," but:

> Busiris and his Memphian chivalry.

To suggest the splendour of an angelic trumpet he invents a periphrasis of vague magnificence:

> Four speedy cherubim
> Put to their mouths the sounding alchemy.

It is partly the associations of the words, partly the music of the vowels that makes his line on the nightingale so lovely :

> She all night long her amorous descant sung.

He does not need for many of his finest effects the thundering sound of learned words : the commonest monosyllables are, in his hands, often the most poetical. The simplest words are enough for the exquisite concluding line of the opening book in *Paradise Regained*, where Christ is left alone in the desert at nightfall :

> He added not ; and Satan, bowing low
> His gray dissimulation, disappeared
> Into thin air diffused ; for now began
> Night with her sullen wing to double-shade
> The desert, fowls in their clay nests were couched,
> And now wild beasts came forth the woods to roam.

VIII

Milton's full power, however, is seen not so much in the details of his workmanship, as in the great resounding passages which succeed each other like billows of the sea. The unit of composition in *Paradise Lost* is not the line, but the verse-paragraph. The first two books consist almost entirely of great passages, some of them a hundred lines or more in length. It is the memory of these verse-paragraphs that stirs the reader to highest admiration. He thinks of Satan's speech to Beelzebub, of the roll-call of the fallen gods, of the building of Pandemonium, of the speeches of Moloch, Belial and Beelzebub, of the occupations in Hell after Satan's departure, of the encounter with Sin and Death—all of these are in the first two Books, and the succession continues, not always on the same marvellous level, but recovering it again and again at intervals through the epic. In such passages alone Milton's full greatness is seen. It is hard to choose between them, but perhaps none better deserves to be known than the Invocation to Light which introduces the first description of Heaven. The poet's thoughts pass naturally from light to his own blindness. He continues:

> Yet not the more
> Cease I to wander where the Muses haunt
> Clear spring, or shady grove, or sunny hill,
> Smit with the love of sacred song ; but chief
> Thee, Sion, and the flowery brooks beneath
> That wash thy hallowed feet, and warbling flow,
> Nightly I visit : nor sometimes forget
> Those other two equalled with me in fate,
> (So were I equalled with them in renown)
> Blind Thamyris, and blind Maeonides,
> And Tiresias and Phineus, prophets old,
> Then feed on thoughts, that voluntary move
> Harmonious numbers ; as the wakeful bird
> Sings darkling, and in shadiest covert hid
> Tunes her nocturnal note. Thus with the year
> Seasons return, but not to me returns
> Day, or the sweet approach of even or morn,
> Or sight of vernal bloom, or summer's rose,
> Or flocks, or herds, or human face divine ;
> But cloud instead, and ever-during dark
> Surrounds me, from the cheerful ways of men
> Cut off, and for the book of knowledge fair
> Presented with a universal blank
> Of Nature's works to me expunged and rased
> And wisdom at one entrance quite shut out.
> So much the rather thou, Celestial Light,
> Shine inward, and the mind through all her powers
> Irradiate, there plant eyes, all mist from thence
> Purge and disperse, that I may see and tell
> Of things invisible to mortal sight.

IX

The lot of another man blind and in adversity is the subject of Milton's last poem. Samson is shown

> Eyeless, in Gaza, at the mill, with slaves.

But the tragedy contains none of the weakness of self-pity. It is the most austere of all Milton's poems. The Hebrew subject cuts Milton off from his richest sources of embellishment, classical mythology, and mediæval romance. The persons of the drama are few : besides Samson, there are only Manoah, his father, Dalila, Harapha—a messenger from the Philistines—a second messenger, and a chorus of Danites. A great outburst by Samson at the beginning of the poem :

> O dark, dark, dark, amid the blaze of noon,
> Irrecoverably dark, total Eclipse
> Without all hope of day !

is followed by a dialogue in which Manoah attempts consolation. Dalila then enters, " like a stately ship," and a bitter scene takes place, in which, as Goethe noticed, Milton does full justice to the woman's case. Then Harapha appears, bearing the command of the Philistine lords. Samson at first contemptuously refuses to obey, but on second thoughts follows the Philistine, leaving behind only Manoah and the Chorus. Suddenly a great noise is heard, followed by human cries, and a man rushes on the stage in wild consternation. He is a Hebrew who has witnessed Samson's last great feat. On hearing the story, Manoah bursts into a cry of triumph :

> Nothing is here for tears, nothing to wail
> Or knock the breast, no weakness, no contempt,
> Dispraise, or blame, nothing but well and fair,
> And what may quiet us in a death so noble.

The last words are spoken by the Chorus, and the tragedy ends, in the Greek manner, on a note of peace :

> All is best, though we oft doubt
>   What the unsearchable dispose
> Of Highest Wisdom brings about,
>   And ever best found in the close.
> Oft He seems to hide His face,
>   But unexpectedly returns,
> And to His faithful Champion hath in place
>   Bore witness gloriously ; whence Gaza mourns
> And all that band them to resist
>   His uncontrollable intent.
> His servants He, with new acquist
>   Of true experience from this great event,
> With peace and consolation hath dismist,
>   And calm of mind, all passion spent.

CHAPTER IX

THE RESTORATION

No year is a more conspicuous landmark in the history of England than 1660. Much of the outburst of joy which greeted Charles on his landing at Dover was due, no doubt, to a feeling that the good old days had returned. But the England of Elizabethan times had disappeared no less assuredly than the repressed and regimented England of Major-Generals. A new set of men were coming into power—the loyal, not to say servile, members of the Cavalier Parliament and the utterly unscrupulous favourites of the Cabal. Even Clarendon, the great champion of the Church of England, could not be endured for long and was driven into exile after seven years of power. Yet his ministry set a permanent mark on his country's life, for his famous " Code " left one great section of the people, the Dissenters, a despised and persecuted body. The Restoration, indeed, was the triumph of a class—the triumph of the Court and the Church. The general relief that Charles had returned was soon followed by a period of bitter animosity between victors and vanquished. Before long, the two great political parties came into being whose rivalry gives the period its peculiar character. The struggle between Whig and Tory colours the literature of the time, as it colours every other aspect of life.

These facts are of particular importance in view of the great change which came over literature about 1660. The Elizabethan age was essentially an age of poetry. Writers appealed to the imagination and the emotions rather than to the reason. Even Milton, in spite of all his public activity, had a soul that " dwelt apart." Dryden, on the other hand, the most eminent of Restoration writers, had none of this grand aloofness. He was accessible to everyone who cared to approach him. His famous habit of sitting at Will's Coffee House in the chair reserved for him, and rewarding a young aspirant in literature with an approving word or a pinch of snuff, is highly typical of the age. Literature, for the first time in England, was becoming social. It was beginning to concentrate upon the daily lives and habits of men. At the same time, authorship was about to become a regular profession. Dryden was in many senses our first great " man of letters " ; and he recognised that it was his business to follow taste as well as to form it.

A change in style was bound to accompany this change in function. The new activities of literature demanded new ways in both poetry and prose. The figurative and intricate blank verse of the Elizabethans was not the right medium for poetry in its more worldly and practical mood. Nor were the rolling periods of a Milton or a Browne fit to be imitated in the columns of the weekly news-letter. Mystery and imagination were now less esteemed than clarity and common sense. It is partly true to say that Dryden prepared the way for the Augustans, in whose hands the new verse and the new prose were brought to perfection. But Dryden and his contemporaries have far more than a merely historical importance. They have left some enduring work of a very high order. Nor is it enough to regard them as forerunners of the eighteenth century : indeed, their own style in both prose and verse was anticipated by writers of a slightly older generation.

I

The really transitional writers were men who lived as the contemporaries of Milton, but were denied his wonderful unity of purpose. Abraham Cowley (1618–1667) was one of those who were born either too early or too late. His reputation at one time was immense. He was an extremely versatile and clever man. He wrote an epic, some plays, Pindaric odes, essays, and lyrics innumerable. He was regarded by many as one of the greatest of poets. Yet, by the beginning of the eighteenth century, his work had fallen so far into oblivion that Pope could ask, " Who now reads Cowley ? "

Yet Cowley is still remembered for three achievements. He was the author of a beautiful elegy on his friend, Mr. William Harvey ; he was one of the founders (with Pepys, Dryden, Evelyn and other writers) of the Royal Society— an institution which thoroughly expressed the spirit of the age ; and he was an early master of the new prose—a prose of short sentences, easy constructions, and plain vocabulary. The Royal Society itself had much to do with this reform. It exacted from its members a " close, naked, natural way of speaking ; positive expressions, clear senses, a native easiness, bringing all things as near the mathematical plainness as they can ; and preferring the language of artisans, countrymen, and merchants before that of wits and scholars."

Cowley's model in prose was the conversation of a well-bred man ; but he remembered the old remark that a perfect prose style would show the reader not how men actually speak, but how they would like to speak. A few sentences from his Essay *Of Myself* will show how modern the work of the newer writers sounds, when compared with that of Milton or Browne :

Even when I was a very young boy at school, instead of running about on holidays and playing with my fellows, I was wont to steal from them and walk into the fields, either alone with a book, or with some one companion, if I could find any of the same temper. I was then, too, so much an enemy to all constraint, that my masters could never prevail on me, by any persuasions or encouragements, to learn without book the common rules of grammar, in which they dispensed with me alone, because they found I made a shift to do the usual exercises out of my own reading and observation. . . . I believe I can tell the particular little chance that filled my head first with such chimes of verse as have never since left ringing there. For I remember, when I began to read, and to take some pleasure in it, there was wont to lie in my mother's parlour (I know not by what accident, for she herself never in her life read any book but of devotion), but there was wont to lie Spenser's works; this I happened to fall upon, and was infinitely delighted with the stories of the knights, and giants, and monsters, and brave houses which I found everywhere there (though my understanding had little to do with all this); and, by degrees with the tinkling of the rhyme and dance of the numbers, so that I think I had read him all over before I was twelve years old, and was thus made a poet.

Two of Cowley's contemporaries, Edmund Waller (1606–1687) and Sir John Denham (1615–1669), are remembered less for their intrinsic merits than for their anticipation of the new style in verse. Waller was the author of some lyrics which combine ease of style with a certain distinction and air of gallantry. The lines *On a Girdle* and *Go, Lovely Rose* are two of the best. It is more important that both Waller and Denham wrote heroic couplets with the precision and neatness which, at the moment, were so wholesome. One great vice of Elizabethan writers had been the habit of pouring forth such an impetuous flood of verse that the rhymes, which ought to serve as landmarks, were almost submerged. Men whose sentences run into a score of lines, some of them ending on trivial words like " of " and " at," fully deserved the strictures of an anonymous seventeenth-century critic. " Verse in those days," he says, " was but downright prose tagged with rhymes. . . ." By making the couplet the unit of verse-composition, by using rhymes only on words which could bear emphasis, and by avoiding every interruption to the easy flow of the lines, Denham and Waller gave English verse the strictness of example which it needed. Some oft-quoted lines of Denham, written as early as 1642, will serve as illustration of the new style. They are from *Cooper's Hill*, and are addressed to the River Thames:

> O, could I flow like thee, and make thy stream
> My great example, as it is my theme;
> Though deep, yet full; though gentle, yet not dull;
> Strong, without rage; without o'erflowing, full.

Denham and Waller were not great poets, but they deserve the praise they received from Dr. Johnson, as the " reformers of our numbers."

II

John Dryden was born in 1631 and died in 1700. As a boy, he came under the last enchantments of the Renaissance ; as a middle-aged man he found true scope for his powers in the political satire. He was thoroughly aware of having been born " out-of-date," or, in his own words :

> Betwixt two ages cast,
> The first of this, and hindmost of the last.

His birthplace was Aldwinkle, in Northamptonshire. He was at school under Dr. Busby at Westminster, and afterwards went to Trinity College, Cambridge. Like Milton, he cherished the idea of excelling in the greatest forms of literature, the tragedy and the epic. Dryden never wrote an epic, though in his last years he solaced himself by translating the *Æneid*. He was not of the stuff out of which epic poets are made. His admiration for great literature was constant, but by nature he was an opportunist. This quality helps to explain both his success and his failure.

Dryden began his career as a poetic commentator on passing events. The death of his kinsman, Cromwell, was the occasion of some *Heroic Stanzas* (1659). Then came the return of Charles, which he celebrated in a congratulatory poem, *Astræa Redux* (1660). The drama having been revived at the Restoration, Dryden brought out two or three plays between 1663 and 1665. In the latter year, the Plague broke out and the theatres were closed. The Great Fire which followed, and the sailing of the Dutch up the Medway, were fresh wonders and provided Dryden with the subject of a new poem, *Annus Mirabilis* (1667). In this work, his style begins to assume the masculine firmness of his maturity, but the poem is disfigured by numerous " conceits." An instance of this

misplaced ingenuity is his consoling quatrain on the burning of old St. Paul's :

> The daring flames peeped in and saw from far
>   The awful beauties of the sacred quire ;
> But, since it was profan'd by civil war,
>   Heav'n thought it fit to have it purg'd by fire.

Like many other Londoners, Dryden found the capital no
tempting place of abode at this time. Moreover, the
Plague made it necessary for the authorities to suspend all
play-acting. He therefore retired into the country, where
he composed the earliest and perhaps the best of his critical
works, *An Essay of Dramatic Poesy* (published in 1667).
The essay is in the form of a dialogue between four persons
interested in the stage, Eugenius (Lord Buckhurst), Crites
(Sir Robert Howard), Lisideius (Sir Charles Sedley), and
Neander (Dryden himself). The essay opens in a delightful manner reminiscent of Plato's dialogues :

It was that memorable day, in the first summer of the late
war, when our navy engaged the Dutch—a day wherein the two
most mighty and best appointed fleets which any age had ever
seen, disputed the command of the greater half of the globe,
the commerce of nations, and the riches of the universe. While
these vast floating bodies, on either side, moved against each
other in parallel lines, and our countrymen, under the happy
conduct of his Royal Highness, went breaking by little and little
into the line of the enemies ; the noise of the cannon from both
navies reached our ears about the City, so that all men being
alarmed with it, and in a dreadful suspense of the event which
they knew was then deciding, every one went following the
sound as his fancy led him ; and leaving the town almost empty,
some took towards the park, some cross the river, others down
it ; all seeking the noise in the depth of silence.

After a time, the four friends hear a " happy omen of
our Nation's victory." Freed from anxiety, their minds
move towards a matter in which they are all interested.
The subject of their discussion is the form of the drama.
Dryden had the greatest admiration for the Elizabethans,
especially Shakespeare, Jonson and Fletcher, but he thought

certain lessons could be learnt from the French, who respected the three Unities of Plot, Place, and Time. Dryden did not propose to extend French authority to England, nor did he think it necessary to go abroad for lessons in dramatic construction. But he welcomed the example and prestige of the French, who, above all peoples, respected the rigours of literary form. Excess had been the vice of the Elizabethans ; and Dryden was determined that the new age, if poorer in invention, should at least have done with the lawlessness and irregularity of its predecessors. In a large measure, he succeeded. He won for criticism its due place in literature ; he made both verse and prose more amenable to reason ; and he fitted literature for its mundane functions. All this he did or helped to do, yet nothing is more characteristic of the man than the sigh, almost of regret, with which, near the end of his career, he looks back on the success of his labours :

> Strong were our sires, and as they fought they writ,
> Conquering with force of arms and dint of wit ;
> Theirs was the giant race before the flood ;
> And thus, when Charles returned, our empire stood.
> Like Janus he the stubborn soil manured,
> With rules of husbandry the rankness cured ;
> Tamed us to manners, when the stage was rude ;
> And boist'rous English wit with art endued.
> Our age was cultivated thus at length ;
> But what we gained in skill, we lost in strength ;
> Our builders were with want of genius curst ;
> The second temple was not like the first.

The lament was just. Literature continued to be cultivated through the eighteenth century with rare assiduity and skill, but for the flowering of the highest poetic genius the times were unpropitious.

III

During the years which immediately followed his Essay, the best part of Dryden's energies was given to the drama. Some of the requisite talents he possessed in full measure. He had skill in devising situations, copious

powers of expression, and a keen though limited knowledge of human nature. But this knowledge came through
observation rather than intuition, and even in the best of
his plays there is evidence of effort. Nevertheless, *The
Conquest of Granada* (1670) and *Aureng-zebe* (1676) are very
fine dramas, while *All for Love* (1678) is a masterpiece.
All of these are " heroic " plays : Dryden has sought to
raise the language and passions to an epic pitch. The
characters clash in the eternal rivalry of war and love.
As human beings, they make little impression on the reader,
but he remembers scenes of violent conflict and frenzied
passion. Almanzor's boast in *The Conquest of Granada* is
typical :

> No man has more contempt than I of breath,
> But whence hast thou the right to give me death ?
> Obeyed as sovereign of thy subjects be,
> But know that I alone am king of me.
> I am as free as nature first made man,
> Ere the base laws of servitude began,
> When wild in woods the noble savage ran.

It is not surprising that, after a time, Dryden began to
doubt the suitability of this style for drama. He " grows
weary of his long-loved mistress, Rhyme," confessing that
there are

> Passions too fierce to be in fetters bound ;
> And Nature flies him like enchanted ground.

So he turned to blank verse, and achieved a great success
in rehandling the theme of *Antony and Cleopatra*. That
All for Love is not eclipsed by Shakespeare, but retains
its place as a very fine tragedy, is the most significant tribute
which can be paid to Dryden's dramatic power.

All this time, Dryden had been unconsciously preparing
himself for a great task. His dramatic practice had given
him absolute mastery over the rhyming couplet. He had
become, as it were, a skilled fencer, and knew how to
parry and attack with precision and lightning speed. The
most famous political satire yet produced, Butler's *Hudibras*
(1663–1678), was too near to burlesque. An opportunity

for employing his art in a new and brilliant way occurred for Dryden in the closing years of Charles II's reign. The king seemed to be losing the popularity with which he had been greeted twenty years earlier, and he was suspected of being a Catholic. The Duke of York, his brother, had openly embraced that religion. Circumstances combined to make the story of a Popish Plot highly plausible, and when the Whigs brought forward their Bill to exclude James from the throne, and make the Duke of Monmouth heir in his place, half the nation was on their side. Dryden belonged to the opposite party, and in a happy moment intervened in the dispute with an ingenious political poem. The Exclusion Bill was passed by the Commons but rejected by the Lords. In July, 1681, Shaftesbury, leader of the Whigs, was imprisoned in the Tower. Dryden's poem *Absalom and Achitophel* was published a week before the the trial. The story of Absalom's plot against David (2 Sam. xiv.–xviii.) presented a striking parallel to the Whig support of Monmouth. The various counsellors of the king gave names to the leaders of the two political parties. Thus Ormond is Barzillai, and Halifax, Jotham. Among the Whigs, Shaftesbury is Achitophel, and Buckingham, Zimri. The parallel is worked out with much ingenuity, but it is not on this account, nor as a narrative, that the work lives, nor yet for its historical value. Its excellence lies in the speeches and spirited verse portraits. Best of all is the description of Buckingham. " The character of Zimri in my Absalom," said Dryden himself, " is, in my opinion, worth the whole poem."

> In the first rank of these did Zimri stand,
> A man so various, that he seemed to be
> Not one, but all mankind's epitome :
> Stiff in opinions, always in the wrong,
> Was everything by starts, and nothing long ;
> But in the course of one revolving moon
> Was chymist, fiddler, statesman, and buffoon ;
> Then all for women, painting, rhyming, drinking,
> Besides ten thousand freaks that died in thinking.
> Blest madman, who could every hour employ
> With something new to wish, or to enjoy !

> Railing and praising were his usual themes,
> And both, to show his judgment, in extremes :
> So over violent, or over civil,
> That every man with him was God or Devil.

So the invective proceeds, concluding with the couplet :

> Thus wicked but in will, of means bereft,
> He left not faction, but of that was left.

Even to-day, the heated emotions of the great political quarrel live in Dryden's forceful verse, and it is easy to conceive the feelings of triumph and rage which the satire must have provoked, when first printed. The characters of Zimri and Achitophel, whether just or not, are among those passages of verse which stamp themselves on the memory.

IV

Dryden's poetry was a great power in his day. The busiest found time to read it ; the most practical could not deny its influence. Its virility and vigour compensate in some measure for its want of the finer and higher beauty. And though Dryden is not one of our chief artists in " poetic diction," he is the master of a rich and copious vocabulary. Coarse in expression he sometimes is, but never insipid.

After the great success of his satires, Dryden continued to find new scope for his skill in verse. His *Religio Laici*, a reasoned defence of the Anglican " via media," was published in 1682, and though the arguments are not new, they are nowhere more interesting than in Dryden's closely-knit couplets. He freely admits his limitations as a poet, at the end of this work, where he says :

> And this unpolished, rugged verse I chose
> As fittest for discourse, and nearest prose.

A few years later, Dryden became a Roman Catholic, and wrote a poem in defence of his new faith. But *The Hind and the Panther*, in spite of some excellent passages, is ruined by its clumsy allegory. The various Churches are represented by animals. Thus, the Roman Catholic Church is a Hind; the Church of England, a Panther; Independency, a Boar; and Quakerism, a Hare. The opening lines, which describe the " milk-white hind immortal and unchanged " wandering through kingdoms which were once her own, are admirable ; but when the animals engage in theological controversy, the allegory becomes absurd.

The last fifteen years of Dryden's life were among the most fruitful, but in worldly fortune his best days were over. William III could not regard with much favour a poet who had so bitterly attacked the Whigs. The Laureateship, which had been conferred upon him in 1668, was now taken away and given to his enemy, Shadwell. But adversity stimulated rather than depressed his genius. He attempted a fresh form of poetry, the Ode, and, after two partial successes, produced a masterpiece in *Alexander's Feast* (1697). There is no subtlety or reserve in this famous poem. It has none of the shyer beauties that shrink from the light. Publicity does not harm it. But, without doubt, the fire has descended from heaven and consumed the offering on the poet's altar.

After translating the Satires of Juvenal—a very congenial task—and the works of Virgil, Dryden began a number of adaptations from Ovid, Boccaccio and Chaucer. These he published in 1700, with a Preface, which is one of the most able of his critical writings. It has a pleasant conversational air, as if the veteran writer were taking us into his confidence. Yet the critical insight is acute, and Dryden never wrote anything better in prose than his praise of Chaucer. Some of the *Fables* are among the best examples of narrative verse in English. Especially good are *Cymon and Iphigenia* and *Theodore and Honoria*, both founded on Boccaccio.

Dryden was one of the most versatile of our greater writers. He gave satire its classical form ; he showed what could be made of the " closed " couplet ; he was a skilful master of the new familiar prose ; and he created a form of criticism in which due recognition of precedent is admirably blended with personal appreciation. To the writer of the eighteenth century, Dryden's name was sacred ; even the achievement of Pope could not eclipse his glory. No one denies that he is a great historic figure in our literature. But if any one feels that in admitting this he has given Dryden his due, let him read over again the best passages in the satires, *All for Love*, the three Odes, the Tales from Boccaccio, and the *Lines to my Dear Friend, Mr. Congreve, on his Comedy called, The Double Dealer*.

V

The age of Dryden was singularly favourable to the cultivation of prose. The playwrights of the Restoration, and diarists, like Samuel Pepys and John Evelyn, have a command of an English style which is clear, easy and unaffected, and above all, free from the abstract and bookish phrases which tend to rob our language of its native simplicity. There was, it is true, a certain cult of French expressions, but many of these truly expressed the spirit of the period. The French words *burlesque*, *badinage* and *ridicule* came into currency during the second half of the seventeenth century, and are a significant inheritance from the age.

The *Diary* of Samuel Pepys (1633–1703), who rose to be Secretary of the Admiralty, was written in cipher, and remained unread at Magdalene College, Cambridge, until the system was interpreted in 1825. Since then it has been one of the most popular of English books. Curiosity is gratified by the privilege of being able to pry without shame into the secrets of so private a document, but the pleasure of reading the Diary is, in part at least, literary. Pepys was a very naïve, observant, ambitious, knowing man—a connoisseur of many arts, and, like many men of his age, a great lover of " projects," scientific and practical. At the same time, his attitude to life makes the Diary one of the most transparent works in literature. To enjoy himself to the full, to rise in the world and to keep a fairly easy conscience, were the chief motives which Pepys knew. Most of his character is contained in this short entry :

This day by God's mercy I am 29 years of age, and in very good health, and like to live and get an estate; and if I have a heart to be contented, I think I may reckon myself as happy a man as any in the world, for which God be praised. So to prayers and to bed.

The style of the Restoration dramatists, on the other hand, is the result of long sifting and re-sifting. Of their various merits, the greatest is the dialogue. The saturnine genius of Wycherley (1640–1715) is most fully expressed in *The Country Wife*, which was performed about 1674; but Wycherley's dialogue has not the sparkle of his brilliant successor, William Congreve (1670–1729), whose plays contain the quintessence of the age's wit. Congreve's besetting fault is the extreme complexity of his plots. But it is enough to be able to follow scene by scene the contests in wit and impudence between the fine ladies and gentlemen and to enjoy their jests and repartees which, in point and finish, have no superior. Congreve's pictures of contemporary manners are excellent. Lord Froth, for instance, in *The Double Dealer*, is an amusing exaggeration of a well-known type. His views on laughter will be seen to anticipate those of the famous Lord Chesterfield :

Lord Froth : I assure you, Sir Paul, I laugh at nobody's jest but my own or a lady's ; I assure you, Sir Paul.

Brisk : How ? how, my lord ? what, affront my wit ! let me perish, do I never say anything worthy to be laugh'd at ?

Lord Froth : O foy ! don't misapprehend me, I don't say so, for I often smile at your conceptions. But there is nothing more unbecoming a man of quality than to laugh ; 'tis such a vulgar expression of the passion ! everybody can laugh. Then especially to laugh at the jest of an inferior person, or when anybody else of the same quality does not laugh with him ; ridiculous ! To be pleased with what pleases the crowd ! Now when I laugh, I always laugh alone.

Brisk : I suppose that's because you laugh at your own jests, egad, ha ! ha ! ha !

Congreve's best stage play is undoubtedly *Love for Love* (1695), but his wit and dialogue shine brightest in *The Way of the World* (1700). Two characters in this play are especially brilliant, Millamant and Mirabell, the Beatrice and Benedick of the Restoration. In the Comedy of

Manners, Congreve is as much Shakespeare's superior as he is his inferior in poetic drama. Of the many passages in *The Way of the World*, which it is a delight to quote, one shall be given—Millamant's enumeration of the terms on which she consents, after infinite delay, to be the wife of Mirabell :

> *Mrs. Millamant :* I won't be called names after I'm married ; positively I won't be called names.
> *Mirabell :* Names !
> *Mrs. Millamant :* Ay, as wife, spouse, my dear, joy, jewel, love, sweetheart, and the rest of that nauseous cant, in which men and their wives are so fulsomely familiar—I shall never bear that—good Mirabell, don't let us be familiar or fond, nor kiss before folks, like my Lady Fadler and Sir Francis ; nor go to Hyde Park together the first Sunday in a new chariot, to provoke eyes and whispers, and then never to be seen there together again ; as if we were proud of one another the first week, and ashamed of one another ever after. Let us never visit together, nor go to a play together ; but let us be very strange and well bred ; let us be as strange as if we had been married a great while ; and as well bred as if we were not married at all.
> *Mirabell :* Have you any more conditions to offer ? Hitherto, your demands are pretty reasonable.
> *Mrs. Millamant :* Trifles,—As liberty to pay and receive visits to and from whom I please ; to write and receive letters, without interrogatories or wry faces on your part; to wear what I please ; and choose conversation with regard only to my own taste ; to have no obligation upon me to converse with wits that I don't like, because they are your acquaintance ; or to be intimate with fools, because they may be your relations. Come to dinner when I please ; dine in my dressing-room when I'm out of humour, without giving a reason. To have my closet inviolate ; to be sole empress of my tea-table, which you must never presume to approach without first asking leave. And lastly, wherever I am, you shall always knock at the door before you come in. These articles subscribed, if I continue to endure you a little longer, I may by degrees dwindle into a wife.

VI

No one will suppose that the gaiety and worldliness of the Restoration writers fully displays the life of the English people even during that gay and worldly age. Two years before Congreve's masterpiece appeared, a severe indictment of current plays was published by Jeremy

Collier, called *A Short View of the Immorality and Profaneness of the English Stage* (1698). There is much that is absurd in this famous work, yet its significance is great. The Restoration drama was in its last days. Wit was not to become extinct in the English people, but in the generation of Addison and Swift it was directed to new uses and embodied in new forms.

But a writer at once greater and more humble than Collier had already raised his voice in the name of godliness. John Bunyan (1628–1688) was one of the many dissenting preachers who suffered under the rigours of Clarendon's code. He was the son of a tinsmith of Elstow, near Bedford, and had fought in the Parliamentarian wars. The death of a comrade who had been shot while serving in his place turned Bunyan's thoughts to serious things. He read the Bible diligently, and became a well-known preacher. At the Restoration, the laws against unlicensed preaching were enforced, and Bunyan spent most of his life between 1661 and 1672 in prison. He is said to have written *The Pilgrim's Progress* during another term of imprisonment in 1675. The book was published in 1678, and has never ceased to be widely read, though even Cowper, a hundred years later, shrank from naming in his verse a work which was considered so " low."

In one sense, *The Pilgrim's Progress* is a book of religious " confessions," in another it is a work of fiction. In representing life under the similitude of a pilgrimage, Bunyan was following an ancient plan, and he seems to be indebted to Spenser for several details of his allegory. But in the execution of his design, Bunyan is an absolutely original artist. His style has one great source, and though he uses the words of the Bible, they have a new flavour in his pages. Of his other books, *Grace Abounding* (1666), with its details of vivid autobiography and deep self-searching, *The Life and Death of Mr. Badman* (1680), a work of warning to the godless, executed in a spirit of sober realism, and *The Holy War* (1682), a record of the siege of " Mansoul " by the forces of evil, are the most remarkable. But none of these can equal *The Pilgrim's*

Progress either in literary art or in universality of interest. Bunyan's great gift as a writer is his power to give life to the figures of his allegory. A single detail is often enough. The chance oath of Apollyon : " I swear by my infernal den," the fact casually let slip that Giant Despair has a wife to whom he goes for advice, give these beings " a local habitation " in the mind of the reader. As a mirror of the times, *The Pilgrim's Progress* contains no pages more striking than those on Vanity Fair, and the passage on the jury which tries Faithful shows the lively character of Bunyan's allegorical art :

Then went the jury out, whose names were Mr. Blindman, Mr. No-Good, Mr. Malice, Mr. Love-Lust, Mr. Live-Loose, Mr. Heady, Mr. High-Mind, Mr. Enmity, Mr. Liar, Mr. Cruelty, Mr. Hate-Light, and Mr. Implacable, who every one gave in his private verdict against him among themselves, and afterwards unanimously concluded to bring him in guilty before the judge. And first among themselves, Mr. Blindman, the foreman, said, I see clearly that this man is a heretic. Then said Mr. No-Good, Away with such a fellow from the earth. Ay, said Mr. Malice, for I hate the very look of him. Then said Mr. Love-Lust, I could never endure him. Nor I, said Mr. Live-Loose, for he would always be condemning my way. Hang him, hang him, said Mr. Heady. A sorry scrub, said Mr. High-Mind. My heart riseth against him, said Mr. Enmity. He is a rogue, said Mr. Liar. Hanging is too good for him, said Mr. Cruelty. Let us despatch him out of the way, said Mr. Hate-Light. Then said Mr. Implacable, Might I have all the world given me, I could not be reconciled to him ; therefore let us forthwith bring him in guilty of death.

CHAPTER X

THE AUGUSTAN AGE

In the last year of his life, Dryden dismissed the seventeenth century with a sigh of relief:

> 'Tis well an old age is out,
> And time to begin a new.

He was glad to bid farewell to the futile wars and the vain intrigues that he had witnessed during his chequered life. If he hoped that the century just beginning would avoid old errors and reveal new virtues, he was in some measure justified. The intense religious bitterness of the past was somewhat assuaged by the Toleration Act, and the political disputes which had rent the nation asunder were never revived in their old acuteness after the compromise of 1689. The feuds of Roundhead and Cavalier were replaced by the milder rivalries of Whig and Tory. The wiser part of the nation had learnt the folly of religious persecution, and although men had no intention of forgoing their cherished privilege of political bickerings, they had resolved not to press these to a tragic issue. The English revolution had come and gone, and few men were anxious to challenge the power of the new Whig aristocracy, or to disturb the solid security of the Established Church. The eighteenth century produced cultured peers and learned bishops. " Philosophy " was in repute, and religious " enthusiasm " in discredit. To such a society, the sovereign merits in literature were elegance, clarity and polish. And the times were such that men of letters had a very large part to play in public life. In the importance of literature, in the close contact between writers and statesmen, and in the general regard for literary tradition, the age of Anne resembles the age of Augustus. The principal names in the Augustan age of English literature are Pope, Swift and Addison. Defoe, a self-made man, of less literary culture, must be regarded by himself.

POPE

I

The chief poet of Queen Anne's reign was an invalid of small stature and delicate constitution, whose bad nerves and cruel headaches made his life, in his own phrase, a " long disease." The writings of Alexander Pope reflect the author's mental and physical constitution. He had not the robustness to execute large designs or to paint pictures of mankind in its multifarious activity. It is wonderful, indeed, that a writer so handicapped should have left on literature any permanent mark at all. But the keen intellectual passion of the man, and his consuming ambition for literary renown, pushed him forward to almost heroic exertions. Quite early in life he saw that correctness of style, in its narrower sense, was an ideal which no English poet had yet pursued consistently and to the end. Pope determined to be the most correct of English poets. His well-to-do parents, he knew, would put him beyond the reach of necessity, and he resolved to make literature his all in all.

At the age of twenty-three, he published his *Essay on Criticism*, a work which reveals to the full many of its author's chief qualities and limitations. The poem was a triumph, and, during the rest of his career, Pope continued to build up a prodigious reputation. He dug for the main currents of poetry channels which lasted for nearly a century. On the great change in taste which came about 1800, his fame suffered an eclipse, and Pope will never be what he was to Dr. Johnson and his other admirers. On the other hand, the nineteenth century disparaged him unduly, and it seems to have been reserved for the present age to strike the mean between worship and contempt, and to see Pope as he was—not indeed as a great poet, nor yet as a mere versifier, but as an artist of genius.

II

Pope's uneventful life, which began in 1688 and lasted till 1744, was passed mostly within a few miles of London, and, during the days of his fame, he lived at Twickenham. Literature and social intercourse were almost the only things for which he cared. He lived for his reputation, and for a few chosen friends, but even his friendships were not secure against his irritable, sensitive and jealous disposition. His first poem of note, the *Essay on Criticism* (1711), challenges comparison with the *Ars Poetica* of Horace, though Pope has in truth far less to say than the Roman poet. The work is one of the last fruits of the Renaissance. Admiration for the classics has become a dogma, almost a superstition, and the writer who does not make them his model is, according to Pope, merely wasting his time. Let him follow the " rules " of composition as discovered by the ancients :

> Those rules of old discovered, not devised
> Are Nature still, but Nature methodised.

But on minute points of style Pope has much to say, and he says it well. In a few effective lines he exposes the folly of those readers whose highest demand from poetry is an insipid harmony :

> But most by numbers judge a poet's song ;
> And smooth or rough, with them, is right or wrong :
> In the bright Muse though thousand charms conspire,
> Her voice is all these tuneful fools admire ;
> Who haunt Parnassus but to please their ear,
> Not mend their minds ; as some to Church repair,
> Not for the doctrine, but the music there.

But many versifiers are ignorant of their business and fail to meet even the simple demands of these readers :

These equal syllables alone require,
Though oft the ear the open vowels tire ;
While expletives their feeble aid do join ;
And ten low words oft creep in one dull line . . .
Then at the last and only couplet fraught
With some unmeaning thing they call a thought,
A needless Alexandrine ends the song
That, like a wounded snake, drags its slow length along.

Pope's next work was in some ways his masterpiece.
Worship of epic poetry, once so rich a source of inspiration,
had now hardened into a convention. Men spoke as if
they knew exactly how an epic was made, and Pope himself, to satirise this vanity, wrote a witty *Receipt to make an
epic poem*. But though the time for a *Paradise Lost* had
gone by, the age of Pope had just that polite and sophisti-
cated love of the classics which would make the travesty
of an epic highly acceptable. A heroic poem celebrating
an event of particular insignificance was a form of jest
which had not yet been attempted by any English writer
of genius. Pope was just the man for the task, and he was
not long in finding a subject. At one of the fashionable
parties of the day, a certain Lord Petre cut off by stealth
a lock of hair from the head of Miss Arabella Fermor.
This was the very theme for Pope, and he set about elabora-
ting it with all the pomp of Virgilian treatment. *The Rape
of the Lock* is a " mock heroic " poem. The invocation,
the description of the heroine's toilet, the journey to
Hampton Court, the game of ombre—magnified into a
pitched battle—all lead up to the moment when the peer
produces the fatal pair of scissors. But the action of
mortals was not enough : Pope knew that in true epics,
the affairs of men are aided and crossed by heavenly powers.
He therefore added four bodies of fairy creatures—Sylphs,
Gnomes, Nymphs and Salamanders—as agents in the story.
Belinda, the heroine, is under the special protection of the
Sylphs, whose devotion, however, is not enough to save
the lock when the peer advances to the attack :

The peer now spreads the glittering forfex wide,
T'inclose the Lock ; now joins it, to divide.

Ev'n then, before the fatal engine closed,
A wretched Sylph too fondly interposed ;
Fate urged the shears, and cut the Sylph in twain,
(But airy substance soon unites again),
The meeting points the sacred hair dissever
From the fair head, for ever and, for ever !

Then flashed the living lightning from her eyes,
And screams of horror rend th'affrighted skies.
Not louder shrieks to pitying heaven are cast,
When husbands, or when lapdogs breathe their last ;
Or when rich china vessels fall'n from high,
In glittering dust and painted fragments lie !

Pope was now well on the road to fame. He was an adept
in the popular style of verse—his couplets have a finish
which is rare even in Dryden's work—and he felt ready
to turn his talents to some great task. For six years he
laboured at a translation of the *Iliad* (1715-1720), a work
now seldom read—it is most un-Homeric—though it
finally established Pope's fame. Five years later came the
Odyssey, a translation in which Pope had two collaborators,
who, like many other men, knew their master's " tune by
heart." Pope's amazing success had created a whole host
of jealous rivals, and he was a man who could not bear to
let any antagonist, however mean, score against him. The
" Grub Street " scribblers had been teasing him for years,
and he resolved to silence them. *The Dunciad* is Pope's
great attack on all kinds of literary incompetence. It is
full of cruel and insulting couplets on his enemies ; but
Pope's pusillanimous concern over small men has brought
its own punishment, for his countless allusions in this
poem to forgotten things now need an antiquary to explain
them. The *Essay on Man* (1732-34) was meant to be a
great philosophical work, and to " vindicate the ways of
God to man." It does nothing of the kind ; but it is full
of brilliant passages and still more brilliant lines, many of
which have become almost a part of English speech. The
habit of satire grew on Pope more and more, and his later
works—*Imitations of Horace*, *Epistles*, and the like—are
chiefly remarkable for their biting attacks on men and
women, their brilliant epigrams and frequent assertions

of their author's high moral aim and superiority to all human littleness.

So complete was Pope's success in imposing his own style on poetry that the reaction, when at last it came, threatened to sweep his whole work away. Yet, now that the waters have subsided, a considerable part of his poetry is seen to be indestructible. For condensing an idea into a line or couplet, Pope has no superior, and almost half his verses have the neatness and point which make an epigram. He disavows all claim to the discovery of new ideas, this not being the province of " wit " or poetry :

> True wit is Nature to advantage dressed,
> What oft was thought, but ne'er so well expressed.

This combination of commonplace thought and perfection of technique has given any number of sayings to our language :

> Who shall decide when doctors disagree ?

> Thou wert my guide, philosopher, and friend.

> Know then thyself, presume not God to scan ;
> The proper study of mankind is man.

> Hope springs eternal in the human breast :
> Man never is, but always to be, blest.

Accident has played a large part in distinguishing such lines above others, and a reader of any of Pope's better poems will see that whole passages might have become proverbial. At times, Pope deliberately restricted himself to a few lines, and his epitaphs, such as that on Newton, are often excellent :

> Nature and Nature's laws lay hid in night :
> God said " Let Newton be ! " and all was light.

He can startle and amuse by his ingenious brevity, as in his picture of female avarice :

> The frugal crone, whom praying priests attend,
> Still tries to save the hallowed taper's end,
> Collects her breath, as ebbing life retires,
> For one puff more, and in that puff expires.

His powers of observation were sharpened by the ills which afflict an invalid in his solitude. He could take but few pleasures, and was almost forced into an attitude of envy towards happier and healthier men. One of the most deplorable incidents in his life was a literary quarrel with the fortunate and, as one would think, unassailable Addison. But Pope's eye detected weaknesses which other men could only vaguely feel, or seeing, could not name ; and the discernment of dislike was perhaps never more forcibly combined with stinging expression than in the portrait of " Atticus." Such couplets as :—

> Damn with faint praise, assent with civil leer,
> And, without sneering, teach the rest to sneer ;

or,

> Like Cato, give his little senate laws,
> And sit attentive to his own applause,
> While wits and templars every sentence raise,
> And wonder with a foolish face of praise,

are so right and " inevitable " that, once read, they cannot be forgotten. Some modern critics have striven to show that Pope was more than a master of satire and epigram, that he could write passages of real passion and lines of almost voluptuous beauty. Such criticism is useful in helping to re-establish Pope's claim to the title of poet, but the general character of his poetry is not open to dispute. Its perfection and felicity keep its memory green, but in true beauty and passion it has been surpassed by many writers to whom custom will allow no higher title than that of " minor " poets.

SWIFT

IV

In originality and intellectual power, Jonathan Swift was by far the greatest writer of his time. To his con-

temporaries he was the formidable pamphleteer whose
pen could endanger governments and discredit treaties.
To many generations of children he has been the author
of one of the most entrancing of fairy stories. To the
lover of literature he is the satirist whose irony and
intellectual rage are like forces of nature—tragic in their
destructive might, uplifting in their exhibition of irresponsible power.

Swift was born in 1667 at Dublin. His family came
from Yorkshire, and he himself was fundamentally English,
though he acquired some of the ways and feelings of the
Protestant colony in Ireland. He was educated at Kil-
kenny School, the " Eton of Ireland," and at Trinity
College, Dublin. His talents were not fully recognised
at the University, and his degree was conferred " speciali
gratia "—a phrase which he humorously interpreted in
later years as a mark of distinction. There was a general
exodus from Ireland during the disturbed year of 1688,
and Swift was among the many who crossed the channel.
He was unsettled about his career, being conscious of
ability, but ignorant how to apply it. His sense of
superiority was unbounded, and it was to be the cause of
bitter disappointments. For a time he was employed as
secretary to Sir William Temple, at whose house, Moor
Park, in Surrey, Swift lived for many years. He thus came
into contact with the great world, for Temple was a diplo-
matist of European reputation. Some account of Swift
reached the ears of King William, who sent the Earl of
Portland to consult him on a certain technicality in the
English constitution. One would have thought that
these were the beginnings of a distinguished career, yet
Swift still remained obscure. He had been ordained priest
in 1695, and received the small prebend of Kilroot in
Ireland. But he could not bear the loneliness of the place :
he resigned the living and returned to Moor Park, where
he remained until Temple's death in 1699.

The years spent at Temple's house deeply influenced
Swift's life. It was there that he made the acquaintance
of Esther Johnson, afterwards famous to the world as

" Stella." At Moor Park, also, Swift wrote his first two important works, *A Tale of a Tub* and *The Battle of the Books*, both published in 1704. The former is a brilliant though somewhat indiscreet satirical narrative on the excesses of Catholics and Puritans as seen from the middle position of the Anglican Church. The story tells how a father left to each of his three sons, Peter, Martin and Jack, a magical coat which would last as long as the wearer needed it. The will enjoined that the coat should be kept intact, without addition or diminution. Of the three sons, Martin is truest to his father's commands. But at first all three brothers compromise with the spirit of the world. One of the most amusing passages in the book is Peter's casuistical argument for decorating his coat with " shoulder-knots," so as to make it more presentable in polite society :

'Tis true, said he, there is nothing here in this Will, *totidem verbis*, making mention of Shoulder-Knots, but I dare conjecture we may find them *inclusive* or *totidem syllabis*. This Distinction was immediately approved by all ; and so they fell again to examine the Will. But their evil star had so directed the matter, that the first syllable was not to be found in the whole writing. Upon which disappointment, he, who found the former evasion, took heart, and said, Brothers, there is yet hopes ; for although we cannot find them *totidem verbis*, nor *totidem syllabis*, I dare engage we shall make them out *tertio modo*, or *totidem literis*. This discovery was also highly commended, upon which they fell once more to the scrutiny, and picked out s h o u l d e r ; when the same planet, enemy to their repose, had wonderfully contrived that a K was not to be found. Here was a weighty difficulty ! But the distinguishing brother . . . now his hand was in, proved by a very good argument, that K was a modern illegitimate letter, unknown to the learned ages, nor anywhere to be found in ancient manuscripts. . . . And by consequence it was a gross mistake in our language to spell Knot with a K, but that from henceforward, he would take care it should be writ with a C ; upon this, all farther difficulty vanished ; Shoulder-Knots were made clearly out, to be *Jure Paterno*, and our three Gentlemen swaggered with as large and as flaunting ones as the best.

The occasion of *The Battle of the Books* was a controversy between ancient and modern learning. The complexities of this dispute have long ceased to awaken much interest, and perhaps it is now chiefly remembered as having given rise to Swift's fable of the spider and the bee. The spider, who is the symbol of modern learning, does nothing but spin webs of sophistry from its own entrails, while the bee, who stands for the ancients, ranges far and wide over the fields, bringing back honey and wax, which provide men with the things they most need—SWEETNESS and LIGHT.

Between 1705 and 1714, Swift played an active part in public affairs. He had originally been a Whig, but owing to his dislike of that party's Church policy, gave his support to Harley and St. John. A powerful writer was, in those days, an indispensable ally of the politician. It was through pamphlets that public opinion was chiefly influenced. The " news-letters " gave little more than a dry summary of events. Parliamentary reporting had not yet begun. The best way, therefore, of appealing to the electorate was through the pen of a " publicist," who could often save or ruin a policy by the power of invective. The position of literary champion to the Tories appealed greatly to Swift. It gave him immense influence, and it flattered his inordinate pride by putting him on a level with the greatest men in the land. " I have taken Mr. Harley into favour again," he writes in his *Journal to Stella*. The Tory chiefs found him so useful that they put up with his overbearing ways, while Swift in secret regarded himself as their master.

The death of Queen Anne and the accession of George the First put an end to Tory ambitions. Swift knew he must renounce his dreams of great place. Under Anne he had been made Dean of St. Patrick's, and had cherished hopes of a bishopric, but the High Church Queen could not forget the irreverent tone of *A Tale of a Tub*. On the fall of the Tories, Swift retired to Dublin, which remained his home for the rest of his life. He hated Ireland, but by making Irish grievances his own, he found a vent for his rage and disappointment. Ireland was oppressed by sumptuary laws, which it was supposed would operate in favour of England. Popular opinion was highly inflammable, and when an Englishman, named Wood, obtained a contract to supply Ireland with a copper coinage of halfpence, it was easy to convince men that the *coup de grâce* would be given to Irish prosperity. Swift wrote a series of pamphlets (*Drapier's Letters*, 1724) so damaging to the Government that the halfpence were withdrawn. This was one of his greatest practical triumphs, but the literary force of his pro-Irish writings reaches its climax in *A Modest Proposal*, a protest against oppression delivered with a fierceness of irony which is appalling.

Ireland, which was Swift's place of exile, was also the scene of his greatest work. The four books of *Gulliver's Travels* were published in 1726. The work immediately became popular, and has remained ever since one of the few books about which every one knows something. Swift lived nearly twenty years more, but his best work was done. His later life was saddened by the death of Stella in 1728, and in his last years he was afflicted by a mysterious disease which clouded his reason and deepened his melancholy. He died in 1745, and was buried in St. Patrick's Cathedral, where the epitaph, composed by himself, tells how its author lies " ubi sæva indignatio ulterius cor lacerare nequit. Abi, viator," it continues, " et imitare, si poteris, strenuum pro virili libertatis vindicem."

v

Gulliver's Travels is both a romance and a satire. Swift's aim, in the first place, was to attack the real world as he knew it, by reducing men and their ways to ridiculous proportions. The Lilliputians, with their pompous ministers of state, their empty honours, and their trivial disputes, are the Englishmen of Swift's day, as seen by a satirist. But very often fiction wins a victory over satire, and Swift tells his story for no other purpose than to indulge his imagination. The opening scene of the

book, for instance, in which Gulliver wakes up to find
his arms and legs fastened to the ground, and his hair
" which was long and thick, tied down in the same
manner," is romance pure and simple. The same
ingenious fancy runs through the whole of the first book,
as when Gulliver describes the shoulders of mutton given
him to eat, which were " smaller than the wings of a lark,"
down to his return to England with some Lilliputian
sheep, which, he hopes, " will prove much to the advantage of the woollen manufacture by the fineness of the
fleeces." The Brobdingnagians, though less delightful
than the Lilliputians, are still good matter for fiction.
The enormous cat which endangers the life of Gulliver
and purrs with a noise " like that of a dozen stocking
weavers at work," is a creature to delight children of all
ages ; so also is the affection of the young giantess,
Glumdalclitch, for her human pet. But in the story
of Brobdingnag, the frown of the satirist is already
becoming portentous, while in the last book—*The
Voyage to the Houyhnhnms*—fancy has become the mere
servant to a terrific onslaught on the whole mass of human
follies.

Swift's irony is the expression of a proud, scornful
temper, and of a critical mind of extreme lucidity. Much
of his work is simply a refutation of the old maxim that
human beings are endowed with reason. Looking at the
religious and political divisions of the world, Swift saw
that these were mostly about matters of secondary importance. The ultimate objects of sound religion and good
government were forgotten in the pursuit of minor ends.
A nice point, like the doctrine of Transubstantiation, was
enough to turn whole provinces into a shambles, while
in England, the bickerings of Whig and Tory had often
made men completely blind to the real interests of the
country. In *The Voyage to Lilliput*, Swift's satire is comparatively genial. His description of the Big-endians and
Little-endians (Catholics and Protestants), who dispute about
the right way to open an egg, is an agreeable pleasantry.
But once he has started his crusade against un-reason,

the spirit of satire possesses him and sweeps him far beyond the region of remediable ills. The awful picture of the Struldbrugs in *The Voyage to Laputa*, is an attack not on human follies, but on the conditions of human life. The miserable creatures who cannot die are a dreadful caricature of mankind, and the description is redeemed only by its astonishing literary power. In *The Voyage to the Houyhnhnms*, the whole background is one of disgust and horror. The picture of the wretched Yahoos and their servitude to the philosophical horses would be unendurable but for the tremendous satire on the crowning offences of mankind against reason. Swift's indictment of law and medicine, though still amusing, has lost some of its force, but the exposure of war is tremendous both in its style and its indignation. Gulliver has just given one of the horses a glowing account of human destructiveness in warfare. The horse, seeing that Gulliver's teeth and nails are feeble weapons of offence, assumes that he has told " the thing which is not " (there is no word among the Houyhnhnms for " lie "). But the missionary of civilization hastens to set him right :

> I could not forbear shaking my head, and smiling a little at his ignorance. And being no stranger to the art of war, I gave him a description of cannons, culverins, muskets, carabines, pistols, bullets, powder, swords, bayonets, battles, sieges, retreats, attacks, undermines, countermines, bombardments, sea-fights ; ships sunk with a thousand men, twenty thousand killed on each side ; dying groans, limbs flying in the air, smoke, noise, confusion, trampling to death under horses' feet ; flight, pursuit, victory ; fields strewed with carcasses left for food to dogs, and wolves, and birds of prey ; plundering, stripping, ravishing, burning and destroying. And to set forth the valour of my own dear countrymen, I assured him, " that I had seen them blow up a hundred enemies at once in a siege, and as many in a ship ; and beheld the bodies drop down in pieces from the clouds, to the great diversion of the spectators."

The character of Swift's irony is unique. It consists in delivering an absurd remark, sometimes the exact opposite of his real meaning, with apparent seriousness. Often he is content with a few contemptuous sentences, as in his comment on the philosophers of Brobdingnag :

> After much debate, they concluded unanimously, that I was only " Relplum Scalcath," which is interpreted literally, ' Lusus Naturae ' ; a determination exactly agreeable to the modern philosophy of Europe, whose professors, disdaining the old evasion of occult causes . . . have invented this wonderful solution of all difficulties, to the unspeakable advancement of human knowledge.

But he loves best to elaborate a preposterous idea with the air of one gravely advancing a useful and practicable suggestion. His greatest triumph in this kind of irony is *A Modest Proposal*. He begins by describing the two great ills of Ireland, extreme poverty and over-population. Having fully stated the social problem, he proceeds with gravity and due attention to detail, to put forward the solution :

> I have been assured by a very knowing American of my acquaintance in London, that a young healthy child, well nursed, is at a year old a most delicious, nourishing, and wholesome food, whether stewed, roasted, baked, or boiled ; and I make no doubt that it will equally serve in a fricassee, or a ragout. . . .
>
> I grant that this food will be somewhat dear, and therefore very proper for landlords, who, as they have already devoured most of the parents, seem to have the best title to the children.

The skill with which the most biting satire is interwoven with the argument is beyond all praise. Point after point is set forth, with the air of one who is advancing a sound business proposition ; and the pamphlet is brought to a conclusion by a remark as shocking to humanity as it is consummate in satire.

VI

Swift, as his relative Dryden assured him, was no poet. None the less, he wrote a great deal of verse, and some of it has at least the merit of letting us see its author's real nature. One of Swift's most characteristic pieces is the poem on his own death (*Lines on the Death of Dr. Swift*). He imagines the feelings with which the news will be greeted by his various acquaintances. First, he touches on his fellow writers:

> Poor Pope will grieve a month, and Gay
> A week, and Arbuthnot a day.

He then passes on to his "female friends," whom he imagines at the card-table:

> My female friends, whose tender hearts
> Have better learn'd to act their parts,
> Receive the news in doleful dumps:
> "The Dean is dead:—(Pray, what is trumps?)
> "Then, Lord have mercy on his soul!
> "(Ladies, I'll venture for the vole.)
> "Six deans, they say, must bear the pall:
> "(I wish I knew what king to call.)
> "Madam, your husband will attend
> "The funeral of so good a friend?
> "No, Madam, 'tis a shocking sight;
> "And he's engaged to-morrow night:
> "My Lady Club will take it ill,
> "If he should fail her at quadrille.
> "He loved the Dean (I lead a heart),
> "But dearest friends, they say, must part.
> "His time was come, he ran his race,
> "We hope he's in a better place."

As usual, a special gibe is reserved for the conclusion, and the last lines of the poem are, in a sense, Swift's final judgment of the world.

> He gave the little wealth he had,
> To build a house for fools and mad,
> And shewed, by one satiric touch,
> No nation wanted it so much . . . .

It is fatally easy, however, to over-emphasise Swift's "misanthropy." In private life he was a sincere friend and a good master. "I hate that animal called man, though I heartily love John, Peter, Thomas and so forth" is one of his most famous and most significant remarks. Because men, in his opinion, have deliberately ignored the teaching of Reason and Nature, they have enslaved themselves to innumerable ills. Swift really was, as his epitaph claims, a champion of human liberty, and his satire is rooted in the strongest, though not indeed the purest, idealism.

ADDISON

VII

Compared with Swift, Addison seems at first sight a figure of quite inferior magnitude. The author of *Gulliver* had no dread of extremes; the essayist of *The Spectator* hated them, and his whole life was a battle for moderation. A man whose motto is μηδὲν ἄγαν may be wise, but is little likely to arouse enthusiasm. Addison's moderation, however, sprang from a real balance of qualities, a natural and beautiful harmony of spirit. There are moments when the equable temper and quiet dignity which are the breath of his style, seem a little insipid. But no one who has read Addison in bulk can help admiring his unfailing sanity, his unsleeping intelligence. His reputation is great, and he deserves it; but as long as he is read in small selections, it will always appear somewhat conventional.

He was born in 1672, the son of a clergyman of some eminence, and after his schooldays at the Charterhouse, settled down for some years to a studious life at Oxford, where he was elected a Fellow of Magdalen. But the opportunity came for a public life, and Addison, leaving the University, attached himself to the Whig party, which was very ready to find work for able writers. His poem, *The Campaign* (1704), written to celebrate the victory of Blenheim, made him a famous man, and his fortunes began to rise rapidly. He became Under Secretary for State, made a grand marriage, and retired from office with a considerable pension. He died in 1719.

His literary work was very miscellaneous. He was famous in his own time as a poet and as the author of a tragedy, *Cato*, but of his verse little is remembered to-day except a few hymns, such as "The spacious firmament on high." His more enduring reputation rests on his work as an essayist, and especially on his contribution to *The Spectator*.

In 1711, Richard Steele, who had already founded *The Tatler*, invited Addison to contribute to a new periodical, called *The Spectator*. The Whigs had just fallen from office, hence Addison was free for literary work. *The Spectator* appeared six times a week, and it contained, besides general news, advertisements and other miscellaneous matter, an essay from one of a few regular contributors, of whom Addison was the most brilliant and inventive. The whole paper consisted only of a small single sheet, so that the length of the essay was necessarily short. Addison soon grew used to the restrictions, and made his contributions as artistic as they were witty. He had read and observed much, and had kept a certain urbane attitude towards life. The need had now arisen for a contributor to furnish comments on things in general to be read by nearly the whole educated public of the time, and there was no one living competent to perform the task half so well as he.

The essays written for *The Spectator* touch on a very wide range of subjects. Some are critical, some are moral, some merely fanciful. Of the critical essays, the most interesting, perhaps, is the fine appreciation of the old ballad *Chevy Chase*. Both in the moral and his literary essays, Addison was the incarnation of good sense and breeding. He laughed at the puerilities of "false wit," and in the same spirit made merry over the childish rivalries of Whig and Tory. Tom Folio, who knows nothing of books but their covers, and the political ladies who advertise their party by their manner of wearing patches, are equally objects of his ridicule. To Addison the world owes much, both in the way of political education and of humanity. He could laugh over the prejudices of the Tory Foxhunter, yet leave his readers in warm admiration for a fine old Englishman. Men grew accustomed to a purer, healthier and more charitable form of wit than that which had amused their grandfathers of the Restoration. They learnt that there was no necessary connection between laughter and immorality, and that fineness of perception was the source of the best humour. Not that Addison always had a moral end in view. He could indulge in irresponsible fancies as well as any man, and perhaps few of his essays gave more delight than *The Adventures of a Shilling*, or *Frozen Words*.

The idea of reports on the members of an imaginary club originated in Steele, who saw that this would be a good way of introducing lively pictures of current manners. Addison took up the notion, and it is through his genius that Captain Sentry, Sir Andrew Freeport and Will Honeycomb are still familiar names in our literature. But his greatest triumph was in the portrait of Sir Roger de Coverley, whose life, as depicted in a succession of essays, makes what may almost be called the first serial English novel. The various papers on Sir Roger at Church, Sir Roger at the Assizes, Sir Roger at the Theatre, and the rest, made the character of the old knight so familiar to readers of *The Spectator*, that when Addison described his death, they must have been affected, as we are, by some of the emotions which accompany the loss of a loved friend. The butler's letter, announcing Sir Roger's end, does equal credit to Addison's wit and his humanity.

Honoured Sir,

Knowing that you was my old master's good friend, I could not forbear sending you the melancholy news of his death, which has afflicted the whole country, as well as his poor servants, who loved him, I may say, better than we did our lives. I am afraid he caught his death the last country sessions, where he would go to see justice done to a poor widow woman and her fatherless children, that had been wronged by a neighbouring gentleman, for you know, Sir, my good master was always the poor man's friend. Upon his coming home, the first complaint he made was, that he had lost his roast beef stomach, not being able to touch a sirloin, which was served up according to custom ; and you know he used to take great delight in it. From that time forward, he grew worse and worse, but still

kept a good heart to the last.   Indeed, we were once in great
hopes of his recovery, upon a kind message that was sent him
from the widow lady whom he had made love to the forty last
years of his life ; but this only proved a lightning before his
death. . . . It was a most moving sight to see him take leave
of his poor servants, commending us all for our fidelity, whilst
we were not able to speak a word for weeping.   As we most of
us are grown grey-headed in our dear master's service, he has
left us pensions and legacies which we may live very comfort-
ably upon the remaining part of our days.   He has bequeathed
a great deal more in charity, which is not yet come to my knowledge, and it is peremptorily said in the parish, that he has left
money to build a steeple to the church ; for he was heard to
say some time ago, that if he lived two years longer, Coverley
church should have a steeple to it.   The chaplain tells everybody that he made a very good end, and never speaks of him
without tears.   He was buried, according to his own directions,
among the family of the Coverleys, on the left hand of his father,
Sir Arthur.   The coffin was carried by six of his tenants, and
the pall held up by six of the quorum ; the whole parish followed
the corpse with heavy hearts, and in their mourning suits ; the
men in frieze, and the women in riding-hoods.   Captain Sentry,
my master's nephew, has taken possession of the hall-house,
and the whole estate.   When my old master saw him, a little
before his death, he shook him by the hand, and wished him
joy of the estate which was falling to him, desiring him only
to make a good use of it, and to pay the several legacies, and the
gifts of charity, which he told him he had left as quit-rents upon
the estate.   The captain truly seems a courteous man, though
he says but little.   He makes much of those whom my master
loved, and shows great kindness to the old housedog, that you
know my poor master was so fond of.   It would have gone
to your heart to have heard the moans the dumb creature made
on the day of my master's death.   He has never joyed himself
since ; no more has any of us.   It was the melancholiest day
for the poor people that ever happened in Worcestershire.
This being all from,

Honoured Sir, your most sorrowful servant,
EDWARD BISCUIT.

P.S.   My master desired, some weeks before he died, that
a book which comes up to you by the carrier, should be given
to Sir Andrew Freeport, in his name.

Another side of Addison's art is represented by his allegorical essays, of which *The Vision of Mirza* is likely always to remain the favourite. Addison makes no attempt to deal with the more violent and deeper emotions. But as a humanist, a fine critic of manners and the master of a faultless style, he has always had, and will long continue to have, many readers to love and admire him.

DEFOE

VIII

The energy and self-reliance of Daniel Defoe would have raised him to eminence in any walk of life. His independence of spirit made him choose literature—an occupation in which he could exercise his originality with the least interference from others. His life was crowded with activity, and his influence as a " publicist " was immense. He stood for moderation in religious disputes, resistance to the aggressive schemes of Louis XIV, and, above all, for Union with Scotland. In the course of his immense activity as a journalist, he acquired that mastery of plain style and circumstantial narrative which enabled him to write the one work by which he is known all the world over—*Robinson Crusoe*.

He was the son of a London butcher, named Foe, and was born in 1661. The grander form of the name he assumed when he was about forty. Being intended for the dissenting ministry, he was educated at Mr. Morton's Academy at Newington Green, where " all dissertations were held in English." He did not enter the Church ; instead, he became a hosier, with a business on Cornhill. This occupation, too, he abandoned, and for a time held a small position under the government of William III, whose policy he had defended in certain pamphlets. When the king and his Dutch favourites were attacked as " foreigners," Defoe replied with his *True-born Englishmen*, an effective piece of rough-hewn verse in which the mixed origin of the English people is held up to ridicule. Though it told against them, the Londoners were delighted with the poem, and bought it in large numbers. From that time, Defoe's fame as an author was established.

When Anne, a known friend of the High Church, ascended the throne, the dissenters were naturally in some fear for their privileges. Defoe hated fanaticism in any form and hastily produced his *Shortest Way with the Dissenters*. The work is a kind of "dramatic monologue" in prose, the speaker being a High Church Tory in a persecuting passion. He warns the Dissenters that their day of grace is over. "Now let us crucify the thieves," he concludes, "and may God Almighty put it into the hearts of all friends of truth to lift up a standard against pride and Antichrist, that the posterity of the sons of error may be rooted out from the face of this land for ever." This was so exact a copy of the language held by High Church extremists, that the public was bewildered. When the Tories discovered that the pamphlet was ironical, they were furious. Defoe was sentenced to a fine and imprisonment, and made to stand three times in the pillory. But he turned the punishment to excellent account, and began studying the ways of thieves and forgers with the greatest zest. All forms of human life interested him, and there was no experience from which he could not profit. On his release from prison, he turned his energies to journalism, and founded *The Review*, a periodical equal in bulk to about two modern leading articles, and combining amusement with instruction. It continued from 1704 to 1713, but Defoe's journalism was not yet at an end. He contributed to a commercial paper called *Mercator*, a monthly paper called the *Mercurius Politicus*, and a quarto-sheet appearing three times a week, called *The Whitehall Evening Post*. As late as 1728, he was projecting a periodical to be named *The Universal Spectator*.

In the midst of these immense labours, Defoe was composing the works of fiction by which he is remembered to-day. From his experience as a journalist, he learned to feel the pulse of the popular taste, and his enormous knowledge of life and facts made him wonderfully adaptable. When the great storm of 1703 swept over England, Defoe was soon ready with *A Collection of the most remarkable Casualties and Disasters which happened . . . both by Sea and Land*. When an epidemic of the plague in 1722 made men recall with alarm the dreadful days of the previous visitation, he brought out his *Journal of the Plague Year*. He had a wonderful gift of circumstantial narrative, and could conceive remote events with such vivid realism, that this *Journal* has sometimes been regarded as a genuine historical narrative. Public curiosity was Defoe's great opportunity. When Jack Sheppard, the notorious robber and prison-breaker, was at last condemned to death, Defoe wrote a story of his life, and gave it out to be the work of the prisoner, and printed at his wish. He even arranged that Sheppard, on reaching the place of execution, should deliver the pamphlet into the hands of a friend as his dying confession. One wonders if any book was ever ushered into the world with so sensational an advertisement. The author, of course, took care that the newspapers should contain a paragraph recording the incident. Defoe had the gift necessary to such a writer of composing his fictions at high speed. *Robinson Crusoe* (1719) was followed by *Duncan Campbell*, *Memoirs of a Cavalier*, and *Captain Singleton*, all produced in 1720. In 1722, came *Moll Flanders*, *A Journal of the Plague Year*, and *Colonel Jack*. *Roxana* was written in 1724, and *A New Voyage round the World* in the same year.

The immediate occasion of Defoe's most famous book was the story of Alexander Selkirk, whose life on a desert island awakened the most lively interest in the year 1719. To imagine how a man could subsist in complete solitude was pleasant employment for the imagination. But it was novel as well as pleasant to read the whole story told by one who knew so much that his fancies read like palpable facts. *Robinson Crusoe* gave its readers not literature but life. In a superficial sense, the book has no style at all. Its sentences are hasty, often formless, sometimes ungrammatical. Yet there are passages in which Defoe's vigorous and exact thinking creates by itself some of the solidest qualities of style. Crusoe's contrivances for his shelter, safety and comfort are as credible as any events in history, and it needs the minutest examination to detect here and there a few inconsistencies in the vast record of facts and details. But Defoe is more than an annalist; there are times when he rises to the height of really great narrative. The description of how Crusoe, after having lived in solitude for many years, discovers a human footprint in the sand, is impressive, after the twentieth reading:

It happened one day, about noon, going towards my boat, I was exceedingly surprised with the print of a man's naked foot on the shore, which was very plain to be seen in the sand. I stood like one thunderstruck, or as if I had seen an apparition. I listened, I looked round me, I could hear nothing, nor see anything. I went up to a rising ground, to look farther. I went up the shore, and down the shore, but it was all one; I could see no other impression but that one. I went to it again to see if there were any more, and to observe if it might not be my fancy; but there was no room for that, for there was exactly the very print of a foot—toes, heel, and every part of a foot. How it came thither I knew not, nor could in the least imagine. But after innumerable fluttering thoughts, like a man perfectly confused and out of myself, I came home to my fortification, not feeling, as we say, the ground I went on, but terrified to the last degree, looking behind me at every two or three steps, mistaking every bush and tree, and fancying every stump at a distance to be a man; nor is it possible to describe how many various shapes affrighted imagination represented things to me in, how many wild ideas were found every moment in my fancy, and what strange, unaccountable whimsies came into my thoughts by the way.

When I came to my castle, for so I think I called it ever after this, I fled into it like one pursued. Whether I went over by the ladder, as first contrived, or went in at the hole in the rock, which I called a door, I cannot remember; no, nor could I remember the next morning, for never frighted hare fled to cover, or fox to earth, with more terror of mind than I to this retreat.

As a less familiar example of his style, one may quote

another crisis in a life history—the description of Moll Flanders's temptation and fall :

Wandering thus about, I knew not whither, I passed by an apothecary's shop in Leadenhall Street, where I saw lie on a stool just before the counter a little bundle wrapped in a white cloth ; beyond it stood a maid-servant with her back to it, looking up towards the top of the shop, where the apothecary's apprentice, as I suppose, was standing upon the counter, with his back also to the door, and a candle in his hand, looking and reaching up to the upper shelf for something he wanted, so that both were engaged mighty earnestly, and nobody else in the shop.

This was the bait ; and the devil, who I said laid the snare, as readily prompted me as if he had spoke, for I remember, and shall never forget it, 'twas like a voice spoken to me over my shoulder, " Take the bundle ; be quick ; do it this moment." It was no sooner said but I stepped into the shop, and with my back to the wench, as if I had stood up for a cart that was going by, I put my hand behind me and took the bundle, and went off with it, the maid or the fellow not perceiving me, or anyone else.

It is impossible to express the horror of my soul all the while I did it. When I went away I had no heart to run, or scarce to mend my pace. I crossed the street, indeed, and went down the first turning I came to, and I think it was a street that went through into Fenchurch Street. From thence I crossed and turned through so many ways and turnings, that I could never tell which way it was, nor where I went ; for I felt not the ground I stepped on, and the farther I was out of danger, the faster I went, till, tired, and out of breath, I was forced to sit down on a little bench at a door, and then I began to recover, and found I was got into Thames Street, near Billingsgate. I rested me a little and went on ; my blood was all in a fire ; my heart beat as if I was in a sudden fright. In short, I was under such a surprise that I still knew not whither I was going, or what to do.

Fiction, which could deal with life as well as this, had, it was clear, a great future before it.

CHAPTER XI

THE EIGHTEENTH CENTURY

POETS AND NOVELISTS

THE age which opened with the accession of George I and closed with the outbreak of the French Revolution, has a character and a spirit which are more definite than those of any other in our literary history. Literature was deeply influenced by the tastes of the small but able body of aristocrats, who dominated the public affairs of the country. These men recognised in the works of Pope a certain harmony with their own thought and temper. Pope revered the classics : so did they. Pope was witty, intellectual, and a minute critic of society. They also were wits, they also talked philosophy and delighted in elegance. The poetry of Pope was easily remembered, rich in quotable passages, and was written in a style which could be passably imitated by even moderate skill. For about a century many writers were content to cast their thoughts in the mould required by the heroic couplet. Of this so-called " classical " poetry, the chief writer in the mid-eighteenth century was Dr. Johnson.

But the life of the English people can never be identified with the limited activities of a particular class. There were many men in England to whom the policy of a Walpole or a Chatham was a matter of small account. One great concern of the people which kings and laws could scarcely touch was religion ; and though the deepest religious emotions slept for many years of the century, they were awakened, as they have never since been awakened, by the wonderful genius of John Wesley. Methodism did

not produce great poetry, but it was the ruling influence
in one of the best poets of the age, William Cowper, and
Cowper's models of style were often writers whom Dr.
Johnson particularly disliked. The love of landscape, too,
was an emotion too fine and too delicate for " official "
verse to express. Men of fashion were not ashamed to
admire " prospects," and some of them, even, were willing
to patronise the Scottish poet, James Thomson, who made
landscape the chief theme of his song. But landscape
poets were not able always to keep their verse within
decent bounds, and towards the end of the century, there
awoke a passion for beauty which shattered the conventional style into fragments. Even the reputation of the
classical writers seemed less inviolable than of old. The
dreadful heresy began to be whispered that perhaps they
might not possess after all a complete monopoly of the
literary and artistic virtues. Renaissance painting, Gothic
architecture and mediæval manuscripts obtained a growing
body of admirers, and even a great scholar like Gray found
it worth while to study the poetry of the " dark ages."
Pope had contemptuously classed Goths with monks as
the foes of polite learning, but towards the end of the
century, the word " Gothic " was used less often as a term
of abuse than as a token of admiration. All these various
tastes developed slowly, and the revolution which they
finally worked was long in coming. " Official " poetry
possessed much superficial brilliance and it enjoyed great
prestige. But if the reader of to-day enjoys it at all, it
will be less for its technical merits than for some human
interest. In Dr. Johnson's verse, for instance, the deep
feelings of the man often break through the smooth disguise
of the conventional manner.

I

The real character of Dr. Johnson,[1] who was Pope's
chief successor, is only in part revealed in his poetry.
He carried on the tradition of the Satire in his two poems

[1] See also pp. 204–209.

London (1738) and *The Vanity of Human Wishes* (1749), both of which are modelled upon Juvenal. Something in the sombre and sincere nature of these two works, especially of the second, endears them to many readers, who can recognise beneath the pompous phrasing, the pulse of a human heart. When Johnson declaimed against the vanity of fame, of long life and of beauty, he was not merely imitating Juvenal's Tenth Satire, but expressing his profound belief that human pleasures are uncertain and unsatisfying. His verse rings truest in his lines on the vanity of literary ambition, and on this passage one may well be content to echo the words of Mr. Birrell, " If this be not poetry, may the name perish ! "

> When first the college rolls receive his name,
> The young enthusiast quits his ease for fame ;
> Thro' all his veins the fever of renown
> Burns from the strong contagion of the gown ;
> O'er Bodley's Dome his future labours spread
> And Bacon's Mansion trembles o'er his head ;
> Are these thy views ?   Proceed, illustrious youth,
> And Virtue guard thee to the throne of Truth.
> Yet, should thy soul indulge the gen'rous heat
> Till captive science yields her last retreat ;
> Should reason guide thee with her brightest ray,
> And pour on misty doubt resistless day ;
> Should no false kindness lure to loose delight,
> Nor praise relax, nor difficulty fright ;
> Should tempting novelty thy cell refrain,
> And sloth effuse her opiate fumes in vain ;
> Should beauty blunt on fops her fatal dart,
> Nor claim the triumph of a letter'd heart ;
> Should no disease thy torpid veins invade,
> Nor melancholy's phantoms haunt thy shade ;
> Yet hope not life from grief or danger free,
> Nor think the doom of man revers'd for thee.
> Deign on the passing world to turn thine eyes,
> And pause awhile from letters to be wise ;
> There mark what ills the scholar's life assail,
> Toil, envy, want, the patron, and the jail.
> See nations slowly wise, and meanly just,
> To buried merit raise the tardy bust.
> If dreams yet flatter, once again attend,
> Hear Lydiat's life, and Galileo's end.

The eighteenth century gave birth to many other works modelled more or less closely on Pope's style, but none have such solid merits as those of Johnson. The more original poets either broke away from Pope's couplet altogether, or else gave it a more liquid music than it has under his own hard control. Above the mass of writers, a few stand out by the refinement of their talent. Four in particular approach the rank of great poets : they are Gray, Collins, Goldsmith and Cowper.

Thomas Gray (1716–1771) was a shy and fastidious man, who lived for nearly the whole of his life as a recluse student. On leaving Eton, he settled at Cambridge where he buried himself in his books, and became, as some said, the most learned man in Europe. His studies were various, but principally literary and historical. He had a few intimate friends, such as Horace Walpole and Richard West, to whom he wrote letters which gave the fullest self-revelation of which he was capable. Matthew Arnold's remark, " He never spoke out," is probably accurate in its suggestion of a man too solitary and shrinking to rise to the full height of his opportunities. Gray suffered from frequent low spirits and had not much capacity for hearty enjoyment. Perhaps he was happiest during his tours through the less known parts of England, and it is worth remembering that he was one of the first men to appreciate the beauty of the Cumberland lakes and mountains. It was a sign of the times that men were glad to vary the monotony of a comfortable life with the thrill of wild or dangerous Nature.

An Elegy written in a Country Churchyard (1751) is one of those poems which have entered so deeply into the fabric of the English mind that it is impossible to view them with detachment. The feelings it expresses are so universal, and the phrasing is so perfect, that it is difficult not to regard it as a thing which has always existed. In one sense, the *Elegy* is a very ordinary poem, in another and deeper sense it is a very original one. As long as men have existed they must have felt the pathos of a life passed in complete obscurity; yet it was reserved for Gray to put this feeling into words of solemn elegiac rhythm that makes them memorable for ever:

> Full many a gem of purest ray serene,
>   The dark unfathomed caves of ocean bear:
> Full many a flower is born to blush unseen,
>   And waste its sweetness on the desert air.
>
> Some village-Hampden, that with dauntless breast
>   The little tyrant of his fields withstood;
> Some mute inglorious Milton here may rest,
>   Some Cromwell guiltless of his country's blood.

The greatness as well as the popularity of the *Elegy* consists in its universal appeal. The solemnity of evening, the simple pathos of human life and the moving associations of a village church set in a homely landscape of southern England are expressed by Gray with a perfection which is beyond praise. Such a poem can never be trite except to the superficial.

Gray's other poems have not the same perfection as the *Elegy*, though there are few of his works over which he did not linger with the minutest care. In his lighter vein, he is best in the *Ode on a Distant Prospect of Eton College*. The conventional phrasing of the age is there used with a happy, playful effect:

> What idle progeny succeed
> To chase the rolling circle's speed,
>   Or urge the flying ball?

His two odes, *The Progress of Poesy* and *The Bard*, have been extravagantly praised and violently abused. Gray was attempting a more genuine kind of poetry than that which was in vogue, and he certainly succeeded in writing two very fine poems. Perhaps the odes scarcely attain to the "sublimity" for which some of their admirers have praised them.

The output of the unfortunate and short-lived William

Collins (1721–1759) was very slight, but he was a genuine lyrical poet, perhaps the best of his time. His most ambitious poem is the spirited *Ode on the Popular Superstitions of the Highlands*, but one likes Collins best when he descends to that simplicity of which he himself sang the praises. In an age of great national confidence and perhaps pardonable boasting (" Rule Britannia " belongs to these years), Collins knew how to celebrate his country's glory with a simple dignity of style and with due recollection of its cost. The modest Ode he wrote " in the beginning of the year 1746 " could not be bettered :

> How sleep the Brave, who sink to rest
> By all their country's wishes blest !
> When Spring with dewy fingers cold,
> Returns to deck their hallowed mould,
> She there shall find a sweeter sod,
> Than Fancy's feet have ever trod.

> By fairy hands their knell is rung,
> By forms unseen their dirge is sung ;
> There Honour comes, a pilgrim grey,
> To bless the turf that wraps their clay,
> And Freedom shall awhile repair,
> To dwell a weeping hermit, there !

In the *Ode to Evening*, a poem deeply saturated with the spirit of the English landscape, Collins's lyrical and descriptive powers are happily blended. All the impressions absorbed from a contemplation of many evenings are here brought together and rendered in phrases of wonderful concentration. By his description of the breathless silence of evening broken only by the " heedless hum " of the beetle as it flies past the traveller ; of the reflection in sheets of still water of the last gleam of light ; and of the sombre beauty of a wide landscape under the rainy, autumn skies, Collins belongs to that group of poets who have felt and described most truly the peculiar beauty of the English countryside. The form of the Ode, which is in short unrhyming stanzas, is both fitting and original.

III

By his literary associations, Oliver Goldsmith (1728–1774) belongs to the circle of Dr. Johnson, but he was too versatile to be regarded simply as a member of a school. His epitaph speaks the plain truth when it describes him as having attempted nearly every kind of writing, and as adorning them all. Goldsmith was not very original in the forms he chose for his poetry. *The Traveller* (1764) and *The Deserted Village* (1770) seem intended, like many of Pope's works, to combine useful reflections with the beauty of poetic language. But even amidst a philosophic account of the different European nations, or a warning to statesmen of the dangers attending a depopulation of the villages, Goldsmith's true genius breaks through the restrictions of his didactic purpose. He was no thinker, but an impulsive, fanciful, wayward poet, open to every charm and impression of beauty which fortune threw in his way. It matters little to literature that he thought fit to declaim against the degeneracy of Continental peoples; the pleasure with which he looked abroad at unfamiliar things still communicates itself in such lines as those on Holland :

> The slow canal, the yellow-blossom'd vale,
> The willow-tufted bank, the gliding sail.

The reflections in *The Deserted Village* are more serious, yet the poem is primarily a work of sentiment and observation. In describing the village parson and the village schoolmaster, Goldsmith is very nearly, if not quite, himself. Sometimes his couplets are of remarkable beauty : that on the smith, for instance, is admirable in its vivid brevity :

> No more the smith his dusky brow shall clear,
> Relax his pond'rous strength, and lean to hear.

The lighter metres probably suited Goldsmith better than the serious heroic couplet. He wrote nothing more finished than the stanzas, " When lovely woman stoops to folly," or more spontaneous than the gay dactylic lines of the unfinished *Retaliation*.

Though William Cowper (1731–1800) was in some respects a typical English gentleman of the eighteenth century, there was something in his character as a writer which seemed to foretell new things. Sensibility is the strength of poets ; but the sensibility of Cowper was of a novel kind. Something in the spirit of the age made the writings of this shy, retiring man strangely attractive to readers of refinement. He fostered, and perhaps created, a new taste. To be moved to tears by Cowper was regarded as proof of a superior nature ; to be insensible to him was a sure sign of mental obtuseness.

Cowper possessed neither the physique nor the disposition to grapple cheerfully with life, though he had, fortunately, a rich vein of humour. At Westminster, where he was educated, his timidity made him the victim of bullying, and schools were to his mind ever after places of cruelty and coarseness. He passed some happy days in reading law and in idling among congenial companions, and all went well until a relative offered to nominate him for a clerkship to the House of Lords. The thought of having to appear for public examination, and of standing in competition against a rival candidate, gradually assumed enormous proportions in his mind; and at last, to escape the ordeal, he actually attempted to commit suicide. All thought of a public career was now given up, and for the rest of his life Cowper lived quietly in the country, most of the time with his friends Mrs. and Miss Unwin, with whom he was on terms of the warmest sympathy. The Unwins lived at Olney in Bedfordshire, where the curate of the parish was the Rev. John Newton, a well-known hymn-writer. Newton had been a slave-owner, but having come under the influence of Methodism, had developed into a zealous and even tyrannical evangelist. He persuaded Cowper to turn his talents to hymn-writing, and the result was the *Olney Hymns* (1779), many of which, such as " Hark, my Soul, it is the Lord," and " God moves in a mysterious way," are as familiar as any in the language. The society of Newton, who made frequent inquisitions into the state of Cowper's soul, was hardly exhilarating, and the poet remained gloomy and depressed. His other poems of this period were somewhat tepid satires—a form of writing for which he had little talent. But the advent of a newcomer to Olney had a miraculous effect on the poet's career. The newcomer was Lady Austen, who quickly changed the current of Cowper's thoughts, and brought his mind back from commonplace moralising to its true function—that of observation and humour. It was Lady Austen who set him to write *The Task*, a poem of no particular plan, but an excellent record of Cowper's most lively feelings. About the same time, he heard the story of John Gilpin, out of which he immediately made the spritely ballad which everybody knows. The letters, as well as the verses which Cowper wrote during these years have a delightful geniality and a wealth of detailed observation which, though slight, is seldom trivial. But the period of happiness soon passed. During the later years of his life, Cowper was again visited by religious melancholy, and though he strove to keep the enemy at bay by translating Homer, he was fighting a losing battle. The pathetic close of his last poem, *The Castaway*, reveals the depth of his depression.

Cowper's strength as a poet lies in description and sentiment. His range is limited both by his temperament and his experience. No one before had described so well the sights and pleasures of domestic life in the country—the warm fire, the hissing tea-urn, the arrival of letters, the labourer trudging through the lanes, the silent countryside under its load of snow. Cowper did not enjoy a soaking in the rain, but all those milder pleasures of the open air which can be enjoyed without much personal discomfort he describes with zest and felicity. The following lines from *The Task* are a pleasing example of his domestic style :

> Hark ! 'tis the twanging horn o'er yonder bridge,
> That with its wearisome but needful length
> Bestrides the wintry flood, in which the moon
> Sees her unwrinkled face reflected bright ;—
> He comes, the herald of a noisy world,
> With spatter'd boots, strapp'd waist, and frozen locks ;

News from all nations lumb'ring at his back.
True to his charge, the close-pack'd load behind,
Yet careless what he brings, his one concern
Is to conduct it to the destin'd inn :
And, having dropp'd th'expected bag, pass on. . . .
    Now stir the fire, and close the shutters fast,
Let fall the curtains, wheel the sofa round,
And, while the bubbling and loud-hissing urn
Throws up a steamy column, and the cups,
That cheer but not inebriate, wait on each,
So let us welcome peaceful ev'ning in.

Cowper's sensitiveness and melancholy enabled him to write elegiac verse which is sincere and pure, though not profound.   His poem on the destruction of a grove of trees :

The poplars are fell'd, farewell to the shade
And the whispering sound of the cool colonnade,

is typical of him ; but on occasion, he could strike a deeper note, and his lines *On the Loss of the ' Royal George'* have the sonorous simplicity which the subject demands.   The most beautiful of his elegiac pieces are the lines *On the Receipt of my Mother's Picture* and the still more affecting poem *To Mary* (Mrs. Unwin).   Good taste, sincerity and clearness of expression are qualities which Cowper's poetry seldom lacks, and though the note of sadness is frequently recurrent, he should also be remembered as the agreeable trifler who could address his dog or describe his pet hare in verses full of charm.   Nature meant much to him.   " Oh, I could spend whole days and nights in feeding upon a lovely prospect ! " he wrote to a friend.   Admirers of Cowper would learn to expect from poetry something very different from what Pope could give them, though they would be spared the ordeal of deciding once for all whether they should return to the safe ways of tradition or go forward to unexplored regions.   Cowper might raise that question, but he would not demand an answer.

Among the more original poets of the century, mention must be made of James Thomson,[1] whose chief work, *The Seasons*, was published between 1726 and 1730 in four parts, *Winter, Summer, Spring,* and *Autumn.*   *The Seasons* is a

[1] See also p. 221.

Nature-poem in Miltonic blank-verse. There are passages in which Thomson is really carried away by his subject; for example, his description of the havoc wrought in a fertile valley by a summer thunder-storm is excellent. But too often he is content with somewhat vague verbal effects, acceptable to an age which admired Miltonic language and was mildly interested in English landscape. A once-famous contemporary of Thomson was the talented and ambitious Dr. Edward Young. He wrote much, and one poem of his enjoyed an enormous reputation. This was *Night Thoughts* (1742–45), a meditative poem in rather prosaic blank-verse. The work is now perhaps unduly neglected. The single line of Young which is universally known :

> Procrastination is the thief of time,

is not a fair specimen of his powers as a writer.

THE NOVELISTS

IV

The complex product of literature which is called a " novel " has many origins, and it is always tempting to look for early novels before the species had really begun to exist. To say nothing of Defoe and Addison, there were books written during the Restoration and even in the reign of Elizabeth, which have been, not unreasonably, called " novels." Prose fiction is of great antiquity, and it is never easy to say what constitutes a genuine novel. The easiest way of settling the question is perhaps the wisest. The works of Richardson and Fielding evidently belong to the same species as those of Scott, Dickens and Thomas Hardy. Of various works by Richardson's predecessors —those of Defoe, for example—no such statement can be confidently made, however clear it is that they possess some, and indeed many, of the qualities of a novel. On the question of plot, characterization and dialogue, and on the relation of all these to each other, Richardson and Fielding held much the same views as the countless novelists who have succeeded them, and the old convention of regarding these two men as the earliest of their class is too convenient and too reasonable to be disputed. Our account of the novel, then, shall begin with Samuel Richardson.

The author of *Pamela* was a short, stout, prosperous bookseller, who had no idea of writing a novel until he reached the age of fifty, when it occurred to him that a collection of fictitious letters might serve the useful purpose of enlightening young people as to the ways of the world. He therefore wrote a story about a servant-girl named Pamela Andrews, who receives advances of love from her master, repels them, is subjected to amazing persecutions, remains firm, and is finally rewarded by an offer of marriage. The whole narrative is told in the form of letters, Pamela being supposed to have a consuming passion for correspondence and time in which to record her adventures down to the minutest particular. It has been calculated that, on some days, she must have been writing for about twenty out of the twenty-four hours.

The success of *Pamela*, which appeared in 1740, encouraged Richardson to follow it up with a second novel, *Clarissa Harlowe* (1747–48), which is his masterpiece. The plot is more complex than that of *Pamela*, and there is a great advance in characterization. The story, however, can be told in a few words. Clarissa Harlowe, in order to escape a hateful marriage into which her parents wish to force her, throws herself upon the protection of her admirer, Lovelace, whom she discovers, when it is too late, to be a scoundrel. The refined cruelty with which the helpless girl is treated finally causes her death, which is avenged on Lovelace in a duel which he is compelled to fight with Clarissa's uncle. Though this sounds simple enough, *Clarissa Harlowe* is one of the most intricate novels in existence. Emotions, good and bad, conflict with each other and strive for mastery like the various currents of a whirlpool. The book is one long story of passion and prayer, entreaty, accusation, intrigue, deception and remorse. The two chief characters, Clarissa and Lovelace, pour forth their hearts in long and agitated letters to the respective friends of their bosom. In what a flutter of spirits the poor heroine is kept may be gathered from the following lines in one of her communications to her confidante, Miss Howe. Clarissa is resisting the wishes of her family that she should marry a detested lover:

In less than a quarter of an hour, up came Betty. I let her in upon her tapping, and asking, half out of breath too, for admittance.

"The Lord have mercy upon us!" said she. "What a *confusion of a house* is this," hurrying up and down, fanning herself with her handkerchief. "Such angry masters and mistresses!—such an obstinate young lady!—such an humble lover!—such enraged uncles!—such—O dear!—dear! What a topsy-turvey house!"

Thus she ran on, while I sat as patiently as I could.

At last, turning to me, "I must do as I am bid. I can't help it. Don't be angry with me, miss. But I must carry down your pen and ink this moment."

"By whose order?"

"By your papa's and mamma's."

"How shall I know that?"

She offered to go to my closet. I stept in before her:

"Touch it, if you dare!"

Up came my cousin Dolly.

"Dear cousin Clarissa," said the good-natured creature, sobbing, "you must—indeed you must—deliver to Betty or to me—your pen and ink."

"Must I, sweet cousin? Then I will to you." And I gave my standish to her.

"I am sorry," said Dolly, "to be the messenger, but your papa will not have you in the same house with him. He is resolved you shall be carried away on Saturday at farthest. And therefore your pen and ink are taken away that you may give nobody notice of it."

And away went the dear girl, very sorrowful, carrying down with her my standish, and all its furniture. As it happened, I had hid half a dozen crowquills in as many different places.

If, as has been said, a novel should "educate the sentiments," Richardson certainly had the right object in view. Many of the tremors and alarms described in his pages now sound ridiculously high-flown. Yet the reader who cannot see how much of the novel arises naturally from the social conditions of the age must be singularly wanting in historical perception. Richardson certainly exaggerated the sentimental fears and scruples which torment his characters ; but his exaggeration is founded on intimate knowledge of humanity, especially of women. In daring to explore some of the secret places of the heart, he made a great contribution to the development of the novel. He did more : he kept the unity of construction, he showed much skill in dialogue, and he created some characters—Lovelace, for instance—who live in the memory of everyone who has read his book Richardson's last novel, in which he attempts to draw the character of a perfect gentleman, was *Sir Charles Grandison* (1753–54).

V

Richardson's chief rival in the art of novel-writing was Henry Fielding, a man in many respects the exact reverse of himself. The author of *Pamela* lived in a world of pleasant illusions, and after the great success of his novel, loved to luxuriate in the adulation of his female admirers. He was quite content with the sentimental view of things, and carefully guarded himself from the raw breath of the outer world. Fielding, on the other hand, a man of family and a magistrate, knew life from first-hand experience of its gross and boisterous, as well as its polite and learned sides. His education at Eton and Leyden, and his early relations with the stage (he wrote several comedies and farces), were good preparation for a novelist's career, but it was Richardson himself who put him on the right path. *Pamela, or Virtue Rewarded*, acted on Fielding in the way in which one-sided books so often act upon men who have eyes to see life for themselves. Fielding was provoked to write a satirical but good-humoured parody of *Pamela*, taking as his hero Joseph Andrews, Pamela's brother, whose adventures were to afford an amusing parallel to those of his sister. But once Fielding had got fairly into the world of parsons and magistrates, of innkeepers and postilions, the novelist in him overcame the parodist and he soon forgot all about Richardson. A more vigorous picture of unregenerate and exuberant old England than that given in *Joseph Andrews* (1742) does not exist. The " plot " matters little : but in describing the miscellaneous company at an inn, the mixed talk in a coach, or the vicissitudes of a journey, Fielding is incomparable. He is also one of the strongest delineators of character among English writers. His portrait of the simple-minded, unworldly, generous and learned Parson Adams is as convincing as it is beautiful. Fielding, in fact, perceived that England was full of in-dividual and often eccentric characters, whose oddities were a veritable mine for the writer of fiction. Dr. Johnson had also noted this fact. " The English nation," he wrote, " produces more originals than all the rest of the world together." It was natural, therefore, that a distinguishing feature of the English novel should be its frequent delinea-tion of extraordinary characters, who, however odd they may appear, are too real to be wholly imaginary.

Fielding's masterpiece, *Tom Jones* (1749), is a far more ambitious work than the slight though excellent *Joseph Andrews*. It is, as its author calls it, in a carefully-worded phrase, a " comic epic in prose." Tom Jones, a foundling, is through a mistake turned out of doors by his benefactor, Squire Allworthy ; he undergoes many hardships, but is at last restored to favour, and marries the constant but long-afflicted Sophia Western. Such, in a sentence, is the story of the book. Fielding took the utmost pains to steer between the commonplace and the improbable, to combine truth with fiction, and nature with art ; to invent enough but not too much ; to learn from literature and to be faithful to experience. Few English writers have thought so wisely about the principles of the novel, but good as Fielding is as a critic, he is far greater as an artist. His power of creating character is masterly, and there is in the book hardly a figure, major or minor, who does not live in the reader's memory with perfect distinctness. The hero and his counterpart Blifil, the one impetuous and warm-hearted, the other cold and discreet; the brutal, blustering, fox-hunting Squire Western, and his book-learned political sister; Parson Thwackum and his rival Square, the philosopher—merely to mention their names is to recall countless incidents and dialogues, tender, violent or absurd. The following conversation on the subject of Sophia Western's marriage illustrates Fielding's vigorous manner. The Squire's sister begins:

"Pray, brother, have you not observed something very extraordinary in my niece lately?" "No, not I," answered Western; "is there anything the matter with the girl?" "I think there is," replies she, "and something of much consequence too." "Why, she doth not complain of anything," cries Western, "and she hath had the small pox." "Brother," returned she, "girls are liable to other distempers besides the small pox, and sometimes possibly to much worse." Here Western interrupted her with much earnestness, and begged her, if anything ailed his daughter, to acquaint him immediately, adding, "She knew he loved her more than his own soul, and that he would send to the world's end for the best physician to her." "Nay, nay," answered she, smiling, "the distemper is not so terrible; but I believe, brother, you are convinced I know the world, and I promise you I was never more deceived in my life, if my niece be not most desperately in love." "How! in love," cries Western in a passion, "in love without acquainting me! I'll disinherit her, I'll turn her out of doors, stark naked, without a farthing. Is all my kindness vor 'ur, and vondness o' ur come to this, to fall in love without asking me leave!" "But you will not," answered Mrs. Western, "turn this daughter, whom you love better than your own soul, out of doors, before you know whether you shall approve her choice. Suppose she should have fixed on the very person whom you yourself would wish, I hope you would not be angry then." "No, no," cries Western, "that would make a difference. If she marries the man I would ha' her, she may love whom she pleases, I shan't trouble my head about that."

Fielding is not a Shakespeare, and his work is not wholly superior to time. *Tom Jones* reveals a world which is simpler, cruder and heartier than our own. But all who value a work of art for its own sake, and do not find our ancestors of two centuries ago so different as to be un-intelligible, will admit Fielding's masterpiece to be rich in the pleasures which a great book can give.

Fielding's last novel, *Amelia* (1751), takes us into a narrower, but also a more amiable world. The book is an attractive story of a woman's devotion to a weak but not worthless husband. One further work, *A Voyage to Lisbon*, is the record of a journey undertaken in a vain search for health. Fielding died in 1754, at the age of forty-seven.

VI

Of the numerous successors of Richardson and Fielding, two at least were men of originality who struck out new paths for themselves. Tobias Smollett, a Scotsman, turned to good account his experience as ship's surgeon on a man-of-war, and in 1748, at the age of twenty-seven, produced his first novel, *The Adventures of Roderick Random*. The book contains some highly realistic descriptions of a young medical student's good and bad fortune on his first introduction to life, and of the brutal ways of seamen in the days of the press-gang. Smollett was a coarse and vigorous writer who well knew the lives of sharpers and adventurers, though he had little insight into the manners of the polite world. His translation of *Gil Blas* acquainted him with one of the greatest of " picaresque " stories and confirmed his natural bias towards that kind of writing. For the next twenty years, he was a busy man of letters, and among many other works produced several novels, of which the best are *The Adventures of Peregrine Pickle* (1751), *The Adventures of Ferdinand, Count Fathom* (1753), and *The Expedition of Humphrey Clinker* (1771). The last-named book is particularly noteworthy both for its graphic picture of Bath society and for its fine collection of odd characters. Smollett was a connoisseur of " originals " (he loves the word), and *Humphrey Clinker* seems planned to bring together as many from different parts of the country as its author conveniently could.

Thackeray's remark about Smollett that "he did not invent much" is probably justified; but he had the talent of selecting from life countless scenes and incidents which he was able to work up into very robust narrative. The novels of Smollett, like those of so many English writers, are in large measure "imaginative reminiscence."

The Rev. Laurence Sterne, sometime Vicar of Sutton-in-the-Forest and Prebendary of York, is one of the strangest figures in our literature. His chief novel, *Tristram Shandy* (finished in 1767), is as much the revelation of its witty and whimsical author as a picture of life. The reader is at the mercy of an irrepressible jester, who, far from relating the fortunes of his hero, does not even suffer him to be born till the end of the book. On perusing this freak among novels, one is suddenly confronted by pages elaborately blackened, or marbled, or entirely blank. Erudition of the quaintest and least verifiable kind meets one at every turn; paths are taken which lead nowhere; hints, allusions and innuendoes, often completely baffling, are scattered broadcast over the whole book. Yet, in spite of all his oddities, the author of *Tristram Shandy* was beyond dispute a novelist of genius. Three at least of his characters, the elder Shandy ("my father"), "my uncle Toby" and Corporal Trim are among the most originally conceived in English fiction. The portrait of Uncle Toby, in particular, with his ridiculous craze for making sham fortifications and his overflowing goodness of heart, has been painted with infinite relish. The best parts of the book, after all, are those in which Shandy learnedly lays down the law, Uncle Toby affectionately contradicts, while the Corporal stands stolidly and respectfully by. Many of such scenes are unforgettable. The following quotation will give some idea of their quality. A disaster has just happened in the christening of the hero, who by the mistake of a messenger has been irrevocably named Tristram instead of Trismegistus:

For my own part, Trim, though I can see little or no difference betwixt my nephew's being called Tristram or Trismegistus, yet as the thing sits so near my brother's heart,

Trim, I would freely have given a hundred pounds rather than it should have happened.—A hundred pounds, an' please your honour! replied Trim, I would not give a cherry-stone to boot.—Nor would I, Trim, upon my own account, quoth my uncle Toby, but my brother, whom there is no arguing with in this case, maintains that a great deal more depends, Trim, upon Christian-names, than what ignorant people imagine— for he says there never was a great or heroic action performed since the world began by one called Tristram—nay, he will have it, Trim, that a man can neither be learned, or wise, or brave.—'Tis all fancy, an' please your honour, I fought just as well, replied the corporal, when the regiment called me Trim, as when they called me James Butler.—And for my own part, said my uncle Toby, though I should blush to boast of myself, Trim, yet had my name been Alexander, I could have done no more at Namur than my duty.—Bless your honour! cried Trim, advancing three steps as he spoke, does a man think of his christian-name when he goes upon the attack?— Or when he stands in the trench, Trim? cried my uncle Toby, looking firm.—Or when he enters a breach? said Trim, pushing in between two chairs.—Or forces the lines? cried my uncle, rising up, and pushing his crutch like a pike.—Or facing a platoon? cried Trim, presenting his stick like a firelock.— Or when he marches up the glacis? cried my uncle Toby, looking warm and setting his foot upon his stool. . . .

The abrupt ending of the scene is quite in Sterne's irresponsible manner.

Sterne wrote only one other novel, *A Sentimental Journey* (1768). For some years, no new novelist of first-rate power appeared in England, but the practice of novel-reading had now become firmly rooted in the upper and middle classes. The popular demand was met by an abundant supply, and plenty of writers appeared who were able to satisfy the popular taste and had little desire to raise it. Two types of novel in particular held the field : the novels of sentiment, of which Henry Mackenzie's *Man of Feeling* (1771) is a famous example, and the novels of terror, of which Mrs. Radcliffe's *Mysteries of Udolpho* (1794) was merely one among many hundreds greedily devoured by the Catherine Morlands [1] of the day.

[1] See p. 253.

CHAPTER XII

THE EIGHTEENTH CENTURY

DR. JOHNSON AND HIS CIRCLE

BETWEEN Pope and Wordsworth there is no English writer who stands out so conspicuously as Dr. Johnson. His personality helps to make eighteenth-century literature a living thing. He was not the greatest or the most original genius of his age. Fielding, Gibbon and Burke, to mention no more, have all left works of higher value than anything of his. Yet so vivid was his figure that there is hardly a single writer of the age whom one does not think of in relation to him. Johnson's admiration for Pope, his dislike of Gray, his enthusiasm for Richardson, his injustice to Fielding, his playful patronage of Goldsmith, his profound respect for Burke, all leave an impression so strong that it is hard—when we are reading Boswell—not to see these great writers through the eyes of their critic. Yet Johnson's literary influence on the abler men of his time was inconsiderable. Some touch of his famous style they may have caught, but it was only in conversation that he really dominated. The idea of his literary dictatorship is a delusion. Goldsmith wrote *The Vicar of Wakefield*, Burke delivered his speeches, Gibbon composed his *Decline and Fall* without Johnson's help, though all were glad to refresh themselves from his wonderful talk. The " age of Johnson," in fact, was one of remarkable achievement: but the use of his name must be understood as a tribute to his greatness as a man, not as the token of superior literary genius. In many ways Johnson was no more than a representative man, an embodiment of eighteenth-century and of English common sense. It is chiefly in the pages of Boswell that one recognises those qualities of mind and character which drew forth so much admiration and love from the greatest men of the age.

I

Apart from his place in Boswell's biography, however, Johnson, both as critic and lexicographer, is a figure of note in our literary history. The greater part of his life— he was born in 1709 and died in 1784—was one long struggle with adversity, and it was only after the publication of his Dictionary, that he began to emerge from obscurity. The degree of LL.D. which is now incorporated with his fame was not conferred until twenty years later. The difficulties with which Johnson had to contend were many. His father, a bookseller at Lichfield, was unable to maintain him for the full number of terms at Oxford, and he left the University without taking a degree. As a boy, he had read insatiably, but his literary knowledge was his only possession, and he had neither the physical nor the moral qualities which bring rapid success. He was large, ungainly, and short-sighted; and he was afflicted by a strange nervous ailment, almost a disease, which made him melancholy when alone and eccentric in company. Before he had won any appreciable success, Johnson married Mrs. Elizabeth Porter, a widow many years older than himself. He had written a tragedy, *Irene*, which he took up to London, and though the work was acted, it brought its author little or no profit. Then followed a period of acute struggle, of which hardly anything is known, though it may be assumed that Johnson suffered all the miseries of an ill-paid literary hack. That he did not succumb is due partly to his sincere religious convictions, partly to his forcible power of self-assertion. One line of his satire, *London*, bears eloquent witness to his experience and reflections :

Slow rises worth by poverty oppressed.

In 1747, Johnson published his *Plan of a Dictionary of the English Language*, which he addressed to the Earl of Chesterfield ; but that illustrious patron of letters and model of aristocratic refinement let the opportunity of helping the obscure scholar go by, and Johnson pushed on his work " without one act of assistance, one word of encouragement, or one smile of favour."

The year 1750 saw the first number of *The Rambler*, a periodical modelled on *The Spectator*, but with little of the wit and spriteliness to which the earlier paper owes its fame. Johnson is a more solid moralist than Addison but has far less invention and a much heavier style. The *Dictionary* appeared in 1755, and Johnson's eminence could now be questioned no longer. The writer of the first English work of its kind, who, with no foundation other than certain Glossaries and " Treasuries," had attempted to cover the whole field of the language, had defined the words and illustrated their meaning by quotations, who had done this work so well that it at once began to give stability to common usage—such a man has an unassailable place in the history of our tongue. Johnson's Dictionary is the basis on which all other lexicographers have worked ; it is the direct ancestor of the greatest of all dictionaries, that which was designed by Sir James Murray and produced at Oxford. The attempt of one man to grapple with so huge a task could not, of course, wholly succeed. Many words are omitted ; the etymologies are imperfect. Some definitions are simply and inexcusably wrong. But Johnson had a way of making even his errors and caprices interesting, and the Dictionary is not only a labour of erudition but a remarkable human document. Johnson's frank admission of his mistake in the definition of " pastern," and his confession of " ignorance, pure ignorance," puts him at once in that little band of scholars whom we know also as men. Nor is one less delighted when he deliberately lets loose a little humour and prejudice into his columns. A " lexicographer " is defined not only as " a writer of dictionaries " but as " a harmless drudge." Johnson was a strong party man and took care that the

Whigs should not escape unscathed. Accordingly, a Tory is described as " one who adheres to the ancient constitution of the State, and the apostolical hierarchy of the Church of England," while the word " Whig " is curtly defined as " the name of a faction." Surely, too, there is some conscious humour in the " Johnsonese " definition of a net, as " a reticulated fabric, decussated at regular intervals."

Johnson's best work as a critic and prose-writer was still to come. In 1759 his mother died, and the author of the first English Dictionary found himself unable to meet the expenses of a funeral. He summoned up all his energy, and, within a week, brought out a work of fiction called *Rasselas*. The book has no claim to rank among novels, but it is a most characteristic work, for it pricks one by one all those bubbles which men vainly pursue in quest of happiness. " Ours is not the best of all possible worlds," says Johnson, in reply to the optimist, and he shows how every scene of life brings its disappointments. Yet, in spite of the sombre tone, *Rasselas* is far from depressing. Its candour and sincerity, its moderate hopes and its central core of religion make it a worthy representative of the best English thought. The book, too, has some lively pages. Nothing Johnson wrote shows him in a happier vein than the chapter on the discomfiture of an inventor, who hoped to fly. The " artist " proves to his own satisfaction that his aim is quite practicable, and busily applies himself to perfecting his pair of wings. There is a delightful curtness in Johnson's manner of describing the inevitable end to this fantastic dream. A year is to be spent in preparing the wings :

The prince promised secrecy, and waited for the performance, not wholly hopeless of success. He visited the work from time to time, observed its progress, and remarked many ingenious contrivances to facilitate motion, and unite levity with strength. The artist was every day more certain that he should leave vultures and eagles behind him, and the contagion of his confidence seized upon the prince.

In a year the wings were finished, and, on a morning appointed, the maker appeared furnished for flight on a little promontory : he waved his pinions awhile to gather air, then leaped from his stand, and in an instant dropped into the lake. His wings, which were of no use in the air, sustained him in the water, and the prince drew him to land, half dead with terror and vexation.

On the accession of George III, Johnson's services to literature at last began to be recognised. He received in 1762 a pension of £300, and a few years later was honoured by an interview with the king. For the rest of his life, Johnson was the great outstanding figure in English literature, and he gave free vent to his passion for social intercourse. His evenings at "The Club," illuminated by his wonderful gifts in conversation and the brilliant circle of men of whom he was the centre, have been made memorable for ever in Boswell's book. The enjoyments of these last years stimulated Johnson's intellectual powers and increased his zest for life. At the age of sixty-four, he undertook, with Boswell, the then arduous journey to Scotland, visiting some of the wildest Highland regions. Both tourists wrote accounts of the expedition, Johnson's being *A Journey to the Western Islands of Scotland* (1775). A few years later, he was asked by some booksellers to furnish prefaces to the works of various English poets. The task caught his fancy, and stirred up the accumulated knowledge of years. The *Lives of the Most Eminent English Poets* (1781) is one of the best books of criticism in the language. It has, of course, the limitations of its author's views. Johnson hated blank verse, and thought the heroic couplet " likely never to grow obsolete." He found the rhymes of *Lycidas* "uncertain" and the " numbers unpleasing"; and he objected to the pastoral form as " easy, vulgar, and therefore disgusting." But the *Lives* of the writers whom Johnson admired, Dryden, Pope and their followers, of his friend, Richard Savage, and of a poet like Cowley, on whom he could fairly exercise all his acuteness, are wonderful in their penetration, knowledge and sententious wisdom. It was natural that biography should be blended with criticism in Johnson's best work, for, in his opinion, books are instrumental to right living and the purpose of literature is to teach men how to enjoy life or to endure it.

II

On the death of Johnson in 1784, various anecdotes of his ways and conversation began to appear, and it was generally felt that his life offered peculiar attractions to the art of the biographer. But the appearance of Boswell's *Life of Samuel Johnson* in 1791 revealed a harmony between the artist and his subject of which no one could have dreamed, and though great things have since been done in biography, Boswell's book is still pre-eminent in its class. The author, a Scotsman, was a born hero-worshipper who for a time attached himself to the Corsican General Paoli after he met Johnson. When he obtained the famous introduction in Mr. Davies's back parlour, Johnson was fifty-four, while Boswell was only twenty-three. The first meeting was not highly auspicious, for the young adventurer met with a severe snub. He persevered, however, won Johnson's affection, and was admitted to the meetings of The Club. He made little attempt to shine in the assembly of famous men, but was content to listen, to remember, and to make provocative remarks designed to draw out the master. His copious memoranda of the Club gatherings formed the basis of his work. Boswell was far more than a patient note-collector; he was a keen observer of human nature, a brilliant literary artist, and, above all, the devoted worshipper of a great man. It is the combination of these qualities that enabled him to draw so firmly the lines of his portraits and to group the figures so well.

Boswell's *Life* is a combination of truth with art. The anecdotes and dialogues have all the marks of genuine history, yet to regard the biographer as a mere transcriber is a great injustice. Throughout his book, one is conscious of the discriminating art which seizes what is significant and rejects the superfluous. Nearly the whole of the

Life is excellent, but there are certain things which, once read, remain in the mind as a possession for ever. Johnson's interview with the king, his dinner with Wilkes, his letters to the unfortunate Dr. Dodd, his unbounded goodness to the tiresome pensioners, his fervent Easter resolutions, his outbursts of merriment, his triumphant repartees— these, and a thousand other things, are all strokes in a picture so vivid and real that Dr. Johnson has become a figure far more living to us than half the phantom beings we meet daily yet never know. Scattered over the whole book are those countless phrases which not only have the ring of genuine literature, but bear the very stamp of their speaker's character. " Clear your *mind* of cant," " Whiggism is a negation of all principle," " My dear Madam, talk no more of this ; nonsense can be defended but by nonsense " —with such abrupt sentences Johnson would clinch an argument or silence an adversary. For his " ingeniously exact analogies " he needed rather more space, but the wording is equally crisp and decisive : " Being in a ship is being in a jail with a chance of being drowned "; " A woman's preaching is like a dog's walking on its hind legs : it is not done well, but you are surprised to find it done at all." Remarks like these are striking enough in print : what their effect was when spoken on the spur of the moment ("No flourishing with the sword," said Sir Joshua Reynolds, "he is through your body in an instant ") one can only imagine, or gather from Boswell. When the biographer has to rely on his own narrative powers, he invariably rises to the occasion. For an instance, the reader need only be referred to the opening or the closing scenes of the friendship between the two men.

III

Of the various writers and wits among whom Johnson practised his formidable powers, none stood in more complete contrast to him than the improvident Irishman of genius, Oliver Goldsmith. As a talker, he was no match for most members of the group, though as a writer he had powers which the best of them might have envied. *The Vicar of Wakefield* (1766), which owed its publication to the intervention of Johnson when its author was in difficulties over his rent, is Goldsmith's one novel, and it is unique in English fiction. It cannot be judged by ordinary standards. A child could expose the absurdity of the plot —a series of ever-increasing disasters suddenly reversed by a turn in fortune's wheel. But such a book as this loses nothing from the naïveté of its construction. In *The Vicar of Wakefield*, the grace of unworldliness, the poetry of rustic life, gently humorous dialogue and ludicrous incident meet and blend in a harmony over which the author's style prevails with unfailing charm. The book is the expression of a nature which criticism could not sophisticate and experience could not sour.

Goldsmith was also the author of two among the few plays of his century which have not grown old. In *The Good-Natured Man* (1768), the treatment is rather uncertain, though there are some admirable scenes. *She Stoops to Conquer* (1773) succeeds as a comedy in spite of its farcical plot. Goldsmith's dialogue is so delightful, his handling of the absurd situations is so spirited, and Tony Lumpkin is so excellent a booby, that the play always pleases, whether acted or read. Another dramatist of Johnson's group, Richard Brinsley Sheridan, surpassed Goldsmith in wit, though he lacked his charm. He wrote and adapted several comedies, of which the best are *The Rivals* (1775), *The School for Scandal* (1777), and *The Critic* (1779). Sheridan owed much to the Restoration drama, but the wit of his dialogue and his brilliant characterisation are his own. The ingeniously contrived scenes, the irresistible comedy of many passages, and the pervading air of gaiety have given his plays a popularity which they have kept for over a century and a half.

IV

The greatest member of Johnson's circle, one of the very few men of whose conversational powers Johnson ever stood in awe, was Edmund Burke (1729–1797). He was an Irishman who, with few advantages but his own talents, won a seat in Parliament in 1765, and almost immediately made his mark. He was associated with Rockingham, who, during his short term as Prime Minister, fought hard for purity of administration in a corrupt and intriguing age. Burke never held high office, though his parliamentary career lasted for over thirty years. He had not, indeed, those gifts of discretion and compliance which were essential to a cabinet minister, and would have stood him in better stead than his vast knowledge and powerful eloquence. Burke was the greatest political philosopher who has ever spoken in the House of Commons. But that there was something both tragic and absurd in his public career cannot be denied. Speeches such as Demosthenes and Aristotle might equally have applauded were delivered to a crowd of irreverent squires who hated to be troubled with long views and profound reasons, and who were wise only by a kind of instinct, the inheritance of their class and race. Burke's philosophy was squandered on the very men who needed it most. Goldsmith saw the comedy of the situation and expressed it in a lively couplet on Burke in *Retaliation* :

> Though fraught with all learning, yet straining his throat
> To persuade Tommy Townshend to lend him a vote.

Burke's chief contributions to literature are the speeches and writings of his public career. They cover a space of some thirty years, the earliest of the major ones being *Thought on the Present Discontents* (1770). In this work, Burke utters his faith in the English constitution as established by the Revolution of 1688. He believes in the principles of limited monarchy—" the triple cord which no man can break "—in which sovereign, peers and commons have each a fixed part to play in the government of the realm. When one encroaches on the functions of the other, as the Executive had done ever since the accession of George III, and most flagrantly in the case of Wilkes, the nicely balanced equipoise is upset, authority is lost, and public evils are certain to arise. At this comparatively early date, Burke's style was somewhat dry and severe, but the work is admirable both as a piece of political analysis and as a reasoned statement of the " old " Whig position.

The critical dispute with the American colonies deeply stirred Burke's feelings both as a statesman and as a patriot. He delivered two speeches in Parliament, *On American Taxation* (1774) and *On Conciliation with America* (1775), which a great authority declares to be " the most perfect manual in our literature, for one who approaches the study of public affairs, whether for knowledge, or for practice." The principles of true statesmanship that broad political expediency stands higher than mere legal right, that the friendship of a powerful people is a richer source of revenue than any taxes grudgingly paid, that an indictment cannot be drawn up against a whole nation, that " force is not an odious, but a feeble instrument," are expressed in these speeches with a fire of conviction and illustrated with a wealth of allusion which the lapse of a century has neither cooled nor dulled. It is needless to praise their wisdom after the quotation from Lord Morley. How much of the spirit of these speeches has illumined and still illumines the best political thought of our country, no student of history or of public affairs can fail to see.

The occasion of Burke's greatest work was the outbreak of the French Revolution. It matters comparatively little that his attitude to this event was partly determined by imperfect information, by prejudice, and by alarm. The misjudgments count for little against the profound verities. As Hazlitt well remarked, " In arriving at one error he discovered a hundred truths." The *Reflections on the French Revolution* (1790) may give a distorted view of a historical event, but by its insight into the foundations of human society, the work is one of the greatest philosophical essays in the language. In it, the deepest lessons of history are opposed to the men who would destroy in a moment the labour of ages. To Burke the structure of society was not a thing which could be grasped by the average intelligent man of a single generation. It was a " great, mysterious incorporation," the work of superhuman wisdom. Men can only attain the perfection of their nature in civil society : the Being, therefore, who had decreed the progress of the race, had decreed the State. " He who had willed the end (man's perfection) had willed the means." To the plausible philosphers—" sophisters and calculators," as he calls them—who spoke and acted as if society were but a machine which could be taken to pieces and put together, Burke replies that it is a living thing, which overshadows many generations of men and binds together past, present and future :

Our political system is placed in a just correspondence and symmetry with the order of the world, and with the mode of existence decreed to a permanent body composed of transitory parts ; wherein, by the disposition of a stupendous wisdom, moulding together the great mysterious incorporation of the human race, the whole, at one time, is never old, or middle-aged, or young, but, in a condition of unchangeable constancy, moves on through all the varied tenor of perpetual decay, fall, renovation, and progression. Thus, by preserving the method of nature in the conduct of the state, in what we improve we are never wholly new ; in what we retain, we are never wholly obsolete.

Nor will Burke admit any but the highest conceptions of man and of the state. In every age when the foundations of society are discussed by the multitude, there will always be men prepared to prove that the nobler parts of our nature—religion, virtue, affection, art—are nothing but excrescences on our real humanity. Such theories Burke sweeps aside in a moment. " Art is man's nature," he affirms, and he proceeds boldly to defend those many acts of duty, affection and courtesy which it may be are the result of " prejudice," but of a prejudice grounded upon true instinct, and wiser than the sophisms which would destroy them. And just as man's higher nature is his real nature, it is right, Burke says, that the state should embrace and assist our loftiest ideals :

Society is indeed a contract. Subordinate contracts for objects of mere occasional interest may be dissolved at pleasure —but the state ought not to be considered nothing better than a partnership agreement in a trade of pepper and coffee, calico or tobacco, or some other such low concern, to be taken up for a little temporary interest, and to be dissolved by the fancy of the parties. It is to be looked on with other reverence ; because it is not a partnership in things subservient only to the gross animal existence of a temporary and perishable nature. It is a partnership in all science ; a partnership in all art ; a partnership in every virtue, and in all perfection. As the ends of such a partnership cannot be obtained in many generations, it becomes a partnership not only between those who are living, but between those who are living, those who are dead, and those who are to be born.

The tone of the *Reflections* differs widely from the reasoned moderation of the earlier speeches, but in imaginative vision the later work is even more striking. As pure literature, too, it must stand higher, for however great is the wisdom of the American addresses, it was the French Revolution that brought out the poetry of Burke's nature. As the Revolution proceeded, and the signs, including the Napoleonic Wars, became more menacing, Burke hardened his heart against hope. He had prophesied that the convulsion of French affairs would end in a military dictatorship, and he foresaw that England would be singled out as the grand foe. These facts must be borne in mind as one notes the growing violence of Burke's later writings, especially the *Thoughts on the Prospect of Peace with the Regicide Directory*. His power of splendid rhetoric, however, did not forsake him. Burke was a supreme master of the oratorical paragraph, in which rhythm, imagery and allusion blend together in a harmony scarcely less splendid than that of the great verse paragraphs of Milton. A fine instance of his art is the famous outburst in the *French Revolution* on the departed age of chivalry. Equally striking, and even bolder in its union of magnificent imagery with bitter scorn, is the culminating paragraph of the *Letter to a Noble Lord*, in which Burke vindicates the British monarchy against the oligarchs at home and the levellers abroad :

Such are *their* ideas ; such *their* religion, and such *their* law. But as to *our* country and *our* race, as long as the well-compacted structure of our Church and State, the sanctuary, the holy of holies of that ancient law, defended by reverence, defended by power, a fortress at once and a temple, shall stand inviolate on the brow of the British Sion—as long as the British monarchy, not more limited than fenced by the orders of the state, shall, like the proud Keep of Windsor, rising in the majesty of proportion, and girt with the double belt of its kindred and coeval towers, as long as this awful structure shall oversee and guard the subject land—so long the mounds and dykes of the low, fat, Bedford level will have nothing to fear from all the pickaxes of all the levellers of France. As long as our sovereign lord the king, and his faithful subjects, the lords and commons of this realm—the triple cord, which no man can break ; the solemn, sworn, constitutional frank-pledge of this nation ; the firm guarantees of each others' being, and each others' rights ; the joint and several securities, each in its place and order, for every kind and every quality of property and of dignity :—as long as these endure, so long the Duke of Bedford is safe : and we are all safe together—the high from the blights of envy and the spoliations of rapacity ; the low from the iron hand of oppression and the insolent spurn of contempt. Amen ! and so be it : and so it will be,

> Dum domus Æneæ Capitoli immobile saxum
> Accolet ; imperiumque pater Romanus habebit.

V

The most striking features in the prose literature of the eighteenth century were clearness of style and a habit of generalisation. It was an age in which philosophers abounded, for a great writer had, to all appearances, made philosophy easy. John Locke, the author of *An Essay concerning Human Understanding* (1690), and the founder of an important school of English thought, wrote on the most abstruse subjects in a style founded on the simplest and commonest words. His successors, Berkeley and Hume, maintained this alliance between philosophy and literature, and thus helped to give metaphysical principles a place in the thoughts of ordinary educated men and women. It seemed easy to use the language of Locke and Berkeley, and to catch their habit of generalisation, though perhaps the metaphysicians of the drawing-room did not contribute to serious thought much more than the unfortunate Soame Jenyns, on whom Dr. Johnson poured such scorn. None the less, the philosophical habit, good or bad, pervaded almost every region of thought. It was an age of "enlightenment," and men turned their skill in analysis upon every subject, confident in their power to banish all mystery from the world. Many leaders of religion allied themselves with the movement, and studied to demonstrate the truths of Christianity by rational evidence.

It was in the atmosphere of "enlightenment" that Edward Gibbon, the greatest historian of the century, was brought up. He was born in 1737, and was sent first to Westminster, then to Magdalen College, Oxford. The picture, in his *Autobiography*, of the University as yet unreformed and at ease, and his descripton of the Fellows with "their dull and deep potations," are among his best-known passages of prose. Gibbon was taught nothing at Oxford, but he had already acquired the faculty of teaching himself, and by his wide reading was unconsciously preparing himself for the great task before him. The chief part of his life was uneventful, for it was occupied by the labour of composition. But his career was not quite devoid of romantic episodes. When a youth, he was converted to Roman Catholicism; but by his father's arrangement he was sent to Lausanne, where a Swiss pastor successfully performed the task of re-conversion. A few years later, he fell in love. His father again intervened, and again overcame opposition. "I sighed as a lover," writes Gibbon sententiously, "but obeyed as a son." For some years after his majority Gibbon pursued the study of literature, but it was not until 1764, as he was wandering among the ruins of the Forum, that he conceived the plan of relating the downfall of the Roman Empire.

Everything conspired to help him in the fulfilment of his idea. He had sufficient means, good health, an equable temperament, a prodigious memory and a wide knowledge of classical and modern literature. He settled down to his immense task, writing first in London, then at Lausanne, and within six years of his death the history was complete. The first volume was published in 1776, the last in 1788. There is something that strikes the imagination in the simply-planned career of this " enlightened " man. Sceptic and rationalist though he was, he has contrived to cast a glow of romance over the four or five capital events of his life ; and the chief of all—the completion of his great work—is described by himself with a simplicity and restraint which are most memorable :

It was on the day, or rather the night, of the 27th of June, 1787, between the hours of eleven and twelve, that I wrote the last lines of the last page in a summer-house in my garden. After laying down my pen I took several turns in a *berceau*, or covered walk of acacias, which commands a prospect of the country, the lake, and the mountains. The air was temperate, the sky was serene, the silver orb of the moon was reflected from the waters, and all Nature was silent. I will not dissemble the first emotions of joy on the recovery of my freedom, and perhaps the establishment of my fame. But my pride was soon humbled, and a sober melancholy was spread over my mind by the idea that I had taken my everlasting leave of an old and agreeable companion, and that, whatsoever might be the future date of my history, the life of the historian must be short and precarious.

The *Decline and Fall of the Roman Empire* is one of the masterpieces of historical literature. Not only is its greatness as a work of art indisputable, but its authority as a history remains, in essentials, to this day. Gibbon begins his narrative proper at the reign of Commodus, and follows the fortunes of the Empire, first as an undivided whole, later as an Eastern State, to the fall of Constantinople in 1453. His subject is the revolution of a world-order. It involves the destinies not of the Roman people only, but of Germany, Africa, Arabia, Persia, and it em-

braces matters of such vast import as the rise of the
Christian Church and of Mohammedanism, the barbarian
invasions and the Crusades. For an age of dissolving
civilization and slowly re-emerging order, Gibbon's
spacious and stately style was admirable. His subject
is likely to remain one which most persons will be satisfied
to study in broad outline, but this is not the only reason
why his work will continue to be read. Gibbon's style
gives distinction to the least attractive parts of his story,
but when he is in his element he writes with extraordinary
gusto, and the rolling periods and elaborate antitheses
become filled with life. Gibbon highly relished his subject. The citizen of a free aristocratic empire, the enlightened philosopher proud of his intellectual liberty,
loved to paint in condescending words a picture of decadence or superstition. The following paragraph on the
son of Marcus Aurelius is a good illustration of the
historian's " immortal affectation " of style :

Elated with these praises, which gradually extinguished the
innate sense of shame, Commodus resolved to exhibit before
the eyes of the Roman people, those exercises which till then
he had decently confined within the walls of his palace and to
the presence of a few favourites. On the appointed day the
various motives of flattery, fear, and curiosity, attracted to the
amphitheatre an innumerable multitude of spectators ; and
some degree of applause was deservedly bestowed on the
uncommon skill of the Imperial performer. Whether he
aimed at the head or heart of the animal, the wound was alike
certain and mortal. With arrows, whose point was shaped
into the form of a crescent, Commodus often intercepted the
rapid career and cut asunder the long bony neck of the ostrich.
A panther was let loose ; and the archer waited till he had
leaped upon a trembling malefactor. In the same instant the
shaft flew, the beast dropt dead, and the man remained unhurt.
The dens of the amphitheatre disgorged at once a hundred
lions ; a hundred darts from the unerring hand of Commodus
laid them dead as they ran raging round the Arena. Neither
the huge bulk of the elephant nor the scaly hide of the rhino-
ceros could defend them from his stroke. Æthiopia and India
yielded their most extraordinary productions ; and several

animals were slain in the amphitheatre which had been seen only in the representations of art, or perhaps of fancy. In all these exhibitions, the surest precautions were used to protect the person of the Roman Hercules from the desperate spring of any savage who might possibly disregard the dignity of the emperor and the sanctity of the god.

CHAPTER XIII

THE EIGHTEENTH CENTURY

LATER POETS

" The languid strings do scarcely move,
  The sound is forced, the notes are few."

So wrote William Blake towards the end of the eighteenth
century. Poetry was not, indeed, in so desperate a case
as he imagined, but if he was thinking of the spirit of the
age and its resistance to new inspiration, he was justly
despondent. The way of the reformer and enthusiast
was certainly hard. A strong phalanx of official criticism
and official poetry stood ready to defend its position
against the disunited attacks of light skirmishers. All
the prestige was on one side. Dryden and Pope were
held to be the legitimate successors of the great classical
authors, and most writers were unwilling to deviate
from a pattern laid down, it was said, once and for all.
Simplicity and naturalness were difficult in an age
convinced that the greatest poetry was always " noble "
and " elevated." Yet men were dissatisfied. Some
indulged in a kind of intellectual truancy among old
ballads, mediæval ruins, and wild landscapes. But the
love of these things was admitted to be but the revolt of
fancy against reason, and it was not until the time of
Wordsworth that the cause of Nature against Tradition
was fairly fought and won. In the meantime, however,
several poets were born who, though not able to effect a
revolution in literature, were strong enough to follow their
own instinct. The genius of Burns and Blake was a force

that could not be repressed or tutored : both were poets who refused " to set their hearts to school."

I

To find new subjects for song, new forms of feeling, new measures for verse, and a fresher poetic language was the desire of many men who lived under the chilling shadow of the old tradition. It was from our own poetic past that the innovators first found the light to lead them to new paths. Many of our older poets were both neglected as authors and despised as models. The Middle Ages were held in special contempt, and though Shakespeare was at the height of his popularity, the earlier Elizabethans were generally ignored as " barbarous " and " Gothic." Spenser, however, was an exception, and there were always some men who took delight in *The Faerie Queene*. About the middle of the century, several writers began to imitate Spenser's stanza and language, and though some produced mere parodies, a few recaptured much of the poet's real spirit. The best of the neo-Spenserians was James Thomson,[1] whose *Castle of Indolence* (1748) must have given a pleasant shock of surprise to men of original taste. A single stanza will show that the work was more than a literary archaism :

> Full in the passage of the vale above,
> A sable, silent, solemn forest stood,
> Where naught but shadowy forms were seen to move,
> As Idless fancied in her dreaming mood.
> And up the hills, on either side, a wood
> Of blackening pines, aye waving to and fro,
> Sent forth a sleepy horror through the blood ;
> And where this valley winded out, below,
> The murmuring main was heard, and scarcely heard, to flow.

The imitations of Spenser were signs of the times. Many men were turning to the architecture, the poetry and the history of the Middle Ages as a means of escape from the frigidity of classicism. Several distinguished writers, such as Horace Walpole and Thomas Gray, were

[1] See also p. 193.

known as connoisseurs in things mediæval, and an enthusiastic though somewhat foolish craze for Gothic architecture was appearing at the same time. The publication in 1765 of Bishop Percy's *Reliques of Ancient English Poetry* produced a great effect. Many people learnt for the first time that an old ballad or a mediæval love-song might appeal to them more directly than the balanced verses which critics were so loud in praising. Imitation ballads soon began to make their appearance, and though Dr. Johnson did all he could by parody and ridicule to check the cult of simplicity (David Garrick himself was a victim), the seed was sown, and within thirty years the *Lyrical Ballads* of Wordsworth and Coleridge were published—the signal or prelude of a poetical revolution.

No one in the century, however, steeped himself so deeply in the spirit of the Middle Ages as the unfortunate boy-poet, Thomas Chatterton. Born in 1752 under the shadow of St. Mary Redcliffe Church at Bristol, and accustomed to pore over the illuminated manuscripts of the muniment room, he acquired a familiarity with the language of the Middle Ages which enabled him to write with ease in a kind of bastard Old English which is often full of a quaint charm. His Chaucerian dictionary and his knowledge of mediæval handwriting made it easy enough to forge some "original manuscripts" of the *Rowley Poems* (really his own composition). He had, meantime, gone up to London to try his fortune, and ultimately, no doubt, would have made a name; but after a series of disappointments he lost hope and took poison, at the age of eighteen.

Chatterton died too young to produce any poetry of great worth. He seems to have had little enough to say, though he created an original style. His best pieces, such as the *Death-Song of Ælla*, have rhythmical and verbal beauty, though not much beside. But historically, Chatterton's importance is considerable. His passionate love of mediæval legend and antique English anticipated the great broadening of taste which took place in the following century. To poets and scholars alike, to Coleridge and Keats, to Rossetti and Morris, the Middle Ages were a source of inexhaustible delight, and to this day the age of Dante and Chaucer continues to enrich our art and our thought. The boy of eighteen who discovered by instinct this new field for the imagination must always be accounted a genius.

II

Just at the time when men were revealing the charm of old words and simple measures, another poet arose to reveal the latent power and the rugged beauty of the Northern English, or, as it is commonly called, the Scottish dialect. Since the time of Dunbar and the other northern Chaucerians, the literature of Scotland had been rather provincial than national. Various writers both of prose and verse had used the native dialect, but they had produced little of enduring literary value. The best Scottish poet of the early eighteenth century, James Thomson, belongs to the purely English tradition, and it would have seemed odd indeed to him to model himself on the obscure poets of his native country rather than on Milton and Spenser. The genius of Burns put the dialect of Scotland on an entirely different footing. He familiarised English readers with scores of words which, odd and puzzling though many were, were accepted for the sake of their rude expressive power. Since the time of Burns, the best Scottish authors have been read over the whole kingdom, and never more eagerly than when most zealously national. From the end of the eighteenth century we may note an awakening interest in local speech and manners—an interest not merely tolerant or amused, but founded on a recognition that the dialect of a peasant may be as tragic or as pathetic as the most stately speeches declaimed by Garrick or Mrs. Siddons.

Robert Burns was the son of a small Ayrshire farmer, and was born in 1759. Nearly his whole life was spent in the Western Lowlands, a district where the covenanting spirit had been all-powerful, and still exacted a rigid observance of religious and moral forms. Burns saw the strength as well as the weakness of the dour, narrow and serious population among whom he lived, but his own nature was cast in a different mould and he was in no danger of becoming one of the " unco guid." He was passionate, impetuous and pleasure-seeking, a warm lover, a good companion, but not his own best friend. He had had something of a literary education, thanks to the generous offices of a young schoolmaster friend, and he soon began to vary the drudgery of farming by writing poems. These quickly acquired great local renown, and Burns was at length induced to try publication. His *Poems, chiefly in the Scottish Dialect* (1786) made him famous. He visited Edinburgh, then the home of a brilliant literary society, and was overwhelmed with attention. Returning to the west, he was constantly dogged by ill-luck, and, eventually, after many losses, gave up farming and accepted a post under the Excise Commission. But intemperance had made him unfit for any regular work, and his last years were degraded and miserable. He died at the age of thirty-seven.

Burns was, above all, a lyrical poet. By his songs he is the national poet of Scotland, but their fire and their elemental passion give them also a unique place in the literature of Britain. There can be no better test of Burns's originality than to read two poems which the editor of the *Golden Treasury* has, with great judgment (as Arnold points out), put in juxtaposition. Goldsmith's " When Lovely Woman Stoops to Folly " is followed by Burns's " Ye Banks and Braes o' bonnie Doon." No words could bring out so well the gulf which separates the two poets. The exquisite artifice of Goldsmith is in one world, the human cry straight from the heart in another. When Burns composed in the polite manner of the eighteenth century he was provincial and vulgar. But his true style was developed out of his practice in finding new words for old national airs. It is in such poems as *Auld Lang Syne, Mary Morison, John Anderson My Jo,* that Burns's memory lives best. Above all, it is his serious love-songs which, in Hazlitt's phrase, " take the deepest and most lasting hold of the mind."

These simple lyrics, however, do not give the full measure of Burns's power. In narrative, in description, in satire, he is as effective as in pure song. The creature of the earth, the ways and manners of men, move him to pity or derision, and he is never more original than in extracting a grim humour or a tender pathos from Scotch peasant life. Nothing before had been written quite like the little poem *To a Mouse*, which has all the finality of true art. In the language and in the stanza of such pieces, Burns was, in fact, the inheritor of a long tradition : but he lifted the stiff, angular Scottish manner out of the provincial rut on to the level of national poetry. Doubtless, many of his pieces are no better than those of the Fergussons and Ramsays who preceded him, but the worth of the best is unmistakable. The grimness of *Death and Doctor Horn Book*, the bizarre mixture of moods in the *Address to the Deil*, and the boisterous satire of *The Holy Fair*, are qualities which conquer the reader at once. For English people, Burns created a new taste. He gave the raciest words, the most daring idioms of his nation a piquantly pleasing flavour, and there are many readers who like Burns best when he gives the reins to his wildest fancies. Certainly he was never more truly creative than in the mad devilry of *Tam o' Shanter*.

III

The character of William Blake (1757–1827), mystic, poet and painter, was one which no country but England could have produced. At first sight, one is tempted to put this extraordinary man in a class by himself ; yet he was not without spiritual affinities in English history. He has something in common with the Quakers and Antinomians of the seventeenth century, and in our own time many men have been strongly attracted by his imaginative boldness and mystical vision. His uneventful life passed between London and Sussex, is meaningless as a clue to his work, for to Blake most of the things which the world calls real had no significant reality whatever. He was a disciple of the Swedish mystic Swedenborg, and inspired by him, built up an esoteric religion which he expounded symbolically in a number of Prophetic Books. These works contain passages of great literary power, but they are too chaotic in form to be regarded as masterpieces of poetry. Blake's genius expressed itself better in his paintings and in his illustrations to various poems, such as the *Divine Comedy* and the Book of Job. Utterly without convention, his art has the power of giving form to phantasmal beings which are superhuman in their force and their simplicity. To Blake, the world of imagination was all in all—a fact which gives the measure both of his strength and of his weakness.

As a poet, Blake has many styles, ranging from the borders of the conventional to the farthest limits of the eccentric. His first volume of lyrics, *Poetical Sketches* (1783), shows him experimenting in several manners. The songs, "My silks and fine array" and "Memory, hither come" are among the most charming products of the Elizabethan revival. In the reflective lyric *To the Muses*, he writes with the chastened beauty of language which is the best feature of his age. But in the *Mad Song* the irregular rhythm and fantastic imagery foreshadow those wild flights of later years which can only be appreciated by a kindred spirit. Blake's next two volumes, *Songs of Innocence* (1789) and *Songs of Experience* (1794), contain the bulk of his good lyrics, as well as others which are documents in the history of his mind rather than treasures of our literature. Blake had now found his own style, which, though unique and often eccentric, is also really original. The poem, "Tiger! tiger! burning bright," a natural expression of childlike wonder at creation, makes an instant and unforgettable impression; and the best of the simpler poems, such as "Piping down the valleys wild" and "Little Lamb, who made thee?" have an undeniable charm. Blake's power of moral vision inspires verses so original that one may overlook the negligent expression with which he is too often satisfied. At times his work has real greatness; and it is curiously significant that this man, who of all English poets trod the most solitary path, should have written the poem which, through its soaring idealism, has deservedly become a second and nobler National Anthem. The two stanzas of *Jerusalem* show Blake's power as a prophet; to illustrate his purely lyrical gift one cannot do better than quote a short poem from the Rossetti MS.:

> Never seek to tell thy love,
>> Love that never told can be;
> For the gentle wind does move
>> Silently, invisibly.
>
> I told my love, I told my love,
>> I told her all my heart;
> Trembling, cold, in ghastly fears,
>> Ah! she doth depart.
>
> Soon as she was gone from me,
>> A traveller came by,
> Silently, invisibly:
>> He took her with a sigh.

A man so exclusively guided by the inward light as Blake could not be fully appreciated in his own generation. Nor can one expect that his critical attitude should have much immediate relation with literary history. He expressed himself clearly, however, on the classical tradition. " We do not want either Greek or Roman models if we are but just and true to our own Imaginations," he writes in the Preface to *Milton*. That Blake, with all his individualism, owed much to native writers is evident from a hundred signs, but nothing shows it more forcibly than his critical remarks, admirable in their sympathy and truth, on that most English of poems the *Prologue to the Canterbury Tales*.

IV

In many respects, the poetry of George Crabbe (1754–1832) presents a complete contrast to that of Blake; and the two men might almost be chosen to illustrate the opposite types of conservative and revolutionary. The man who was befriended by Burke and praised by Jeffrey in the *Edinburgh Review* might seem free enough from all taint of iconoclasm; and the poet who clung to the heroic couplet after Wordsworth and Coleridge had finished their best work would appear to be excluded from the list of innovators. Nor was Crabbe, in any of the superficial senses of the word, at all original. He accepted without demur the " official " style of the eighteenth century, and he is, indeed, nearer to the tradition of Pope than either Goldsmith or Cowper. In Crabbe's work, however, all this is totally unimportant. His language and technique count for nothing. If he is read at all, it is for the sincerity of his observation, for his unfailing loyalty to truth. Crabbe was a lifelong student of English rustic life, especially those aspects of it which poets had for long either ignored or idealised.

> I paint the Cot,
> As Truth will paint it, and as Bards will not,

he says in *The Village*; and he shows us, with unwavering fidelity, all the unlovelier side of country life, its sombreness and also its meanness. Yet there is much that is vital in Crabbe's poetry, and its vitality springs straight from the English soil. Byron's eulogy, " Nature's sternest painter, yet the best," he scarcely deserves. It is by his reliance on simple fact that Crabbe became a poet; and though often prosaic in this reliance, he well deserves a place among those who are held to have led the " return to Nature."

After a youth of struggle, Crabbe became known to Burke, and through his interest was made curate of Aldeburgh in 1781. From 1783 till his death he occupied a succession of livings, in the Midlands and in the West, and for the greater part of his life he wrote voluminously. The chief of his early poems were *The Library*, *The Village* and *The Newspaper*, the last of which was published in 1785. Then came a long silence, and the critics regarded

Crabbe as a poet whose work was done. In 1807, how-ever, he reappeared with *The Parish Register*, and the poems which followed, *The Borough* (1810) and *Tales in Verse* (1812), contain much of his best work. The record of Crabbe's life suggests that of a clergyman in easy cir-cumstances who took to poetry as a recreation. But the impression is misleading, for the formative years of his life were those he spent on the barren Suffolk coast, as servant in the family of a country doctor, and as surgeon in the small coast town of Aldeburgh. It was then that Crabbe came to know the struggling life of the poor from within, the ways of smuggler and poacher, the hard-headed sense of the small farmer, the monotonous look of the Suffolk lanes, and the dreary mud-stretches of the shore.

Crabbe's earlier poems were discursive and ethical, in the manner dear to his age. *The Village* is analogous to *The Vanity of Human Wishes*, both of them testimonies, from men who know the facts, against an easy optimism. It is, indeed, the unvarying truth of Crabbe's observation that keeps his work alive. He can describe the dreariest scenes in words of sad sincerity which convince, even if they do not please :

> Lo ! where the heath, with withering brake grown o'er,
> Lends the light turf that warms the neighbouring poor ;
> From thence a length of burning sand appears,
> When the thin harvest waves its wither'd ears ;
> Rank weeds, that every art and care defy,
> Reign o'er the land, and rob the blighted rye :
> There thistles stretch their prickly arms afar,
> And to the ragged infant threaten war ;
> There poppies nodding, mock the hope of toil ;
> There the blue bugloss paints the sterile soil.

During Crabbe's long interval of silence, public taste in literature underwent a complete change. It would appear that in these years he tried to bring himself into line with the newer fashions. Certainly he wrote a good deal of prose fiction, though he destroyed it all in despair. But his nature was too stubborn to mould itself anew, and when he re-emerged as an author, it was seen that he had merely developed the talent for narrative verse of which he had given many signs in his earlier poems. All else is unchanged. The memories of the Suffolk coast and the struggling poor remain, though these are now the material for verse narrative. Conservative critics welcomed the return of a poet so eminently sober and sane ; but to the volatile public who were just beginning to intoxicate themselves on the new romance, Crabbe appeared a very humdrum poet. Superficially, they were right. Crabbe is certainly not exciting. Even his humour (as in *The Learned Boy* and *The Preceptor Husband*) is grim, and his tragic tales (as *Resentment* and *Peter Grimes*) deal mostly with dull suffering or sordid cruelty. But time has been kind to Crabbe, and many to-day who care little for the poetic romances of Scott and Byron return to *The Borough* and *Tales of the Hall* with an unfailing appetite. Lovers of realism have delighted in Crabbe's unvarnished truth, and several great men have placed him high among their favourite authors, perhaps for his stable wisdom and a humble acceptance of life, which enable him to tell a plain tale without marring it.

Crabbe's early memories of the Suffolk coast continued to inspire some of his best verse even in his later maturity. Perhaps the strongest of all his descriptions is one in the poem *Peter Grimes*, a sombre story of a fisherman who murdered his apprentices and ended his days in madness. The following lines describe his misery between the crimes and their retribution :

> When tides were neap, and, in the sultry day,
> Through the tall bounding mud-banks made their way,
> Which on each side rose swelling, and below
> The dark warm flood ran silently and slow ;
> There anchoring, Peter chose from man to hide,
> There hang his head, and view the lazy tide
> In its hot slimy channel slowly glide ;
> Where the small eels that left the deeper way
> For the warm shore, within the shallows play ;
> Where gaping mussels, left upon the mud,
> Slope their slow passage to the fallen flood ;—
> Here dull and hopeless he'd lie down and trace
> How sidelong crabs had scrawl'd their crooked race ;

Or sadly listen to the tuneless cry
Of fishing gull or clanging golden-eye;
What time the sea-birds to the marsh would come,
And the loud bittern, from the bull-rush home,
Gave from the salt-ditch side the bellowing boom:
He nursed the feelings these dull scenes produce,
And loved to stop beside the opening sluice;
Where the small stream, confined in narrow bound,
Ran with a dull, unvaried, sadd'ning sound;
Where all, presented to the eye or ear,
Oppress'd the soul with misery, grief, and fear.

CHAPTER XIV

WORDSWORTH AND COLERIDGE

THE year 1789 will always be regarded as one of the land-marks in human history, and the period which closed some twenty-six years later continues to exercise a fascination which the tremendous events of the Great War have not appreciably weakened. History tells no tale more wonderful than that of which the first chapter was the meeting of the Three Estates at Versailles, and the last, the flight of Napoleon from the field of Waterloo. A spirit was abroad which we may recognise in the most diverse characters of that age. The men of 1789, like those of the Renaissance, felt themselves in the dawn of a new era. Napoleon, Beethoven and Wordsworth were alike in this at least, that they resolved to found their work on principles true for all time. That genius could dispense with rules, that Nature was a better guide than precedent, was the faith in which the great men of that age lived and acted. No wonder the young poet who beheld the new spirit in the might of its epiphany acclaimed the vision of

> human nature seeming born again.

The position which England occupied during these critical years naturally affected the outlook of her imaginative writers. The great awakening of literature which was heralded by the *Lyrical Ballads* was not caused by Continental events, though it was, no doubt, quickened by them. The Revolution, after all, was French and not English. Englishmen reacted violently to the stirring events abroad, but as often in alarm as in congratulation. Fox applauded the Revolution, but Burke execrated it.

Time also wrought great changes. In 1789, there were plenty of Englishmen who felt and were not afraid to say that, by casting off her old government, France had set a great example to mankind. In 1806, many had already changed their minds, and of those who thought as before, most were either dispirited or silent. The epoch which began with the Revolution and ended with Napoleon had, indeed, two different effects upon the English mind. It broadened and it intensified. It set up new rights and it strengthened old loyalties. It created new faith in mankind, new desires for human brotherhood, new confidence in individual effort, and it also strengthened the sense of nationality and recalled men to pieties and duties which they had half forgotten. Some of our writers were equally affected by both movements. Wordsworth, Coleridge and Southey, for instance, began their lives as revolutionaries, and ended them as patriots. Shelley, on the other hand, was a democrat from first to last, while Scott was never shaken from his old-fashioned Toryism. Byron, with fewer convictions than any of these men, felt the unrest and turmoil of the time though he scarcely understood its deeper currents : Keats, the latest-born and shortest-lived, was the purest artist, the least distracted of all from devotion to poetry. Among the prose writers, Hazlitt kept his revolutionary faith, mingled with worship of Napoleon, till the end, while Jeffrey, the most powerful of the reviewers, stood firm for Conservatism.

I

William Wordsworth, the first of the new writers, was the son of an attorney living at Cockermouth in Cumberland, and was born in 1770. His childhood was spent under the spell of one of the loveliest regions in the world. The steep fells, secluded dales and silent lakes of Cumberland were in easy reach of Cockermouth, and he grew up

Fostered alike by beauty and by fear.

At Hawkshead, where he was at school, he was in the

heart of the Lake country. With many free hours to dispose of, he boated, skated, and rambled far and wide over the fells. When he left Hawkshead at the age of seventeen, he had sown the seeds of a love of Nature as intense as man ever possessed. His relatives sent him to St. John's College, Cambridge, where he showed a strong disinclination to systematic study, though he read widely on his own account. He was passionate and self-willed, and though not unsocial, he knew that his deeper nature could never grow except in solitude. A turning-point in his career was reached in the summer of 1790, when he set out to visit France with a Cambridge friend. The moment he landed, Wordsworth was carried away by the signs of hope and gladness on every side :

> The senselessness of joy was then sublime!

Crossing France on foot, the two friends penetrated into Switzerland, where Wordsworth's love of mountain scenery revived in all its strength. The memories of the tour were afterwards preserved in one of his early poems, *Descriptive Sketches*. On his return to England, the thought of France haunted him day and night, and in 1791 he was " lured forth " to a second and even more eventful visit. This time, he really committed himself to the revolutionary cause. He attended debates, made close friendships, and if he could have had his way would have thrown in his lot with the Girondin party.

But now events in France took a bad turn, and in 1794 the climax of tyranny was reached in the Reign of Terror. The disappointment of his hopes threw Wordsworth into the deepest despondency. The Revolution had become his religion, and with the failure of the Revolution, the main hope for man seemed to have vanished. Fortunately for Wordsworth, he had two devoted and highly-gifted friends, both of them warmly attached to him, and both firm believers in his poetic future. One was his sister Dorothy, whose love of natural beauty was as tender as her brother's and almost as strong. The two set up house at Racedown in Dorsetshire, and there, by degrees, the poet recovered his joy in the sights and sounds of the open air; and in these simple pleasures found a beginning of new hopes and new purposes. About the same time he met Samuel Taylor Coleridge, then at the height of his powers, and already an admirer of Wordsworth, whose early poems he had read. The breadth of Coleridge's philosophical ideas, and his glowing schemes for rebuilding thought and reviving poetry gave Wordsworth just the stimulus he needed. One day, the two friends set off on a walking-tour over the Quantock Hills, and the plan was proposed of collaborating to bring out a small volume of poems. Both had already published verse, but neither had found his characteristic manner. They had been groping in the twilight; now they suddenly emerged into full day. The fruit of the expedition was *Lyrical Ballads* (1798), a volume to which Coleridge made the best single contribution (*The Ancient Mariner*), though Wordsworth's pieces were more numerous. The little collection was far from perfect, but the originality of both writers was beyond dispute.

Wordsworth had now found his true path. He had become the poet of Nature; and henceforth he was to show how the world of earth and sky can feed the poet's mind with passions purer and scarcely less intense than those created by the sight of great towns and the complex life of civilization. He was to become the poet of men and women too, but of men living under the eye and in the presence of Nature. For such poetry, a simple home in some little community among his own lakes and mountains was all that Wordsworth needed, and, by a stroke of miraculous good fortune, the means were provided. A legacy left by an admirer enabled Wordsworth and his sister to settle at Dove Cottage, Grasmere, and this valley, with its neighbourhood, became their home for the rest of the poet's long life. In 1807, the best of his shorter works appeared in a book entitled *Poems in Two Volumes*, and in 1814 he published *The Excursion*. By this time his best work was already done, and though he continued to compose, much of his later verse is uninspired and even conventional. His great autobiographical poem, *The Prelude*, was finished in 1806, but Wordsworth continued to revise it at intervals, and it was not published until 1850, the year of his death. During his early and middle life, the poet's work was derided by most of the reviews and ignored by the public; but he had a few discerning admirers of great ability. By degrees, opinion completely changed. His appointment to the Laureateship in 1842 was the sign of his victory. Since his death, Wordsworth's greatness has been recognised more and more clearly, not in England only, but over much of the civilized world.

II

The most casual reader of Wordsworth cannot fail to be struck by his originality. He stands before us in all the simplicity of the pure poetic character. Most great poets, hitherto, had made some apparent concession to the world in their choice of subject. Even Milton, the most independent of men, had not thought of setting his judgment against that of educated opinion: he deliberately sought for the grandest theme, " Things unattempted yet in prose or rhyme." Wordsworth, however, was resolved to stand or fall by his poetic merits alone. To the prestige of the past, to the prosaic judgments of the ordinary man, to the subtle aid of literary convention, he was determined to owe nothing. It is not surprising that the man who stood in awe before a child, or a mountain shepherd, or an old leech-gatherer, should have outraged a generation of critics proudly conscious of their high civilization. To most men, the simplicity of Wordsworth's poetry seemed like an affront. Even so discerning a reader as Hazlitt admitted that he must be either inspired or mad.

Much of Wordsworth's verse is still a stumbling-block to many readers, and there is no poet whose work gains so much by a wise selection. But when all possible deductions have been made, the quantity of first-rate poetry remaining is still abundant. In his lyrics, above all, Wordsworth's greatness is apparent. If in poetry we look for the rightness of phrase that admits of no question, the naturalness so absolute that a poem once read becomes in a moment a familiar friend, Wordsworth, at his best, has no superior. Language can scarcely be at once more simple and more full of feeling than in these stanzas from one of the " Lucy poems " :

> Three years she grew in sun and shower,
> Then Nature said, " A lovelier flower
>   On earth was never sown ;
> This child I to myself will take ;
> She shall be mine, and I will make
>   A lady of my own.
>
> " She shall be sportive as the fawn
> That wild with glee across the lawn
>   Or up the mountain springs ;
> And hers shall be the breathing balm,
> And hers the silence and the calm
>   Of mute insensate things.
>
> " The stars of midnight shall be dear
> To her ; and she shall lean her ear
>   In many a secret place
> Where rivulets dance their wayward round,
> And beauty born of murmuring sound
>   Shall pass into her face."
>
> Thus Nature spake—The work was done,—
> How soon my Lucy's race was run !
>   She died, and left to me
> This heath, this calm, and quiet scene,
> The memory of what has been,
>   And never more will be.

The variety of Wordsworth's lyrical verse is astonishing. He can stir the deepest emotions by the simplest means, but he is master, too, of all the nobler resources of our language. The sonnet, with its strict curtailment of " too much liberty," suited him perfectly, and he followed Milton's example of extending the use of the form to all the moods of a poet's mind. The best of Wordsworth's sonnets are among the greatest of English lyrical poems. Some of the finest, the sonnet *On the Extinction of the Venetian Republic*, the one *To Toussaint l'Ouverture*, the one entitled *London, 1802,* and many others "dedicated to Liberty," help to swell the glory of the volumes of 1807. But Wordsworth kept his faculty for writing fine sonnets till almost the end of his life. The indifferent series on the River Duddon is redeemed by the splendid *Afterthought,* and as late as 1833 he could write the beautiful sonnet beginning, " Most sweet it is with unuplifted eyes." It is in the sonnets and the odes that the grander side of Wordsworth's nature is most visible. No English writer of the last two centuries can equal him in that austere spiritual beauty which criticism calls " the sublime." The grandeur and awe of his own mountains informs those verses of " sinewy strength " so justly admired by Coleridge, and the *Ode to Duty* raises thought to the heavens themselves. The crown of Wordsworth's lyrical work is, no doubt, the *Ode on the Intimations of Immortality,* where the elevation of the style is softened by a charm of rhythm which he did not often achieve. But in the *Ode* Wordsworth is celebrating one of his most cherished beliefs, that our earliest intuitions are the truest, and that the lot of those is happy whose maturity is not severed from their childhood :

> Hence, in a season of calm weather,
> Though inland far we be,
> Our souls have sight of that immortal sea
> Which brought us hither,
> Can in a moment travel thither,
> And see the children sport upon the shore,
> And hear the mighty waters rolling evermore.

III

But Wordsworth was more than a lyrical poet; he justly claims to be the poet of Man, of Nature, and of Human Life. Though limited in his view of humanity, he has revealed some of the deepest springs of life; and he explored anew some of the fundamental relations of men and women to each other and to the world around them. That Wordsworth was self-centred is true to this extent, that other men interested him chiefly as they partook of the poetic character. But this is only half the truth, for poets, in Wordsworth's sense, were not rare—at least among the mountains and dales which alone he professed to know. The boy of Winander, who " blew mimic hootings to the silent owls " and then listened for their reply was, Wordsworth would have us believe, not wholly exceptional in his sudden awakening to the beauty of Nature :

> Then sometimes, in that silence, while he hung
> Listening, a gentle shock of mild surprise
> Has carried far into his heart the voice
> Of mountain torrents ; or the visible scene
> Would enter unawares into his mind
> With all its solemn imagery, its rocks,
> Its woods, and that uncertain heaven received
> Into the bosom of the steady lake.

Nor is the affection of *The Brothers*, or the paternal love of *Michael*, in any way out of the course of Nature. " These are the cords of man," Wordsworth seems to say ; and in the simple pieties of rustic life he finds a surer foundation for faith in mankind than in the dazzling hopes created by the French Revolution. And though civilized society is often a sorry spectacle, in solitude men may be sublime. Wordsworth loves to show his characters ennobled by some overwhelming emotion, like the mother in *The Affliction of Margaret* ——, or as lonely figures dwarfed in body but magnified in spirit by the grandeur of Nature, like the leech-gatherer in *Resolution and Independence*. The old man and his surroundings make a single picture :

> As a huge stone is sometimes seen to lie
> Couched on the bald top of an eminence ;
> Wonder to all who do the same espy,
> By what means it could thither come, and whence ;
> So that it seems a thing endued with sense :
> Like a sea-beast crawled forth, that on a shelf
> Of rock or sand reposeth, there to sun itself ;
>
> Such seemed this Man, not all alive nor dead,
> Nor all asleep—in his extreme old age :
> His body was bent double, feet and head
> Coming together in life's pilgrimage ;

As if some dire constraint of pain, or rage
Of sickness felt by him in times long past,
A more than human weight upon his frame had cast.

Himself he propped, limbs, body, and pale face,
Upon a long grey staff of shaven wood :
And, still as I drew near with gentle pace,
Upon the margin of that moorish flood
Motionless as a cloud the old Man stood,
That heareth not the loud winds when they call ;
And moveth all together, if it move at all.

Just as Man and Nature in this poem form a harmony, so it is the harmony of his own spirit with the universe that is the theme of Wordsworth's greatest Nature-poems. It is this that gives such intense spirituality to the *Lines written above Tintern Abbey*, to *Yew-Trees*, and to the Lines on the Simplon Pass,[1] where sky and crag, wind and waterfall merge into an overwhelming unity :

Tumult and peace, the darkness and the light—
Were all like workings of one mind, the features
Of the same face, blossoms upon one tree,
Characters of the great Apocalypse,
The types and symbols of Eternity,
Of first, and last, and midst, and without end.

IV

Wordsworth gave much thought to the theory of poetry, and though his literary sympathies were narrow, his criticisms are well worth reading for the light they throw on his own aims and attitude. It is in the *Preface* to the *Lyrical Ballads* that he explains his views most fully. He presented to the world a reasoned defence of both the subjects and the style of his poetry. By virtue of its eloquence and depth of thought the *Preface* is a memorable work, though on certain points palpably one-sided.

As a critic, Wordsworth's principal aim was to reassert the independence of the poet. Poetry, like the poet himself, is the creation of Nature rather than of learning or criticism. It is the innate, not the acquired qualities that

[1] In *The Prelude*.

are important; and if this now sounds a platitude, it is so, largely because Wordsworth's *Preface* and his example have achieved their object. A Poet, he says, is " a man . . . endowed with more lively sensibility, more enthusiasm and tenderness, who has a greater knowledge of human nature, and a more comprehensive soul, than are supposed to be common among mankind." This truth, when recognised, struck down the idol of literary convention which had been blindly worshipped for so long. But when Wordsworth says, " Poetry is the spontaneous overflow of powerful feelings," one feels that he is approaching debatable ground. One cannot help comparing it with the motto of Keats : " Easy composition, laborious correction." It is, however, in speaking of poetic language that Wordsworth most evidently exaggerates his case. So zealous is he for purity of diction, so opposed to the " gaudiness and inane phraseology " then often affected, that he will allow poetry no claim to a vocabulary of its own. " There neither is, nor can be," he says, " any *essential* difference between the language of prose and metrical composition." It was easy for Coleridge to show the fallacy of this statement by simply referring to Wordsworth's own practice in nearly all his better poems.

Yet Wordsworth was more right than wrong, and he effectively put an end to the use of " false poetic diction," the worst of all the diseases which have afflicted English poetry. To address the sun as " rosy Phœbus " or to call fish the " finny prey " is now regarded as at best a rather poor witticism. But for many years such language had passed current as " noble " and " elevated," and those who employed it fondly conceived themselves to be the poetic descendants of Milton.

v

In the personality of Samuel Taylor Coleridge there is so much that is fascinating that it is difficult not to linger over his life. Yet Coleridge's career was too uncertain and too broken to have such significance for literary history as Wordsworth's. As a man, Coleridge is the more interesting of the two, but he lacked Wordsworth's strength of purpose, and he was never in the same way a "dedicated spirit." A sentence from the epitaph written by himself confesses the melancholy truth :

> Beneath this sod
> A poet lies, or *that which once seem'd he.*

By the time he was thirty, he had written all his best poetry and was already lamenting his loss of the "shaping spirit of Imagination." He lived more than thirty years longer, always a profound thinker, often a great critic, but never more than a minor poet.

He was born in 1772, the son of a Devonshire clergyman, and even as a small child showed a great fondness for reading. "I became a dreamer," he says, "and acquired indisposition to all bodily activity." After his schooldays at Christ's Hospital (made familiar in one of Lamb's best essays), he went to Jesus College, Cambridge, where his brilliant classical scholarship won him some distinction. But his revolutionary and unorthodox opinions found less favour. He also fell into debt, and for a time played truant from the University, enlisting as a private in the Light Dragoons. He finally left Cambridge without a degree, and went forth into the world as a general reformer of society and a missionary of the Gospel of Truth. His scheme of "Pantisocracy and Aspheterism"—a plan for founding a communistic society of educated men and women in the wilds of America—was preached in 1794, and was typical of the man and the age. But Coleridge's powers of mind and speech raised him far above the level of ordinary theorists, and on several younger men who heard him he made an impression which altered the whole course of their lives. He clearly possessed a marvellous intellectual magnetism. To the censorious Hazlitt, he was "the only man who ever taught him anything." To Wordsworth, he was "the most wonderful man he had ever known."

Coleridge's full poetic strength was not revealed until

1797. He had written a good deal of verse, but not with his full energy, and much of his time had been given to preaching and journalism. He had married in 1795, but between him and his wife there was no real sympathy, and until he met the Wordsworths he was never perfectly understood or appreciated. The complete harmony of mind existing between the three friends made the weeks spent together in Somerset the happiest period of their lives, and to both Coleridge and Wordsworth joy was the best stimulus to poetic creation. *The Ancient Mariner* was finished and *Christabel* begun before the little society broke up. To Coleridge, such days of real achievement never came again. The poetic impulse revisited him for some time to come, and he continued at intervals to embark on magnificent schemes of literature. But the habit of taking opium, which he had acquired some years before, began to grow upon him, and to a nature which at best was one of " indolence, capable of energies," nothing could be more disastrous. He wandered from place to place, ill and self-reproachful, and at last got involved in a miserable quarrel with Wordsworth. Still, however, his wonderful powers continued to find new admirers, and his public lectures in London in 1811 were, in Byron's phrase, " a sort of rage." A few years later, he published his *Biographia Literaria*, which, amid certain garrulous pages, contains some of the most suggestive criticism in this or any language. In 1816, Coleridge found what he was seeking— " a physician who will be not only firm but severe in his regimen." Thanks to the care of Dr. Gillman of Highgate, the opium habit was overcome. At Highgate Coleridge continued to live until his death in 1834. He was much visited by literary men, to some of whom he was a kind of oracle. The new schools of theological thought were especially indebted to his teaching. He had long since returned to an orthodoxy based upon the philosophy of Kant, and his influence on the leaders both of Broad Church and High Church thought was far-reaching and profound.

Amid the very small body of great poetry left by Coleridge, *The Rime of the Ancient Mariner* occupies a peculiar position. It is his "one perfect and complete achievement." Few poems in the world have so much the power of an incantation or spell. Leaving the rest of the reader's faculties under a trance, it gives his imagination the experience of a marvellous waking dream. It is in this power of wizardry that Coleridge is unique. There are moments in his other poems, *Christabel* and *Kubla Khan*, when he gives glimpses of even greater potency, but the poet is unable to guide us out of the mysterious world he has created. *The Ancient Mariner* is more than a dream, it is a revelation. As in many great poems, meanings are hinted at which cannot be directly expressed. The torments of the mariner's voyage suggest the experience of a soul separated from humanity :

> Alone, alone, all all alone,
>   Alone on a wide wide sea !
> And never a saint took pity on
>   My soul in agony.

Such an accent of heart-felt suffering raises the poem above the level of mere fantasy. To read *The Ancient Mariner* is to pass through a dream in the midst of life and to find life in the midst of a dream.

In *Christabel* and *Kubla Khan* one must be content with the magic of rhythm and words, but from Coleridge at his best it would be strange to ask for more. From a historical point of view, there was nothing new in the treatment of metre in *Christabel*. But Coleridge made so free a use of "substitution" that he seemed to have discovered a new and delightful form of verse. The "*Christabel* metre" moved both Scott and Byron to enthusiasm, and they strove to imitate it—with a measure of success which brings out by contrast Coleridge's exquisite ear for verse. Other poets are masters of a grander and more varied music, but none has so subtle a sense of haunting and mysterious rhythms. Where, one may ask, do familiar English words seem so new, so strange, and so melodious as in these lines from the beginning of *Christabel*?

> She stole along, she nothing spoke,
>   The sighs she heaved were soft and low,
> And naught was green upon the oak,
>   But moss and rarest mistletoe :
>   She kneels beneath the huge oak tree,
>   And in silence prayeth she.
>
> The lady sprang up suddenly,
>   The lovely lady, Christabel !
> It moaned as near, as near can be,
>   But what it is, she cannot tell.—
>   On the other side it seems to be,
>   Of the huge, broad-breasted, old oak tree.
>
> The night is chill; the forest bare ;
>   Is it the wind that moaneth bleak ?
> There is not wind enough in the air
>   To move away the ringlet curl
> From the lovely lady's cheek—
>   There is not wind enough to twirl
>   The one red leaf, the last of its clan,
>   That dances as often as dance it can,
>   Hanging so light, and hanging so high,
>   On the topmost twig that looks up at the sky.
>
> Hush, beating heart of Christabel !
> Jesu, Maria, shield her well !
>   She folded her arms beneath her cloak,
>   And stole to the other side of the oak.
>   What sees she there ?

Few readers of *Christabel* and *Kubla Khan* can avoid speculating on what Coleridge might have done, had his moral strength been greater. But it may be that the peculiar beauty of his verse owes its very existence to his passive and dreamlike nature. Coleridge, with a resolute will, might have been a better man, but he would not be the Coleridge we know—a poet unmatchable in his own region, a man whose charm survives, unmistakable and unique, in all the records of his life and words.

CHAPTER XV

THE EARLY NINETEENTH CENTURY

THE NOVEL AND THE ESSAY

On the eve of Sir Walter Scott's publication of *Waverley* in 1814, the English novel appeared to have fallen on evil days. No branch of literature is subject to more diseases than the art of fiction. The success of Fielding and Smollett gave the novel popularity, but not all the critical chapters of *Tom Jones* could educate the public in the principles of good novel-writing. Many readers wanted nothing better than to be melted into tears or terrified into hysterics ; and their demands were eagerly met by a generation of writers far inferior to the early novelists. The success of Horace Walpole's " Gothic romance," *The Castle of Otranto* (1764), prepared the way for other works of crime and mystery. Some, such as the best novels of Mrs. Radcliffe and Charles Robert Maturin, had real power ; but the number of absurd stories of this class has thrown a lasting reproach on the Minerva Press and the " Tales of Terror " which issued from it. These novels, however, at least indicate the existence of a strong craving. Readers wanted fiction to open a new world to them, as exciting and strange as their own was flat and familiar. They wanted " romance " —a natural desire, which the satire of Jane Austen and Eaton Stannard Barrett [1] could not destroy. It was Scott's achievement in the next generation to create a better taste and to meet its demands. *The Castle of Otranto* had fantastically foreshadowed the historical novel : *Waverley* and its successors established it as a great literary type.

[1] Author of *The Heroine ; or, Adventures of Cherubina* (1813).

Many of the opportunities which lay before the writer who could combine history with fiction were revealed before Scott began to produce his famous series of romances. Jane Porter's *Thaddeus of Warsaw* (1803), for instance, had a great success, and her *Scottish Chiefs* (1810) spread her fame as far as Russia. Maria Edgeworth's *Castle Rackrent* (1800), and her other Irish stories, showed how well national customs might serve the purpose of a novelist who knew them from within. Scott did not at once discover where his real strength lay. He began his literary life as a collector of old ballads and an author of poetical romances. *Marmion* (1808), *The Lady of the Lake* (1810) and their companions were written in the short leisure of a very busy life, and they bear all the marks of rapid composition. Scott could produce good, stirring verse, and at times, as in the Flodden passages of *Marmion*, he wrote with splendid energy and fire ; none the less, the sudden appearance of Byron and the partial eclipse of Scott by his superior light proved, in the long run, to be fortunate events. Scott's strength as a poet lay in his short lyrics, such as " Proud Maisie " : for purposes of narrative, prose, which allowed him to use the vernacular, gave him wider scope than verse. Several years before the date of *Marmion* he had written some chapters of a prose romance, called *'Tis Sixty Years Since*, and had shown the manuscript to a friend. But the friend's opinion was unfavourable ; the story was abandoned, and the manuscript was put away and forgotten. Some years later, Scott rediscovered the unfinished story by accident, and this time the opinion of his critics was more encouraging. The book was completed with great speed and published in 1814, under the title of *Waverley, or 'Tis Sixty Years Since*. Its success, which was brilliant, is a landmark in literary history. Except Jane Austen, no novelist of the first rank was then writing, and her vogue, like her field, was narrowly restricted. On the other hand, Scott, or rather, " the Great Unknown," quickly became a national institution. Though occupied for about half his time as Clerk of the Sessions at Edinburgh, he flung himself into the business of novel-writing, and for a time kept well above an average of a novel a year. *Guy Mannering* and *The Antiquary* appeared in 1815, *Old Mortality* in 1816, *Rob Roy* in 1817, *The Heart of Midlothian* in 1818, *The Bride of Lammermoor* and *The Legend of Montrose* in 1819. Scott then made a raid into English history, and produced *Ivanhoe* (1820), and though he returned to Scotland in *The Monastery* (1820), he chose southern subjects for *Kenilworth* (1821), *Peveril of the Peak* (1823), and *Quentin Durward* (1823). In the midst of writing *Woodstock* (1826), he heard news which left him a broken man. The publishing firm of Ballantyne and Constable, of which Scott was a partner, went bankrupt; Scott felt his honour involved, and the rest of his life was one unceasing struggle to meet the claims of creditors. He succeeded by dint of heroic effort. *Woodstock* was finished, and the long series of novels was continued. But the joy had gone out of his work, and the later books bear many signs of labour. His health broke under the strain, and a journey which he took to Italy failed to restore him. He died in 1832 at Abbotsford, the beautiful home which he had built on the banks of the Tweed.

II

In the eyes of most men whose chief reading years lay between the battle of Waterloo and the accession of Queen Victoria, the literature of their own time could be summed up in two names, Byron and Scott. Scott's reputation survived the nineteenth century almost unimpaired, though writers of brilliant talent arose to give the novel passion, seriousness, satire and poetry, unequalled before. It must be confessed that the admiration which Scott has received has often been conventional. The lovableness of the man, the wholesomeness of his stories, and his vast historical learning have given him a high prestige among parents and teachers : he has been an excellent writer to recommend to the young. Yet a cool survey of his work reveals many inequalities, and many faults. The art of novel-writing, more than any other department of literature, has improved since Scott's time, and criticism to-day sees defects which passed without comment in the epoch of Jeffrey and Lockhart. Formerly Scott's critics were too lenient ; at present many are too severe. To discriminate between the good and bad qualities of his work is no easy task, yet the attempt must be made.

The qualifications which Scott possessed for uniting history with fiction were in some ways unique. Being a man of affairs as well as a man of letters, he handles matters of state with a sureness not common among novelists, and on all the ordinary business of public life—its litigations, its ambitions, its quarrels—he writes with the authority of real knowledge. Moreover, he was acquainted with many spheres of life. In Edinburgh and in London he was received in the highest society, yet he never lost the habit of frankly conversing with the shepherds and cottars of his own Border hills. His store of anecdotes was immense, and indeed, many of his best episodes are but anecdotes enlarged and adapted. No novelist, perhaps, has possessed so wide a knowledge of history, and the history which Scott knew was that which served him best. He cared little for the wider political issues, and his history may be said to lack " seriousness " ; but of the colour of history, the costume, the armour, the legends, the gossip, the superstitions of past ages, his knowledge was inexhaustible. For sketching the outline of a remote period and filling in its more striking colours, he has no superior. *Ivanhoe*, with all its defects, is still the best picture of early Norman England in fiction, as *Quentin Durward* is of France under Louis XI. Above all, Scott had the gift, without which all of these acquirements would have availed nothing, of telling a good story. The rind of superfluity and introduction is often thick, but the fruit is there, as solid and wholesome as one could wish.

A story of adventure in a vivid historical setting—if that is all one asks, Scott supplies it in *The Talisman*, in *Kenilworth*, and indeed in nearly all the books he wrote.

But it is not much to ask, and there are many writers who meet it as well and with greater liveliness of style. The truth is that there were two Scotts, the writer of superficial romance in a commonplace and often laborious style, and the border minstrel to whom his native ground and its inhabitants were endeared by memory and knowledge, and enriched by a poetic romance only awaiting an interpreter to become fine literature. In the first capacity, Scott gave his audience what they wanted—skilfully, but without much passion or depth or beauty of style ; in the second, the subject carried him away, and he depicted the Scottish character in a hundred forms and varieties with all the skill of imaginative appreciation. As a purveyor to the public, he could write as tastelessly as this :

Some very indifferent twopenny ale, and a glass of excellent brandy crowned our repast ; and, as our horses had, in the meantime, discussed their corn, we resumed our journey with renovated vigour.

Compare this dull, mechanical English with almost any dialogue in broad Scots, and it is hard to believe both issued from the same pen. And there is as much difference between the lip-service paid to the " unrivalled " and " inimitable " view from Richmond Hill and the heartfelt praise of the bleak Solway Firth and the wild hills of Lammermoor.

III

Many writers have owed much to the circumstances of their epoch and upbringing. That Scott became the interpreter of his native land to the rest of the world was due in part to the moment of his birth. The most brilliant intellectual period of Scotland—the age of Hume, Robertson and Adam Smith—though just passing away, could still give a great stimulus to literary effort. Edinburgh was justly proud of its culture : its writers were, some of them, men of European reputation ; and just beyond the city walls lay a region almost unknown to the rest of the world, full of strange survivals from the age of Knox and the Covenanters, and inhabited by a race tenacious of local customs and speaking a rude but expressive dialect which would have been utterly unintelligible to London ears. All the Tory in Scott went out in sympathy to this ancient world, soon, as he feared, to be transformed by the new industrial spirit. The poet and historian in him saw in countless traditions, memories, turns of speech and habits of thought the remains of a half-barbarous, yet half-heroic age—an age of feuds and loyalties, of cruel persecution and of selfless devotion. It is the vitality of his Scotch characters, the rhythm and phrase of their dialogue that keeps his novels alive. It is true that he often paints surface-portraits only, but how lively they are, how convincing in their humanity !

It is these portraits that give the Scottish novels their superiority over the rest. Again and again, critics have passed in review the long troop of characters whom Scott has endowed with enduring life—Dugald Dalgetty in *The Legend of Montrose*, Jeanie Deans in *The Heart of Midlothian*, the Headriggs, mother and son, in *Old Mortality*, Caleb Balderstone in *The Bride of Lammermoor*, Peter Peebles and Joshua Geddes in *Redgauntlet*, Andrew Fairservice in *Rob Roy*—to name a few at random. Such figures as these are Scott's great contribution to literature, and by them the imagination may still be enriched and surprised. How nobly his peasants could speak on occasion is shown nowhere better than in a famous passage from *Waverley*, where Maccombich addresses the court after his condemnation at the Carlisle assizes :

Evan Maccombich looked at him with great earnestness, and, rising up, seemed anxious to speak ; but the confusion of the court, and the perplexity arising from thinking in a language different from that in which he was to express himself, kept him silent. There was a murmur of compassion among the spectators, from an idea that the poor fellow intended to plead the influence of his superior as an excuse for his crime. The Judge commanded silence, and encouraged Evan to proceed.

" I was only ganging to say, my lord," said Evan, in what

he meant to be an insinuating manner, " that if your excellent honour, and the honourable Court, would let Vich Ian Vohr go free just this once, and let him gae back to France, and no to trouble King George's government again, that ony six o' the very best of his clan will be willing to be justified in his stead ; and if you'll just let me gae down to Glennaquoich, I'll fetch them up to ye mysell, to head or hang, and you may begin wi' me the very first man."

Notwithstanding the solemnity of the occasion, a sort of laugh was heard in the court at the extraordinary nature of the proposal. The Judge checked this indecency, and Evan, looking sternly around, when the murmur abated, " If the Saxon gentlemen are laughing," he said, " because a poor man, such as me, thinks my life, or the life of six of my degree, is worth that of Vich Ian Vohr, it's like enough they may be very right ; but if they laugh because they think I would not keep my word, and come back to redeem him, I can tell them they ken neither the heart of a Hielandman, nor the honour of a gentleman."

There was no further inclination to laugh among the audience, and a dead silence ensued.

IV

Scott had many imitators who soon became busy in the wide fields of history which he had left untouched. Moreover, his romantic pictures of the Middle Ages had a great effect on the popular imagination, and some have maintained that the Oxford Movement and the Catholic Revival were largely due to the Waverley Novels. Very different has been the influence of Jane Austen, whose work, quietly matured in a Hampshire vicarage, lies wholly apart from the great highway of history, whether literary or political. Something, no doubt, she owed to the women novelists who preceded her, especially to Fanny Burney, whose first and brightest book, *Evelina* (1778), gives a delightfully fresh picture of life as seen by a young lady of true breeding and keen senses. But Jane Austen's own work did not invite imitation. There was nothing in it which could be exploited or vulgarised. Her books dealt with everyday life, not only of the quietest kind, but with everyday life from which all that is violent, all that is disgusting, has been eliminated. A lady may sprain her ankle, and even fall some height on to a pebbly beach, but in Jane Austen's world these are the worst ills that flesh is heir to. Her men and women are, indeed, not averse to marrying; they spend long evenings at each other's houses; they ride in carriages or on horseback through the country lanes, and picnic in picturesque surroundings; the younger even dance while their elders play backgammon—but of whatsoever lies outside the borders of gentility, Miss Austen appears to be wholly ignorant. Her books were nearly all published within a few years of the battle of Waterloo; yet the even tenor of life is such that save for the gleam here and there of a scarlet coat, the rulers of the world might have entered into a compact for perpetual peace.

Since Miss Austen's time, the novel has won so many triumphs and unfolded such rare experiences, such mighty passions, that one may ask why any reader should enter this tame, familiar little world seen from the windows of a country parsonage. The answer lies wholly in Miss Austen's art. There is no insipid propriety, no fatiguing folly, no pretty vulgarity which she cannot animate with interest. You must submit to confinement, but you cannot complain of unreality. In her comparatively early work, *Northanger Abbey*, there is some mild farce; but the story of Catherine Morland's silly fancies and her discovery of a supposed crime in a totally innocent house where she is visiting, is quite funny as a satire on the romance of mystery, and the character-drawing is already solid. *Sense and Sensibility* (1811), a novel of contrasted natures, suffers a little from its abstract plan: Elinor Dashwood, the sensible, and Marianne, the sensitive, are conceived just a trifle too much as types; but they are individuals as well, and poor Marianne's successive disillusionments make good material for comedy. In *Pride and Prejudice* (1813), Jane Austen is really herself, and there are many who think this her best novel. Certainly she has no livelier scenes than some in this book, such as Mr. Collins's marriage-proposal and the discomfiture of Lady Catherine de Bourgh. Elizabeth Bennett is a delightful heroine, and her sisters' characters are discriminated with the nicest observation. Mrs. Bennett is one of Jane Austen's victims ; but that is partly because of her injustice to Elizabeth. One could not wish common-mindedness to be better punished than in her outburst on hearing that this slighted daughter has, after all, made a grand match :

"Good gracious ! Lord bless me ! only think ! dear me ! Mr. Darcy ! Who would have thought it ? And is it really true ? Oh, my sweetest Lizzy ! how rich and great you will be ! What pin-money, what jewels, what carriages you will have ! Jane's is nothing to it—nothing at all. I am so pleased—so happy ! Such a charming man ! so handsome ! so tall !—Oh, my dear Lizzy ! pray apologise for my having disliked him so much before. I hope he will overlook it. Dear, dear Lizzy ! A house in town ! Everything that is charming ! Three daughters married ! Ten thousand a year ! Oh, Lord ! what will become of me ? I shall go distracted."

Each of Miss Austen's three remaining novels is, in its way, a masterpiece. *Mansfield Park* appeared in 1814, *Emma* in 1816, and *Persuasion* in 1818, a year after its writer's death. Opinions may differ as to the relative merits of these books, and readers are not unaffected by their personal feeling for the heroines. Thus, the affectionate but shrinking Fanny Price, in *Mansfield Park*, has her admirers, but there are some who find her too low-spirited and submissive. That Miss Austen does not succeed well with her male characters is undeniable. Perhaps the only man who is wholly at home in her world is Mr. Woodhouse, the valetudinarian of weak nerves and perfect manners, whose severest remark in the whole course of *Emma* is, it is said, a mild rebuke of a young man's thoughtlessness in leaving the door open, and who ventures to recommend to his guests at dinner a boiled egg, with the strict proviso that it is prepared by his own cook.

But, for many women of the upper middle class, the little world of social relationships was, a century or so since, that in which they " found their happiness or not at all."

Jane Austen's women, as she draws them, are exact, minute and consistent. They have their own vocabulary, mode of thought, and turn of phrase, and every word they speak is in character. Into the portraits of her heroines, Emma Woodhouse, Anne Elliott and the rest, she has put her best art, and that they are so subtly different from each other is, after all, the supreme proof of her powers. By their side are the minor figures—Miss Bates, Mrs. Norris, Lady Bertram, and their like—as distinct and individual as can be. And with what simple means Jane Austen gains her effects! One instance of her economy in words shall be given. Lady Bertram, the mistress of Mansfield Park, is a good-natured but utterly indolent and pampered woman. For a long time we see nothing of her; when next she appears it is after a succession of tragic family disasters. We follow Fanny Price back to the afflicted house, half expecting its mistress to be completely changed :

By one of the suffering party within they were expected with such impatience as she had never known before. Fanny had scarcely passed the solemn-looking servants, when Lady Bertram came from the drawing-room to meet her; came with no indolent step; and, falling on her neck, said, " Dear Fanny ! now I shall be comfortable."

Thus, having thrown the reader off his guard, Miss Austen quietly reminds him that Lady Bertram is Lady Bertram still, and closes her chapter.

V

It was natural that the Essay, like every other form of imaginative literature, should be affected by the new spirit of the age. Just as the poets were launching out on an uncharted sea with nothing but their poetic instinct to guide them, so the essayists strove to transcend the known rules of art and to produce the pure essence of literature. Wordsworth had taught that a " thinking heart " will find " a tale in everything "; and similarly the essayists, as often as not, chose their subjects with all the licence of caprice. Since Bacon's time, essays had usually discussed matters of some general interest or importance. Lamb and Hazlitt were as capable as any men of serious writing, but they hated to appear the slaves of method. In their hands, the essay was drawn away as far as possible from the formal treatise with its clear headings and logical arrangement. Subjects were chosen, not as themes to be developed but as starting-points for flights of imagination ; and the author is content to display the skill of his gyrations, without any thought for his orderly progress towards an anticipated conclusion. In a word, the essays of Lamb and Hazlitt are the intimate self-revelations of their authors. Each might have said in the language of Montaigne : " I write but myself and my essence."

The reader of essays so full of personal reminiscence, so strong in their personal flavour as Lamb's, is at a great disadvantage without some introduction to his author. He soon finds, however, that though Lamb's style is highly complex, his life was simple—a life divided between drudgery at an office, and relaxation among books and friends. The events of Lamb's life can be recorded in a few lines. Born in 1775, the son of John Lamb, clerk to a Bencher of the Inner Temple, he was sent to Christ's Hospital at the age of seven and remained there until he was fourteen. He obtained a clerkship in the East India Company, and during " six-and-thirty years " was tied to office-work for " eight, nine, and sometimes ten hours a day." When Lamb was twenty-one, a frightful domestic tragedy occurred. His sister Mary killed their mother in a fit of madness. After confinement in an asylum, Mary Lamb was released, but only on condition that Charles should act as her custodian. Literary work was Lamb's chief solace in these gloomy years, but it was a long time before he made any mark. He was devoted to the older English authors, and wrote an " Elizabethan " play, *John Woodvil*—a work without dramatic qualities. The *Tales from Shakespeare* (1807), however, and the *Specimens of English Dramatic Poets contemporary with Shakespeare* (1808), were well received, and the second was quite a new thing in literary appreciation. But it was not until 1820 that

Lamb found his true style. In that year, the *London Magazine* was begun, and Lamb, already known as a poet and critic, was asked to become a contributor. The *Recollections of the South-Sea House* was the first essay of Elia, and the series was continued until a volume of twenty-five essays was ready for publication. Lamb retired from the East India House ten years before his death, which occurred in 1834.

"I am a bundle of prejudices—made up of likings and dislikings—the veriest thrall to sympathies, apathies, antipathies." So writes Lamb of himself; and it is because his "likings and dislikings" are so strong, because they are so genuinely intuitive, and not reasoned or intellectual, that his essays are so distinct a revelation of himself. He admits that his "little sketches" are "anything but methodical," but he knows that that is their strength. The whole fabric of the essays is wrought out of impressions and memories, and the sentences follow each other by laws of association known only to the author himself. The vocabulary is a record of his wanderings among old books, and his very rhythms have an echo of the seventeenth century. That essays so individual should carry the reader with them and impose their author's own taste and experience upon him proves the depth of Lamb's humanity and the fineness of his literary tact. It is natural enough that a sketch so universal in its feeling as *Dream Children ; a Reverie*, should make an immediate appeal ; but it is wonderful that "Mrs. Battle" and "C. V. Le G——," and "Mackery End in Hertfordshire," and indeed all the "partial illuminations" and "embryo conceptions" of the essays should harmonize together in the author's scheme of self-expression. For his style, Lamb had no guide but his own instinct, and only a fine sureness could have enabled him to write so artificial a paragraph as this without stumbling in word or rhythm :

Sacred, and, by me, never-to-be-violated, secrets of Poverty ! Should I disclose your honest aims at grandeur, your makeshift efforts of magnificence ? Sleep, sleep, with all thy broken keys, if one of the bunch be extant; thrummed by a thousand ancestral thumbs; dear, cracked spinnet of dearer Louisa! Without mention of mine, be dumb thou thin accompanier of her thinner warble! A veil be spread over the dear delighted face of the well-deluded father, who now haply listening to cherubic notes, scarce feels sincerer pleasure than when she awakened thy time-shaken chords responsive to the twitterings of that slender image of a voice.

Fully to enjoy a style so elaborate and reminiscent as this, one must, perhaps, have some of Lamb's own literary tastes. Most readers, probably, will find that the best approach to Elia is through the autobiographical passages, of which almost every essay has some. Lamb, like Wordsworth, found something poetical, almost sacred in his earliest memories. "While childhood, and while dreams reducing[1] childhood, shall be left," he writes, " imagination shall not have spread her holy wings totally to fly the earth." Some of his best essays, *Christ's Hospital Five-and-thirty Years Ago*, for instance, and *My First Play*, are merely autobiography transformed by the most delicate touch of fancy and sentiment. The whole of his life affords him material—his holidays, his relatives, his love of London, the clerks of the East India House. His most sustained, and, in some ways, his most memorable piece of autobiography is *The Superannuated Man*. The whole essay is excellent, and it would be impossible to surpass the taste with which he has controlled and disguised the deep feeling of the central passage. He has described his long years of service at the office-desk, and now comes to the moment of his release :

Independently of the rigours of attendance, I have ever been haunted with a sense (perhaps a mere caprice) of incapacity for business. This, during my latter years, had increased to such a degree, that it was visible in all the lines of my countenance. My health and my good spirits flagged. I had perpetually a dread of some crisis, to which I should be found unequal. Besides my daylight servitude, I served over again all night in my sleep and would awake with terrors of imaginary false

[1] *I.e.* "bringing back."

entries, errors in my accounts, and the like. I was fifty years of age, and no prospect of emancipation presented itself. I had grown to my desk, as it were, and the wood had entered into my soul.

My fellows in the office would sometimes rally me upon the trouble legible in my countenance; but I did not know that it had raised the suspicions of any of my employers, when, on the fifth of last month, a day ever to be remembered by me, L——, the junior partner in the firm, calling me on one side, directly taxed me with my bad looks, and frankly inquired the cause of them. So taxed, I honestly made confession of my infirmity, and added that I was afraid I should eventually be obliged to resign his service. He spoke some words of course to hearten me, and there the matter rested. A whole week I remained labouring under the impression that I had acted imprudently in my disclosure; that I had foolishly given a handle against myself, and had been anticipating my own dismissal. A week passed in this manner—the most anxious one, I verily believe, in my whole life—when on the evening of the 12th of April, just as I was about quitting my desk to go home (it might be about eight o'clock), I received an awful summons to attend the presence of the whole assembled firm in the formidable back parlour. I thought now my time is surely come, I have done for myself, I am going to be told that they have no longer occasion for me. L——, I could see, smiled at the terror I was in, which was a little relief to me—when to my utter astonishment, B——, the eldest partner, began a formal harangue to me on the length of my services, my very meritorious conduct during the whole of the time (the deuce, thought I, how did he find out that? I protest I never had the confidence to think as much). He went on to descant on the expediency of retiring at a certain time of life (how my heart panted!), and asking me a few questions as to the amount of my own property, of which I have a little, ended with a proposal, to which his three partners nodded a grave assent, that I should accept from the house, which I had served so well, a pension for life to the amount of two-thirds of my accustomed salary—a magnificent offer! I do not know what I answered between surprise and gratitude, but it was understood that I accepted their proposal, and I was told that I was free from that hour to leave their service. I stammered out a bow, and at just ten minutes after eight I went home—for ever. This noble benefit—gratitude forbids me to conceal their names—I owe to the kindness of the most munificent firm in the world—the house of Boldero, Merry-weather, Bosanquet, and Lacy.

Esto perpetua!

VI

Little need be said about the life of William Hazlitt (1778–1830), whose work one reads not so much to know its author, as to enjoy the stimulus of his enthusiasms and the force of his thoughts. He felt to the full the stirring spirit of the time, and nourished himself on what was best in the new literature. He had a genius for intellectual enjoyment, and it was his life-work to be " preaching the joys of good books, good plays and good pictures." Sincerity is the keynote of his writings, a sincerity which often becomes censorious, for Hazlitt was a sharp-tempered man and a good hater. Nature and education alike made him an individualist : " I am not to be browbeat or wheedled out of any of my settled convictions—If to ' be wise were to be obstinate,' I might set up for as great a philosopher as the best of them, for some of my conclusions are as fixed and as incorrigible to proof as need be." In a man less gifted, this attitude would breed nothing but an irritating perversity. But Hazlitt loved so many good things and loved them with such " gusto " (his own word), that his very prejudices are stimulating. He chose that form of writing in which an individualist has the greatest liberty—the Essay.

Hazlitt wrote some hundreds of essays, and delivered scores of lectures. In so large a mass of writing there must needs be many inequalities, yet the number of dull pages is wonderfully small. It was, in fact, impossible for a man of such acute perceptions to be flat or commonplace. Few writers have been so free from any form of intellectual superstition. Hazlitt often admires, but his admiration never rises or falls into worship, and even his praise is often double-edged. No one can anticipate what he will say next, yet he is free from the vanity of paradox-hunting. Abrupt his style is often, but never insipid. He has the openness of mind which produces the finest scholarship, and coupled with this, the sensibility of an artist. At one time he had practised painting, and his experience stood him in good stead as a writer. " The humblest painter," he says, " is a true scholar ; and the best of scholars—the scholar of Nature." His detestation of false scholarship is well expressed in his essay *On the Ignorance of the Learned*, and it would be hard to find a more concise indication of his tastes than the following paragraph :

The most sensible people to be met with in society are men of business and of the world, who argue from what they see and know, instead of spinning cobweb distinctions of what things ought to be. Women have often more of what is called *good sense* than men. They have fewer pretensions ; are less implicated in theories ; and judge of objects more from their immediate and involuntary impression on the mind, and, there-fore, more truly and naturally. They cannot reason wrong ; for they do not reason at all. They do not think or speak by rule ; and they have in general more eloquence and wit, as well as sense, on that account. By their wit, sense, and eloquence together, they generally contrive to govern their husbands. Their style, when they write to their friends (not for the book-sellers), is better than that of most authors.—Uneducated people have most exuberance of invention and the greatest freedom from prejudice. Shakespeare's was evidently an uneducated mind, both in the freshness of his imagination and in the variety of his views ; as Milton's was scholastic, in the texture both of his thoughts and feelings. Shakespeare had not been accustomed to write themes at school in favour of virtue or against vice. To this we owe the unaffected but healthy tone of his dramatic morality. If we wish to know the force of human genius we should read Shakespeare. If we wish to see the insignificance of human learning, we may study his commentators.

How keen were Hazlitt's powers of enjoyment one may learn from such essays as *My First Acquaintance with Poets*, *On the Feeling of Immortality in Youth*, or *On Going a Journey*. His style, if imitated, would be unbearably irregular and discontinuous. In his hands, the abruptness is concealed by his alertness of mind and the felicity of the sharp, ringing sentences. Any wilfulness of manner may be pardoned in a writer who can communicate his relish of consummate skill so well as Hazlitt does in his praise of John Cavanagh :

Died at his house in Burbage Street, St. Giles's, John Cavanagh, the famous hand fives-player. When a person dies who does any one thing better than any one else in the world, which so many others are trying to do well, it leaves a gap in society. It is not likely that any one will now see the game of fives played in its perfection for many years to come—for Cavanagh is dead, and has not left his peer behind him. It may be said that there are things of more importance than striking a ball against a wall—there are things, indeed, that make more noise and do as little good, such as war and peace, making speeches and answering them, making verses and blotting them, making money and throwing it away. But the game of fives is what no one despises who has ever played at it. It is the finest exercise for the body, and the best relaxation for the mind. The Roman poet said that " Care mounted behind the horseman and stuck to his skirts." But this remark would not have applied to the fives-player. He who takes to playing at fives is twice young. He feels neither the past nor future " in the instant." Debts, taxes, " domestic treason, foreign levy, nothing can touch him further." He has no other wish, no other thought, from the moment the game begins, but that of striking the ball, of placing it, of *making* it ! This Cavanagh was sure to do. Whenever he touched the ball there was an end of the chase. His eye was certain, his hand fatal, his presence of mind complete. He could do what he pleased, and he always knew exactly what to do. He saw the whole game, and played it ; took instant advantage of his adversary's weakness, and recovered balls, as if by a miracle and from sudden thought, that every one gave for lost. He had equal power and skill, quickness and judgment. He could either outwit his antagonist by finesse, or beat him by main strength. Sometimes, when he seemed preparing to send the ball with the full swing of his arm, he would by a slight turn of his wrist drop it within an inch of the line. In general, the ball came from his hand, as if from a racket, in a straight, horizontal line ; so that it was in vain to attempt to overtake or stop it. As it was said of a great orator that he never was at a loss for a word, and for the properest word, so Cavanagh always could tell the degree of force necessary to be given to a ball, and the precise direction in which it should be sent. He did his work with the greatest ease; never took more pains than was necessary; and while others were fagging themselves to death, was as cool and collected as if he had just entered the court. His style of play was as remarkable as his power of execution. He had no affectation, no trifling. He did not throw away the game to show off an attitude or try an experiment. He was a fine, sensible, manly player, who did what he could, but that was more than any one else could even affect to do. His blows were not undecided and ineffectual—lumbering like Mr. Wordsworth's epic poetry, nor wavering like Mr. Coleridge's lyric prose, nor short of the mark like Mr. Brougham's speeches, nor wide of it like Mr. Canning's wit, nor foul like the *Quarterly*, nor *let* balls like the *Edinburgh Review*.

(From *The Indian Jugglers*.)

Hazlitt had his full share of conflict and disappointment, as well as some serious defects of character. It is the intellectual zest revealed in his writings that explains the last words he ever spoke, "Well, I've had a happy life."

VII

As an essayist, Thomas de Quincey (1785–1859) had two great advantages—the memory of a varied life, crowded with strange and occult experiences, and the possession of a style which, at its best, is hauntingly beautiful, and at its worst, has the flavour of very pleasant gossip. His mind and nature were many-sided. By education, he was a scholar, and he never lost contact with the learned world. But while he was still a boy at Manchester Grammar School he fell in love with the poetry of Wordsworth, and this enthusiasm gave his mind a new "orientation." He speaks with pride of his discovery. "Was I then, in July 1802, really quoting from Wordsworth? Yes, reader; and I only in all Europe." Through the new poetry, he entered into wide regions of thought and speculation, and began to acquire the critical and philosophical ideas which help to make him so suggestive a writer. In the same year, 1802, he ran away from school, as described in the *Confessions*, and, for many months, wandered unknown, first among the mountains of Wales and later in the London streets.   Though he was discovered by his friends and sent, in 1803, to Worcester College, Oxford, the effects of his vagabondage remained to the detriment of his health, and to relieve his physical sufferings he began to take opium. By inclination, no doubt, De Quincey would have passed his life between study and dreaming, but fortunately it became necessary for him, when he was about thirty-six, to begin writing for money.   He became the editor of the *Westmoreland Gazette*, and, in 1821, began composing the *Confessions of an English Opium Eater*.   For the rest of his life, he was immersed in authorship, pouring forth reviews, criticisms, essays—an invaluable contributor to magazines, for there was nothing on which he could not write with a show of authority, no subject which he could not suffuse with the magic of his style.   Literary toil did not dispel the element of mystery which always hung about him.   As the guest of Christopher North, we are told :

His wants, indeed, were simple, and, in one sense, regular ; a particular joint of mutton, cut according to a certain mathematical formula, and an ounce of laudanum, made him happy for a day.   But in the hours when ordinary beings are awake he was generally to be found stretched in profound opium-slumbers upon a rug before the fire, and it was only about two or three in the morning that he gave unequivocal symptoms of vitality, and suddenly gushed forth in streams of wondrous eloquence to the supper parties detained for the purpose of witnessing the display.

Most of De Quincey's life was spent in the north of England or in Scotland.

The basis of De Quincey's style was a wonderful sense of prose-rhythm.   He was in the best sense a rhetorician ; and the skill with which he vitalizes his matter by the varied pace and temperature of his sentences is akin to the actor's art of throwing life into the words of a speech.   But De Quincey was more than a master of eloquence.   His reading was vast, and though not always accurate himself, he never forgot what scholarship was, or lost his respect for it in others.   His love of fine logical distinctions may seem pedantic at times, but to be subtle was, with him, almost an instinct. He delighted to contemplate vast and vague catastrophes, like that commemorated in *The Revolt of the Tartars*, and to record astounding adventures like the history of *The Spanish Military Nun*. He can write with the appearance of erudition about the darkest enigmas, as in his paper on *Judas Iscariot*, and he can make game of the methods and materials of learning, as in that superb piece of extravagance, *On Murder considered as one of the Fine Arts*. De Quincey is one of the founders of sensational literature of the higher kind. No one knew better how to keep the reader in suspense, to play on his nerves, to insist on the significance of an apparently trivial word or deed. The supreme instance of this is in *The English Mail-Coach*, where all the powers of prose are drawn upon to create an atmosphere of impending calamity. From the actual circumstances of the accident, De Quincey's elusive imagination turns away ; and the vision of the frail little gig lying across the path of the ponderous coach is consummated not in the material crash but in a succession of magnificent verbal variations played upon the theme of Sudden Death.

Among De Quincey's many qualities as a writer, one stands out unique, his mastery of " impassioned prose." Like all great artists in rhetoric, he holds in reserve certain powers of eloquence for supreme occasions. In his power to lift prose to the level of a lofty ode or chorus, he equals the great masters of the seventeenth century. An absolute control over the resources of verbal rhythm combined with recollections of obscure suffering give certain pages of De Quincey's work a fascination which never loses its power. Here is one of the great paragraphs on opium-dreams at the end of his *Confessions* :

Then suddenly would come a dream of far different character —a tumultuous dream—commencing with a music such as now I often heard in sleep—music of preparation and of awakening suspense. The undulations of fast-gathering tumults were like the opening of the Coronation Anthem ; and, like *that*, gave the feeling of a multitudinous movement, of infinite cavalcades filing off, and the tread of innumerable armies. The morning was come of a mighty day—a day of crisis and of ultimate hope for human nature, then suffering mysterious eclipse, and labouring in some dread extremity. Somewhere, but I knew not where—somehow, but I knew not how—by some beings, but I knew not by whom—a battle, a strife, an agony, was travelling through all its stages—was evolving itself, like the catastrophe of some mighty drama, with which my sympathy was the more insupportable from deepening confusion as to its local scene, its cause, its nature, and its undecipherable issue. I (as is usual in dreams where, of necessity, we make ourselves central to every movement) had the power, and yet had not the power, to decide it. I had the power, if I could raise myself to will it ; and yet again had not the power, for the weight of twenty Atlantics was upon me, or the oppression of inexpiable guilt. " Deeper than ever plummet sounded," I lay inactive. Then, like a chorus, the passion deepened. Some greater interest was at stake, some mightier cause than ever yet the sword had pleaded, or trumpet had proclaimed. Then came sudden alarms ; hurryings to and fro ; trepidations of innumerable fugitives, I knew not whether from the good cause or the bad ; darkness and lights ; tempest and human faces ; and at last, with the sense that all was lost, female forms, and the features that were worth all the world to me ; and but a moment allowed—and clasped hands, with heart-breaking partings, and then—everlasting farewells ! and, with a sigh such as the caves of hell sighed when the incestuous mother uttered the abhorred name of Death, the sound was reverberated—everlasting farewells ! and again, and yet again reverberated—everlasting farewells !

And I awoke in struggles, and cried aloud, " I will sleep no more ! "

CHAPTER XVI

BYRON—SHELLEY—KEATS

It is commonly said that no poet receives due recognition in his own lifetime. The career of Byron would alone be enough to refute this assertion. No English poet worthy of the title ever attained so great a fame in so short a time. His vogue was in part due to adventitious things—his distinguished birth, his handsome face, and, later, to the scandalous whispers which thrilled as much as they shocked. But Byron's poetry was not only talked about—it was read, quoted, imitated and really understood by men and women to whom the verse of other men made little appeal. Byron had the gift of making his most commonplace readers feel that they too had a touch of romance somewhere in their being, and this is one great secret of his success.

It was inevitable that a writer so much admired in his own generation should suffer from a reaction in the next. Byron went much out of fashion during the Victorian age, and Matthew Arnold's prophecy that in 1900 he would be ranked with Wordsworth as one of the two greatest writers of his age was assuredly not fulfilled. To-day, his reputation stands somewhat higher than it did at the beginning of the century; yet how much of his poetry is of really enduring value is a question on which even now no two critics would easily agree.

I

George Gordon Noel, afterwards sixth Lord Byron, was born in 1788, of a family which can be traced to the Conquest. The fates contrived to bestow on the poet a very mixed collection of gifts. The ancient name which he inherited was sullied by some ugly stories current about his immediate predecessor in the title. His handsome appearance was marred by a clubbed foot of which he was morbidly ashamed. His mother, foolishly fond, was a most injudicious parent, and it was perhaps no great misfortune for the poet when she died " in a fit of rage brought on by reading an upholsterer's bill." Byron was sent to Harrow, where his gifts were evident enough, though they were perhaps rather showy than solid. He formed some passionate friendships, and made a name for an independence of spirit not wholly free from insolence. He also acquired some facility in verse-writing, and before he went to Cambridge had become the victim of a disappointment in love—an event powerfully described much later in *The Dream*. *Hours of Idleness*, an early volume of verse published in 1808, showed its author already adopting one of his favourite poses :

> Weary of love, of life, devoured with spleen,
> I rest a perfect Timon, not nineteen.

The verses were attacked in *The Edinburgh Review* ; whereupon Byron produced his *English Bards and Scottish Reviewers* (1809), a poetic satire of the order founded by Dryden, though evidently the work of a more dashing and much younger writer. Byron surveys the whole field of contemporary letters ; he upholds the more conservative writers, such as Rogers, author of *The Pleasures of Memory*, and Campbell, the poet of some stirring national songs, but he dismisses the more original men in a few smart couplets. There is cleverness enough, of a superficial kind, in his attack on Wordsworth :

> Who both by precept and example shows
> That prose is verse and verse is merely prose.

A long journey to the Near East, in the course of which he visited Athens and Constantinople and swam the Hellespont, gave Byron something to write about, and the first two cantos of *Childe Harold's Pilgrimage* (1812) were the fruit of his travels. The success of the poem was extraordinary. " I awoke," he says, " to find myself famous." The lapse of a century has somewhat abated the force of these two early cantos. But it is not difficult to see why they delighted the poet's own generation. In the brief comments on famous names and places, the contempt for things ordinary, and the romantic enthusiasm for greatness and glory, there is a high-handedness of treatment which must have been dazzling enough while it was still novel. For the rest, *Childe Harold* succeeded by not soaring too high. It " was just on the level of its age." From that time onwards, the public bought any verse which Byron chose to publish.

His next attempt was in the domain of the tale in verse, a field in which Scott had already won success. Byron's *Giaour* (1813), the first of the series, easily eclipsed the fame of *Marmion*. The story is simple enough. The hero, a renegade Christian, steals the mistress of a Mussulman, Hassan, who, however, contrives to avenge himself by drowning her. The Giaour returns, kills Hassan, and then enters a monastery. The poem abounds in words redolent of the Levant, such as caïque, tophaike, jerreed, ataghan, calpac, which delighted romantic readers living a sheltered English life ; and the perils of the wild country with its violence, its hatred, its fanaticism had all the attraction of the unknown. The central figure, above all, was mysteriously fascinating :

> Not oft to smile descendeth he,
> And when he doth 'tis sad to see
> That he but mocks at Misery.
> How that pale lip will curl and quiver !
> Then fix once more as if for ever ;
> As if his sorrow or disdain
> Forbade him e'er to smile again.

In this portrait it was easy to imagine a certain resemblance to the noble author himself.

The Giaour was followed by *The Bride of Abydos*, *Lara*, *The Siege of Corinth*, and *Parisina*, all of them bearing a strong family likeness to each other. They appeared between 1813 and 1816, the years of Byron's greatest popularity, when society idolised him, young men of fashion made him their model, and the Byronic curl of lip became a recognised mark of superiority. But a catastrophe was at hand. In 1815, Byron made a marriage from which his friends anticipated no very happy results. Their worst fears were fulfilled. Lady Byron left her husband in the following year, and the most scandalous stories were soon afloat. He was compared, says his biographer, "to Sardanapalus, Nero, Tiberius, the Duke of Orleans, Heliogabalus and Satan." Society turned against him, and England ceased to be a habitable place. He left it for ever, and the rest of his life was spent in various parts of the Continent—in Switzerland first, then in Italy ; finally, for a short time, in Greece, where he died.

This adversity was the salvation of Byron's poetry. It forced him to throw aside affectation and to seek for his own natural tone. In the poems of the next few years, he is using his own voice, that voice of alternating seriousness and flippancy, passion and scorn, which is the best thing which Byron, as a poet, has to give. "His more serious conversation," wrote Shelley, "is a sort of intoxication ; men are held by it as by a spell." Byron's problem as an artist was to find the right medium for this essential part of himself. As he passed through Switzerland, the story of the patriot Bonnivard's long imprisonment came into his mind, and he composed his admirable *Prisoner of Chillon* (1816), with its stirring prefatory sonnet, " Eternal Spirit of the chainless Mind ! " About the same time, he wrote the first of several imperfect dramas, *Manfred* (1817), as well as *Darkness*, a sombre poem in blank verse, which reveals the depth of tragic imagination in Byron's nature. But the chief work of this period was the second half of *Childe Harold* (cantos iii and iv, 1816–1818). The advance which Byron had made in a few years is most striking. His humanity had deepened, his style had more force and, above all, his descriptive power had reached maturity. " Description," he said truly, " is my forte." The Waterloo stanzas, the address to the ocean, the descriptions of Venice, of the Alpine storm, and of the Coliseum, are fine instances of Byron's turbulent power and vivid observation. Nor can one deny the strength of his famous stanzas on the Dying Gladiator :

> I see before me the Gladiator lie :
>   He leans upon his hand—his manly brow
> Consents to death, but conquers agony,
>   And his droop'd head sinks gradually low—
>   And through his side the last drops, ebbing slow
> From the red gash, fall heavy, one by one,
>   Like the first of a thunder-shower ; and now
> The arena swims around him—he is gone,
> Ere ceased the inhuman shout which hail'd the wretch who won.
>
> He heard it, but he heeded not—his eyes
>   Were with his heart, and that was far away ;
> He reck'd not of the life he lost nor prize,
>   But where his rude hut by the Danube lay,
>   *There* were his young barbarians all at play,
>   *There* was their Dacian mother—he, their sire,
>   Butcher'd to make a Roman holiday—
> All this rushed with his blood—Shall he expire
> And unavenged ?   Arise ! ye Goths, and glut your ire !

II

A long period of dissipation in Venice wrought a further change in Byron's poetry. He began to cultivate a style of light cynicism and mocking disillusionment. He gave up the Spenserian stanza, which had suited the graver moods of *Childe Harold* and adopted the *ottava rima* of Italian poetry, a measure which he handled with consummate ease. In this new style, he was greatly aided by his skill in rhyme. No one, perhaps, has been so ingenious in the discovery of double and triple rhymes as Byron, and he made no secret of his somewhat boyish satisfaction on writing such a couplet as :

> But—oh ! ye lords of ladies intellectual,
> Inform us truly, have they not hen-peck'd you all ?

Beppo was Byron's first poem in the lighter vein, and while he was still at Venice he began to write the early books of his masterpiece, *Don Juan* (published 1819–24). Meantime, his conduct and writings were giving great offence in England. His exile had not diminished the sale of his works. Readers continued to buy them and be shocked. Public opinion was most seriously perturbed by his drama *Cain*, which was as vehemently praised by the rebel Shelley as it was condemned by the staid and orthodox Southey. This work is, in fact, Byron's finest drama; but Southey, an excellent man and painstaking poet, was in no mood to recognise merit in a poem which represents the world as being governed by tyrannical might. Nor could he approve of the treatment of Cain, whose bewildered helplessness when the mysteries of the universe are revealed to him cannot but create some sympathy in the reader, a feeling which is heightened by the pronouncement of the sinner's tremendous doom. Southey, as Poet Laureate, felt bound to protest in the name of religion; and he denounced Byron as chief of the " Satanic School " of poetry. This attack gave Byron his opportunity; and his answer to the indictment was one of the most effective pieces of poetic ridicule ever written. Southey had recently made himself vulnerable by an absurd laudation of George III, in a poem on that monarch's entry into heaven entitled *A Vision of Judgment*. Byron's reply to his antagonist was a poem on the same subject and with the same title, but written in a style of parody which pours ridicule not only on the whole conception, but on every foible in the character of the unfortunate Laureate, especially his conversion from extreme republicanism to almost fawning loyalty. The parody begins by describing George III's arrival at the gates of heaven, through which he is about to enter when Lucifer suddenly appears to claim possession of the king. A dispute arises, and witnesses are called. George's fate still hangs in the balance, when the devil, Asmodeus, unexpectedly arrives with the living body of Southey which he has seized on the shores of Derwentwater. The Laureate is only too delighted to bear testimony before such an audience :

He had written praises of a regicide;
   He had written praises of all kings whatever;
He had written for republics far and wide,
   And then against them, bitterer than ever;
For pantisocracy he once had cried
   Aloud, a scheme less moral than 'twas clever;
Then grew a hearty Anti-Jacobin—
Had turned his coat—and would have turn'd his skin.

Attention is now drawn from the king to the garrulous poet, who improves the occasion by a timely proposal:

He had written Wesley's life:—here turning round
   To Satan, " Sir, I'm ready to write yours,
In two octavo volumes, nicely bound,
   With notes and preface, all that most allures
The pious purchaser; and there's no ground
   For fear, for I can choose my own reviewers:
So let me have the proper documents,
That I may add you to my other saints."

Satan, however, declines the offer; but determined to have audience, the Laureate draws forth a manuscript:

and no
Persuasion on the part of devils, saints
Or angels, now could stop the torrent; so
   He read the first three lines of the contents;
But at the fourth, the whole spiritual show
   Had vanish'd, with variety of scents,
Ambrosial and sulphureous, as they sprang,
Like lightning, off from his " melodious twang."

The poet is knocked down by St. Peter's keys and falls into his own lake:

As for the rest, to come to the conclusion
   Of this true dream, the telescope is gone
Which kept my optics free from all delusion,
   And show'd me what I in my turn have shown;
All I saw farther, in the last confusion,
   Was, that King George slipp'd into heaven for one;
And when the tumult dwindled to a calm,
I left him practising the hundredth psalm.

III

Don Juan, which was finished in 1823, is without doubt Byron's greatest as well as his longest work. The poem, as his biographer says, *is* Byron. All the man's qualities are there—his cynicism, his disquiet, his vast experience of life, his bursts of tenderness and passion, his unfailing cleverness, his bitter mockery. His descriptive power is there too, and Byron never wrote anything more wonderful than his stanzas on the storm in Canto ii. Throughout the poem, there is the sigh of disillusionment, the sense of premature age. One would have thought the author of *Don Juan* had little more to live for ; and in a sense this is true, for he had little more to write. But the greatest action of his life was still to come. The news that the Greeks had risen against their Turkish oppressors stirred all the nobler qualities in Byron's nature. Whatever else he had mocked at, he had never mocked at the spirit of Hellas or of freedom. He had energy still ; and though he did not live to see victory, he accomplished enough to leave an undying name among the Greeks, before he died of fever at Mesolonghi. His enthusiasm for Greek independence was the inspiration of his last poem, and no man ever wrote his own epitaph more fittingly than Byron in the lines *On this day I complete my thirty-sixth year* :

> 'Tis time this heart should be unmoved,
>   Since others it has ceased to move :
> Yet, though I cannot be beloved,
>   Still let me love !
>
> My days are in the yellow leaf ;
>   The flowers and fruits of love are gone ;
> The worm, the canker, and the grief
>   Are mine alone !
>
> *   *   *
>
> But 'tis not *thus*—and 'tis not *here*—
>   Such thoughts should shake my soul, nor *now*,
> When glory decks the hero's bier,
>   Or binds his brow.

> The sword, the banner, and the field,
>   Glory and Greece, around me see !
> The Spartan, borne upon his shield,
>   Was not more free.

>   *   *   *

> If thou regrett'st thy youth, *why live ?*
>   The land of honourable death
> Is here :—up to the field, and give
>   Away thy breath !

> Seek out—less often sought than found—
>   A soldier's grave, for thee the best ;
> Then look around, and choose thy ground,
>   And take thy rest.

IV

Percy Bysshe Shelley, like Byron, was a writer whose life as well as his verse was the expression of his poetic nature. Like Byron, too, he was a rebel. But he was a man of much finer mould, and an inflexible will and wide-ranging intellect were hidden beneath an almost feminine delicacy. He was the descendant of an old family living at Field Place, near Horsham, and was born in 1792. As a child, his intelligence and beauty attracted equal notice, and he is said to have " learned the classic languages almost by intuition, while he seemed to be spending his time in dreaming." At Eton, he was distinguished by his warm affections and his queer hobbies. His peculiar delight was in chemical experiments of an abstruse kind, and they were conducted with a want of method which made his study a centre of considerable danger. On entering University College, Oxford, he began that extraordinary career, partly pathetic, partly ludicrous, partly tragic—of which one can only say that it is impossible to judge it by ordinary standards. Shelley's life, above that of all other men, proves that the most generous worship of ideal goodness and ideal beauty is compatible with thoughtless and even heartless action when the idealist is brought face to face with the minor vexations of men. Shelley was wholly without worldly wisdom, yet he was in a violent hurry to reform the world. At Oxford, he came under the influence of the "advanced" thinkers, Hume and the French materialists, and immediately conceived it his duty to enlighten the whole bench of bishops. He wrote and distributed a pamphlet called *The Necessity of Atheism*, confident that his views were irrefutable and would work a speedy revolution. The result was very different. Shelley was summoned before the Fellows of his College, questioned about the tract and ultimately sent down from Oxford, to his equal surprise and distress. The same penalty was inflicted upon his friend, Jefferson Hogg, who had generously claimed a share of the blame.

This was the first of many actions which, being compounded of idealism and folly, began in hope and ended in disaster. In a fit of generosity, Shelley married Harriet Westbrook, a school-friend of his sister's, in order to rescue the girl from the alleged " tyranny " under which she was suffering. But the marriage was a tragic mistake. Harriet was commonplace, superficial, and rather vulgar. After three years of married life, husband and wife separated, and two years later, Harriet brought her troubles to an end by drowning herself in the Serpentine. Meantime, Shelley had conceived a great admiration for the " philosopher " and novelist William Godwin, and had fallen in love with his daughter. It was just before his separation from Harriet, while the thought of Mary Godwin was in his mind, that he wrote the first of his really beautiful lyrics, " Away ! the moor is dark beneath the moon." The two concluding stanzas will show the quality of this melodious poem :

The cloud shadows of midnight possess their own repose,
    For the weary winds are silent, or the moon is in the deep :
Some respite to its turbulence unresting ocean knows ;
    Whatever moves, or toils, or grieves, hath its appointed sleep.

Thou in the grave shalt rest—yet till the phantoms flee,
    Which that house and heath and garden made dear to thee erewhile,
Thy remembrance, and repentance, and deep musing are not free
    From the music of two voices and the light of one sweet smile.

Shelley's unfortunate encounters with life turned his thoughts more and more to poetry. At one time, he had had schemes of practical reform, and in the months immediately after his marriage, he threw himself into the agitation for Catholic Emancipation, being convinced that " anything short of unlimited toleration and complete charity with all men is wrong." He never lost the spirit of the reformer ; but he gradually learnt that the best service he could perform to Truth and Beauty, was to clothe his ideas in words, and leave time to scatter his thoughts over the universe. His early poem, *Queen Mab*, has many marks of immaturity, but *Alastor* is at once characteristic of its author's thought and a splendid piece of blank verse. The title of this work is taken from the Greek name of a dæmon, which drives its victim into desert places. Indefinite in outline, and often obscure, *Alastor* is really a piece of poetic autobiography. A clue to its meaning is given in the motto from St. Augustine :

> Nondum amabam, et amare amabam,
> quærebam quid amarem, amans amare.

Alastor describes the infinite aspirations of the idealist. The hero is a poet who has fed his youth on the most lofty speculations, and conceived unlimited ideas of goodness and beauty. In a dream he beholds " a veiled maid," whom at first he believes the realization of all that he had imagined. He yields at first to irresistible joy, but the unreality of the vision is soon forced upon him. He continues a wanderer and a solitary, consumed by his dream of the impossible, and shunning all human intercourse. There is no escape from his disillusionment but by death, and he dies amid wild Alpine scenery of fantastic terror and beauty.

V

The beauty of *Alastor* owes much to the mountains of Switzerland, which Shelley had seen in the Autumn of 1814. Two years later, he was in Switzerland again, and for a time made one of a little group of writers collected there.

Others were Byron and M. G. Lewis, author of a popular sensational story called *The Monk*. Another member of the party was Mary Godwin—subsequently the wife of Shelley, who made the visit memorable by writing her weird, supernatural tale *Frankenstein*. In 1818, Shelley left England for ever, and from this time onward was a wanderer in Italy, sometimes at Rome, sometimes at Pisa, and finally at Spezia. Away from the vexations of home, and in a land he loved, Shelley's poetic genius quickly ripened. His spirit had a kinship with light and fire, and under the blue of Italian skies he created a poetry of nature expressive of his own imagination. A line from the *Stanzas written in Dejection* might be quoted as the quintessence of Shelley's graceful and radiant imagery :

> I see the waves upon the shore,
> *Like light dissolved in star-showers, thrown.*

In the *Lines written among the Euganean Hills*, his descriptive power has full scope. His pictures remind one of Turner. He has the same love of dazzling light, of the cloud patterns, of the depth of skies, of spires and pinnacles lit by the sun. Shelley sees the Venetian sunrise in all its Turnerian splendour :

> Lo ! the sun upsprings behind,
> Broad, red, radiant, half-reclined
> On the level quivering line
> Of the waters crystalline ;
> And before that chasm of light,
> As within a furnace bright,
> Column, tower, and dome, and spire,
> Shine like obelisks of fire,
> Pointing with inconstant motion
> From the altar of dark ocean
> To the sapphire-tinted skies.

Equally beautiful in its descriptions is *The Sensitive Plant*, a poem which contains an exquisite expression of Shelley's love of nature. His stanzas on the lady's garden reveal to perfection the refinement and delicacy of his imagination. The pictures of the " pied wind-flowers," the lily of the vale with its tremulous bells, " the broad water-lilies," the " starry river-buds " and the other flowers of spring have an almost overpowering sweetness. As usual, Shelley is not content with mere description, and the Sensitive Plant is an obvious type of the soul athirst for beauty :

> For the Sensitive Plant has no bright flower ;
> Radiance and odour are not its dower ;
> It loves, even like Love, its deep heart is full,
> It desires what It has not, the Beautiful !

Perhaps the greatest of all his nature-poems is the *Ode to the West Wind*, where, in lines of impetuous speed, he likens his spirit to the wild force of approaching winter, which destroys that it may " quicken a new birth."

VI

Although Shelley's peculiar excellence is in the lyric, the intellectual greatness of his work can be fully seen only in his longer poems, most of which are, indeed, lyrical in conception. Perhaps the finest of all is *Adonais* (1821), his elegy on the death of Keats. Shelley himself had a justly high opinion of this work. " *Adonais*," he said, " in spite of its mysticism, is the least imperfect of my compositions." The poem certainly takes rank among the three great elegies in English, and the sustained flight of its impassioned verse gives it, perhaps, a unique place in our literature. It opens in the manner of the Sicilian elegies, on a repeated note of lamentation. The poet's imagination lingers about the bier to which the " quick Dreams " and " passion-wingèd Ministers of thought " who had served Adonais in his life, come trooping. Other beings lament the dead poet, " All he had loved, and moulded into thought," Morning, Spring, and his " spirit's sister," the " lorn nightingale." Finally, come the poet's own con-temporaries, Byron, " the Pilgrim of Eternity," Moore from the wilds of Ierne, and " midst others of less note," Shelley himself, a " frail Form, a phantom among men." The poem pauses a moment to fling a line of scorn at the reviewer who—as Shelley supposed—had hastened Keats's death,

> Live thou, whose infamy is not thy fame !

and then the note suddenly changes from lamentation to triumph.   Adonais " is not dead," " He has outsoared the shadow of our night " :

> He lives, he wakes—'tis Death is dead, not he ;
> Mourn not for Adonais.—Thou young Dawn,
> Turn all thy dew to splendour, for from thee
> The spirit thou lamentest is not gone ;
> Ye caverns, and ye forests, cease to moan !
> Cease, ye faint flowers and fountains, and thou Air,
> Which, like a mourning veil thy scarf hadst thrown
> O'er the abandoned Earth, now leave it bare,
> Even to the joyous stars which smile on its despair !

The exultant stanzas which follow affirm the poet's transcendent idealism :

> The One remains, the many change and pass ;
> Heaven's light for ever shines, earth's shadows fly ;
> Life, like a dome of many-coloured glass,
> Stains the white radiance of Eternity.

From this point the elegy proceeds to its conclusion in verses of supreme eloquence.

VII

Of the other long poems of Shelley, *The Cenci* and *Prometheus Unbound* (both 1819) are the most remarkable. *The Cenci* is a drama of hideous and unnatural wickedness, and although there are weaknesses in the earlier scenes, the work is redeemed by the great power of the last act, in which Beatrice Cenci and her mother, guilty only in law, are led to their execution. *Prometheus Unbound* is a cosmic drama on the captivity and final deliverance of man's champion and friend. The poem is Shelley's great indictment of tyrannical might. Prometheus had given strength and dominion to Jupiter, " with this law alone, ' Let man be free '." Jupiter has accepted the power but ignored the condition. He has become the oppressor of earth and has bound Prometheus to a precipice in a ravine of icy rocks, whither from time to time come legions of tormenting furies. A mysterious power named Demogorgon is destined one day to overthrow Jupiter and leave his throne for ever vacant; and there is also a " Spirit of the Hour," whose approach will be the signal for the tyrant's doom. At the beginning of the third act, the car of the Hour arrives, and Demogorgon draws near to pronounce the irrevocable sentence. In vain Jupiter pleads for mercy. " Oh," he cries,

> " That thou wouldst make mine enemy my judge,
> Even where he hangs, seared by my long revenge,
> On Caucasus ! he would not doom me thus.
> Gentle, and just, and dreadless, is he not
> The monarch of the world ? "

The words are true, for on the fall of the tyrant the spirit of Prometheus is enthroned in the universe. Earth exults in the new law of Love, and in the deliverance of man, for whom she prophesies a reign of unlimited knowledge, power and joy :

> The lightning is his slave ; heaven's utmost deep
> Gives up her stars, and like a flock of sheep
> They pass before his eye, are numbered, and roll on !
> The tempest is his steed, he strides the air ;
> And the abyss shouts from her depth laid bare,
> " Heaven, hast thou secrets ? Man unveils me ; I have none."

The poem finally returns to the victory of Love over tyranny, and the concluding lines are a pæan in praise of the divine endurance of Prometheus :

> To suffer woes which Hope thinks infinite ;
> To forgive wrongs darker than death or night ;
> To defy Power, which seems omnipotent ;
> To love, and bear ; to hope till Hope creates
> From its own wreck the thing it contemplates ;
> Neither to change, nor falter, nor repent ;
> This, like thy glory, Titan, is to be
> Good, great and joyous, beautiful and free ;
> This is alone Life, Joy, Empire and Victory.

Adonais was one of Shelley's last works. In the follow-ing year (1822), his life came to a sudden and tragic end. He was living at the Villa Magni, on the Gulf of Spezia. With characteristic imprudence, he ventured on a sea voyage in a small vessel, accompanied only by a friend and a sailor-boy. The boat disappeared into a mist, and shortly after, the Ligurian Sea was swept by a terific storm. Some days of fearful suspense were passed by Mrs. Shelley, but at length all hope was abandoned. A week after the storm, the bodies were cast up on the shore.

Shelley was under thirty when he died, and hence but a small part of his poetic promise was fulfilled. His poems, especially the longer ones, have, notwithstanding their beauty, many defects of style. Shelley was a hasty writer, and one can well understand how Keats, a far more deliber-ate artist, should have urged him to " load every rift with ore." It is in his shorter lyrics that Shelley is really supreme —such pieces as " On a poet's lips I slept," " O world, O Life, O Time," " Music when soft voices die," " Life of Life, thy lips enkindle," and with these must be included a few longer poems, such as the *Ode to a Skylark*. These are pieces which every lover of English poetry comes to know by heart. But there is another side of Shelley's work which no reader ought to ignore. Shelley was as earnest as Wordsworth in his endeavour to arrive at a true theory of poetry ; and his critical essay, *A Defence of Poetry*, is a work of high creative thought. To Shelley, as one might expect, the essential nature of poetry is far more important than any details of form. He regards poetry as akin to all the other works of man's creative spirit. Music, sculpture, and even just laws are manifestations of the same power. Only poetry has an advantage over all these in that its material, language, is itself the work of imagination. The noble panegyric on poetry in the essay is not mere rhetoric ; it is a confession of faith from one whose life was dedicated to the quest of truth and the expression of beauty. Happy is the man who can write thus of his own age and his own art :

The literature of England has arisen as it were from a new birth. We live among such philosophers and poets as surpass beyond comparison any who have appeared since the last national struggle for civil and religious liberty. . . . It is impossible to read the compositions of the most celebrated writers of the present day without being startled with the electric life which burns within their words. They measure the circumference and sound the depths of human nature with a comprehensive and all-penetrating spirit, and they are themselves perhaps the most sincerely astonished at its manifestations ; for it is less their spirit than the spirit of the age. Poets are the hierophants of an unapprehended inspiration ; the mirrors of the gigantic shadows which futurity casts upon the present : the words which express what they understand not ; the trumpets which sing to battle and feel not what they inspire ; the influence which is moved not, but moves. Poets are the unacknowledged legislators of the world.

IX

The life of John Keats (1795–1821) was shorter even than that of Shelley. Yet in his little span of years he made as great strides towards perfection in his art as perhaps any other man has ever done in so brief a time. Keats was above all things a poet. It is doubtful whether any other man has ever lived whose nature was more entirely and essentially poetical. Readers of his poetry must needs be interested in a life so brilliant, so brave, so pitifully short. Yet Keats was not a man whose biography, like Wordsworth's or Byron's, throws light upon some of the deepest currents of the age. Wordsworth besides being a poet was a political thinker ; Coleridge was a metaphysician ; Shelley was a reformer and idealist. But Keats was a poet and nothing else ; the whole of his vital energy went into his art. In writing of his work, the historian of literature must be content for once to be wholly a critic.

John Keats came of a family which, though self-respecting and diligent, had very few claims to be called cultured. His father was the head ostler in a livery stable, and the boy was the eldest of four children. He was sent to school at Enfield, where he was well taught, and must have obtained some knowledge of great literature, for he translated the *Æneid* into English. Before he was quite sixteen he left school and was apprenticed to a surgeon. But he kept up an acquaintance with the son of his head-master, and one day from this friend he borrowed *The Faerie Queene*. The language of Spenser revealed to Keats the vast world of poetry; and about the same time his eyes were opened to the beauty of nature, for even in the neighbourhood of Edmonton there were green fields and blue skies. These two new passions began to play havoc with his medical studies. With the encouragement of some literary friends at Hampstead—members of the circle of John Henry Leigh Hunt—he brought out a small volume of verse in 1817. The book passed without notice, but Keats felt that he had taken the decisive step, and now definitely decided upon a literary career. A small legacy inherited from his grandmother made this plan not wholly imprudent.

Having now plenty of leisure to write, Keats set to work on a long poem, *Endymion*, which was published with a few other pieces in 1818. In an almost deprecatory preface, the young poet admits that this work is " a feverish attempt, rather than a deed accomplished," and it is true that any reader who tries to follow the fortunes of Endymion in his love for the moon-goddess is almost certain to be baffled in the endeavour. But the poem must not be judged as a narrative. It is rather a riot of poetic phrases, a labyrinth of images, with here and there, as in the *Hymn to Pan*, lines of consummate expression. *Endymion* was savagely dealt with in *Blackwood's Magazine* and *The Quarterly Review*; and as Keats read the articles soon after he had returned, over-fatigued, from a walking-tour in Scotland, it is possible that their severity may have hastened the fatal consumption which was shortly to attack him. He had, however, a year of marvellous achievement to look back upon; for within this short time, he had produced nearly all the works which compose his last volume. The *Poems* of 1820 are Keats's enduring monument. They include the three narratives, *Isabella*, *The Eve of St. Agnes* and *Lamia*; the unfinished epic, *Hyperion*; the odes, *La Belle Dame sans Merci*, and a few sonnets. To Keats, with fresh poetic schemes in his mind, and the knowledge that he would never live to fulfil them, the wonderful volume seemed but a trifle. But his whole life was now embittered by illness. Early in 1820, he had caught a severe chill, and shortly after, alarming symptoms appeared. To escape the English winter, he made a voyage to Italy, accompanied by his devoted friend, Joseph Severn. But no efforts could stay the progress of the disease, and Keats died in the February of 1821. He was buried in the Protestant Cemetery at Rome, where the remains of Shelley were laid a year later.

X

It is generally agreed that the two chief forms of great poetry are the Epic and the Tragedy. To write an epic, a poet must have command of a great subject and must possess skill to deal with it worthily. To write a tragedy, he must be able to delineate the mightier passions. Though Keats knew well enough that he was scarcely of an age to write either epic or tragedy, the idea of " great poetry " was ever before him, and the two versions of *Hyperion* are both splendid efforts to reach unattainable heights. Yet though Keats did not possess the Titanic strength to design and execute an entire epic, he had, even at his early age, complete mastery over one branch of poetic art. In choice of phrase and descriptive power he was often as near perfect as a poet can be.

At an early age, Keats fell in love with the poetry of the English language and the beauty of the English landscape. These two passions determined his career and made him, above all things, the master of the expressive phrase and the revealer of beauty. The mixed origin of English and its wealth of short significant words make it one of the most expressive and therefore one of the most poetical languages in existence. Few men, however, have had so deep an insight into its resources, or such skill to extract the last drop of poetic essence from them as Keats. "He looked on fine phrases," it was said, "like a lover." He knew that if language is to be truly expressive, it must seem slightly unusual. It is in his adjectives that the poet has the fullest scope for originality : " l'epithète rare," as a French critic said, " voilà la marque du poète." On almost every page of Keats there are instances of the felicitous epithet. Look, for example, at these seven lines from the *Ode on Melancholy* :

> But when the melancholy fit shall fall
>   Sudden from heaven like a weeping cloud,
> That fosters the droop-headed flowers all,
>   And hides the green hill in an April shroud ;
>   Then glut thy sorrow on a morning rose,
>   Or on the rainbow of the salt sand-wave,
>   Or on the wealth of globed peonies. . . .

Here, three at least of the epithets, *weeping, droop-headed,* and *globed,* give the very essence of the thing described ; and even the common word *green,* as Keats uses it, has a significance more than ordinary. He does not, indeed, depend on words rare in themselves, and in the last of these four lines from *The Eve of St. Agnes,* the description is as graphic as it can be, though the means employed are simple :

> A chain-droop'd lamp was flickering by each door ;
>   The arras, rich with horseman, hawk, and hound,
> Flutter'd in the besieging wind's uproar ;
> And the long carpets rose along the gusty floor.

But when Keats puts forth the whole of his strength, the effect is astonishing. Where, out of Shakespeare, are flowers described with such concentrated loveliness of language as in the *Ode to Psyche* ?

> I wander'd in a forest thoughtlessly,
>   And, on the sudden, fainting with surprise,
> Saw two fair creatures, couched side by side
>   In deepest grass, beneath the whisp'ring roof

Of leaves and trembled blossoms, where there ran
  A brooklet, scarce espied :
'Mid hush'd, cool-rooted flowers, fragrant-eyed,
  Blue, silver-white, and budded Tyrian,
    They lay calm-breathing on the bedded grass.

The lines on the " moving waters " in the last sonnet, and the simile of the " branch-charmed " oaks in *Hyperion* are but two instances among many others of Keats's command over phrases, of which every word is a revelation of beauty.

XI

But Keats was not merely a poet of splendid details. His education by beauty—he had no other teacher—taught him to seek poetry in other forms than the sensuous phrase and the luxurious image, to which the softer side of his nature inclined. " I have loved the principle of beauty in all things," he wrote ; and through the whole of his poetic life he was endeavouring to extend the boundaries of beauty into new regions. His poem, *Isabella*, which is an attempt to turn a somewhat repellent story into a thing of beauty, shows both his ambition and his immaturity. The opening stanzas in which the love of Isabella and Lorenzo is revealed to each other are full of charm ; and the description of the two brothers' determination to thwart the match is written with energetic imagery. But a little later, Keats's love of a poetical metaphor causes him to throw dramatic propriety to the winds. It is not thus that a villain planning murder would seek to entice his victim into his clutches :

" To-day we purpose, aye, this hour we mount,
  To spur three leagues towards the Apennine ;
Come down, we pray thee, ere the hot sun count
  His dewy rosary on the eglantine."

Yet in spite of lapses in taste and weaknesses in handling, the narrative has some powerful moments. The dramatic contrast between Isabella's gay parting from her lover and the grim opening of the next stanza is most effective :

"Good-bye! I'll soon be back."—" Good-bye!" said she ;—
And as he went she chanted merrily.

So the two brothers and their murder'd man
Rode past fair Florence. . . .

The appearance of Lorenzo's ghost to Isabella, and her journey with the old nurse to the scene of the crime, are on the same high level. And the poem reaches its climax in a stanza of tragic intensity :

> She gaz'd into the fresh-thrown mould, as though
>   One glance did fully all its secrets tell ;
> Clearly she saw, as other eyes would know
>   Pale limbs at bottom of a crystal well ;
> Upon the murderous spot she seem'd to grow,
>   Like to a native lily of the dell ;
> Then with her knife, all sudden, she began
> To dig more fervently than misers can.

The rest of the poem, Isabella's cherishing of Lorenzo's head in a pot of basil, the discovery of the secret by the two brothers, and their flight from Florence, falls somewhat below this standard, and the conclusion is, unfortunately, feeble. Yet *Isabella*, and *Lamia*—the story of a serpent which, under the form of a woman, beguiles a young man into marriage—though not perfect, are both remarkable experiments in narrative. They show that it was not foolish in Keats to cherish the hope of one day writing " a few fine plays."

XII

In *The Eve of St. Agnes*—a poem of slender narrative, but surpassingly beautiful in its descriptions—*La Belle Dame sans Merci*, a few sonnets, and, above all, the odes, the art of Keats is seen in perfection. Of the odes, those *To a Nightingale*, *On a Grecian Urn*, and *To Autumn*, stand out above the rest, and are among the masterpieces of poetic art. It is needless to ask which is the finest ; but for the purpose of quotation in a literary history of England, the choice is not hard. It has often been remarked how deeply our landscape has influenced our imaginative literature; and in *Autumn* Keats has written to the glory of Nature a poem which for richness and colour has never been surpassed. The ode was composed in the fields near one of the most ancient centres of English civilization, Winchester, on a Sunday evening in September 1819:

To Autumn

1

Season of mists and mellow fruitfulness,
   Close bosom-friend of the maturing sun;
Conspiring with him how to load and bless
   With fruit the vines that round the thatch-eves run;
To bend with apples the moss'd cottage-trees,
   And fill all fruit with ripeness to the core;
     To swell the gourd, and plump the hazel shells
   With a sweet kernel; to set budding more,
And still more, later flowers for the bees,
Until they think warm days will never cease,
     For summer has o'er-brimm'd their clammy cells.

2

Who hath not seen thee oft amid thy store?
   Sometimes whoever seeks abroad may find
Thee sitting careless on a granary floor,
   Thy hair soft-lifted by the winnowing wind;
Or on a half-reap'd furrow sound asleep,
   Drows'd with the fume of poppies, while thy hook
     Spares the next swath and all its twined flowers:
And sometimes like a gleaner thou dost keep
   Steady thy laden head across a brook;
   Or by a cyder-press, with patient look,
     Thou watchest the last oozings hours by hours.

3

Where are the songs of Spring? Ay, where are they?
   Think not of them, thou hast thy music too,—
While barred clouds bloom the soft-dying day,
   And touch the stubble-plains with rosy hue:
Then in a wailful choir the small gnats mourn
   Among the river sallows, borne aloft
     Or sinking as the light wind lives or dies;
And full-grown lambs loud bleat from hilly bourn;
   Hedge-crickets sing; and now with treble soft
   The red-breast whistles from a garden-croft;
     And gathering swallows twitter in the skies.

CHAPTER XVII

THE VICTORIAN AGE: CRITICS AND HISTORIANS

The " Victorian Age " is a phrase so often on our lips that one would imagine its meaning to be quite simple and definite. Yet the reign of the Queen was, in fact, far from a unity, whether regarded as a political period or as an epoch of civilization. It was crowded with events, rich in notable works, and susceptible, during its course, of so many changes that its end seems scarcely to belong to the same order as its beginning. The phrases " Early " and " Late " Victorian testify to a general sense that " Victorianism " is a term of vague and uncertain meaning ; and the idea that there are divisions in time more important than the dates of the Queen's reign is confirmed by a survey of the chief events in political and literary history.

The political historian has little difficulty in fixing the chief landmarks. The First Reform Act of 1832, the Repeal of the Corn Laws in 1846, and the Second Reform Act of 1867, followed by the return of Gladstone to power two years later, indicate very clearly the limits of several historical periods. In politics, the years 1820–1832 were a time of suspended animation. That England was fast turning from an agricultural into a manufacturing country was a fact of which the Tory statesmen either denied the truth or ignored the importance. Consequently, the reform of the constitution, already overdue, was delayed until 1832 ; then and then only was the way open for new experiments in constructive politics. In literature, the years 1820–1832 were also singularly barren. Wordsworth, who, like Wellington, dreaded revolution and opposed reform, published his *White Doe of Rylstone* in 1815, and thenceforward wrote little of note during all the thirty-five years which remained to him. The younger men, who might have enriched the period, died in its opening years— Keats in 1821, Shelley in 1822, Byron in 1824. Seldom were the prospects of poetry more blank. Nor did the future of the novel appear much brighter. Scott was still writing, but his powers were visibly in decline, and there was no one among the younger writers worthy to succeed him.

Soon after 1832, however, the features of a new age begin to take shape with growing distinctness. The Reform Act gave the middle classes the power which they had long coveted, and the Repeal of the Corn Laws conferred an immense advantage upon the manufacturing interest. Though the years 1839, 1840 and 1841 were long remembered with horror by the poor in the north of England, immense strides were being made in the accumulation of wealth. In spite of the Factory Acts and Mines Acts, it was the golden age of the employer. To men of much energy, some capital, and little heart, no period has ever offered brighter prospects. The Great Exhibition of 1851 stood as witness to the world of England's industrial greatness ; and the following years saw a further application of the principles of Free Trade. It was not until 1867 that the power of the middle class in politics was threatened by the enfranchisement of the artisan ; and it was not until 1870 that the Education Act admitted a responsibility in the State for the mental welfare of its poorest citizens.

The great age, then, of middle-class supremacy, the age of "laissez-faire," of unrestricted competition, extended from about 1832 to 1870 ; and it was during this period that the writers commonly called "the great Victorians" produced their principal works. Tennyson's first important volume, *Poems*, appeared in 1832, and the following year saw Carlyle's *Sartor Resartus*. Dickens's earliest work, *Sketches by Boz*, was published in serial form in 1833, and the literary career of Thackeray began about 1837.

By 1870, some of these men, as well as several younger writers, had already finished their work. Tennyson, Ruskin and Carlyle continued to write for some years longer, but they did little to alter their reputation, and, meantime, new fashions in verse and prose were coming into existence. The year 1870 was the last of Dickens's career, and Thackeray died in 1863. Browning, who continued to write prolifically until his death in 1889, produced nothing after 1869 to equal *The Ring and the Book*, and most readers would probably agree that his finest period is that which begins with *Dramatic Lyrics* (1842), and ends with *Dramatis Personæ* (1864). The literary career of the three Brontës falls wholly within the years in question ; and of George Eliot's novels, only the latest, *Middlemarch* (1872) and *Daniel Deronda* (1876), fall outside it. A few years before 1870, a startling portent had appeared in the literary heavens, a sign that a new order in poetry had begun. This was the publication of Swinburne's *Atalanta in Calydon* (1865), followed in the next year by the more famous *Poems and Ballads*. In 1871 Thomas Hardy's *Desperate Remedies*, with *Under the Greenwood Tree* (1872), announced the career of a new novelist. George Meredith had been writing for some years almost unobserved by the reading public : his first novels to attract general notice were *Beauchamp's Career* (1876) and *The Egoist* (1879). Swinburne, Meredith and Hardy are, perhaps, the three most eminent writers of the later Victorian age. Hardy is, in some senses, a poet of the twentieth century.

Yet, although the " Early " Victorian writers were the children of the new industrial age, they were far from being in sympathy with its spirit. On the contrary, they were, for most of their time, in conscious revolt against it ; and the abandonment of " laissez-faire " in legislation was largely due to their efforts. Inevitably, however, they were all affected by the spirit of the age, and with one at least of its qualities they heartily sympathised. It was an age of individualism, and they themselves were individualists. All were men and women of marked originality in outlook, character or style. In Macaulay, there was much of the energy and enterprise of the " self-made " man. Tennyson loved to sing the praises of sturdy independence. Ruskin felt himself a voice crying in the wilderness and gloried in it. In Dickens's books there are, perhaps, more " originals " than in those of any other novelist in the world. The Brontë sisters pursued their lonely path in life with the pride and endurance learnt at the Haworth parsonage. Carlyle and Browning cultivated a manner full of eccentricity ; and even Thackeray, though more regular in style than his contemporaries, loved to follow a haphazard path in the conduct of his stories, indulging in unbounded licence of comment and digression.

One only of these writers seemed satisfied with the condition of England in the early nineteenth century. This was Macaulay, for whom the success of his *Essay on Milton*, published in 1825, was the first step in a career brilliant by its achievement both in letters and in administration. Neither by temperament nor by experience was Macaulay moved to find fault with the world he lived in. He saw the country " growing richer and richer," and that was enough. Of the " early Victorian " writers, he alone was himself a complete " early Victorian."

I

Throughout his life, Thomas Babington Macaulay (1800–1859) displayed those mental and moral qualities which impress the world and dismay competitors. Somewhat short and sturdily built, he was made for work ; and his memory was such that a fact once known, or a line once treasured, was never forgotten. Both his parents were " strong-minded " persons, and the intellectual progress of their son began almost at birth. He could read at the age of three. At seven, be began a compendium of universal history. At eight, he wrote a treatise to convert the natives of Malabar to Christianity, and planned a poem on Olaus Magnus, the supposed ancestor of the Macaulays. From this time to the end of his life, reading and writing were as natural to him, and almost as indispensable, as breathing. At Cambridge he won a brilliant reputation for classical learning, and was elected a Fellow of his College. Soon after, he entered political life, and in 1830 he was returned to Parliament as member for Calne. He had, however, already begun his series of brilliant essays, and in 1825 contributed to *The Edinburgh Review* his Essay on Milton, which drew from Jeffrey, the editor, the admiring remark, " The more I think, the less I can conceive where you picked up that style." He became a commissioner of the board of control in 1832, but found time for literary work by rising at 5 a.m., and writing before breakfast. Many of his essays were the product of these early hours. Having been appointed to a seat on the Supreme Council for India, he sailed in 1834, and remained abroad for four years. His work in India has been of enduring importance, and must have been exhausting, yet he still found time to read enormously—in classics, modern literature, history and fiction. On his return home, he began his *History of England*, and in 1842 published the *Lays of Ancient Rome*. From this time onwards, till the end of his life, writing was his chief occupation. He re-entered Parliament after an interval of some years, in 1852, but his health had now become too uncertain for the excitement of politics, and his best energy was given to the History. He died in 1859, leaving only a fragment of the colossal work he had planned.

II

The reader of Macaulay's Essays need not go far before perceiving the main qualities of their writer's mind—his energy, his optimism, his knowledge, his cleverness, as well as his faults of taste and numerous limitations. It is clear that Macaulay's views on life and literature, on religion and politics, were formed quite early, and that though capable of development, they could not be radically changed. Being thus spared the pain of shocks, and the weakness of doubts, he writes with extreme assurance ; and his power of argument and wealth of illustration are such that he often appears, on the surface, invincible and omniscient. As an essayist, he is at his best on historical subjects, and especially excels when writing on post-Reformation events. Here he is on his own ground, and some of the essays, like that on Sir William Temple, give a pleasant foretaste of the *History*. Macaulay's strength lies in graphic description, in the massing of details, in the rapid painting of bold backgrounds. Hence the brilliance of the Essays on Clive and Warren Hastings, which the writer's knowledge of Indian affairs enabled him to pack full of telling descriptions, like that most vivid account of the Black Hole of Calcutta. For the analysis of motive and character, his mind was not fine or speculative enough ; but he can describe with spirit the energetic career of a man like Chatham, and the passage on the great orator's funeral is a piece of noble rhetoric. With his love of effect, Macaulay rejoices at the chance of caricature, and the picture of the garrulous Duke of Newcastle is executed with obvious relish. For the same reason, he loves pointed comparisons : the intercourse of Frederick the Great with Voltaire provides an opportunity for contrast and antithesis, in which he indulges without measure. Though many of the essays are not unexceptionable as history, nearly all have, to an extraordinary degree, the power of stimulating an interest in their subject.

As a critic, Macaulay's defects are serious, but he has some brilliant qualities. From one fault at least he is wholly free—that of half-heartedness. His energy in attacking confused thought or muddled metaphor is almost ferocious, and no one who has once read it can forget the annihilating effect of his Essay on Mr. Robert Montgomery. Much of Macaulay's originality lies in his power of expansion. His comparison between the definiteness of Dante and the vagueness of Milton is not very profound as criticism ; yet the fact is undeniable, and Macaulay's elaboration of it could not be bettered. On writers who may be treated half historically—Addison, for instance, and Fanny Burney—he is generally successful, and his gifts as a social historian stand him in good stead. He can sympathise, too, with Bacon, for he ardently believed in the same gospel of progress. But in his endeavour to exalt Bacon at the expense of a rival thinker, Macaulay is grossly unfair to Plato, and exposes his own metaphysical shallowness. To the finer qualities of imagination, style and character, he is often insensible. He fails to do justice to Dr. Johnson, and instead of praising his sterling qualities, exaggerates his oddities. He endeavours too much to make every sentence emphatic—an unworthy object, and not attainable without sacrifice of truth. Lord Chesterfield, he says, in the Essay on Johnson,

was by no means desirous to see all his carpets blackened with the London mud, and his soups and wines thrown to right and left over the gowns of fine ladies and the waistcoats of fine gentleman, by an absent, awkward scholar, who gave strange starts and uttered strange growls, who dressed like a scarecrow, and ate like a cormorant.

The exaggeration implied in the phrase " *all* his carpets," in the choice of the verb " thrown," and in the comparison with the scarecrow and cormorant is an indictment not of Johnson's manners, but of his critic's taste. Macaulay's chief defect is unconsciously revealed in one of his own remarks. " No man," he says, " whatever his sensibility may be, is ever affected by Hamlet, or Lear, as a little girl is affected by the story of little Red Riding Hood." True, perhaps : but the quality of an impression is as important as its force.

III

In his *History of England*, Macaulay had hoped to cover the whole period between the reign of James II and the Reform Act of 1832, thus building a secure monument to the glories of limited monarchy. That he should have executed only a small part of the scheme is not surprising. The scale is too vast for one lifetime, yet it is the minuteness of the work and its wealth of detail that give the History its unique value. Macaulay's ambition was to make his work as interesting as a novel, and he succeeded. The chapter on the state of England in 1685 must surely rank among the masterpieces of social history. The great narratives—the Battle of Sedgemoor, the Bloody Assize, the Trial of the Seven Bishops, the Siege of Londonderry, the Massacre of Glencoe—move us as if these were matters of which we had never heard, with consequences still uncertain. That Macaulay should not have been encumbered by his vast material is one of the greatest proofs of his skill. In the chapters on James II, for example, the broad issue is kept in view with the utmost clearness. Every page brings the sovereign's deposition perceptibly nearer.

The main defect of the work is obvious—so obvious as to lose half its evil, for the writer's Whig prejudices cannot escape or mislead a child. Moreover, Macaulay's endeavour to be always interesting sometimes lowers the dignity of history. Not only does it betray him into caricature, but it makes his whole method seem somewhat superficial. No shortcomings, however, can outweigh the merits of the work, and Macaulay's place among the great historical artists is secure.

IV

Thomas Carlyle (1795–1881), in spite of his five years' seniority, was much later than Macaulay in making his mark. It would be difficult to name two writers more sharply contrasted. In education, in outlook, in temperament and in style they were completely different. Carlyle, the son of a stone-mason living at Ecclefechan in Dumfriesshire, was brought up in an atmosphere of stern Calvinism, and he soon learnt to look upon life as a battle to be fought with the weapons of industry, character and intellect. His early manhood was passed in teaching and miscellaneous writing : it was years before he found his true vocation. His essays, written in the regular reviewing style on the German authors of whom he had made a special study, were full of sound information and useful criticism ; but they wanted unusual brilliance to commend them, and as yet, the subjects did not commend themselves. The years were passing by, and Carlyle was beginning almost to think himself a failure, when at last he produced an original and characteristic book, *Sartor Resartus* (1833–34). This work belongs to the large class of imaginative auto-biographies, but both by its fantastic style and its philosophy it was different from anything that had yet appeared in England.   Carlyle had managed to express the meditations which were deepest in his mind in a manner which conveys all the fire and force, all the light and darkness which they possessed for himself.   He stands before the world, a prophet with a new gospel.   From the French philosophers of the eighteenth century he had learnt a complete scepticism in religion, and he now bids the world to have done with hypocrisy and " shams."   This part of his gospel is conveyed in the chapter called *The Everlasting No*.   By the German philosophers he had been taught to find in the nobler instincts of man, especially in conscience, a divine authority, and on this foundation he builds the constructive part of his teaching, *The Everlasting Yea*. Readers of the book must have found much of it obscure, but it was evident at least that Carlyle was preaching a gospel of earnestness and sincerity.   That the manner of a prophet is dark is, perhaps, no great objection, provided he appears sufficiently inspired.

Carlyle now settled in London, and began to write the history of the French Revolution.   The manuscript was finished and ready for the publisher, when it was destroyed by the mistake of a maidservant, who used it to light a morning fire.   Carlyle re-wrote the whole work, and it appeared in 1837.   Its success was far greater than that of *Sartor Resartus*, and it made its author famous.   About the power of *The French Revolution* as a work of literature, there can be no question, though its value as a history is doubtful. But a great historical drama is, perhaps, of as much value to the world as a scientific record ;   and to Carlyle, the Revolution was a genuine tragedy after the Greek model, involving the fortunes of a whole people.   A great nation, submitting to a gigantic " sham " (such, to Carlyle, was the " *ancien régime* ") is drawn by Nemesis through an agony of five terrific years, at the end of which it is at last purged of its evil. Little is said about the great constructive work of the Revolution; and the sequence of events is hard to follow. But such merits must not be looked for in Carlyle. Instead, he gives us an impression of dim and vast upheaval. Against a dark background, certain scenes stand out as if written in fire. Such are the Procession of the Notables, the King's Flight to Varennes, the Death of Charlotte Corday, the Execution of Robespierre. Carlyle, like Macaulay, laid great emphasis on the literary side of history. Its task, he held, was " to make the past and the distant a thing of here and now." His success was as great as Macaulay's, though achieved by different means; and there are chapters in *The French Revolution* as graphic as any in the whole range of historical literature.

The Revolution gave ample scope to Carlyle's descriptive powers, but in some respects the subject did not attract him. For one thing, it was destitute of a great commanding figure. Secondly, it was the triumph of democracy. Carlyle distrusted democracy and he admired great men. His next subject was taken from a century which gave birth to heroes and turned with horror from the leveller. He had long contemplated a work on Cromwell, and at one time thought of writing his life. But a study of the Protector's letters and speeches gave him such a sense of the man's greatness, that he changed his plan and restricted himself to the more modest task of editor. *Oliver Cromwell's Letters and Speeches* (1845), however, must certainly be included among Carlyle's historical works. The connecting links between the letters and speeches form a considerable bulk, and we are conscious of the editor's mind at every page. The work is a monument to Carlyle's care and judgment, and its authority as a history has not been seriously impaired. But its finest quality is the portrait it gives of its hero. Hitherto, Cromwell had been regarded, for more than a century, as a " great, bad man " : Scott himself had accepted this view in *Woodstock*. Carlyle's book destroys the myth of Cromwell's hypocrisy, and establishes his human as well as his political greatness.

Between these two histories, Carlyle delivered a series of lectures, published later as a book entitled *Heroes and Hero-Worship* (1841). Taught by his German masters to believe in the "Zeit-Geist" or Spirit of the Age, he sought out a number of representative "heroes" in whom the "Time-Spirit" most clearly mirrored itself. Odin, Mahomet, Dante, Shakespeare, Dr. Johnson, and others are chosen as examples; and the treatment of each "hero" is a skilful blending of history and biography. This interpretation of the past flattered the individualism of the Victorian audiences, and they were quite willing to adopt Carlyle's enthusiasm for heroes. But they had no intention of replacing the power of the middle classes by the dictatorship of the "strong man," and Carlyle's contempt for "ballot-box" politics in *Past and Present* was put down to the eccentricity of genius.

Carlyle's most ambitious work, *The History of Frederick II of Prussia* (1858–65), was not his greatest success. He took the utmost pains to arrive at accuracy, and travelled over Frederick's battlefields. But compared with his earlier histories, the book is tedious; and Carlyle obviously found the War of the Austrian Succession and the Seven Years' War much less inspiring than the Puritan Revolution. When he died in 1881, his greatness was recognised in America and Germany as well as in England. His eccentric style—founded in part on the Lowland speech of his father—had ceased to irritate, and was admired for its virility, its humour, its flashes of poetry. Though appearing sometimes to exalt Might over Right, his books became a great moral force. He preached the gospel of work and the duty of strenuous endeavour. Perhaps his teaching might best be summed up in one of the precepts of *Sartor Resartus* : "Do the duty which lies nearest thee."

v

John Ruskin (1819–1900), one of the greatest masters of English prose, was also one of the most acute critics of his age. But partly through a defect of nature, partly through the fault of his education, he never commanded the attention which was his due. " I tell men their plain duty," he said, with both truth and humour, " and they tell me that my style is charming." He was the only son of a wealthy wine merchant, and was brought up in strictly evangelical beliefs. He had little schooling, and so was free to accompany his father on journeys of business to the houses of customers. At times, the family would visit the Continent, and travel by road in the leisurely manner of those days. The boy thus became acquainted, in the best possible manner, with the landscape of England, the old buildings of France, and the Swiss mountains. The elder Ruskin was an admirer of Turner, and possessed several of his paintings. His son carried the same taste almost to adoration ; and when, one day, he read in a review that Turner was " out of Nature," he was raised, he says, " to the height of black anger." It was this sense of injustice that led him, some years later, to write *Modern Painters*. At Oxford, Ruskin formed some valuable acquaintances, but did not receive the mental discipline he most needed. When he left the University he was still something of a precocious boy, acute and learned in some things, simple and ignorant in others. He began, almost at once, to write his vindication of Turner, a work which involved an examination of the principles of art, and a consideration of nearly all great painters from Giotto onwards. The five volumes of *Modern Painters* (1843–1860) form one of the most suggestive works on æsthetics to be found anywhere, for Ruskin's love and understanding of the beautiful are almost unmatched. His evangelical upbringing, however, made it impossible for him to separate Beauty from Religion ; and his endeavour to prove that " all great art is praise " leads him into many inconsistencies, and some strange judgments. But his insight into art is so keen that his very errors are instructive. Even his remarks on Rembrandt, to whom he is most unfair, are not valueless. Art criticism in England was at a very low ebb when *Modern Painters* appeared, and a book which not only discussed the relations of painting with history, religion and social conditions, but was well-informed on matters of technique was of high importance. Nothing in the book, however, was so praiseworthy as its style. The descriptions of Alpine scenery, the appreciations of great paintings such as Turner's "Slave Ship" and Tintoretto's "Crucifixion" are among the most eloquent passages of prose in our literature. The caustic denunciations of bad art, such as the analysis of Wouvermans' "Landscape with a Hunting Party," are hardly less effective. Scattered through the book are digressions, some of them in Ruskin's finest critical manner. One of the best is the chapter on "Vulgarity"; and a good second is the controversial but suggestive discussion of the "Pathetic Fallacy."

VI

Examination of the principles of art gradually led Ruskin to the study of social ethics. Architecture, he found, even more than painting, indicated the state of a nation's health. *The Seven Lamps of Architecture* (1849) is one of the least ornate of Ruskin's books, but it is one of the best reasoned. Some such work was much needed, for the artistic conscience of the nation suffered the most hideous buildings to be erected without protest. Ruskin at least made it clear that there was something ignoble in a pillar intended to adorn rather than support, and that a form of moulding suitable to a Greek temple might be out of place in a shop-counter; though some of his injunctions, especially that of lavish expenditure for its own sake, fell on deaf ears. *The Stones of Venice* (1851–1853) expanded and enforced the teaching of the *Seven Lamps*. The book is second only to *Modern Painters* in its wealth of beautiful descriptions; and the chapter called "The Nature of Gothic" is equal to anything Ruskin ever wrote.

The publication of *Unto this Last* (1860) was a landmark in Ruskin's career. From this time onwards he wrote little on art and devoted himself to discussing the ills of society. *Unto this Last* is an attack on the prevalent system of political economy. Ruskin's definition of the "valuable " as " that which leads to life," and his contention that the same wages should be paid to all workmen, irrespective of the amount and quality of their work, seemed to the Cobdenites and Utilitarians pernicious nonsense. A storm of protest was raised, and the publication of the book in *The Cornhill Magazine* was discontinued. Ruskin took no pains to soften his paradoxes, and some of his suggestions were provokingly unpractical. None the less, the book was a timely protest against unrestricted competition (the law of Devil-take-the-hindmost, as Ruskin called it), and its literary skill was so great that the sound part of its teaching began to bear fruit. It was, indeed, an acute and eloquent attack on heartless economics. The books by which it was followed, *Sesame and Lilies* (1865) and *The Crown of Wild Olive* (1866), show Ruskin as a popular educator, clear in argument and skilful in illustration. They consist of lectures, of which one of the best, " Of Kings' Treasuries," is an attempt to define the nature of good literature, and contains a famous exposition of a passage in *Lycidas*. Ruskin was made Professor of Fine Art at Oxford in 1869, and, except for a short interval, occupied the chair until 1884. His last work, an autobiography called *Præterita*, opens with some interesting pages of reminiscence ; but Ruskin's powers were failing and he never finished the work. He died at Coniston, the home of his later years.

VII

Ruskin's greatness as a stylist gives him a very high place in English literature. Though his upbringing was in some respects unfortunate, it was favourable to his future as a master of prose. As a child, he was made to study the Bible every day, and to learn long passages by heart. This training, as he admits, was the foundation of his style. Secondly, his habit of close observation and drawing made him dissatisfied with any vagueness of expression ; and his descriptions have the same definiteness as a draughtsman's minute studies from life. Further, his powers of analysis were sharpened by the practice they received in his early theoretical writings, such as the first two books of *Modern Painters*. By the time he came to write *Unto this Last*, Ruskin was in control of an instrument which, for fineness, lucidity and beauty has never been outmatched in English.

In his later writings, he allowed himself to wander disconcertingly into the byways of knowledge and fancy; and at Oxford, he gained a reputation for incoherence. But on subjects which he thoroughly understood, Ruskin is one of the clearest of writers, and he has also a wonderful power of insight. No one, for instance, should visit the Spanish Chapel at Florence without having first read his interpretation of the frescoes. On subjects outside art, his strength lies in aphorism rather than in systematic thought. A paragraph like the following gives a good idea of Ruskin's attitude towards life :

There are three things to which man is born—labour, and sorrow, and joy. Each of these three things has its baseness and its nobleness. There is base labour, and noble labour. There is base sorrow, and noble sorrow. There is base joy, and noble joy. But you must not think to avoid the corruption of these things by doing without the things themselves. Nor can any life be right that has not all three. Labour without joy is base. Labour without sorrow is base. Sorrow without labour is base. Joy without labour is base. (From *Time and Tide*.)

His descriptions of mountain and wave, of forest and cloud are among the most beautiful in English prose. Rhythm and vocabulary are both perfect. The following is a picture of Alpine scenery from *Modern Painters* :

Such precipices are among the most impressive as well as the most really dangerous of mountain ranges ; in many spots inaccessible with safety either from below or from above ; dark in colour, robed with everlasting mourning, for ever tottering like a great fortress shaken by war, fearful as much in their weakness as in their strength, and yet gathered after every fall into darker frowns and unhumiliated threatening ; for ever incapable of comfort or of healing from herb or flower, nourishing no root in their crevices, touched by no hue of life on buttress or ledge, but, to the utmost, desolate ; knowing

no shaking of leaves in the wind, nor of grass beside the stream,
—no motion but their own mortal shivering, the dreadful
crumbling of atom from atom in their corrupting stones;
knowing no sound of living voice or living tread, cheered
neither by the kid's bleat nor the marmot's cry; haunted only
by uninterpreted echoes from far off, wandering hither and
thither, among their walls, unable to escape, and by the hiss of
angry torrents, and sometimes the shriek of a bird that flits
near the face of them, and sweeps frightened back from under
their shadow into the gulph of air; and, sometimes, when the
echo has fainted, and the wind has carried the sound of the
torrent away, and the bird has vanished, and the mouldering
stones are still for a little time,—a brown moth, opening and
shutting its wings upon a grain of dust, may be the only thing
that moves, or feels, in all the waste of weary precipice, darkening
five thousand feet of the blue depth of heaven.

VIII

The writing and criticism of poetry was the province of
Matthew Arnold[1] (1822–1888), son of Dr. Arnold of Rugby,
and his election to the Chair of Poetry at Oxford was a
fitting recognition of his powers. But Arnold's wide
interests went far beyond the technical and æsthetic side
of poetry. He was an active man with many friends and
occupations; a student, too, of the best contemporary
thought, and an enthusiast for his country's welfare, as
became his father's son. It was natural that Arnold should
regard poetry as a " criticism of life," and that his own
literary criticism should have in view the promotion of
culture, as well as the interpretation of letters. His best
work is contained in the two volumes of *Essays in Criticism*
(1865 and 1888), and in the lectures *On Translating Homer*
(1861). The articles on Wordsworth, Byron and Keats,
though not infallible, have gone far towards determining
the true rank of these poets; and many of Arnold's
sentences, like that on Keats, " he is with Shakespeare,"
have long been recognised as critical dicta against which
there is no appeal. Few critics are more sparing of praise
than Arnold; and his high-handed and jaunty dismissal

[1] See pp. 325–327.

of various esteemed authors caused him to be accused of intellectual snobbery. One of his critical methods is particularly severe. He will quote a line from Homer, Dante, Shakespeare or Milton, and then ask if the author under discussion can write verse of the same " accent." Yet although this procedure falls heavily on all but the greatest writers, it was not adopted without reason. Arnold hated the fulsome praise of third-rate poets, for he knew—no man better—the rarity and worth of really great poetry, and he saw that in a democratic age the false estimate of literature is a serious social evil. Among the best of Arnold's essays are those on wide subjects, such as " The Function of Criticism at the Present Time," " The Literary Influence of Academies," and " The Future of Poetry."

Arnold's chief work of general criticism, *Culture and Anarchy* (1869), expands the views on life and society which are hinted at in the literary essays. He principally addresses the middle classes, " the Philistines," as he gaily calls them, for he abandons the " Barbarians " of the upper class as impervious to ideas, and passes by the " Populace " as scarcely able to read and write. The good-natured but pointed satire on the shortcomings of the Philistine are extremely diverting, though times have changed. The love of tea-meetings and Exeter Hall, the complacent pride in " our unrivalled Anglo-Saxon breed," and the hideous industrial town which was the Philistine's chief visible work form an excellent target for Arnold's serious pleasantry. He grants that the middle-class Victorian had energy, that he had drawn great moral strength from the Old Testament, but where, he asks, is that love of ideas for their own sake, which is the best fruit of culture ? England, no doubt, is prolific in men of genius, but even a Ruskin has lapses into extravagance, through want of a stricter intellectual conscience. To qualify the " Hebraism " of the Philistine, Arnold recommends the cultivation of the " Hellenistic " virtues, and these he describes, in a phrase borrowed from Swift, as " Sweetness and Light." So, too, England has been rich in poetry, for that is the work of energy and imagination; but the prose of the average educated man falls far below the level it reaches in France, for the virtues of prose are "regularity, uniformity, precision, balance," the results of that clear thinking which we have neglected to cherish. The historical value of Arnold's general criticism is already great, and it will increase. The fine quality of his prose, its grace, wit and rhythm, would keep his best criticism alive even without its other merits.

IX

During the nineteenth century, many historians flourished whose works were of high literary merit, and often not far below those of Macaulay and Carlyle in prose style. It was an age of works planned on a large scale and written with more literary art than many of the specialist monographs of our own time. One of the most learned historians of the century was Henry Hallam, author of *A View of the State of Europe during the Middle Ages* (1818), and *A Constitutional History of England* (1827). Henry Thomas Buckle's unfinished *History of Civilization in Europe* (1857–1861) was an attempt at a philosophical treatment of the subject. The style is clear and picturesque, but many of the generalisations are untrustworthy. James Anthony Froude, a great figure in his day, has also a name for inaccuracy. Yet his chief work, *A History of England from the Fall of Wolsey to the Defeat of the Spanish Armada* (1856–1870), is still a standard book, and his *Short Studies on Great Subjects* (1867–1883) is one of the best collections of historical essays in English. W. E. Hartpole Lecky was the master of an agreeable style, and few books on the Dark Ages are so readable as his *History of European Morals from Augustus to Charlemagne* (1869). His most ambitious work—still an authority—was the *History of England in the Eighteenth Century* (1878–1890). J. R. Green's *Short History of the English People* (1874) is remarkable for its high literary finish, and for its introduction of a strong human interest into the national story. Other great historical names of the century are Freeman, Gardiner, Stubbs and Maitland.

Many of the leaders of nineteenth-century thought were men whose style, apart from their ideas, entitles them to a place in literary history. Thanks to the system of classical education still prevalent, the men who became famous in religious, scientific and political thought had all had some literary training. In general, the early Victorians created new ideas, the later Victorians popularised and applied them. A great political thinker and a leader of the Utilitarians was John Stuart Mill (1806–1873), whose essay *On Liberty* (1859) was a charter of political individualism. He was known as an " advanced " writer, and his work *The Subjection of Women* (1869) marks the beginning of extensive changes in national life. His most interesting work, probably, is his *Autobiography* (1873), which, though severely written and as nearly impersonal as such a work can be, is a fine record of a mind dedicated through its whole history to public service. The chief religious movement of the century was that which began at Oxford under such men as Keble, Pusey and Newman. It gave birth to some highly cultivated prose, especially in *Tracts for the Times*, begun in 1833. But its chief gift to literature was the *Apologia pro Vita Sua* (1864) of J. H. Newman, written after he had entered the Roman Catholic Church, in answer to a clumsy charge of dishonesty brought against him by Charles Kingsley. Newman's book, composed under deep emotion, reveals his fine and subtle nature with a fulness which makes it one of the best autobiographies in the language. Pain and indignation alone could have moved Newman to make his great " confession." Of his other works, *The Idea of a University* (1852–58) and *A Grammar of Assent* (1870) have, perhaps, most general interest. In scientific thought, there was one book of outstanding importance, Charles Darwin's *Origin of Species* (1859), the great classic on the theory of natural selection. It provoked much opposition, but its effect could not be withstood, and the idea of evolution gradually spread beyond the boundaries of biology into nearly every region of thought and speculation.

Later Victorian literature was marked by the eminence

of the "publicist," the man who strove to extend ideas which deserved a field of operation outside small circles of specialists. The theories of Darwin, for instance, were ably expounded by T. H. Huxley in *Man's Place in Nature* (1863) and other works. A writer of great name in his day, a student of many sciences, and a philosopher supposed to be always in the van of thought was Herbert Spencer, whose reputation has since greatly declined. Two disciples of French philosophy, Frederic Harrison and John Morley, exercised much influence in the later half of the century. Morley's books *Voltaire, Diderot* and *Rousseau* are remarkable for their vigorous and eloquent prose. His chief work was the *Life of Gladstone*.

A few writers remain to be mentioned who busied themselves exclusively with literature and art. The *Imaginary Conversations* (1824–53) of Walter Savage Landor, a series of dialogues between persons famous in many lands and ages, do not quite succeed in re-creating the past, and are to be prized chiefly for the stateliness and precision of their prose. Landor's imaginary characters are somewhat statuesque, and the dialogues want motion and life ; but his style has always a chaste elevation, and sometimes the warmth and fervour of poetry. He is a somewhat lonely figure in literature, and his long life made him a link between the age of Wordsworth and the age of Browning. Among the later Victorian critics, Walter Pater (1839–1894) and A. C. Swinburne (1837–1909) are the most notable. Pater's essays are the work of one long accustomed to the finest æsthetic experiences. He has loved all forms of art for their own sake, and has found beauty in many byways of painting and literature. His style is infinitely studied, a pattern of words curiously chosen and cunningly arranged. It displays in every detail the fineness of his taste, but wants variety, strength and, at times, one might add, humanity. His principal works are *Studies in the History of the Renaissance* (1873), *Imaginary Portraits* (1887), *Appreciations* (1889), and *Greek Studies* (1895). One of his best books is a philosophical novel, *Marius the Epicurean* (1885).

Most of Swinburne's criticism is the fruit of passionate

enthusiasm, and, at its best, shows a fine intuition into the qualities of his subject. He rarely wrote on any author whom he did not love almost to adoration. On men who had not then received their due, such as Blake, Chapman, and other contemporaries of Shakespeare, he has many illuminating things to say, but his praise is apt to swell into rhapsody, and he is at times the slave, rather than the master, of his rhetoric. His range was very wide, and some of his best articles were on the novel. Most of his criticism was written between 1868 and 1894.

x

The following extract from Newman's *Idea of a University* is quoted, partly as a specimen of Victorian prose at its best, partly for the historical interest of its matter :

It is almost a definition of a gentleman to say he is one who never inflicts pain. This description is both refined and, as far as it goes, accurate. He is mainly occupied in merely removing the obstacles which hinder the free and unembarrassed action of those about him ; and he concurs with their movements rather than takes the initiative himself. His benefits may be considered as parallel to what are called comforts or conveniences in arrangements of a personal nature : like an easy chair or a good fire, which do their part in dispelling cold and fatigue, though nature provides both means of rest and animal heat without them. The true gentleman in like manner carefully avoids whatever may cause a jar or a jolt in the minds of those with whom he is cast ;—all clashing of opinion, or collision of feeling, all restraint, or suspicion, or gloom, or resentment ; his great concern being to make every one at their ease and at home. He has his eyes on all his company ; he is tender towards the bashful, gentle towards the distant, and merciful towards the absurd ; he can recollect to whom he is speaking ; he guards against unseasonable allusions, or topics which may irritate ; he is seldom prominent in conversation, and never wearisome. He makes light of favours while he does them, and seems to be receiving when he is conferring. He never speaks of himself except when compelled, never defends himself by a mere retort, he has no ears for slander or gossip, he is scrupulous in imputing motives to those who interfere with him, and interprets everything for the best. He is never mean or little in his disputes, never takes unfair advantage, never mistakes personalities or sharp sayings for arguments, or insinuates evil which he dare not say out. From a long-sighted prudence, he observes the maxim of the ancient sage, that we should ever conduct ourselves towards our enemy as if he were one day to be our friend. He has too much good sense to be affronted at insults, he is too well employed to remember injuries, and too indolent to bear malice. He is patient, forbearing, and resigned, on philosophical principles ; he submits to pain, because it is inevitable, to bereavement, because it is irreparable, and to death, because it is his destiny. If he engages in controversy of any kind, his disciplined intellect preserves him from the blundering discourtesy of better, perhaps, but less educated minds ; who, like blunt weapons, tear and hack instead of cutting clean, who mistake the point in argument, waste their strength on trifles, misconceive their adversary, and leave the question more involved than they find it. He may be right or wrong in his opinion, but he is too clear-headed to be unjust ; he is as simple as he is forcible, and as brief as he is decisive. Nowhere shall we find greater candour, consideration, indulgence : he throws himself into the minds of his opponents, he accounts for their mistakes. He knows the weakness of human reason as well as its strength, its province and its limits. If he be an unbeliever, he will be too profound and large-minded to ridicule religion or to act against it ; he is too wise to be a dogmatist or fanatic in his infidelity. He respects piety and devotion ; he even supports institutions as venerable, beautiful, or useful, to which he does not assent ; he honours the ministers of religion, and it contents him to decline its mysteries without assailing or denouncing them. He is a friend of religious toleration, and that, not only because his philosophy has taught him to look on all forms of faith with an impartial eye, but also from the gentleness and effeminacy of feeling, which is the attendant on civilization.

CHAPTER XVIII

THE VICTORIAN AGE: POETRY

THERE can be no doubt about the high quality of much Victorian poetry. No one, of course, could maintain that the verse of 1840–1870 matches that of 1590–1640; nor were the Victorian poets the equals of their immediate predecessors. Yet the age of Tennyson does not fall so very far short of the age of Wordsworth, and in some respects it is superior. The later poets were less original in their work, but they were also less unequal. The best poetry of Wordsworth and Coleridge, of Keats and Shelley, was produced in the period of early manhood. The poetry of 1840–1870 is the product of riper years: Tennyson and Browning maintained their greatness in middle life. In the supreme quality of "inspiration" the earlier age stands higher. The elemental simplicity of Wordsworth, Keats's passionate sense of beauty are, both of them, poetic qualities higher than anything in Tennyson's age. The peculiar excellence of the Victorians lies in the variety and range of their merits. Their work is the product of natural talents greatly improved by cultivation. It is both complex and civilized. Tennyson, Browning and Arnold were all born poets; yet all illustrate the truth of Ben Jonson's saying, "A good poet's made as well as born." All three were "humanists," and despised the narrow creed of "Art for Art's sake." Though honouring poetry, they knew that life is greater.

The later generations of Victorian poets, Rossetti and Morris, who came first, Swinburne and Meredith, who followed shortly after, and the host of others who appeared in the later years of the century, possessed no man of the stature of Tennyson and Browning. Swinburne, the greatest of the younger poets, though marvellous in the technique of verse, wanted the wide humanism of the earlier Victorians. For Rossetti, Morris and Meredith, poetry was but one means of self-expression, and much of their strength was spent in other directions. Later still in the reign, new poets appeared, such as Mr. Bridges and Mr. Kipling; but these, though in part Victorians, have done much of their work in the twentieth century.

I

The publication of Tennyson's volumes of 1842 was a noteworthy event in English literary history. The volumes were less revolutionary than the *Lyrical Ballads* of 1798, less sensational than Swinburne's *Poems and Ballads* of 1866. Nothing so good had appeared for many years, and the *Poems* were seen to be not only fine in achievement, but rich in promise. It was a dull time for poetry. Some great men of the past lived still, but their days for writing had long gone by. Of the newer voices, men like Ebenezer Elliott, known for his *Corn-Law Rhymes* (1831), and Thomas Hood, author of *The Song of the Shirt* (1843), attracted notice by the poignancy of their complaints; but such verse was of social rather than literary importance. Tennyson had been familiar to a select few for many years when his volumes of 1842 were published; but it was only then that the reviews and the nation at large recognised the advent of a new poet.

Alfred Tennyson, born in 1809, passed his childhood at Somersby Rectory in Lincolnshire, the home of his father, Dr. George Clayton Tennyson. There was much in Tennyson's early life to foster both his imagination and his intellect. Out of doors, he would wander over the rolling Lincolnshire wolds, ending in the desolate coast of the North Sea. Indoors, there were lessons from the Doctor, a learned man and a traveller; and it must have been partly due to his teaching that three of his sons became poets. Just before leaving home for Cambridge, Alfred and Charles Tennyson brought out a volume of verse called *Poems by Two Brothers*.

At Cambridge, Tennyson formed one of an able group of men who called themselves " The Apostles." The society met to discuss politics, biology, metaphysics and literature ; and no doubt Tennyson owed much of his wide culture to his membership of this set. He won a University prize for his poem *Timbuctoo*, and in 1830 published a volume, *Poems, chiefly Lyrical*, which attracted some slight notice in the literary world. The best piece in the book is that delightful poem, *Mariana in the Moated Grange*. Tennyson left Cambridge with the resolution to make poetry his profession ; and in the retirement of Somersby he prepared his volume of 1832, a collection including among other pieces, *The Lady of Shalott*, *Œnone*, *The Palace of Art*, *The Lotus Eaters*, *The Dream of Fair Women*, and *The May Queen*. The book was enthusiastically received at Cambridge, but the world at large was indifferent and even hostile. A review in the powerful *Quarterly* was particularly malicious.

Tennyson was disappointed ; but the blow was nothing to that which fell in the following year. His chief friend, Arthur Hallam, a young man of great promise, died suddenly at Vienna : and the poet, immersed in dreams of beauty, was suddenly brought face to face with the cruellest reality of life. The grief of the bereavement first found expression in the lines, " Break, break, break " ; later, in the brooding verse of *The Two Voices* ; and later still, when the sorrow had at last spiritualised his whole view of life and the universe, in *In Memoriam*. Tennyson had to struggle through nine gloomy years of depression and silence before the success of his *Poems* (1842) gave his prospects a brighter look. The Reviews this time were loud in their praise, and they recognised that Tennyson was not merely a graceful singer, but an interpreter of life. " It was the heart of England even more than her imagination that he made his own." Most of the pieces, *Morte d'Arthur*, *St. Simeon Stylites*, *Ulysses*, *The Vision of Sin*, were new ; but certain of the older poems, *The Lotus Eaters*, for instance, and *The Lady of Shalott*, reappeared in an improved form.

Some critics have held that after 1842, Tennyson's poetic powers declined, that he merely applied his skill in verse to purposes of narrative and discussion, and underwent no new imaginative experience of the highest kind. This view finds some support in *The Princess* (1847); though Fitzgerald and Carlyle went too far when they " gave up all hopes " of Tennyson after the poem. *The Princess* is a piece of beautiful patch-work, or as its title calls it, " a medley." It has no imaginative or emotional unity. It is half fanciful, half didactic. Its topic, the higher education of women, was a matter of great contemporary importance, and Tennyson's thesis that " woman is not undevelopt man, but diverse " no doubt deserved stating. But the story of the women's college which finally dissolves under the power of love was difficult to handle seriously; and the poet admits that in trying to please both " the mockers and the realists " he may have pleased neither himself nor them. A doubtful success was achieved in the *Idylls of the King*, the first of which, *Enid*, *Vivien*, *Elaine*, and *Guinevere*, appeared in 1859. Tennyson's re-handling of the Arthurian legends robs the stories of their old simplicity, and gives them an ethical colouring wholly foreign to their true spirit. Apart from this, Tennyson does not take kindly to the duties of a narrative poet. In *Elaine*, for instance, he describes with lavish detail the emblazonry of Sir Launcelot's shield and the desolate scenery through which he rides, but he shuns the dust and heat of the tournament. The *Idylls* were highly popular, and Tennyson continued the series in the following years. But the central work of his career was *In Memoriam* (1850). Its roots are in the grief at Hallam's death, seventeen years before; and it anticipates in its grander sections the lofty philosophical poems of Tennyson's later life. The year of *In Memoriam* was also the year of Tennyson's marriage and his appointment to the laureateship in succession to Wordsworth.

For the rest of his life Tennyson, now recognised as the chief of living poets, lived amid beautiful surroundings in the south of England, first at Farringford, in the Isle of Wight, later at Aldworth in Surrey. He published *Maud* in 1855, a poem attacked in the reviews, but warmly praised by Ruskin and Jowett; and other volumes of verse continued to follow at intervals. His dramas, of which *Queen Mary* (1875) was the first, were designed " to complete the line of Shakespeare's chronicle-plays which end with the commencement of the Reformation." Though he wrote less as he grew older, Tennyson's lyrical powers never failed him. He was eighty when he wrote *Crossing the Bar*, and the hardly less beautiful *Silent Voices* was written in the last year of his life. Many new poets had arisen since Tennyson's appointment to the Laureate-ship, and Browning, especially, was regarded by some as his equal or superior. But when he died in 1892, Tennyson was still looked upon by the nation at large as the chief among Victorian poets, and it seems unlikely that this judgment will ever be reversed.

II

Tennyson owed much of his contemporary fame to the variety of his work. His verse was an instrument which could express every mood, from the airiness of a cradle-song to the sonorous sorrow of a funeral ode. He could write for the many in the sentimental strains of *The May Queen*, and for the few in the noble verse of *Ulysses* and *Tithonus*. He could express a national emotion with spirit and fire as in *The Charge of the Light Brigade*; he could delight men of science by his minute observation, as in the lines on the dragon-fly in *The Two Voices*; and he could win the approval of philosophers by the profound experience of his elegiac and reflective verse. With this wide range he had also a perfection of technique which made his English not only wonderfully expressive but free from every offence of harshness and monotony.

Tennyson had all the qualities of a successful laureate, but he was also a poet whose original sense of beauty and fine talent for lyric give him a high place among the masters of English verse. Some of his shorter pieces, such as " Break, break, break," " Tears, idle tears," *In the Valley of Cauteretz* and *Crossing the Bar*, have a distinction of music and imagery which places them among the finest English songs. Though this quality of lyrical emotion is seldom so perfect as in these few pieces, it was one of Tennyson's most constant gifts, and it pervades nearly the whole of *Maud*—a poem of astonishing variety in music and feeling. Moreover, Tennyson is a master of imaginative description. A good example for quotation is his fragment, *The Eagle*—a poem of six lines, which once read leaves a picture which cannot be forgotten :

> He clasps the crag with crooked hands ;
> Close to the sun in lonely lands,
> Ring'd with the azure world, he stands.
>
> The wrinkled sea beneath him crawls ;
> He watches from his mountain walls,
> And like a thunderbolt he falls.

This quality, too, is not occasional in Tennyson : it is his constant characteristic ; his weakest poems are redeemed by some flashes of it. It is found in its richest form in the volumes of 1842, some pieces of which, such as *A Dream of Fair Women*, are almost wholly composed of imaginative descriptions. *Œnone* also has a fine array of pictures, like that suggested by the scenery of the Pyrenees :

> The long brook falling thro' the clov'n ravine
> In cataract after cataract to the sea.

The Lady of Shalott, The Gardener's Daughter, Morte d'Arthur are all rich in splendid descriptions ; but perhaps the finest of all poems in this class is *The Lotus Eaters*. Words can hardly be more beautiful or more expressive than in such a stanza as this :

> A land of streams ! some, like a downward smoke,
> Slow-dropping veils of thinnest lawn, did go ;
> And some thro' wavering lights and shadows broke,
> Rolling a slumbrous sheet of foam below.

They saw the gleaming river seaward flow
From the inner land : far off, three mountain tops,
Three silent pinnacles of aged snow,
Stood sunset-flush'd : and, dew'd with showery drops,
Up-clomb the shadowy pine above the woven copse.

It is also a part of Tennyson's praise that he interpreted the spirit of his age. As we see the life of Augustan Rome in the poetry of Virgil, and of mediæval Florence in that of Dante, so the life of Victorian England lives in the verse of Tennyson. That he sometimes condescended to facile sentiment and trivial prettiness is undeniable ; but these things are not any more " Victorian " than some very noble qualities. It was fitting, for instance, in an age of much general culture and many fine scholars, that the most eminent poet should do honour to Dante and Milton, to Catullus and Lucretius in lines of felicitous appreciation ; that he should address Virgil in a majestic style so faithfully echoing his own :

Thou that sëest Universal Nature clothed by Universal Mind :
Thou, majestic in thy sadness at the doubtful doom of human kind ;

Now thy Forum roars no longer, fallen every purple Cæsar's dome—
Though thine ocean-roll of rhythm sound for ever of Imperial Rome.

It was fitting, too, that the prevalent belief in progress should be both expressed and interrogated in the two poems, *Locksley Hall* and *Locksley Hall, Sixty Years After*. In an age when the vast and the minute in nature were coming into man's ken, it was a worthy extension of the province of poetry to draw imagery, as Tennyson did, from the new knowledge. Above all, the conflict between the materialistic and the spiritual interpretations of life is reflected more clearly in the poetry of Tennyson than any-where else in our literature. There are no lines more tragic in *In Memoriam* than those in which the poet contem-plates the terrible implications of complete materialism. And it is one of the most touching things in poetry to see, in *Vastness*, how, after the lapse of years, the same gloomy thoughts were still haunting the poet, until dispelled in the

last line by the belief he had striven for ever since the death
of Hallam :

> Peace, let it be ! for I loved him, and love him for ever :
> the dead are not dead but alive.

Tennyson did not solve the problems of his age, but he felt
them as only a great man could.

III

The life of Robert Browning (1812–1889) has far less
significance for literary history than Tennyson's. It was
long, happy and uneventful, but it was not spent in intimate
contact with his country's life. Browning did not study
the soul of England so much as the soul of man. There
was something slightly foreign or at least cosmopolitan
about him. He left school at the age of fourteen ; he
had none but the slightest contact with any University.
He was brought up in a world of books and works of art,
and after his marriage with Elizabeth Barrett, much of his
time was passed in Italy. He was a man of vast knowledge,
but his studies were unorthodox, and he loved the by-
paths of learning. He had less practice than most writers
in the elementary drill of expression ; and it was natural
that his first poems, being packed with thought and
erudition, should be quite beyond the comprehension of the
ordinary reader. For a large part of his life, Browning was
regarded as hopelessly " obscure " ; and although he always
had some admirers, his career was far advanced before his
true greatness was generally recognised.

Browning published several volumes of verse before he
discovered the form of expression which really suited him.
His early poems, *Pauline*, *Paracelsus* and *Sordello*, are works
of promise rather than of performance. In his dramas, of
which *A Blot in the 'Scutcheon* is perhaps the finest, one feels
that the mind of a gifted writer is not employed to the best
end. But the *Dramatic Lyrics* (1842) and *Dramatic
Romances* (1845) are as successful as they are original ; and
the appearance of *Men and Women* (1855) was a further

triumph on the same lines. Browning continued to follow his own methods in *Dramatis Personæ* (1864), and in *The Ring and the Book* (1868–69), which was his greatest and most ambitious effort. But certain faults of haste and carelessness had now appeared in his work, and, moreover, the poet in Browning seemed giving way to the lover of intellectual and psychological analysis. In his later works, such as *The Inn Album* (1875) and *Pacchiarotto* (1876), there is a want of formal beauty ; and from this time onwards, true poetry appeared in his work in flashes only, as in the splendid epilogue to *Asolando*, a poem written in the last years of his life. Browning died at Venice.

IV

The forms of poetry which Browning made peculiarly his own were the Dramatic Lyric, the Dramatic Romance and the Dramatic Idyl. These three titles are Browning's own, and in all his " dramatic " poems he suggests a definite situation in place or time, or both. Thus, even so simple a song as " Kentish Sir Byng," indicates the period of the Civil War and the martial loyalty of the speaker. Browning puts the whole of a poem into the mouth of one man or woman, and no one, before or since, has given so wide a range to the poetry of the first person. The *Dramatic Lyrics* and *Romances* are speeches uttered in the crisis of a life, and most of them express a whole dramatic situation. *The Laboratory*, for instance, gives utterance to the rage of a wronged woman ; and she pours out her passions to an apothecary who is preparing the poison by which she will avenge herself on her lover and her rival :

> He is with her ; and they know that I know
> Where they are, what they do : they believe my tears flow
> While they laugh, laugh at me, at me fled to the drear
> Empty church to pray God in for them !—I am here.

The *Soliloquy in a Spanish Cloister* expresses the disgust and irritation caused by daily contact with an unsympathetic nature. *My Last Duchess* is the speech of an Italian aristocrat who is making negotiations for a second marriage; and as he stands before the smiling portrait of his last wife, he nonchalantly reveals the history of a secret crime. His lady's facile good nature had aroused his jealousy, and the smile so freely given to all the world became her destruction :

> O, sir, she smiled no doubt,
> Whene'er I passed her ; but who smiled without
> Much the same smile ?   This grew ; I gave commands ;
> Then all smiles stopped together.

Browning's wonderful knowledge of life and manners in different countries and ages enabled him to invent scores of dramatic situations, and to give each of them a colouring both vivid and distinct.

The *Dramatic Lyrics* and *Romances* seldom extend to more than a few hundred lines, and many, by their style and metre, give the feeling of tense or vigorous action.   The three riding poems, for instance, *How they brought the Good News from Ghent to Aix*, *The Last Ride Together*, and *Through the Metidja*, all move vigorously, though with different speed and emotion.   In *Men and Women* the emphasis is less on action, more on character.   Most of the poems are in blank verse, as being more appropriate to analysis and reflection.   The men and women are generally somewhat complex beings.   Even the simple-hearted Fra Lippo Lippi has arrived at a subtle theory of art far in advance of his age ; while Bishop Blougram, hero of the masterly *Apology*, is one of the most ingenious sophists in literature.   A short analysis of *Andrea del Sarto* will illustrate Browning's method.   The speaker, a painter, now nearing old age, sits looking from his window in Florence out " to yonder sober pleasant Fiesole."   He has been called " faultless," so skilful is his brush.   A picture by Raphael hangs in the studio, and Andrea points out that there is a fault in the painting of the arm.   But though he can correct minute defects, he has lost, or never possessed, the shaping spirit of imagination :

> All is silver grey,
> Placid and perfect with my art—the worse !
> *(He points to the copy of Raphael's painting).*
> That arm is wrongly put—and there again—
> A fault to pardon in the drawing's lines,
> Its body, so to speak : its soul is right,
> He means right—that, a child may understand.
> Still, what an arm ! and I could alter it.
> But all the play, the insight and the stretch—
> Out of me ! out of me !

Gradually we learn that the painter's limitations are subtly connected with a moral weakness. His reflections are uttered in the presence of a woman, Lucrezia, for whose sake, we learn, he had many years since stolen some money entrusted to him for the purchase of pictures by the King of France. Lucrezia has long lost all affection for the painter —a more favoured admirer is, in fact, waiting without, as Andrea knows—but she keeps up a cold-hearted connection with him for the sake of his presents. To his art she is utterly indifferent. She has carelessly allowed her skirt to smear one of his pictures ; and when he recounts a glowing compliment once paid him by Michelangelo, she has not enough interest to listen :

> What he ? why, who but Michael Angelo ?
> Do you forget already words like those ?

he exclaims in mild protest. He is too weak to overcome his infatuation. The only signs that he is not wholly degraded are his sense of his condition and his feeling for great art. The poem ends with Andrea's dismissal of Lucrezia to the " cousin," who has given a signal of his impatience from without.

In *The Ring and the Book* Browning stretched the use of the dramatic monologue to its farthest possible extent. The poem is founded on a crime perpetrated in Italy towards the end of the seventeenth century. Many persons are involved in the story—the murderer, Count Guido Franceschini, his young wife, Pompilia, a priest and several others. Each, in a long monologue, delivers his or her view on the events ; and finally the Pope, to whom the condemned Count has appealed, sums up the whole situation and passes judgment. Intellectually, *The Ring and the Book* is probably Browning's greatest poem, and few works bring home so forcibly to the reader the complexity of human life and the relative nature of human justice. But in execution the poem is very uneven. While parts of it, such as Pompilia's monologue, are as natural as anything Browning wrote, others display the habit of his later age to versify unpoetical matter.

v

As a poet, Browning cares little for harmonious or regular beauty. He cares little, even, for the poetry of language. Few of his poems arise out of, or lead up to, a phrase of sheer verbal felicity. His words are poetic not for what they are, but for what they mean. He is, indeed, more heedless of harsh consonantal combinations than many prose-writers. What he loved was the expressive word, the characteristic detail. He strove to give an appropriate setting to each of his miniature dramas, and his success in this is beyond praise. In *Up at a Villa—Down in the City*, the appearance of the Italian hill-country is given in a few lines of energetic description :

What of a villa ?   Though winter be over in March by rights,
'Tis May perhaps ere the snow shall have withered well off the heights :
You've the brown ploughed land before, where the oxen steam and wheeze,
And the hills over-smoked behind by the faint grey olive-trees.

Is it better in May, I ask you ?   You've summer all at once ;
In a day he leaps complete with a few strong April suns !
'Mid the short sharp emerald wheat, scarce risen three fingers well,
The wild tulip, at end of its tube, blows out its great red bell
Like a thin clear bubble of blood, for the children to pick and sell.

In a Spanish poem, *How it Strikes a Contemporary*, he describes the deep shadows on the walls and the Moorish architecture. In *An Epistle*, he notes the animals of the Syrian desert, the lynx with its yellow eyeballs. Browning has no fear of the ugly and grotesque provided they are significant. He delights in the weird sights through which

Childe Roland has to make his way to the Dark Tower—the leering cripple, the miserable horse with every bone a-stare, the ugly rivulet that crosses his path, " So petty yet so spiteful," the ground churned up as by the feet of savages, the grass growing as scant as hair in leprosy. Rarely is such expressive ugliness of language to be found as in that remarkable poem *Caliban upon Setebos*, where Browning reveals the cunning, the cruelty, the fawning terror of a savage mind. It is thus that the island-creatures appear to Caliban's keen animal eye :

> [Setebos] made thereat the sun, this isle,
> Trees and the fowls here, beast and creeping thing.
> Yon otter, sleek-wet, black, lithe as a leech ;
> Yon auk, one fire-eye in a ball of foam,
> That floats and feeds ; a certain badger brown
> He [1] hath watched hunt with that slant white-wedge eye
> By moonlight ; and the pie with the long tongue
> That pricks deep into oakwarts for a worm,
> And says a plain word when she finds her prize,
> But will not eat the ants ; the ants themselves
> That build a wall of seeds and settled stalks
> About their hole—He made all these and more,
> Made all we see, and us, in spite : how else ?

VI

Though Browning speaks through the mouths of his various men and women, he clearly has a very definite attitude towards life, and the shortest survey of his work would be imperfect without some remarks on his " teaching." He is above all things an " optimist " ; and when carried away by enthusiasm he gives utterance to a soaring faith in the ultimate satisfaction of human effort :

> There shall never be one lost good ! What was shall live as before ;
> The evil is null, is nought ; is silence implying sound ;
> What was good shall be good, with, for evil, so much good more ;
> On the earth the broken arcs : in the heaven, a perfect round.

But the counterpart to this optimism is an insistence on a certain magnanimity. Men must have the courage of

[1] Caliban generally speaks in the third person.

their convictions : they must stake all if they are to win all. *The Statue and the Bust* ends with a warning from the fate of two lovers who hesitated to take the step which would have led to their union, until their whole lives oozed away in a mere dream. For once, Browning adds his own comment to the story :

> And the sin I impute to each frustrate ghost
> Is, the unlit lamp and the ungirt loin.

Abt Vogler and *Rabbi Ben Ezra*, though dramatic monologues, both evidently express moods of Browning's own. He is equally in sympathy with the idealism of the scholar in *A Grammarian's Funeral*. This man is one of the heroes of the Renaissance. Having seen at a distance the glories of Greek literature, he begins by labouring to elucidate the minute details of grammar. His youth wears away ; his eyes become like lead ; diseases menace him prematurely. What of that ? He has settled the functions of *Hoti* and *Oun* and *De*, and other tasks lie thick before him. In the midst of his toil he dies, and his disciples who had vainly besought him to take a little rest, carry him proudly to his grave on the hill-top. A great failure is better than a mean success, and the poem ends on a note of triumph :

> Here's the top-peak ! the multitude below
>   Live, for they can, there.
> This man decided not to Live but Know—
>   Bury this man there ? . . .
> Lofty designs must close in like effects :
>   Loftily lying,
> Leave him—still loftier than the world suspects,
>   Living and dying.

VII

During their long lives, Tennyson and Browning enjoyed an almost sacred leisure and devoted the whole of it to poetry. Matthew Arnold,[1] on the other hand, was a busy educationalist and man of letters. His best poems

---

[1] See pp. 305–307.

were written in the earlier half of his life, and though he attempted several long works he was most successful in comparatively short pieces. His tragedy in the classical manner, *Merope*, betrays signs of effort; his two short epic "episodes," *Sohrab and Rustum* and *Balder Dead* want spontaneity, though they have many beautiful details. It is in his reflective poems, and in a few lyrics and sonnets, that Arnold is at his best. He is above all an elegiac poet.

There are two deep strains of feeling in Arnold's poetry— a melancholy dissatisfaction with his age and a love of natural beauty. At times he looked back wistfully to the centuries of faith, when the dogmas of religion were held to be as demonstrable as the propositions of geometry. At times he looked forward with distrust to the days of advanced democracy and new forms of belief. His own days, he felt, had fallen on an age of transition, and he himself was

> Wandering between two worlds, one dead,
> The other powerless to be born.

A few of the last generation had borne up against the evil spirit of the times; and in his *Memorial Verses* he names three great poets of latter-day Europe who had given a new meaning to life—Goethe, "Physician of the Iron Age," Byron, and now, last of all, Wordsworth:

> Ah! since dark days still bring to light
> Man's prudence and man's fiery might,
> Time may restore us in his course
> Goethe's sage mind, and Byron's force:
> But where will Europe's latter hour
> Again find Wordsworth's healing power?
> Others will teach us how to dare,
> And against fear our breast to steel:
> Others will strengthen us to bear—
> But who, ah who, will make us feel?
> The cloud of mortal destiny,
> Others will front it fearlessly—
> But, who, like him, will put it by?
>
> Keep fresh the grass upon his grave,
> O Rotha! with thy living wave.
> Sing him thy best! for few or none
> Hears thy voice right, now he is gone.

Though Arnold finds little to praise and much to criticize in his own age and country, an unfailing charm still lingers for him among the hamlets and hedges of England. Away from books and cities he is a new creature. One region in particular he has made classic ground by the beauty of his two finest poems, *The Scholar Gipsy* and *Thyrsis*. The first is the fullest revelation of Arnold's poetic nature. It begins with a meditation on the wanderings of a scholar of old days who had forsaken Oxford and joined the gipsy tribe that he might learn their secrets and some day give them to the world. All the loveliness of the neighbourhood enters into the verse as the poet follows in imagination the scholar's footsteps over the familiar ground. The reader need know nothing of Oxford to delight in "the stripling Thames at Bab-lock-hithe," or the "warm green-muffled Cumner Hills," or the "line of festal light in Christ-Church Hall." Then the poet turns abruptly to the contrast between the happy wanderings of the scholar and the "strange disease of modern life," the "sick hurry" and "divided aims" of his own generation. The simile with which the poem closes is one of the most beautiful Arnold ever wrote, and he was famous for that form of poetical adornment.

Thyrsis, a lament on the death of another Oxford poet, A. H. Clough, is a companion elegy to *The Scholar Gipsy*. Again the sentiment and landscape of Oxford enter into the poetry. For these two elegies, Arnold invented a new stanza, somewhat similar to that of Keats's odes, and the measure, as a quotation from *Thyrsis* will show, is capable of a fine plangent music :

> So, some tempestuous morn in early June,
>> When the year's primal burst of bloom is o'er,
>> Before the roses and the longest day—
> When garden-walks and all the grassy floor
>> With blossoms red and white of fallen May
>> And chestnut-flowers are strewn—
> So have I heard some cuckoo's parting cry
>> From the wet field, thro' the vext garden-trees,
>> Come, with the volleying rain and tossing breeze :
> " The bloom is gone, and with the bloom go I."

Elizabeth Barrett (1806–1861), who lived the life of a recluse student till she was forty, and then married Robert Browning, against the will of her family, is a writer whose reputation is bound to vary much with the fluctuations of taste. Though a true poetess and a woman of high intellectual gifts, she has not that unfailing power of characteristic style which conquers time. Nor was she faultless in the technique of expression. Her ear was defective, and the rhythms of her verse are often strangely displeasing. These defects come out clearly in her most ambitious work, *Aurora Leigh* (1857), a story of contemporary life in blank verse. When Mrs. Browning adopted more exacting metres, her level of workmanship was much higher. In *Casa Guidi Windows* (1851), for example, she is saved from her worst defects by the difficulties of the *terza rima*. One of her works, at least, is above the changes of taste, the collection of *Sonnets from the Portuguese* (1847). Deeply charged with feeling, swift and impulsive in their movement, the expression of a nature both passionate and refined, the collection is one of the great sequences in our poetry. The sonnet beginning, " I tell you, hopeless grief is passionless," illustrates the intensity of feeling and expression which is Mrs. Browning's finest poetic quality.

Another poetess of the nineteenth century, Christina Rossetti (1830–1894), is known chiefly for her sonnets and shorter poems, though, in *Goblin Market* (1862), there is a profusion of fancy not to be contained within narrow limits. There is, however, a higher quality in the restrained style of her meditative and religious pieces. Thanks to her fine ear for the music of verse and her delicate sense of language, she wrote a number of pieces which, though subdued in tone, are nearly faultless in expression. An example of her style at its best is the sonnet beginning : " Remember me when I am gone away." She was one of the best religious poets of the century, and a typical piece like the one beginning, " Does the road wind uphill all the way ? " is not more touching in its sentiment than exquisite in the taste of its wording.

IX

It was the aim of Tennyson and Browning to make poetry the expression of their fullest imaginative and intellectual life. Though the delicacy of Tennyson's work suffered somewhat from his conscious obligation to the highest interests of his age ; and though Browning confesses in *One Word More* that it is an occasional relief to write for his wife alone and not for the world, the gain to poetry in the generous humanism of these writers far outweighed the loss. The merits as well as the defects of early Victorian poetry were largely due to this frank admission of the services which it owed to humanity. In the later Victorians there was a reaction against this attitude. They insisted that poetry is an art, that the poet's chief, perhaps his only debt, is to his artistic conscience. In the 'sixties, the cry " Art for art's sake " began first to be heard ; and though the new movement fostered a delight in fine technique, it weakened the connection between poetry and life. " It matters little what a poet says," was the new contention, " provided that he says it well."

The life and work of Edward Fitzgerald (1809–1883) somewhat anticipated the spirit of later Victorianism. He was a lifelong friend of Tennyson, and it is significant that he was one of the critics who noted a falling-off in Tennyson's work after the volumes of 1842. He himself was a solitary student devoted wholly to literature. He published little until he was fifty, and then, in 1859, brought out his first translation of the *Rubáiyát* of the Persian poet, Omar Khayyám. A second version appeared and then the final one (1872), now known word by word to hundreds of poetry-lovers. That the fame of a writer should rest wholly on one work, and that work a translation of a rather short poem, is one of the strangest facts in literary history. But Fitzgerald's *Rubáiyát* is one of those rare poems which make the idea of perfection seem for a while a

real and tangible thing. The novel music of the stanza
and the peculiar turn of phrasing both harmonise perfectly
with the spirit of the poem :

> I sometimes think that never blows so red
> The Rose as where some buried Cæsar bled ;
> That every Hyacinth the Garden wears
> Dropt in its Lap from some once lovely Head.

The popularity of *The Rubáiyát* has not been wholly due
to the literary merits of the translation. Its mingling
of the voluptuous with the pessimistic exactly suited late
Victorian taste, and it was natural that the generation which
produced the poems of Swinburne and the novels of Hardy
should delight in Fitzgerald.

Dante Gabriel Rossetti (1828–1882), whose life was
passed between painting and poetry, was the founder of the
pre-Raphaelite Brotherhood and exercised a deep influence
on the art of the century. He drew his inspiration very
largely from the Middle Ages. His early poem, *The
Blessed Damozel*, marks a new phase in the cult of mediæval-
ism. It brings out the romance of intense religious
sentiment. It also impresses the imagination by its
picture of love frustrated by infinite distance. Rossetti's
translations collected in *The Early Italian Poets* (1861),
show a close sympathy with the passionate mysticism of
love as expressed by Dante and his contemporaries. It is
in his ballads and his sonnets, especially in the sequence
called *The House of Life*, that Rossetti's poetry is at its best.
Sonorous in their music, and rich in symbolical imagery,
the sonnets seem at first to outshine all others by the
brilliance of their colour. Rossetti undoubtedly achieved
a high standard of finish, and the best of the sonnets, such
as the one beginning, " The lost days of my life," are
superb. Sometimes, however, the means employed seem
out of proportion to the effect produced. Rossetti's
resources of rhythm and language are magnificent ; but
other men have written sonnets at least as fine with simpler
words.

William Morris (1834–1896), also a pre-Raphaelite, and a
mediævalist, was in other ways a great contrast to Rossetti

both as a man and a painter. He had little interest in the mystical poetry of the Middle Ages, but a great love of its romance, its architecture, its high standard of craftsmanship. Mediæval France and mediæval England attracted him more than mediæval Italy; and his first volume of verse, *The Defence of Guenevere and other Poems* (1858), showed how much romance might be drawn from the old literature of northern Europe by one who was in real sympathy with its spirit. A poem like *The Haystack in the Floods* brings the reader into much closer contact with actual life in the Middle Ages than anything in Keats or Tennyson; and in this particular piece there is a concentration of feeling and expression which Morris never surpassed. As he grew older, his writing became more fluent and less intense. His delight in the whole vast field of classical and mediæval legend led him into writing more verse than could possibly have the memorable strength of true poetry. Moreover, he came to regard composition as a kind of craft demanding honest labour rather than inspiration. *The Life and Death of Jason* (1867) and *The Earthly Paradise* (1868–70) are admirable for two high qualities—their author's skill in direct narrative and his eye for description. The *Prologue* to *The Earthly Paradise*, a record of imaginary voyage and discovery in the fourteenth century, is full of passages in the glowing colours so beloved by pre-Raphaelite painters. In the large collection of stories which form the body of the poem it is pleasant to see the spirit of two arts happily blended; and the rich tapestry of a narrative like *Atalanta's Race* gives a high idea of Morris's skill. In the weaker pages of *The Earthly Paradise* one cannot forget that its author's aims as a writer were not very exacting. He wished to give the charm of old stories a place in modern English literature, and both by his original verse, and by his translations from Anglo-Saxon, Old Norse and other languages he did this; but one regrets his loss of the concentrated style of earlier days. In *The Earthly Paradise* he was often content to be, in his own phrase,

The idle singer of an empty day.

Fortunately, his enthusiasm for the literature of the North inspired him to stronger efforts. *The Story of Sigurd the Volsung* (1877) is a fine attempt to render the great Norse epic into English verse.

X

Many who passed their young manhood in the 'sixties of the last century kept through the whole of their lives a vivid recollection of the excitement created by the appearance of Swinburne's *Poems and Ballads* in 1866. Those who, some twenty years before, had accepted Tennyson as the great poet of the age somewhat resented the hardihood of this upstart who, though possessing high technical skill, cared nothing for restraint and dignity. To Arnold who, no doubt, found many of his lines somewhat empty of meaning, he was " a young pseudo-Shelley." Serious persons were perturbed by his blatant heterodoxy. The young, however, were carried away by the passion of his verse, his intoxicating rhythms, and the new prospects of beauty which seemed to be opening for English poetry.

Swinburne first became known by his *Atalanta in Calydon* (1865), a poetic drama distingushed by some great choruses, especially the one that opens, " Before the beginning of years." Other examples of drama followed, among them *Bothwell* (1874) and *Mary Stuart* (1881), both on a period of history in which Swinburne was passionately interested. For most readers, however, Swinburne is, above all, a lyrical poet ; and many of his early admirers who followed his career throughout its course were obliged to admit that he never surpassed, perhaps never equalled, the *Poems and Ballads*. In such poems as *Laus Veneris*, *The Garden of Proserpine*, the *Hymn to Proserpine*, *The Triumph of Time*, *Itylus* and *Dolores*, the qualities of Swinburne's imagination are expressed in their richest form, and much that he wrote afterwards seemed only a repetition of images and ideas already familiar. A passion for intellectual freedom was one of Swinburne's deepest instincts ; and it found fine expression in his

332

Freeman
Drinkwater.
M. Baring "a poem ensures
immortality — any in [a] book"
(Georgian Poetry)
" In Memoriam" will take its
place among [the] gt. Elegies:
Thyrsis Lycidas, Adonais."
W. J. Turner.

"Why We Should Read
S.P.B. Mais
(Grant Richards)

N Books & their Writers
Ibid.

A. Meynell.   Evelyn Underhill
Dora Sigerson   (mystic)
Iris Tree.
Sheila Kaye-Smith
J.C. Squire — Mais calls "ablest
                    literary critic alive)
Siegfried Sassoon.

Nichols. (Squire calls "the Bull" one of finest
Hodgson   poems of our generation)
                    sympathy.
Harold Monro (quaintly humorous)

Masefield. (colloquial)
Lascelles Abercrombie (intellectual)
Chesterton — ballad.
De la Mare. (seductive,
                    wizardry)
W.H. Davies (childish simplicity
        (Squire's "Paradise")
                    Books in General
W.J. Turner   Tricks n Trade"
R. Graves
Pitson

two volumes on the Risorgimento, *A Song of Italy* (1867) and *Songs before Sunrise* (1871). Two other volumes of *Poems and Ballads* appeared in 1878 and 1889. By this time, Swinburne's power of lyrical invention was failing, but his love of metrical experiment was inexhaustible. *Studies in Song* (1880) is a display of the most varied technical skill, and *A Century of Roundels* (1883) shows astonishing facility in a French form of verse, till then rarely attempted in English. Swinburne's *Tristram of Lyonesse* (1882) is a notable attempt to do justice to a great story which has baffled many writers. He continued to publish volumes of poetry till nearly the end of his life. He died in 1909.

It is in the music of verse that Swinburne is pre-eminent. When once asked at an Oxford gathering, which English poet had the best ear, he answered, " Shakespeare without doubt ; then Milton ; then Shelley ; then, I do not know what other people would do, but I should put myself." This claim, made in all simplicity, was not extravagant. Swinburne is one of the great masters in metrical technique. He was not a revolutionist in verse. He was true to the fundamental principles of English metre, but he handled familiar forms of line with a freedom which seemed to reveal their latent melody for the first time. In *The Garden of Proserpine*, for instance, he uses a stanza which, having been adopted by both Dryden and Keats, was fairly well established in English poetry : but the music which Keats and Dryden had drawn from it seems crude beside Swinburne's subtlety :

> Here, where the world is quiet ;
> Here, where all trouble seems
> Dead winds' and spent waves' riot
> In doubtful dreams of dreams ;
> I watch the green field growing
> For reaping folk and sowing,
> For harvest-time and mowing,
> A sleepy world of streams.

The first impression created by this stanza is surprise at an unsuspected beauty in English rhymes. There had been nothing quite like this flexibility of verse in all the long line of Swinburne's predecessors. Something of the same novel beauty is revealed in his language. Swinburne was not one of the great masters of poetic diction; but he gave a new turn to familiar words. In his hands, language of Biblical simplicity is invested with a new poetic impressiveness. He can tune it to many emotions: in this stanza he gives it the accent of melancholy resignation with exquisite skill:

> You have chosen and clung to the chance they sent you,
>   Life sweet as perfume and pure as prayer.
> But will it not one day in heaven repent you?
>   Will they solace you wholly, the days that were?
> Will you lift up your eyes between sadness and bliss,
> Meet mine, and see where the great love is,
> And tremble and turn and be changed? Content you;
>   The gate is strait; I shall not be there.

Though some of Swinburne's metrical feats seem mere *tours de force*, the taste and felicity he shows always command respect. His mastery of rhyme enabled him to handle forms of stanza which would have baffled the skill of almost any other poet. *Faustine*, for instance, whatever its merits as a poem, is an astounding display in the feat of finding numerous rhymes to one word.

Though much of Swinburne's poetry, especially that of his later years, seems unsubstantial and almost empty of meaning, he is far more than a mere technician in verse. He has intense poetic enthusiasms—love of the sea, for instance, and admiration for certain literary masters, Victor Hugo, Baudelaire, Charles Lamb. His hatred of tyranny, his somewhat voluptuous paganism, are genuine poetic impulses. When, in *Hertha*, he sings the birth and destiny of man, he is a great poet.

CHAPTER XIX

THE VICTORIAN AGE: THE NOVEL

THE theme of most novels in the eighteenth century had been contemporary life and manners. Scott had enlarged the novelist's sphere by giving his stories a historical setting, and other writers, such as William Godwin, had seen that fiction might serve the purpose of political propaganda. The Victorians, however, went much farther; and a succession of brilliant writers, variously endowed, showed it was possible to adapt the novel to almost all purposes of literature whatsoever. To know the intellectual life of the period one need hardly go outside the sphere of fiction. The sermon, the political pamphlet, the philosophical discourse, the social essay—all were shown to be susceptible of novel form. Some novels were autobiographies in disguise; some were almost poems in prose. Novel-reading was one of the chief occupations of the educated public, and material had to be provided for every taste. The theatre, which might have been expected to rival fiction as a source of imaginative entertainment, had fallen on evil days, and did not begin to revive till the latter half of the century.

I

There are three reasons for regarding Charles Dickens as the representative novelist of the age. In wealth of invention he was, at the lowest estimate, inferior to no living writer. Secondly, he surpassed all other novelists in popularity, and was read with equal relish by the learned and ignorant. Thirdly, he wrote most of his books " with a purpose " : hence they help to give " an abstract and brief chronicle of the time." Though bearing on every page marks of the writer's idiosyncrasies, and though datable in every chapter as " early Victorian," they have suffered little from the lapse of time or the change in manners. For they have, in a pre-eminent degree, the virtue of vitality.

Dickens was born in 1812, his father being a clerk in the Navy Pay-Office. The family, which was in financial difficulties during most of Dickens's boyhood, moved from place to place, and at length settled at Camden Town, in " a mean, small tenement, with a wretched little back garden abutting on a squalid court." Dickens received little school-education at any time ; and it ceased altogether when his father was arrested for debt and sent to the Marshalsea. Then followed the saddest days of Charles Dickens's life. He was obliged to work in a blacking manufactory at Old Hungerford Stairs, where the coarseness of his companions nearly drove him to despair.

" No words," he wrote, " can express the secret agony of my soul as I sunk into this companionship ; compared these everyday associates with those of my happier childhood ; and felt my early hopes of growing up to be a learned and distinguished man, crushed in my breast."

Better times came at length. Dickens was sent back to school for a while, and later entered the office of an attorney. By learning shorthand he was able to do some reporting ; and his next step was to offer some short articles to a magazine. These began to appear in 1833 as *Sketches by Boz*, and in 1836 *The Pickwick Papers* were announced. The serial publication began on a modest scale, but before it was finished the issue of each new number was almost a national event. " Of part one," we are told, " the binder prepared four hundred ; of part fifteen his order was for more than forty thousand." There was a lull in fiction at the moment of *Pickwick's* appearance. Bulwer Lytton, Disraeli and Harrison Ainsworth were writing, but had made no great mark as yet. Dickens became at a leap the most popular living novelist; and though the next few years brought forward some formidable rivals, his primacy was uncontested—except, perhaps, by Thackeray—till the end of his life. *Pickwick* was finished in 1837, and Dickens straightway began *Oliver Twist*, his first " novel with a purpose." The attack on the administration of the Poor Law was followed by the exposure of bad private schools in *Nicholas Nickleby*, an unequal novel, with some excellent scenes of grim humour and some feeble attempts at social satire. *The Old Curiosity Shop* and *Barnaby Rudge* were his next two books, the one a romance coloured largely by the popular sentimentality of the time, the other a historical novel on the Gordon Riots. The overdrawn pathos of Little Nell was highly acceptable in both England and America.

In 1842, Dickens visited America, and on his return recorded his somewhat crude impressions in *Martin Chuzzlewit*, a novel otherwise remarkable for Mrs. Gamp, a comic creation whose humour quite eclipses the author's satire on bad nursing. About the same time, he began his *Christmas Books*, a series which has done much to foster the genial spirit of Christmas time. Dickens's overflowing goodness of heart was no small cause of his popularity. " Who can listen," wrote Thackeray of *A Christmas Carol*, " to objections regarding such a book as this ? It seems to me a national benefit and to every man or woman who reads it a personal kindness." For some time, Dickens gave his energy to journalism, but a new novel, *Dombey and Son*, was finished in 1848, and it was followed in 1850 by *David Copperfield*, commonly regarded as Dickens's greatest work, and, in any case, notable for its large element of autobiography. Whatever the merits of *Copperfield*, Dickens's powers were showing no decline, and the books of his last twenty years are at least equal to their predecessors. *Bleak House* (1852–53) proves that Dickens had more to gain than to lose from advancing years. The book has less abounding vivacity than the earlier novels, but it is much riper in experience and its variety is immense. Its onslaught on the old Court of Chancery is one of

Dickens's most vigorous pieces of social criticism; and his next book, *Hard Times* (1854), has an equally serious purpose. It is a grave study on the problems of capital and labour: some of its details were drawn from a strike at Preston, which Dickens visited for the purpose. *Little Dorrit*, finished in 1857, preserves its author's dismal memories of the Marshalsea Prison in some scenes of much truer pathos than the exaggerated descriptions of Little Nell and Paul Dombey. For the next few years, much of Dickens's energy was consumed in the public readings from his novels which he gave in England and America. The enthusiasm displayed by the audiences was without bounds, but the readings were too exhausting for the performer, and probably shortened his life. His last four books, however, *A Tale of Two Cities*, *Great Expectations*, *Our Mutual Friend* and the unfinished *Edwin Drood*, are among his very best, and each shows that its author's imagination was nearly as fruitful as ever. Dickens died in 1870, leaving the issue of his last story a mystery which has aroused endless conjecture.

II

That Dickens was a " self-made " author was no obstacle to his popularity in an age which loved individual enterprise and " self-help." On the art of construction, Dickens's ideas were certainly elementary. The origin of his novels was the vivid idea of certain scenes and characters. " I thought of Mr. Pickwick," he said; and provided Mr. Pickwick could be introduced in a number of ludicrous situations, his creator did not care about much else. Many of his books seem no more than a patchwork of the gay, the melodramatic and the sentimental—the author's one concern being that no single strain should predominate. As he grew older, he strove to give his novels some unity. In *Martin Chuzzlewit*, for instance, the idea of selfishness runs through the whole story; *Dombey and Son* is written against pride. But the old defect remains. We still feel that the books are too much of a " variety entertainment." It was, indeed, impossible for

Dickens to overcome the temptations inherent in serial publication.

But Dickens has one merit which silences criticism—the merit of superlative vitality. Whether his characters are " true to life " or not, they are alive in his pages. " It has the life and soul in it of fifty human beings," said Leigh Hunt of Dickens's face ; and the face was the index of the mind. His good characters, indeed, are not often convincing ; but no novelist has such power of impressing moral or physical defects on the imagination of his readers. The grotesque characters, Quilp, Smallweed and other members of this class ; the evil ones, Bill Sikes, Jonas Chuzzlewit, Rogue Riderhood ; the vulgar ones, Squeers, Noah Claypole, Mrs. Gamp, are as intensely conceived as any human beings in fiction. We do not ask whether such persons are real, for the imagination accepts them involuntarily. Or, if the question crosses our mind, we may remember that England, in Dickens's day, as in Johnson's and Smollett's, was still a country of " originals."

In the vividness of his descriptive passages, Dickens is unsurpassable. He does not, like Meredith or Hardy, give the poetry of a scene ; he gives the scene itself. Let any one read the description of Marseilles in the burning heat of the sun, at the beginning of *Little Dorrit* ; or the description of the choking fog filling the Court of Chancery in *Bleak House* ; or of the terrible slum, Tom All Alone's, in the same book ; or of the dismal Essex marshes in *Great Expectations* ; or of the Thames riverside scenes in *Our Mutual Friend*—let any one read these, and he will see that in this branch of the novelist's art, Dickens is supreme. Nor is this intensity occasional—it pervades the whole of his books. Dickens did nothing by halves. He described no human face, no London alley, no lawyer's chamber which his imagination did not see as vividly as if they stood before the bodily eye. We believe in Dickens's fantastic exaggerated world while we are reading his books, because he believed in it himself.

William Makepeace Thackeray, whose name is so often coupled with that of Dickens, has little in common with him beyond being his contemporary. He belongs neither to the school of social reformers, nor to the novelists who resembled Dickens in their love of the fantastic and sensational. Thackeray's qualities were just those which Dickens lacked. By birth and education he was able to depict those classes of society which Dickens never understood, and he had that sense of literary style only to be obtained by one who has lived long under the influence of the best books.

Thackeray, who was born in 1811, and educated at the Charterhouse and at Trinity College, Cambridge, was long in finding his true sphere in literature. Being the heir to a sufficient fortune, he did not choose any regular profession. But having got rid of all his inheritance in a year or two, he turned to literature for his livelihood. He contributed to *Punch*, and he wrote one or two novels, such as *The Great Hoggarty Diamond* (1841) and *The Luck of Barry Lyndon* (1844), the second a powerful " picaresque " story. Thackeray was, by nature, an indolent man, and discriminating critics saw that he could write something far more solid than he had yet done, if he would " put forth all his strength." In 1847-48, he brought out a really great book, *Vanity Fair*. This was followed by *Pendennis* (1850), *Henry Esmond* (1852), and *The Newcomes* (1855). His next novel, *The Virginians* (1859) shows some falling-off in power—not a surprising fact, as Thackeray's mind was distracted by political ambitions ; and his last novels, *Lovel the Widower*, *The Adventures of Philip* and *Denis Duval* do not reach the standard of his great days. Like Dickens, Thackeray appeared on the public platform after he was famous, and his lectures on *The English Humorists of the Eighteenth Century* were an important social event in London. He died in 1863.

The outstanding merit of Thackeray's novels is their reality. Of the best scenes in *Vanity Fair*, one can only say, "This is life itself." Not that Thackeray uses the photographic method of the realist: he sifts his material and keeps only that which is to the purpose. *Vanity Fair* is a book which is true in two ways. It is true to human nature in general, and true to the manners of the Regency in particular. Becky Sharp belongs to no age. Whenever she appears, whether it is at Miss Pinkerton's Academy, or at the Sedleys' table, or at Queen's Crawley, or at Gaunt House, or in the fatal scene with Lord Steyne when her career in high society is brought to a sudden close, it is the naked human interest that grips us. But the background to all these vivid tableaux is hardly less important. Thackeray has, to a wonderful degree, the power of creating a real historic atmosphere. The complex social life of London with its scandal and its vanities and its flunkeys; the distraction and alarm at Brussels at the height of the Waterloo campaign, are essential parts of the scheme, and no praise is too high for the sense of actuality which Thackeray produces.

Pendennis and *The Newcomes* have much the same qualities as *Vanity Fair*. The social atmosphere is conveyed with equal brilliance, though the central figures are less interesting. Blanche Amory, for instance, falls short of her predecessor, Becky Sharp. Thackeray's great success after *Vanity Fair* was *Henry Esmond*. No English writer has had in fuller measure the gifts of a historical novelist; and no period would have suited Thackeray so well as the reign of Queen Anne. The book is less brilliant than *Vanity Fair*, but the beauty of its style is a more than equal merit. To the simple elegance of Augustan prose, Thackeray added a touch of romance which is his own. In certain scenes the dialogue is consummate, as in the chapter where Lady Castlewood contests with the Duke of Hamilton her daughter's right to receive presents from Esmond. And Esmond's interview with Lady Castlewood after his return from the wars is more moving in its beauty of feeling and style than anything else in Thackeray, with the possible exception of Colonel Newcome's death. The scenes in which historical figures, Marlborough, Swift and Addison, appear, form an excellent background to the main story, of which Beatrix Esmond is the central light.

None of Thackeray's books, unfortunately, is free from desultory passages. Digressions, moral, satirical and historical, delay the progress of events in both *Vanity Fair* and *Henry Esmond*. He is essentially a novelist of social life. His portraits of " clubmen " like Major Pendennis are perfect ; of the influence of solitude or nature on the character he seems to know nothing. He is the Victorian successor of Fielding. Both were civilized men of the world with a strong vein of satire in them. If Thackeray has faults of construction from which Fielding at his best was free, he has also scenes of a higher beauty than Fielding ever attained to.

IV

THE SOCIAL AND POLITICAL NOVEL

Benjamin Disraeli has a strong claim to be called the most eminent among our political novelists. Since his time, many writers have discussed some aspect of public affairs under the guise of fiction, but Disraeli made the political novel his peculiar province, and he wrote little else. Moreover, his novels have a special interest as foreshadowing the political programme of one who always felt destined to play a conspicuous part in public life. *Vivian Grey* (1826), his earliest novel, attracted some notice ; but his reputation rests principally on *Coningsby* (1844) and its immediate successors. In *Coningsby*, Disraeli takes stock of the political situation created by the Reform Bill, and the book is filled with portraits of men and women eminent in the 'thirties. *Sybil* (1845), his next book, is perhaps his best. Its sub-title, *The Two Nations*, suggests its theme, namely, the great social cleavage wrought in the country by the Industrial Revolution. The powerful picture of squalid life in a manufacturing town should dispose of the popular idea that Disraeli can only depict " high life." The book contains some suggestive discussions on the mediæval system of society, and Disraeli's main contention is that the upper classes should cease to be merely ornamental and should recover their ancient position as leaders of the nation. The animated dialogues, with their rich fund of ideas lightly suggested, make the best of Disraeli's books agreeably stimulating. *Sybil* was followed by *Tancred* (1847), and in his later years, Disraeli wrote *Lothair* (1870) and *Endymion* (1880).

Mrs. Gaskell (*née* Stevenson) is best known for *Cranford* (1853), a book which invests the quiet village life of some spinster ladies with a delicate charm and humour. But much of her work was of a much sterner kind. Mrs. Gaskell had an intimate knowledge of industrial England, and her story of Manchester life in *Mary Barton* (1848) is remarkable not only for its picture of want and suffering, but for its vindication of the strong Lancashire character. *North and South* (1855) describes the two divisions of Victorian England as they existed in all their startling contrast—the ancient life of the agricultural villages with their old-fashioned charm, and the newly-created industrial North, crude in its sudden transformation. Mrs. Gaskell's sympathetic understanding of the northern character comes out clearly in her *Life of Charlotte Bronte* (1857); and the book gives not only a fine study of the novelist, but a memorable account of the Yorkshire moors and their half-wild inhabitants. The best of Mrs. Gaskell's other books are *Ruth* (1854), *Sylvia's Lovers* (1863), and *Wives and Daughters* (1864–66). Mrs. Gaskell's most striking gift, perhaps, was her genuine and unforced pathos—a quality strongly shown in *Ruth*. But her quiet and truthful observation of character makes nearly all her books worth reading.

Charles Kingsley was as deeply concerned with the social injustice of the time as Mrs. Gaskell; but he had less knowledge of working men, and did not realise how much solid strength of character is diffused among the industrial districts. His two social novels, *Yeast* (1848) and *Alton Locke* (1850), betray the alarm and indignation of a generous impulsive nature brought face to face with grim realities. Their author's impressible feelings and inflammable imagination made him a vivid describer; but he had no great power of creating memorable characters. Kingsley formed one of the small group of men, who, accepting Carlyle's gospel of earnest work, but remaining more orthodox than their master, became known as " Christian Socialists." In his historical novels, *Hypatia* (1853) and *Westward Ho!* (1855), there is plenty of local colour and graphic incident: and the epic description of the Armada shows what a fine prose style Kngsley could command on great occasions. *Two Years Ago* (1857) is an exciting romance of contemporary life.

V

IMAGINATIVE AUTOBIOGRAPHY :
GEORGE BORROW

In George Borrow, the independence of character of which so many Victorians boasted was carried to an excess which would have been preposterous in an ordinary man, and is sometimes absurd enough even in him. But Borrow was a man of extraordinary gifts and extraordinary experiences; and as his power of telling his own stories almost invariably makes literature of a high order, he had no need to go outside his own life for the material of his " novels."

He was a prolific writer, but his various compilations and translations are of small account. His first remarkable book, *The Bible in Spain* (1843), was published in his fortieth year. It is ostensibly a report on his labours as representative of the British and Foreign Bible Society; but in fact it is a record of travel and incident, which, heightened by imaginative exaggeration, is as marvellous as an oriental romance. Borrow's life in Spain was, indeed, not without incident. He was imprisoned in Madrid; and his facility in Spanish as well as his love for odd characters led him much farther off the beaten track than any discreet traveller would have ventured. But for Borrow there is romance in everything. An old woman directing him on the way, a taciturn Jew met by chance in the gathering darkness, are so described that their lightest words seem fraught with significance. An interview with a Spanish official who reads Bentham seems one of the strangest dialogues ever held between men. Borrow's life in Spain was full of adventures; but to hear him describe is an adventure in itself. Hence, there is scarcely a dull moment in the book.

In *Lavengro* (1851), the author's movements are confined to the British Isles, but the incidents are at least as remarkable as those of *The Bible in Spain*. The title of the book is the name given to Borrow by the gipsies on account of his proficiency in their cant phrases and his knowledge of languages in general. *Lavengro* is no more than a collection of incidents and dialogues; but from a writer who gives us the conversation between himself and Mr. Petulengro about "the wind on the heath"; and the description of Byron's funeral; and the encounter with the old apple-woman on London Bridge; and the meeting with the Welsh preacher who has committed the unpardonable sin; and the battle with the Flaming Tinman, and the conversation with Isopel Berners, it would be ungrateful, indeed, to ask for more. Of Borrow's other works, *The Romany Rye* (1857), a continuation of *Lavengro*, falls but little below his two best books; and the lover of Borrow will be glad to read *Wild Wales* (1862), though its quality as compared with that of *Lavengro* is but as moonlight to sunshine.

VI

THE BRONTËS

In all the external circumstances of her life, Charlotte Brontë was as unlike George Borrow as any one could be; yet as writers, the two have several points of resemblance. Both were persons whose vivid imagination turned their own lives into a romance. Both had moods of morbid sensibility. Both could write with an eloquence of description which gives prose the warmth and colour of poetry. In Charlotte Brontë, however, there was a depth of human passion wholly wanting in Borrow.

The events in her life are soon chronicled. She was born in 1816 and brought up in the solitude of her father's parsonage at Haworth, near Bradford. Her two sisters, Emily and Anne, and her brother, Branwell, were all gifted persons, and Emily was a woman of genius. As it was necessary for the daughters to earn their living as governesses, Charlotte and Emily went for a time to Brussels to improve their French; and there Charlotte met a M. Héger, the original of M. Paul Emanuel, with whom Lucy Snowe falls in love in *Villette*. Charlotte Brontë's first novel, *The Professor*, is founded very largely on these early experiences. Her first published book, *Jane Eyre* (1847), soon made its mark, and it has appealed to every fresh generation by its poetry and its passion. *Shirley* was published in 1849, and her last book, *Villette*, in 1853. Meantime, life at Haworth had been darkened by calamity. Branwell, after much misery and folly, drank himself to death. Anne, the author of two novels, died of consumption; and in the year following the publication of her great book, *Wuthering Heights* (1847), Emily ended her short and troubled life. Charlotte enjoyed a few months of happiness after her marriage, and then her health also failed, and she died in 1855. The father of this gifted family, the Rev. Patrick Brontë, survived for some years at Haworth after the death of all his children.

As a story, *Jane Eyre* is ordinary enough. Mr. Rochester's inauspicious first marriage, which is revealed while he stands at the altar with his new bride, is ostensibly the pivot of the whole novel. But for the melodrama which surrounds this mystery, no discriminating reader will care a jot. It is the chapters which reveal the writer's own nature, her power of intense suffering, her stoical endurance, her capacity for joy that make *Jane Eyre* a great book. Charlotte Brontë is the real heroine of the book : she is Jane Eyre. The rigours of Jane's life at school, her betrothal to Rochester and the agony of their separation are written in words of fire. There are pages, such as those on Jane's meeting with Rochester in the garden, on the evening of their betrothal, which have all the beauty of a lyrical poem; the tremulous ecstasy of the writer enters into the very words. Yet *Jane Eyre* is by no means a fault-less work. The behaviour of the fashionable Blanche Ingram, for instance, is ludicrously improbable, and, in the tamer parts of the book, the style is marred by frequent pedantries. But these are the defects of Charlotte Brontë's qualities. Like her sisters, she was self-taught, and knew little of the world; her naïveté is the other side of her genius.

Shirley, though less autobiographical than *Jane Eyre*, is also in part founded on the writer's own experience. The book wants the intensity of her other works, though the background of Yorkshire characters and industrial strife is excellent. *Villette* is a return to something like auto-biography. Lucy Snowe's life at Mme. Beck's school and all her many encounters with M. Paul Emanuel are described with that poignant mixture of joy and suffering which is Charlotte Brontë's peculiar quality. The agonised suspense of the last chapter is one of the great passages in English fiction, not only for its human feeling, but for the heart-searching rhythms of its prose.

Emily Brontë's one novel, *Wuthering Heights*, is regarded by some as equal to her sister's best work. The atmo-sphere is darker, the suffering is crueller, the passions more fierce. Emily's nature was more tragic than her sister's, but it was also less rich. It is not the least of Charlotte's merits that she usually kept her balance, and even a certain gaiety and humour. To write, often with the accent of great poetry, on the eternal subjects of life and death was the gift of both sisters—with what simple strength of style may be illustrated by a short quotation from *Shirley*:

But, Jessie, I will write of you no more. This is an autumn evening, wet and wild. There is only one cloud in the sky; but it curtains it from pole to pole. The wind cannot rest: it hurries sobbing over hills of sullen outline, colourless with twilight and mist. Rain has beat all day on that church tower: it rises dark from the stony enclosure of its graveyard: the

347

nettles, the long grass, and the tombs all drip with wet. This evening reminds me too forcibly of another evening some years ago : a howling, rainy autumn evening too—when certain who had that day performed a pilgrimage to a grave new-made in a heretic cemetery, sat near a wood-fire on the hearth of a foreign dwelling. They were merry and social, but they each knew that a gap, never to be filled, had been made in their circle. They knew that they had lost something whose absence could never be quite atoned for so long as they lived : and they knew that heavy falling rain was soaking into the wet earth which covered their lost darling ; and that the sad, sighing gale, was mourning over her buried head. The fire warmed them ; Life and Friendship yet blessed them ; but Jessie lay cold, coffined, solitary—only the sod screening her from the storm.

<h2 style="text-align:center">VII</h2>

<h1 style="text-align:center">ANTHONY TROLLOPE : GEORGE ELIOT</h1>

The novels of Anthony Trollope were very numerous ; and after the lapse of many years an interest is being shown in several of his books which the world had almost forgotten. But it is not likely that the general opinion as to his best works will undergo much change. Trollope will always be known chiefly as the author of the " Barchester Series "—a collection of six novels, the actions of which revolve round the Cathedral Close of Barchester. The first of the cycle, *The Warden* (1855), introduces some of the main cathedral characters, the formidable Archdeacon Grantly, for instance ; but the central character of the book, the Rev. Septimus Harding, is a man made rather to endure than to act, and on that account the whole novel is somewhat slight. *Barchester Towers* (1857) is perhaps the best of the series. The rivalry between the Bishop's wife, Mrs. Proudie, and the Bishop's chaplain, Mr. Slope, provides Trollope with some very lively scenes ; and there is not a dull moment whenever the henpecked Bishop is on the stage. Three other Barchester novels, *Dr. Thorne* (1858), *Framley Parsonage* (1861), and *The Small House at Allington* (1864), followed, each with characters and interests new as well as old, and the series was closed with *The Last*

348

Chronicle of Barset (1867). Trollope is perhaps at his best in parts of this last book. The tragic figure of Mr. Crawley, a clergyman wrongly accused of theft, is surely Trollope's greatest portrait; and the sudden death of Mrs. Proudie after a quarrel with the Bishop, has the reality of the finest imaginative writing. If this book were of uniform excellence, it would certainly be Trollope's masterpiece. *Orley Farm* is, perhaps, the best of Trollope's books outside the Barchester series, and he wrote several others of nearly the same quality.

As a novelist, Trollope belongs to the school of Thackeray. Men and women in their relations to each other as parent and child, as husband and wife, as friends, as enemies, as lovers, gave him all the material he needed. Most of his characters belong to the well-to-do classes. Out of their position in life, their property and connections, their mutual rivalries and alliances arise the entanglements which form the plots of his novels. In the most successful of his books, Trollope confined himself to these matters. He describes the affections and motives of ordinary people with close fidelity. Those who are interested in the simple dramas which arise out of the very conditions of civilized life will find both truth and humour in Trollope.

It is her wider sympathy and deeper penetration that make George Eliot a greater writer than Trollope. To have drawn a clergyman merely as a social being without reference to his religious faith would have seemed to her a somewhat trivial thing. She was a born novelist, but she was also a profound student; and she strove to show the part played in life not only by the ordinary emotions, but by great ideas and enthusiasms. Her earliest work of fiction, *Scenes of Clerical Life* (1857), consists of three short stories, of which the best, *Janet's Repentance*, deals with the influence of an evangelical clergyman on the mind of a woman whom suffering gradually made susceptible to his teaching. Apart from its deep human interest, the story gives a vivid account of life in provincial England during the middle years of the last century. Many characters meet in *Adam Bede* (1859), the shrewd and homely, the frail and erring, the fervently religious, and the book contains some beautiful descriptions of country life, but it is surpassed by *The Mill on the Floss* (1860), one of the finest studies every written of the plain English character, with its doggedness, its humour, its moral strivings. The main subject of *Silas Marner* (1861) is the experience undergone by a narrow, earnest soul after a religious crisis. This work is much shorter than most Victorian novels, and George Eliot's art gains greatly from enforced concentration. The book shows in miniature all her peculiar gifts as a novelist. *Silas Marner* is the last of George Eliot's works which seem written for the sheer joy of creation. In *Romola* (1863), a story of Italian life in the late Middle Ages, the effort to create a historical background of perfect accuracy wears a certain appearance of strain, and the scenes in which Romola, Tito and Tessa play their domestic drama bring out by their superior qualities the want of spontaneity in the chapters on state intrigues. Yet *Romola* is a fine historical novel ; and though George Eliot is not at her ease with a swashbuckler like Dolfo Spini, her portrait of Savonarola is finely sympathetic. *Middlemarch* (1871–2), her longest book, has all the ripeness of experience, and the task of portraying English provincial life in its upper circles with the complex relations of squire and doctor, artist and scholar, was one for which George Eliot was well fitted. The interest of the book, however, is not quite uniform, and nothing else in it can quite equal the story of Dorothea Brooke and the erudite Mr. Casaubon, for whom she is at first prepared to sacrifice herself, in such fatal ignorance of his character and of life in general. None of George Eliot's books is without moments of marvellous human interest, but in her later works there are some stretches of dreary writing. This is especially true in *Felix Holt* and *Daniel Deronda*.

George Eliot's view of life was a serious one. Many of her best-drawn characters are men and women who live in the light of some high ideal or under the sway of some strong ambition. There is room in fiction for a novelist who really understands what part religion and intellect play in life, and none is more worthy to fill it than George Eliot. She has, however, an insight into many kinds of character which are neither religious nor intellectual. Hetty Sorrel is as well drawn as Dinah Morris; Mrs. Poyser is as much alive as Romola or Maggie Tulliver. George Eliot's habit of sometimes relying on her reading rather than her intuition has, in recent years, weighed heavily against her reputation. But no rational criticism can deny her a place among the six or seven greatest novelists of the century.

VIII

THE LATER VICTORIAN NOVEL: STEVENSON

The more original novelists of the later Victorian epoch were all to some extent in reaction against the work of their predecessors. The use of fiction as a medium for discussing serious problems did not at all meet with the approval of Robert Louis Stevenson (1850–1894), whose imagination dwelt naturally in romance and adventure. In regarding the novel as intended above all things to amuse, Stevenson could quote many great names as his authority. His originality lay in raising to the level of real literature stories of pure adventure, in which the maturer emotions are generally subordinate. Stevenson approached fiction as a deliberate and conscious artist in words. He had, in his own phrase, " played the sedulous ape " to various masters of style. His early book, *Travels with a Donkey* (1879), showed that his literary masters had enabled him to form a distinct manner of his own, which was, however, agreeably full of reminiscence. In the studied choice of his language and his delicate care for the associations of words, Stevenson has some affinity with Pater and the other leaders of the " æsthetic " movement in literature.

His greatest success was in the short story, his two best collections of which are *The New Arabian Nights* (1882) and *The Merry Men* (1887). Some of his stories, such as *Thrawn Janet*, are in their main character, sensational;

351

others, like *Will o' the Mill*, are full of poetic charm ; others again, like *Providence and the Guitar*, are made up out of surprise and coincidence. But in Stevenson's work, the literary handling is a chief feature. In the sinister *Thrawn Janet*, for instance, the masterly use of the Scots dialect is as skilful an achievement as the grotesque horror of the story. *Treasure Island* (1883) and *Kidnapped* (1886) frankly belong to the class of boys' books. But Stevenson's style has renewed for grown-up people a primitive form of literary pleasure which they might well have feared to be lost to them for ever. In *Dr. Jekyll and Mr. Hyde* (1886), the psychological and the sensational are effectively blended : the book is in one sense a splendid " thriller," but all possible crudity is dispelled by a treatment which is at once fine and serious. Stevenson's faculty for writing good stories with a literary turn was apparently inexhaustible ; but in his last book, *Weir of Hermiston* (1896), he went further, and had written the first chapters of a fine tragedy, when his death stopped its completion.

Stevenson's books appealed highly to the generation of readers immediately after his death. But his work is of a kind that is greatly subject to fluctuations in taste. It can never be denied, however, that he could tell a good story superlatively well ; and that a mixture of courage and sensibility in his nature give his works virility and charm.

IX

MEREDITH

The work of George Meredith stands apart from most fiction of the century. He did not follow any established tradition, nor did he found a school. His main teachers were not novelists, but philosophers and poets. His mind was highly selective. He confined himself principally to the upper classes of society ; and his attitude towards life is that of the thinker and poet. Much of his own best writing, indeed, was in verse ; and *Love in the Valley*, and certain " sonnets " of the sequence *Modern Love*, are among the most beautiful poems of the age. In his novels, he cared little for incident or plot on their own account, but

352

used them principally to illustrate the activity of the " Comic Spirit." Meredith loves to trace the calamities which befall those who provoke Nature by obstinately running counter to her laws. A certain balance and sanity, a fine health of body and soul are, in his view, the means prescribed by Nature for the happiness of man. Many of his poems, *The Woods of Westermain*, for instance, give expression to his " philosophy " of high courage and spiritual valour. The men and women of his novels are mostly persons of mental alertness and high animal spirits ; and it is the various infatuations of such people that give rise to the " comic " situations which it was his delight to study.

The Ordeal of Richard Feverel (1859), though one of Meredith's earliest books, is one of his best. Its main theme is the ill-advised upbringing of an only son by a well-meaning but too officious parent. Sir Austin Feverel's intentions are, in the first place, excellent, but they are so ill-suited to the nature of any boy that the father is converted, against his will, into his son's worst enemy. The situation is one such as Meredith loved, but in this book the issue is rather tragic than comic. For the rest, the novel contains some chapters of high poetic beauty. *Evan Harrington* (1861) is much more conventional in its style, and the humorous situations which arise out of the social snobbery of the Harrington family have much of the ordinary Victorian flavour. Only in Meredith, there is a more conscious concentration on the comic issues. Where Dickens and Thackeray would have been content to plan broadly and trust to the inspiration of the moment, Meredith calculates point after point with minute care. *Rhoda Fleming* (1865), *Sandra Belloni* (1864), *Harry Richmond* (1871), and *Beauchamp's Career* (1876), all have in a large measure the best qualities of Meredith's art. Intellectual brilliance, a ruthless exposure of social foibles, and an occasional poetic intensity of style are in all these books ; and though Meredith has no fear of poignant scenes—there are several in *Rhoda Fleming*—he is for ever vigilant against sentimentality. The climax of his art was reached in *The Egoist* (1879), the most perfect illustration of what Meredith meant by " comedy." The interplay of character and circumstance which leads on to the complete discomfiture of Sir Willoughby Patterne, is one of the neatest things in English fiction. In this book, too, are some of Meredith's best-drawn characters, not only the Egoist himself, but Clara Middleton, Lætitia Dale, and that very natural boy, Crossjay Patterne. Unfortunately, the style of *The Egoist* is marred by a straining after brilliance which leads sometimes to affectation, sometimes to obscurity. Latterly, Meredith found it impossible to write with any approach to simplicity, and this is the more to be regretted since some of his latest books, *Diana of the Crossways* (1885), for instance, and *One of Our Conquerors* (1891), show their author at his best as a commentator on human nature.

X

HARDY

George Meredith wrote with the trained consciousness of a literary artist; and though he had less creative power than Dickens, he also made fewer concessions to popular taste. Thomas Hardy (1840–1928) was, like Meredith, a poet as well as a novelist, and he resembled him also in aiming at the highest standard of literary excellence. He also followed the method of an artist; and the influence of his example on the technique of the English novel has certainly been to the good.

Hardy's true manner was first revealed in *Under the Greenwood Tree* (1872), a book which its author describes as " a rural painting of the Dutch school." The story is slight; but the description of Dorsetshire landscape and character show an intimacy with the life of old rustic England such as scarcely any other writer has ever possessed. The members of the Mellstock choir speak a language as expressive as it is quaint, and their stiff country attitudes are brought as vividly before us as the trees that line the Dorest lanes, at which the author has looked so long and with such discerning eyes. In *A Pair of Blue Eyes* (1873), the sombreness of outlook which afterwards became a fixed habit with Hardy makes its first appearance. He is fond of involving his characters in a web of calamity from which there is no escape ; and though, in this book, the fate of Elfride Swancourt is painfully pathetic, it is the separate scenes that linger longest in the memory, such as the marvellously told adventure at the " Cliff without a Name." This book was an excursion into Cornwall ; in *Far from the Madding Crowd* (1874) Hardy returned to the heart of Wessex and to its true-bred inhabitants, whom he understood so much better than any other beings under heaven. *The Return of the Native* (1878) has claims to be regarded as his greatest novel. Certainly he never wrote anything finer than the grand opening description of Egdon Heath ; and the spirit of that sombre Dorset upland pursues the story to its culminating tragedy. The whole conception of the book is poetic ; and such incidents as the game of dice played by the light of glow-worms, and Mrs. Yeobright's fatal walk over the heath after her visit to her son's cottage must be viewed as details in a profound study of the relation between the life of man and the life of nature. *The Trumpet-Major* (1880) is a much slighter book, but it is one of Hardy's successes, and its use of local traditions surviving from the Napoleonic wars is admirable. *The Mayor of Casterbridge* (1886), which followed two works of little merit, is perhaps the most picturesque of all Hardy's books and its succession of scenes founded on old Dorset customs and incidents is masterly in the extreme. Moreover, Michael Henchard, the hero of the story, is the most strongly conceived of all Hardy's characters. *The Woodlanders* (1887) is a book of more subdued beauty : its peculiar charm lies in its closeness to the soil. The very spirit of the woodland earth seems to live in the instincts and feelings of Giles Winterborne and Marty South. *Tess of the d'Urbervilles* (1891) is popularly regarded as the crown of Hardy's work in fiction. The story of Tess's life and death is powerfully tragic, though the handling is here and there sensational. But no lover of what is characteristic in Hardy can deny that the book contains some of his finest things—the life of Tess at Talbothays, for instance, the dairy-farm with its maids and men, and above all, the desperate flight of Tess with Angel Clare to Stonehenge. The last of Hardy's great novels, *Jude the Obscure*, appeared in 1896. Here his tragic vision is at its darkest ; and the reader who rebels against so gloomy a picture of life is acting under a healthy impulse. None the less, most of Hardy's best qualities are here, and the power of the book is immense.

Thomas Hardy is one of our great local poets. All that is most ancient in the life of Wessex, all that is most typical of its men and its villages, its superstitions and memories, was part of his very being. When he describes the " crusted characters " of the alehouse or church choir, the ways of the " reddleman " or " tranter," a " skimmity-ride " or a cider-making, a quack doctor or a village prophet, above all, in his pictures of ancient landmarks, heath and tower and barrow, he seems to utter the spirit of immemorial England, and his style assumes a fine impersonality. It is his saturation in the life of Wessex that gives his poems their power. In some important respects, his talents as a novelist were limited. His success in creating characters outside the rustic circle is not great. His style in both verse and prose has several faults and only one constant virtue—sincerity. Much of his vast drama on the Napoleonic wars, *The Dynasts*, is prosaically written, though the vividness of the descriptions makes the work, as its author intended, " eminently readable." For breadth of outlook, perfection of style, knowledge of the wider world, we must go to other men. But as one of the voices of rural England, changing and unchangeable, Hardy's place among the more enduring of our writers is secure.

CHAPTER XX

SOME FEATURES OF CONTEMPORARY LITERATURE

THE man who stands at distance from a mountain-range has little difficulty in singling out its highest peak. The man who stands on the mountain itself often sees nothing more than a chaos of rocks and boulders, so that he almost doubts whether his upland station has any unity, or is other than a mass of hillocks. It is impossible to write the literary history of an age when we are in doubt as to its real shape and features. A man like Dryden stands out so clearly among his contemporaries of the Restoration and forms so evident a link in the chain of peaks behind and before, that his work may safely be taken as the epitome of his epoch. But who is the Dryden of our own age? Is it Mr. Shaw, or Mr. Wells, or Mr. Kipling, or some other writer equally known or wholly obscure? Is there, indeed, any representative author at all among us? Have the literary giants been succeeded by a race of men, more numerous, indeed, but of smaller stature? Such questions may give rise to endless debate, but no one alive can settle them. Literary history cannot be extended into our own time, for history demands perspective, and among our contemporaries we can move only by guesswork. Yet, notwithstanding the mistakes of omission and commission which cannot be avoided, some attempt must be made to continue the story on the same lines as before—to continue it only, for happily the conclusion is still invisible in the distance.

I

The long prosperity of Queen Victoria's reign culminated in the brilliance of her Diamond Jubilee in 1897.
Her life itself was to close amid the gloom of the Boer War,
but of this calamity few men as yet saw any sign. The
decade between the jubilees of 1887 and 1897 not only
witnessed the death of Browning, Tennyson and other
Victorians, but developed very decided literary tastes of
its own. By the younger critics, Tennyson was already
regarded as old-fashioned. They found him insular and
" moral," and had little sympathy with his idealism. The
cry of Art for Art's sake, first heard some thirty years before,
had now become almost a dogma, and the most applauded
writers were those who aimed at a superfine and exquisite
beauty. The chief organ of the new æsthetic movement
was the " Yellow Book," with which the names of Oscar
Wilde and Aubrey Beardsley are associated. But the movement spread far, and few of the better writers in the 'eighties
and 'nineties escaped its influence. Alike in the verse of
Mr. A. E. Housman and the prose of Edmund Gosse, one
may see that instinctive care for the right word and the right
phrase which gives style its perfect finish. But the results
of the æsthetic movement were very various. The
preoccupation with form, to the exclusion of matter, was
felt to be both affected and un-English. " Mr. Punch "
was unwearied in his mockery of the æsthetes ; and in
regarding them as indifferent to our higher traditions, that
watchful guardian of the national welfare was mainly in the
right. The closing years of the century were, indeed,
critical of most things. Men were dissatisfied with Church
and State, with the political and social system, with the
universe, and with themselves. The whole foundations of
our civilization were questioned in Samuel Butler's Utopian
romance *Erewhon* (1872). The inequality of rich and poor
was denounced with a clear-sighted bitterness in the novels
of George Gissing, and more quietly in his autobiographical
book, *The Private Papers of Henry Ryecroft* (1903). William
Hale White (" Mark Rutherford ") wrote some novels

during the 'eighties, on his deliverance from what he regarded as the dead hand of Puritan beliefs, and the same notes of scepticism and sadness are in many works of the time. Other writers openly gave way to the blackest despair, notably James Thomson, in *The City of Dreadful Night* (1874). In spite of the virile verse of W. E. Henley (1849–1903) and the rich mystical imagination of Francis Thompson (1859–1907), it appeared as if literature were forming an alliance with destructive thought, or abandoning itself to sheer *ennui*. From abroad, however, new teachers were being proclaimed : to the novelist the example of Tolstoi was held up, to the dramatist that of Ibsen. We may sum up by saying that in the closing years of the century literature as a profession was in high esteem : its artistic and intellectual aspects were fully appreciated ; only it had for a time lost contact with the real life of the nation.

II

It has been the great achievement of Mr. Rudyard Kipling to restore the connection between imaginative literature and the vital activities of England. Though educated at home, Mr. Kipling's real career began in India, and it was as the spokesman of the Anglo-Indian that he first became known as a writer. When a young man, living in the North-Western district of India, he expressed a wish " to live with the Army for a time, and go to the frontier to write up Tommy Atkins." The wish was fulfilled ; and the first results of Kipling's new life were *Departmental Ditties* (1886) and *Plain Tales from the Hills* (1888). Both verse and prose were warmly welcomed in India, for no one had yet expressed the Anglo-Indian point of view with a tithe of such vigour ; but in England, too, the books were appreciated, for Kipling clearly understood the art of the short story, and his verse, with all its short-comings, was at least alive. The *Plain Tales from the Hills* were certainly unequal ; but no one could miss Kipling's wonderful sympathy with the British soldier, as shown, for instance, in his pictures of Privates Mulvaney, Ortheris and Learoyd.

Most of Kipling's later work has been on the lines of these early books. In *The Light that Failed* (1891) and *Kim* (1901) he attempted the full-length novel, and the second of these, with its graphic descriptions of the external shows of Indian life, is possibly his masterpiece. *Stalkey and Co.* (1899), founded on his own boyhood at the United Services College, Westward Ho, is one of the very few school stories which have any claim to rank as literature. But his most striking success has always been in the short story; and in his various collections, *The Jungle Book* (1894), *The Day's Work* (1898), *Just So Stories* (1902), with their successors, the power of his imagination is best shown—both its grasp of hard material facts and its skill in creating a kind of new folk-lore, dear to most children and to many older readers.

Historically, the importance of Kipling is great, for he, above all writers, has given voice to the spirit of the new imperialism. His *Recessional* expressed an undercurrent of deep national feeling in the brilliant days of the Diamond Jubilee, and few poems of the last half-century are so certain of a long life. No one can resist the resonant and even disturbing power of the language. The sentiment of the poem, more akin to the Old Testament than to the New, is quite characteristic of the author, and Kipling really has some of the spirit of an ancient Jewish patriot. He is wholly in sympathy with the half-inarticulate, half-irrational virtues which built the British Empire, and his interest in all forms of vigorous action, in peace or war, on land or in the air, is unbounded. His sphere is the strife and endurance of man. Of the more subtle and intellectual natures he shows little knowledge, nor does he much regard the place of theory and analysis in modern life. His early style in prose and verse was sometimes crude and blatant; but in his later work there is a finer note, due in part, no doubt, to his increasing love of Southern England, and his sense of the poetry in its landscape and associations.

III

Mr. Bernard Shaw may be regarded as a popular enter-
tainer, or as a serious thinker, or as a brilliant dramatist.
He is all three ; but his ideas are the life of his work. It is
they that sparkle in the prose of his prefaces, and give point
to the dialogues of his plays. He is a teacher who hates to
be dull, and he has chosen the drama as the chief instrument
for his teaching. Thereby the stage has profited greatly
and its intellectual value been immensely increased. Mr.
Shaw is a critic of life first, and a playwright only second.
His power to represent character has many limitations,
and his men and women are often the mouthpiece of ideas
rather than creations of flesh and blood swayed by emotion.
" I write plays," says Mr. Shaw, quite clearly, " with the
deliberate object of converting the nation to my opinions."
Fortunately, this matters less than it might, as Mr. Shaw is an
adept in the technique of the stage.

Mr. Shaw, who was born in 1856, began his literary
career as a novelist ; but after publishing four books of
small merit, gave up that form of writing on the ground that
he had no taste for " popular art." He was more con-
genially employed in writing his books on Socialism ; but
political thought, however freshly conceived, did not by
itself give sufficient play to Mr. Shaw's versatile mind.
Nor was æsthetic criticism quite his sphere, though *The
Quintessence of Ibsenism* (1891) and *The Perfect Wagnerite*
(1898) are both important works. The stage itself was
Mr. Shaw's true ground. There, his wide observation of
life, his witty phrasing, his crisply written dialogue and his
clever stage-craft enabled him to write a series of comedies
which as sheer entertainments are not easy to beat. The
first of Mr. Shaw's plays to be successfully produced was
Arms and the Man (1894), a piece intended to show that
" romance is the great heresy to be swept off from art and
life." The scene is laid in Bulgaria : and the fun arises
out of the conflict between the heroine's conception of war
as chivalrous and romantic, and the view of a Swiss officer
(afterwards her successful lover), in whose eyes it is a mere

profession and rather an inglorious one. The play was published a few years later with two others, each of them enlarged by the elaborate stage-directions which help to make Mr. Shaw's plays such lively reading. "Three Plays for Puritans" were produced during the next few years and published in 1901. In *Man and Superman* (1903), where woman is shown as the pursuer and not the pursued, there is just that mingling of paradox with realism in which Mr. Shaw delights; and beneath the laughter of the play there is a serious "motif"—the application of biology to the improvement of the human race. Mr. Shaw's plays now succeeded each other rapidly. Any accepted view afforded him a butt. In *The Doctor's Dilemma*, for instance, the credulous faith of the public in the medical profession received a rude shock; and the little conventions of family life were held up to ridicule in *Fanny's First Play*. Mr. Shaw continued to write both during and after the war; but in his later plays there is more open seriousness and less irresponsible mirth. *Back to Methuselah*, an immense and unequal drama on salvation through longevity, is introduced by an admirable preface on Mr. Shaw's intellectual history; and in *St. Joan*, a great story is revived in the light of an individual interpretation. Years do little to impair Mr. Shaw's freshness: in *The Intelligent Woman's Guide to Socialism* (1928) there is nearly as much vitality as ever.

Mr. Shaw belongs to that order of social and political critics among whom Voltaire stands highest in world literature. Both are true humanists, and both, though apparently destructive, are really among the architects of the social order. It is Mr. Shaw's great praise, like Voltaire's, to have written brilliantly in the cause of common sense. There are few things in human life from eating to love-making on which he has not something both sensible and witty to say. On the questions of religion, morality, and beauty, however, his voice speaks with less conviction. In his early days, he learnt from his teacher, Samuel Butler, the "necessity of a conscientious Laodiceanism in religion."[1] The fact indicates certain limitations in Mr. Shaw's grasp

[1] See J. W. Cunliffe: *English Literature during the last Half-Century.*

of life. Those who think that these limitations are of little account may well accept him as an intellectual master ; others will exclude him from the list of major prophets, though grateful for his contribution to the gaiety of nations.

IV

Though a less original thinker than Mr. Shaw, Mr. H. G. Wells has greater powers of imaginative creation. He combines the gifts of the novelist and the teacher. The future has always been as much his sphere as the present, and of late years he has added the whole of the historical past. Nothing daunts him, however remote. He has that stimulating gift of the teacher—the power to be always annexing new provinces of knowledge. Mr. Wells is the mirror of our changeable, inquiring age. His influence is due largely to his vast mass of acquired information, and the confident dexterity with which he displays it. Force and clearness are the two great qualities of his style.

The character of Mr. Wells's work has been partly determined by his early circumstances. His education had to be won by a hard struggle. He had already begun to earn his living when a scholarship enabled him to enter the Royal College of Science at South Kensington, where he came under the influence of Huxley. His training in zoology made Mr. Wells a champion of the new learning, and he has since become a severe critic of the traditional subjects and methods of education. In the early 'nineties, however, when Mr. Wells first came before the world as a writer, he was known chiefly as one who had made the methods and speculations of science a source for gratifying the prevalent taste for sensational literature. His earlier romances, *e.g. The Time Machine* (1895) and *When the Sleeper Wakes* (1899), are brilliant experiments in blending science with fiction. They were not the first of their kind ; but Mr. Wells's combination of technical knowledge with his power of startling description gave him an advantage over most competitors. There is a more lasting value in the novels which Mr. Wells based upon sober reality. He knew the drabness, the deprivations, and the humour of lower middle class life, and he had always loved to observe the various ways of speech among the illiterate and half-educated. *Love and Mr. Lewisham* (1900) and *Kipps* (1905) are both successful examples of that class of novel in which autobiography forms the basis and imagination the super-structure. The practice gained from writing these books was next applied to a series of novels dealing with topics of the day. *Tono-Bungay* (1909), a book on a huge advertising hoax, was followed by *The New Machiavelli* (1911), a political novel, and by *Mr. Britling Sees It Through* (1916), one of the best books yet written on the early days of the Great War. Latterly, the zeal of the popular teacher has somewhat encroached on Mr. Wells's enthusiasm for fiction. An excursion into theology was not particularly fortunate, but his *Outline of History* (1920) is, in spite of some dubious statements, a noteworthy attempt to prove that a world-state is the only logical consummation to the political experiments of past ages.

The richly-productive and versatile career of Mr. Wells is very typical of the age, and he has won many disciples by his gift of highly plausible prophecy. Some of his books, however, seem too hastily improvised, and his style, like his thought, often wants distinction. His own claim, we are told, is that he has " jogged the young, and started them on experiment, and taught them zest."

V

SOME MODERN POETS

Poetry has for centuries been the highest mode of expression which the English people have possessed. It is, however, an art which stands to suffer from modern life. The tendency of civilization has long been to raise the intelligence of the many, but also, it would appear, to reduce the opportunities for highly creative work. Certain forms of literature may profit by the change—criticism, history, and many kinds of miscellaneous prose. But the highest forms of literature will suffer. In the poetry of the twentieth century these changes are clearly reflected. The quantity of good verse written is great, but its scope is generally limited and its ambitions are modest. In the longer forms of poetry, the limitations of the age are very distinctly felt.

The last years of the nineteenth and the early years of the twentieth century were rich in writers whose verse was marked by a sure and conscious mastery in the technique of expression. A typical writer of the age was Sir William Watson, who both as a sonneteer and as an elegiac poet has written work of high distinction and beauty. A fine combination of literary culture and poetic feeling is also found in the work of Edmund Gosse, Andrew Lang, W. S. Blunt, Lawrence Binyon and many others. Perhaps the highest place of all among the scholar-bards belongs to the Poet Laureate, Mr. Robert Bridges, who has for many years been writing verse of infinite metrical variety and flawless taste. Some of Mr. Bridges' lyrics are of rare beauty—" Awake, my heart, to be loved," " There is a hill beside the silver Thames," the ode " A coy inquisitive spirit, the spirit of wonder," to name a few—and much that he has written is scarcely inferior. Besides being skilled in verbal music, Mr. Bridges is a master of the descriptive phrase. The quality of his lines on a view of warships :

> Those murderous queens walking in Sabbath sleep,
> Glided in line upon the windless deep,

pervades much of his work ; and in his highly finished narrative poem, *Eros and Psyche*, the level of description is admirably sustained. Mr. Bridges is the poet of Beauty and Joy. His work owes much to a very fine culture, so much, indeed, that its qualities are apt to elude the less literate reader. Although Mr. Bridges uses the simplest language, the feelings to which he appeals are often rather subtle. But all whose taste is already formed must value his poetry for its unfailing refinement, and honour its author for his devotion to the highest ideals of his art.

There is another order of contemporary poets whose

work is less dependent upon literary culture. Perhaps there is no living writer whose work is so essentially poetical as Mr. A. E. Housman, author of two small volumes of verse, *The Shropshire Lad* (1896) and *Last Poems* (1922). The style of these pieces is simple, but it is perfect. Housman is a poet swayed by an impulse altogether deeper than his conscious mind, and his words have a power of suggestion far beyond their visible meaning. The phrasing may well be called " inevitable " in some of his best lyrics—in *Bredon Hill*, for instance, or the lines *To an Athlete Dying Young*, or those beginning, " Into my heart an air that kills." Some of the deepest feelings of the age are uttered in the lines, " On Wenlock Edge the wood's in trouble." Another recent poet of original power is Rupert Brooke (1887–1915), whose career was suddenly brought to an end by the War. His poetical quality appears in the swift and passionate verse of his sonnets, like *Failure*, and those written in the early days of the War, such as " Now, God be thanked Who has matched us with His hour," and " If I should die, think only this of me." He often strikes a modern note in the daring frankness of his language, which a certain quality of real strength or humour generally redeems from mere violence. James Elroy Flecker (1884–1915) has, above all things, a poet's love of expressive words. He endeavours, like Keats, to " load every rift with ore," but he does so entirely in his own way, and he is the creator of an original poetic style. His effective use of proper names—Samarkhand, Famagusta—is typical of his verbal art. Modern poets are by no means reluctant to experiment in their language, but there are few who unite boldness and taste in so happy a proportion as Flecker.

A skilful evocation of the suggestions latent in language is one of the most striking features of contemporary lyrical verse. Mr. Masefield, for instance, has written some lyrics of extraordinary verbal felicity, especially the famous " Quinquireme of Nineveh." He has also shown great skill in devising new rhythms, an art in which Mr. de la Mare likewise excels. Few living poets have written verse at once so original, so natural and so expressive as that of *The Listeners*. Mr. de la Mare has also rekindled the recollections of childhood in the hearts of his readers by a charming waywardness of fancy, which though not deeply serious is wholly enchanting. He is one among several living writers—Sir Henry Newbolt, J. C. Squire, W. H. Davies, Lascelles Abercrombie, Harold Munro, Ralph Hodgson—to name a few—who have enriched the present age with a remarkable number of genuine and spontaneous lyrics.

In the poetry of Mr. W. B. Yeats there is a quality which makes a strong appeal to many of the present generation. He has revealed the romanticism latent in the misty regions of Celtic lore and tradition, and by so doing has found a new home for the imagination of those who wish to take refuge from the harshness of our mechanical age. The modern poet will often lead his readers farther afield than his predecessors did in the last century. C. M. Doughty, for instance, carries us back to the earliest days of our island's civilization (in *The Dawn in Britain*) ; others like Hardy and W. H. Hudson love those ancient relics and monuments which give " a sense of the continuity of the human race." Others, again, like Edward Thomas, discover an imaginative sympathy with the unchanging ways of animal life. The crudities of industrial civilization do not offer the poet an attractive subject, though the crudities of the War were sometimes put into language and verse of the starkest realism. But the War also gave birth to many gracious pieces founded on poignant regrets for the lost beauties of life.

The longer poem does not flourish particularly well in an age which is sensitive to the offence of prosaic qualities in verse. But among contemporary poets, Mr. John Masefield is conspicuous for his great success in the art of poetic narrative. In *The Everlasting Mercy* (1912) there is some uncertainty of treatment, and the author had not yet discovered where his real strength lies. By degrees, he concentrated more and more on the description of mere action, rapid, vigorous and intense. His poem, *Dauber*, in which an artist undergoes the rigours of seamanship, gives a real sense of conflict with tremendous forces ; but his greatest success is *Reynard the Fox*, a thrilling narrative of the chase chiefly from the fox's point of view. In his other poems, Mr. Masefield sometimes loses his poetic sense of words and things, and is content to regard common men as they regard themselves. In *Reynard*, this realism serves a purpose, for it points the contrast between the coarseness of the human beings and the fineness of the animal. Mr. Masefield has also written some admirable poetic dramas, such as *Philip the King* (1914).

VI

THE NOVEL

The novel still occupies a dominant position in our literature. The many fresh distractions of modern life make wonderfully little difference to its popularity. Neither the revival of the theatre, nor the growth of the cinema, nor the development of broadcasting, has appreciably lessened its vogue. To judge from the output of novels, their quantity and variety, there are few classes of the community which do not read them. Mr. Hugh Walpole alludes to a recent critic who " insisted that there were at least a hundred and fifty living novelists, men and women, whose work was worthy of serious attention." Even allowing for an exaggeration in this estimate, it must evidently be a bold man who dogmatizes about the condition of the novel to-day. Here, more than anywhere, certainty is unattainable.

One great change, however, which has taken place in the novel during the last fifty years is clear enough. It has become a work of much more conscious art. The novelist has ceased to be a pioneer working by rough-and-ready methods, and is expected to aim with some precision at the desired result. There is less freedom, perhaps, for creative genius, but there is more demand for deliberate skill. A modern novelist must keep to his business, and avoid the digressions, in which his predecessors loved to indulge ; and, moreover, his characters must work out their destiny in a world in which we can really believe. Secondly, the novelist is expected to see life steadily and to tell the truth without flinching. The spirit of the age condemns nothing more than " hypocrisy." The result is that the novel has become both more of an art and more of a science : objective truth is demanded as well as rigorous construction. Among the older novelists whose work is written more or less in agreement with these principles, three stand out above the rest—Mr. John Galsworthy, Mr. Arnold Bennett and Joseph Conrad.

Mr. Galsworthy, who was born in 1867, has cultivated the drama, the short story and the novel with eminent success. He is one of the closest observers of manners and loves to watch the varying shadows which the changing years cast on the surface of life. His chosen region is that in which he was born and bred—the upper-middle class ; and alike in his plays and novels, the faults which arise from worldly success—narrowness of outlook, hardness of heart, and the like—are the mainspring of the action. Mr. Galsworthy had been publishing some eight or nine years before he wrote *The Man of Property* (1906), now the first novel of *The Forsyte Saga*. The idea of a family or clan, all the members of which, though differing widely, have a certain tenacity and instinct for worldly success, brings Mr. Galsworthy's great knowledge and observation into play. Few characters are introduced from outside the family : the Forsyte world is self-contained and self-sufficient, and the little group who, though in it, are not of it, are far from enviable. Soames Forsyte, the central figure of the Saga, is also the quintessence of the family virtues and vices. His career is the epitome of a large part of English society in all its crowded history through some thirty years. And it is noteworthy that the man who is shown to us at first as hard and repellent appears, in the latest additions to the Foryste series, as a figure of rock-like stability in a world of change. Mr. Galsworthy is certainly one of the finest artists in contemporary fiction. His best scenes imprint themselves on the memory like etchings wrought with a few deft and unerring strokes. His style, always pure, sometimes attains a high beauty, as in that little masterpiece, *Indian Summer of a Forsyte*.

A boyhood cast in a region distinguished from the rest of the world by ways and speech of its own is one of the best gifts which Fortune can bestow on a future novelist. This gift was granted to Mr. Arnold Bennett, who was born in 1867 near Hanley, one of the Five Towns of the Potteries. After some years spent in miscellaneous literary work, Mr. Bennett resolved to devote himself wholly to novel-writing. His strength was first fully shown in that powerful study of contrasted destinies, *The Old Wives' Tale* (1908) ; then again in *Clayhanger* (1910), which, with its sequel, *Hilda Lessways* (1911), is perhaps his masterpiece. Mr. Bennett has a joy in creating and a zest in describing which prove him a born novelist. There are scenes in *Clayhanger*— a study of provincial life in the last century—as convincing in their reality as anything in English fiction. It is Mr. Bennett's merit, as has been well said, " to see freshly the things of life we take for granted." His range is wider than that of a " regionalist," yet he is most himself in the Five Towns. Everything in the grim streets and provincial houses is a little strange, yet it is all obviously true. In Mr. Bennett's best books there are many tragic incidents ; but he has written a number of lighter novels which are full of amusing " humours." Of his more recent works, *Mr. Prohack* (1922), a book on the " new rich " and the " new poor," is probably the most notable.

The work of the Polish-born Teodor Jozef Konrad Korzeniowski (1856–1924), known to the world as Joseph Conrad, is among the most original in the whole realm of fiction. Conrad's life was one of the strangest. It was dominated at the beginning by two forces. One of these was the sea, which enticed him from prospects of a comfortable life in Poland and transformed him into a Master Mariner of the British Merchant Marine. The other was the English language, with which, by his own description, he fell in love at first sight. Novel-writing became his occupation by a conspiracy of forces ; and almost against his will he found himself engaged on *Almayer's Folly*, the first of his stories, which appeared in 1895. *Lord Jim* (1900) was a riper work, and was followed, among others, by *Nostromo* (1903), *Under Western Eyes* (1911), *Victory* (1915), and *The Shadow Line* (1917). Besides novels, Conrad wrote a number of short stories, and an auto-biographical sketch called *Some Reminiscences*.

Most readers, on their first acquaintance with Conrad, experience a sense of strangeness. His method is unusual, and sometimes difficult. Simple narration would not do justice to Conrad's view of life as a complex and often self-contradictory affair. The events of his stories are frequently presented from more than one standpoint, and their sequence in time may remain obscure until the last pages of the book are reached. But the substance of Conrad's novels is so original that one cannot in fairness quarrel with his methods. His stage is a very large part of the globe. He himself has no fixed roots in any soil, and if he is more at home in one place than another, it is on ship-board. His descriptions of the sea, in calm and tempest, create a sense of reality such as only a few great poets have rivalled, and no one writes with more wealth of experience. One wonders whether a storm has ever been described with so mighty a *crescendo* as in *Typhoon*. Most of Conrad's men and women are sojourners over the earth, and the heroes among them are generally engaged in some great conflict. A thinly-disguised barbarism, as in *Nostromo* and *Victory*, the suspicion and tyranny of the Tsarist régime, as in *Under Western Eyes*, and again and again the unappeasable sea—such are the forces against which his characters are pitted ; and in the relentless struggle it is necessary above all things that men should be loyal to each other, to humanity. The test is severe ; and many, not really ignoble at heart, fail to stand it. Conrad loves to explore the secret places of the heart ; and some of his best books describe the making-good of men who have failed once under a sudden temptation. It is so with Lord Jim in the novel called after him, and with Razumov, the Russian student, in *Under Western Eyes*. Novels so conceived almost take on the character of prose epics ; and, though many of Conrad's books by reason of their narrower scope must rather be termed " sea-sagas," nearly all have the strength and sincerity of stories sprung from the heroic age.

The novel-form, like other kinds of literature, is being subjected to ceaseless experiment. Before the War, the " psychological " novel was much in vogue, and in Henry James, an American writer who assumed British nationality, it has one of its greatest masters. An offshoot of the psychological novel is the minute autobiographical novel, of which Mr. Compton Mackenzie's *Sinister Street* was a notable example, and frequently imitated. Some of the best features of contemporary fiction, its sense of form, its insistence on candour, its analysis of character, are well represented in the work of Mr. Hugh Walpole, who, like many writers of the day, is concerned with the theory of the novel as well as with its practice. Among other leading novelists are Mr. D. H. Lawrence and Miss Sheila Kaye-Smith, and there are others rapidly rising to the same position. No branch of fiction is more flourishing than the short story, and some fine instances of the art have been produced during the century. Prose fiction is now wholly free ; and although there are numerous writers who use the form without any artistic scruple, there is also a wide-spread sense of what a novel should be. That sense, one may hope, will preserve the liberty of the form from abuse.

VII

DRAMA

The revival of drama is one of the most striking features of recent literature. There were great actors and great poets living in 1870, but the glory of the stage was in temporary eclipse. Many persons entertained a prejudice against the theatre, inherited from Puritan times ; and among writers, some, like Tennyson and Browning, clung to vain hopes for a revival of great poetic drama ; others,

like Dickens and his friend Wilkie Collins, were content to
refashion popular novels to the needs of the stage. The
writer who would revive the art of the drama and make it
once more hold up the mirror to nature was slow to
appear. But in the last decade of the century some able
men, well versed in stagecraft, skilful in dialogue and keenly
observant of contemporary manners, began to make the
theatre once again a living institution. The technique of Sir
Arthur Pinero and Henry Arthur Jones, the wit and polished
dialogue of Oscar Wilde (in such plays as *The Importance
of being Earnest* and *Lady Windermere's Fan*), helped to
restore to the drama its due place in the world of literature.

But the work of Pinero and Wilde was, intellectually,
somewhat slight; another element was needed. It was
largely through the efforts of William Archer and Sir
Edmund Gosse, the popularizers of Ibsen, that the stage
began to play again an important part in the cultural life
of England. The work of Ibsen revealed the immense
dramatic wealth latent in the social and moral problems of
the day. Mr. Bernard Shaw learnt this lesson and adapted
it to uses of his own. Among other masters of the new
drama, one of the most versatile in talent and serious in
purpose is Mr. John Galsworthy. He has been writing
plays at intervals for a score of years and more, and some of
his pieces are among the best of the modern stage.

The Silver Box, which was first performed at the Royal
Court Theatre in 1906, gave a clear foretaste of Mr. Galsworthy's subsequent work. The action of the play, in
which the power of money is shown as shielding the rich
from penalties to which the poor are liable, is quite typical
of Mr. Galsworthy's point of view. The manners of
modern life in a well-to-do household, a very poor one, and
a London police-court are drawn with fine observation and
occasional saturnine humour. The whole piece is an
efficient " problem play." Mr. Galsworthy achieved
another success in *Strife* (produced in 1909), a sombre
tragedy on an industrial dispute. The ironical conclusion
is very characteristic. A long strike has at last ended after
much misery :

TENCH (*staring at Harness—suddenly excited*): D'you know, Sir,—these terms, they're the *very same* we drew up together, you and I, and put to both sides before the fight began? All this—and—and what for?

HARNESS (*in a slow, grim voice*): That's where the fun comes in!

Justice contains some powerful law-court and prison scenes, but it also bears traces of the sentimental humanitarianism so common just before the War. In *The Eldest Son* (1912), Mr. Galsworthy returned to a characteristic theme—the inconsistencies of those who live by a strict code of honour in their own class, but judge quite differently for those " beneath " them. The more recent plays, such as *The Skin Game* and *Loyalties*, show Mr. Galsworthy's dexterous stagecraft at its best, but they also reveal the limitations of his work. In *Loyalties*, for instance, there seems something arbitrary in the tragic conclusion to a plot in which some characters are little more than embodiments of a single idea. A world of men and women who are half abstractions may well lend itself to comedy, gay or grave; but for a tragic ending one surely needs to feel that the characters belong to a real world, not to one which has been artificially simplified so as to enforce an important lesson.

The great feature of Sir James Barrie's work is its irresistible charm. A delicate and wayward fancy, a humour and melancholy all his own—these are his gifts to the theatre, and they are such that it is unnatural to ask for more. Yet Barrie admits that he has his " practical and canny " as well as his " fanciful " side; and, indeed, a man less practical could never play so cunningly on the sensibilities of his audience. The first of Barrie's successful plays were *Quality Street* and *The Admirable Crichton*, both of them produced in 1903. Like many plays of the century, *The Admirable Crichton* is a social satire; but its fancy and humour, and its all-pervading sentiment penetrate the satire with poetic charm. The idea of a rather silly household containing but one true man—the butler—is one that might have occurred to any writer; but the manner in which every mood, every feeling latent in this situation is brought to the surface is as original as it is delicate, and the whole style is so buoyant that it bears its burden of thought as lightly as air. *Quality Street*, though a slighter piece, is a charming example of the mingled pathos and humour of which Barrie is a master. In *Peter Pan*, now at last published, fancy creates a world of its own though it builds on human emotions ; and to the same blending of a fairy-tale with real life, Barrie returns in the wholly delightful war-piece, *A Kiss for Cinderella* (1916). In *Mary Rose* (1920) we are taken into still stranger regions, and the author seems no longer to aim at that nice balance of thought and feeling, which is so great a merit of his earlier plays.

Among other works of the century, certain Irish plays occupy a very high place. *Cathleen ni Houlihan* and the other works of Mr. W. B. Yeats opened a new and mysterious source of dramatic emotion, but the finest results of the Celtic revival are, surely, the plays of Mr. J. M. Synge. The strange moral setting of *The Playboy of the Western World* (1907), in which parricide is accounted for righteousness, cannot disguise the naked force of the conflicting emotions, or the fascinating rhythms of the dialogue. Synge's strength appears even more impressively in his one-act plays, especially in *Riders to the Sea*, a tragic sketch of sombre intensity. Another feature of modern drama is the revival of the historical play, Mr. John Drinkwater's *Abraham Lincoln* (1918) being a noteworthy example.

VIII

PROSE

Matthew Arnold once asked why it was that the " journeyman-work " of literature was " so much worse done here than it is in France." This reproach has now to a large extent been removed. Books of general information, short monographs by authorities, and the like, are better written in England now than at any previous time.

375

The wisdom of scholar and historian is available in prose which neither overtaxes the mind nor offends the taste. On the other hand, the vogue of the highly individual style seems to have passed. The best prose of to-day is the product of intellect and culture rather than of creative imagination, and there are few living authors who are to be read chiefly " for their style."

Something, however, of the " æsthetic " tradition of the 'eighties and 'nineties survived into the early years of the present century. The aptness and elegance of Sir Edmund Gosse's prose are known to all who have made any study of the best current criticism ; and the same blending of ease and erudition marks the varied works of Andrew Lang. Gosse has also a place in the history of thought, for his fascinating little autobiography *Father and Son* did much to mould the contemporary notion of " Victorianism." Two writers whose prose, though slight in bulk, is exquisite in quality are Francis Thompson and Mrs. Meynell, both of them essayists as well as poets. The essays of Mr. Augustine Birrell are the fruit of a robuster culture and more active life ; but they have also that lightness of touch which marks so much later Victorian work. Austin Dobson's books reflect his studies, which lay equally among literature and manners, and his style has the easy elegance so much admired in his beloved eighteenth century. The essays of Mr. E. V. Lucas have something of the same quality but are more waywardly fanciful. His *Life of Charles Lamb* (1904) is a monument of admiration to the lover of wit and poetry to whom he is much akin in spirit. The essay has now a regular place in the higher journalism ; and it is pleasant to see year by year collections of articles and sketches which made their first appearance in the columns of a newspaper.

The work of Mr. G. K. Chesterton is distinguished by a certain philosophical consistency which gives it a place apart. The unceasing sparkle of paradox and epigram which illuminates his pages might be tedious if their author were concerned merely to display his infinite cleverness. But though modern in expression, Mr. Chesterton's ideas are connected with a very ancient order of thought. His Catholicism is not like that of most other Catholics. By him its truth is discovered afresh every day in the adventures and wanderings of his active mind. His love of paradox is merely the mask of his consistency, and amid the changes of the modern world he stands for the sanity of the ages. Mr. Chesterton is a versatile writer, and he has made a mark both as a novelist and as a poet ; but his real province is the criticism of life and letters. His early book *Browning* (1903) leaves an impression rather of its author's own cleverness than of the qualities of its subject. His *Dickens* (1906) is a more solid work, and its many brilliant passages are really suggestive. Mr. Chesterton is at his best, perhaps, when moving unfettered in his favourite regions of speculation ; and he has written nothing more serious and more characteristic than the Confession of Faith, called *Orthodoxy* (1908). Another Catholic man of letters, Mr. Hilaire Belloc, has done some distinguished work both as an essayist and a historian. His writings are marked by vigour of thought, a power of graphic description, and a rich experience of life.

Many important works of criticism have been produced during the century, some of them genuine contributions to literature. The fine quality of Sir Walter Raleigh's books on Shakespeare, Milton, Wordsworth and Johnson, have given them a vogue beyond student-circles, and his *Letters*, recently published, seem worthy to take a place with those of Horace Walpole and the vivacious writers of his generation. Another critic whose work seems likely to outlast his own age is Mr. A. C. Bradley, author of *Shakespearean Tragedy*, a masterpiece of sympathetic judgment, profound thought and lucid exposition. Criticism needs the rarest qualities to keep it fresh, otherwise one might predict a long life for the writings of several other scholars still living or recently dead.

The years succeeding the War were a tempting season in which to take stock of the recent past and forecast the immediate future. Of the many books which gave expression to the mood of reaction following the War, one of the best was C. E. Montague's *Disenchantment*, a record of the four years, full of vivid reminiscences and written with a certain bitter calm. The *Outspoken Essays* of W. R. Inge, Dean of St. Paul's, made a deep impression by their incisive style and their unflattering picture of the future. One of the most brilliant of living prose-writers is Mr. Lytton Strachey, whose skill in short biography is without precedent in our literature. Whether Mr. Strachey is perfectly just to all the famous men and women whose lives he narrates may be doubted; but the best history, it is said, is written with a bias, and Mr. Strachey certainly has the art of making his pages live. Moreover, he has a gift of convincing portraiture, and those who have read his Life of Florence Nightingale in *Eminent Victorians* are relieved for ever of the doubt whether that half-mythical figure was really a woman of flesh and blood. Of Mr. Strachey's recent book, *Elizabeth and Essex*, one need only say that it not unworthy to follow *Queen Victoria*.

INDEX

A

INDEX

INDEX

INDEX

D

Dactylic Metres, 94
Daffodils, To, 123
D'Alembert, 110
Daniel Deronda, 292, 350
Daniel, Samuel, 35
Dante, 16, 22, 223, 295, 306, 318
Darkness, 270
Darwin, Charles, 308, 309
Dauber, 367
David Copperfield, 337
Davies, William H., 367
Dawn in Britain, The, 367
Day's Work, The, 360
Death and Dr. Horn Book, 225
Death of the Duke of Wellington, Ode on the, 104
Death-Song of Ælla, The, 222
Decamerone, Il, 22
Decline and Fall of the Roman Empire, The, 203, 217–219
Defence of Guenevere, The, 331
Defence of Poetry, A, 282
Defoe, Daniel, 161, 179–183, 194
Dekker, Thomas, 86
De la Mare, Walter, 366
Denham, Sir John, 147, 148
Denis Duval, 340
Departmental Ditties, 359
De Quincey, Thomas, 263–266
Descriptive Sketches, 234
Deserted Village, The, 190
Desperate Remedies, 292
Diana of the Crossways, 354
Diary, the, of Samuel Pepys, 155
Dickens, Charles, 194, 291, 292, 293, 335–339, 373
Dickens (Chesterton's), 377
Dictionary, Johnson's, 205, 206
Diderot (Morley's), 309
Disenchantment, 378
Disraeli, Benjamin, 336, 342, 343
Distant Prospect of Eton College, Ode on a, 188
Divina Commedia, La, 22, 226
Dobson, Austin, 376
Doctor Faustus, 61, 84
Dr. Jekyll and Mr. Hyde, 352
Doctor's Dilemma, The, 362
Doctor Thorne, 348
Doctrine and Discipline of Divorce, On the, 115

Dolores, 332
Dombey and Son, 337, 338
Don Juan, 102, 272, 274
Donne, John, 118, 121, 126, 127, 128
Double Dealer, The, 156
Doughty, C. M., 375
Drake, Sir Francis, 8
Dramatic Lyrics, 292, 319–321
Dramatic Romances, 319–321
Dramatis Personæ, 292, 320
Drapier's Letters, 170
Drayton, Michael, 40, 91, 123
Dream, The, 268
Dream Children ; a Reverie, 257
Dream of Fair Women, The, 314
Dream of the Rood, The, 6
Drinkwater, John, 375
Dryden, John, 13, 38, 91, 100, 103, 144–146, 148–155, 160, 207, 220, 333, 357
Duchess of Malfi, The, 87
Dunbar, William, 223
Duncan Campbell, 181
Dunciad, The, 164
Duty, Ode to, 238
Dynasts, The, 356

E

Eagle, The, 317
Early Italian Poets, The, 330
Earthly Paradise, The, 331
East Midland Dialect, the, 3, 31
Ecclesiastical History, The, 7
Edgeworth, Maria, 247
Edinburgh Review, The, 228, 268, 294
Education, Tractate of, 115
Edward I, 69
Edward II, 84, 85
Edward the Confessor, 42
Edwin Drood, 338
Egoist, The, 292, 353, 354
Elaine, 315
Eldest Son, The, 374
Elegiac Stanzas on Peele Castle, 101
Elegy, Gray's, 101, 187, 188
Eliot, George, 292, 349–351
Elliott, Ebenezer, 313
Elyot, Sir Thomas, 105
Elizabeth, Queen, 34
Elizabeth and Essex, 378
Eminent Victorians, 378
Emma, 254

INDEX

INDEX

INDEX

INDEX

INDEX

INDEX

PRINTED IN ENGLAND BY WILLIAM CLOWES AND SONS' LIMITED, BECCLES.